Tolstoy or Dostoevsky

by the same author

THE DEATH OF TRAGEDY

IN BLUEBEARD'S CASTLE: Some Notes Towards
the Re-Definition of Culture

EXTRATERRITORIAL: Papers on Literature and
the Language Revolution

THE SPORTING SCENE: White Knights of
Reykjavik

George Steiner

TOLSTOY
OR
DOSTOEVSKY

An Essay in Contrast

FABER AND FABER
London Boston

First published in England in 1960
by Faber and Faber Limited
3 Queen Square London WC1
First published in Faber Paperbacks in 1980
Printed in Great Britain by
Whitstable Litho Ltd Whitstable
All rights reserved

In Memoriam: Humphry House

British Library Cataloguing in Publication Data

Steiner, George, b. 1929
    Tolstoy or Dostoevsky.
    1. Dostoevskiĭ, Fedor Mikhaĭlovich – Criticism
    and interpretation
    2. Tolstoy, Leo, Count – Criticism and
    interpretation
    I. Title
    891.7'3'309   PG3328.Z6

ISBN 0-571-11626-4

Preface to this Edition

This is a young man's book. It was written, as first books ought to be, out of sheer compulsion. It was my conviction that Tolstoy and Dostoevsky tower over the art of fiction; that their pre-eminence entails certain fundamental points about western literature as a whole (so far as the Russian novel may be said to belong to this literature); and that the reader's inevitable preference of the one master over the other will define a whole philosophic and political stance. These propositions had overwhelmed me; and this book was written in order to share with others a vehement and necessary awareness.

Twenty-one years later, I still subscribe to these convictions, though I would now qualify them. The magnitude of the Tolstoyan and Dostoevskyan performance still seems to me unmatched. But there are in Proust categories of intelligence, of psychological acuity and philosophic discovery which make of the *Remembrance of Things Past* an indispensably central act. T. S. Eliot spoke of the ways in which Dante and Shakespeare divide our world between them. Proust seems to me a party to this division, knowing as much of evil as does the *Commedia* and no less of grace and music as do Shakespeare's late plays.

If I were to rewrite this study, moreover, I would want to show that there are possibilities, though rare and unstable, of a congruence between the antithetical worlds of Tolstoy and Dostoevsky, that there can, momentarily as it were, be refusals to choose between them. The case I have in mind is that of Kafka to whom Tolstoy's *Death of*

Ivan Ilych and Dostoevsky's *Letters from the Underworld* were equal sources of vision, for whom the metaphysical melodrama of *Crime and Punishment* proved no less seminal than the epic parable in Tolstoy's *Snowstorm*. In particular, I would want to argue that Kafka's economy is underwritten by the preceding prodigality of the two Russians.

Translated into other languages, this book has elicited much discussion. I have learned from my critics, of course. But I remain unrepentant on what has been the most controversial point: my "working metaphor" (it was no more than that) in respect of the "Legend of the Grand Inquisitor" in *The Brothers Karamazov*. The analogies between the tragic casuistry of the Inquisitor and certain fundamental propositions in the counter-theology of the later Tolstoy *are* at once uncanny and substantial. Dostoevsky's antennae for the motions of spirit in other men were of a rare force of exactitude and anticipation. We know his meditation on Tolstoy to have been frequent and most intense. This meditation leaves only oblique traces in his published writings. Hence my conjecture. More generally, I remain convinced that there is much still to be understood about the reciprocal awareness of the two giants and about the interactive pressures which this awareness, externally so barren, exercised on their works

When I wrote *Tolstoy or Dostoevsky*, the dominant bias of literary studies, both in Britain and the United States, was that of the "new criticism" as engendered by the practices of "close reading" in I. A. Richards and William Empson. Such reading bore on passages of "complex" lyric verse didactically excised from their biographical, historical or ideological context and matter in the name of a rigorous purity of formal response. I sought to show that these "new critical" techniques could not handle material of the scope and hybrid character offered by the novels of Tolstoy and Dostoevsky. Such material exceeded not only the performative means of "practical criticism"; it demanded just those philosophic, political, biographical and social perspectives which the "new critics" had repudiated in their rejection of historicism, of Marxism, of literary biography and sociology. Above all, it seemed to me that the close readers of poetic "protocols" had turned their backs on the cardinal relations between literary form and world-view, between style and the metaphysics which it transcribes. But it is just these relations which give to great literature its enduring significance and summons to interpretation. Lukács's insistence on "totality", F. R. Leavis's focus on the moral substance of the novel, Sartre's postulate that a writer's techniques always refer us back to his metaphysics, seemed to me vital pointers.

In 1980, such sentiments seem absurdly gentle. Today, it is not the "new critics", with their personal commitment to poetry, with their scrupulous delight in the text (R. P. Blackmur, Allen Tate were my teachers), who set the tone. It is the byzantine practitioners of "dissemination" and of "deconstruction". With each modish wave of structuralist-semiotic decomposition, the actual literary text recedes further from autonomy, from the truth of felt being. At numerous points on the critical–academic spectrum, the poem, the passage from the novel, the scene from the play, have become nothing more than contingent occasions for the display of analytic acrobatics in a house of mirrors. The Narcissist arrogance (the semiotic anatomist is axiomatically more intelligent, more knowing, more important than the text on which he operates), the espousal of a pseudo-scientific jargon, the covert thrill of violence implicit in current interpretative methods, raise larger issues. They confirm a crisis in humane literacy, in humanistic values, whose roots touch on the troubled centre of our political and social condition.

Be that as it may: a plea for the "old criticism" has now taken on a polemic immediacy beyond any it had in 1959. More than ever before, certain banalities need to be reiterated. The poet, the playwright, the novelist are the *raison d'être* for criticism and interpretation. The writer matters far more than the critic, who is at best a loving, clairvoyant parasite. The interpreter who exploits his text for self-display is betraying his sole function. Great literary texts are not self-contained word-games. They are life-forms embedded in the person of their authors in the entire physical, spiritual, social realities of the age. They are not an arbitrary cat's-cradle of internal allusion, but utterance outward (the essential distinction is that between mirrors and windows). The capacity of major literature to alter our personal and communal existence, to reshape the landscape of our being, is evident. Equally evident is the metamorphic process which major literature undergoes over successive generations of centuries of response. But the final source of this capacity, of this radiant energy, defies analytic paraphrase. Thus it is the special, if limited, dignity of useful criticism to challenge, to labour against the "mystery" of classic creation while, at the same time, giving to this mystery and to its executive realization a more precise authority and presence. *Tolstoy or Dostoevsky* was written in service to this paradoxical, always frustrated obligation. Its re-issue may be timely.

G. S.
Geneva, 1980

Acknowledgments

TO Allen Tate and Archibald MacLeish for having made possible crucial stages of apprenticeship; to Sir Isaiah Berlin and E. T. Williams for having encouraged the project at the outset; to R. P. Blackmur for the constant education of his presence and for having been willing to look at another man's work on a subject of which he is himself a master; to Mrs. L. B. Turkevich for making one's ignorance of Russian seem a personal as well as a professional loss; to Sir Llewellyn Woodward, Alexandre Koyré, and Harold Cherniss for their many kindnesses while the work was in progress; to Griffith Edwards and Michel Gourévitch for their loyal assertion that they would like to read the book when it was done; to James Billington, who read proofs and brought to that tedious task his acute judgment and wide knowledge of Russian history and literature; above all, to Dr. J. Robert Oppenheimer and the Institute for Advanced Study for allowing me a year and a half under matchless conditions in which to complete the job.

The vexations endured in these matters by one's wife and immediate family are beyond acknowledgment.

G. S.

THANKS are due to the following publishers for permission to quote from the specified books: Jonathan Cape Ltd., *The*

Letters of T. E. Lawrence, edited by Edward Garnett; J. M. Dent & Sons Ltd., the Everyman's Library editions of Charles James Hogarth's translations of Dostoevsky's *Poor Folk* and *Letters from the Underworld*; Librairie Gallimard, *Carnets de Tolstoi et Carnets de Dostoevsky*; Hogarth Press, the Mansfield–Woolf–Koteliansky translation of Gorky's *Reminiscences* and *Stavrogin's Confession*; William Heinemann Ltd., the Constance Garnett translations of Dostoevsky's *The Brothers Karamazov*, *The Idiot*, and *The Possessed* and Tolstoy's *Anna Karenina*; Methuen & Co. Ltd., H. D. F. Kitto's *Form and Meaning in Drama*; The Oxford University Press, the Aylmer Maude translations of Tolstoy and T. E. Lawrence's translation of *The Odyssey*.

Illustrations

Tolstoy or Dostoevsky

NOTE ON DATES

All dates that refer to the lives and works of Tolstoy and Dostoevsky are given in the Old Style—i.e., twelve days earlier than Western European dates. G. S.

✸ 1 ✸

*Ein Buch wird doch immer erst gefunden, wenn
es verstanden wird.*
GOETHE *to* SCHILLER, *May* 6, 1797

LITERARY criticism should arise out of a debt of love. In a manner evident and yet mysterious, the poem or the drama or the novel seizes upon our imaginings. We are not the same when we put down the work as we were when we took it up. To borrow an image from another domain: he who has truly apprehended a painting by Cézanne will thereafter see an apple or a chair as he had not seen them before. Great works of art pass through us like storm-winds, flinging open the doors of perception, pressing upon the architecture of our beliefs with their transforming powers. We seek to record their impact, to put our shaken house in its new order. Through some primary instinct of communion we seek to convey to others the quality and force of our experience. We would persuade them to lay themselves open to it. In this attempt at persuasion originate the truest insights criticism can afford.

I say this because much contemporary criticism is of a different cast. Quizzical, captious, immensely aware of its philosophic ancestry and complex instruments, it often comes to bury rather than to praise. There is, indeed, a vast amount that requires burial if the health of language and of sensibility is to be guarded. Instead of enriching our consciousness, instead of being springs of life, too many books hold out to us the temptations of facility, of grossness and ephemeral solace. But these are books for the compulsive craft of the reviewer, not for the meditative, re-creative art of the critic. There are more than a "hundred great books," more than a thousand. But their number is not inexhaustible. In distinction from both the reviewer and the literary historian, the critic should be concerned with masterpieces. His primary function is to distinguish not between the good and the bad, but between the good and the best.

Here again, modern opinion inclines to a more diffident view. It has lost, through the loosening of the hinges of the old-established cultural and political order, that serenity of assurance which allowed Matthew Arnold to refer, in his lectures on translating Homer, to the "five or six supreme poets of the world." We would not put it that way. We have become relativists, uneasily aware that critical principles are attempts at imposing brief spells of governance on the inherent mutability of taste. With the decline of Europe from the pivot of history, we have become less certain that the classical and western tradition is pre-eminent. The horizons of art have retreated in time and in space beyond any man's surveyance. Two of the most representative poems of our age, The Waste Land and Ezra Pound's Cantos, draw on Oriental thought. The masks of the Congo stare out of the paintings of Picasso in vengeful distortion. Our minds are shadowed by the wars and bestialities of the twentieth century; we grow wary of our inheritance.

But we must not yield too far. In excess of relativism lie the germs of anarchy. Criticism should recall us to the remembrance of our great lineage, to the matchless

4

tradition of the high epic as it unfolds from Homer to Milton, to the splendours of Athenian, Elizabethan, and Neo-classical drama, to the masters of the novel. It should affirm that if Homer and Dante and Shakespeare and Racine are no longer the supreme poets of the whole world—it has grown too large for supremacy —they are still the supreme poets of that world from which our civilization draws its life-force and in defence of which it must take its imperilled stand. Insisting upon the infinite variety of human affairs, on the role of social and economic circumstance, historians would have us discard the old definitions, the long-founded categories of meaning. How can we, they ask, apply the same title to the *Iliad* and to *Paradise Lost*, separated as they are by millennia of historical fact? Can "tragedy" signify anything if we use it at once of *Antigone*, of *King Lear*, and of *Phèdre*?

The answer is that ancient recognitions and habits of understanding run deeper than the rigours of time. Tradition and the long ground-swell of unity are no less real than that sense of disorder and vertigo which the new dark ages have loosed upon us. Call epic that form of poetic apprehension in which a moment of history or a body of religious myth is centrally engaged; say of tragedy that it is a vision of life which derives its principles of meaning from the infirmity of man's estate, from what Henry James called the "imagination of disaster." Neither definition will do in respect of exhaustiveness or inclusion. But they will suffice to remind us that there are great traditions, lines of spiritual descent, which relate Homer to Yeats and Aeschylus to Chekhov. To these criticism must return with passionate awe and a sense of life ever renewed.

At present, there is grievous need of such return. All about us flourishes the new illiteracy, the illiteracy of those who can read short words or words of hatred and tawdriness but cannot grasp the meaning of language when it is in a condition of beauty or of truth. "I should like to believe," writes one of the finest of modern critics, "that there is clear proof of the need, in our particular society a greater need than ever before, for both scholar and critic to do a particular job of work: the job of putting the audience into a responsive relation with the work of art: to do the job of intermediary." [1] Not to judge or to anatomize, but to mediate. Only through love of the work of art, only through the critic's constant and anguished recognition of the distance which separates his craft from that of the poet, can such mediation be accomplished. It is a love made lucid through bitterness: it looks on miracles of creative genius, discerns their principles of being, exhibits these to the public, yet knows it has no part, or merely the slightest, in their actual creation.

These I take to be the tenets of what one might call "the old criticism" in partial distinction from that brilliant and prevailing school known as "the new criticism." The old criticism is engendered by admiration. It sometimes steps back from the text to look upon moral purpose. It thinks of literature as existing not in isolation but as central to the play of historical and political energies. Above all, the old criticism is philosophic in range and temper. It proceeds, with most general application, on a belief particularized by Jean-Paul Sartre in an essay on Faulkner: "the technique of a novel always refers us back to the metaphysic of the novelist [*à la métaphysique du romancier*]." In works of art are gathered the mythologies of thought, the heroic efforts of the human spirit to impose order and interpretation on the chaos of experience. Though inseparable from aesthetic form, philosophic content—the entry of faith or speculation into the poem—has its own principles of action. There are numerous examples of art which moves us to performance or conviction through its proposal of ideas. To these modes contemporary critics, with the exception of the Marxists, have not always been attentive.

The old criticism has its bias: it tends to believe that the "supreme poets of the world" have been men im-

[1] R. P. Blackmur: "The Lion and the Honeycomb" (*The Lion and the Honeycomb*, New York, 1955).

6

pelled either to acquiescence or rebellion by the mystery of God, that there are magnitudes of intent and poetic force to which secular art cannot attain, or, at least, has not as yet attained. Man is, as Malraux affirms in *The Voices of Silence*, trapped between the finiteness of the human condition and the infinity of the stars. Only through his monuments of reason and artistic creation can he lay claim to transcendent dignity. But in doing so he both imitates and rivals the shaping powers of the Deity. Thus there is at the heart of the creative process a religious paradox. No man is more wholly wrought in God's image or more inevitably His challenger than the poet. "I always feel," said D. H. Lawrence, "as if I stood naked for the fire of Almighty God to go through me—and it's rather an awful feeling. One has to be so terribly religious, to be an artist." [2] Not, perhaps, to be a true critic.

Such are some of the values I would bring to bear on this study of Tolstoy and Dostoevsky. They are the two greatest of novelists (all criticism is, in its moments of truth, dogmatic; the old criticism reserves the right of being so openly, and of using superlatives). "No English novelist," wrote E. M. Forster, "is as great as Tolstoy—that is to say has given so complete a picture of man's life, both on its domestic and heroic side. No English novelist has explored man's soul as deeply as Dostoevsky." [3] Forster's judgment need not be restricted to English literature. It defines the relationship of Tolstoy and Dostoevsky to the art of the novel as a whole. By its very nature, however, such a proposition cannot be demonstrated. It is, in a curious but definite sense, a matter of "ear." The tone we use when referring to Homer or Shakespeare rings true when applied to Tolstoy and Dostoevsky. We can speak in one breath of the *Iliad* and *War and Peace*, of *King Lear* and *The Brothers Karamazov*. It is as simple and as complex as that. But I say again that such a statement is not sub-

[2] D. H. Lawrence to Ernest Collings, February 24, 1913 (*The Letters of D. H. Lawrence*, New York, 1932).

[3] E. M. Forster: *Aspects of the Novel* (New York, 1950).

ject to rational proof. There is no conceivable way of demonstrating that someone who places *Madame Bovary* above *Anna Karenina* or considers *The Ambassadors* comparable in authority and magnitude to *The Possessed* is mistaken—that he has no "ear" for certain essential tonalities. But such "tone-deafness" can never be overcome by consequent argument (who could have persuaded Nietzsche, one of the keenest minds ever to deal with music, that he was perversely in error when he regarded Bizet as superior to Wagner?). There is, moreover, no use lamenting the "non-demonstrability" of critical judgments. Perhaps because they have made life difficult for artists, critics are destined to share something of the fate of Cassandra. Even when they see most clearly, they have no way of proving that they are right and they may not be believed. But Cassandra *was* right.

Let me, therefore, affirm my unrepentant conviction that Tolstoy and Dostoevsky stand foremost among novelists. They excel in comprehensiveness of vision and force of execution. Longinus would, quite properly, have spoken of "sublimity." They possessed the power to construct through language "realities" which are sensuous and concrete, yet pervaded by the life and mystery of the spirit. It is this power that marks Matthew Arnold's "supreme poets of the world." But although they stand apart through sheer dimension—consider the sum of life gathered in *War and Peace, Anna Karenina, Resurrection, Crime and Punishment, The Idiot, The Possessed,* and *The Brothers Karamazov*—Tolstoy and Dostoevsky were integral to the flowering of the Russian novel in the nineteenth century. That flowering, whose circumstances I shall consider in this opening chapter, would seem to represent one of the three principal moments of triumph in the history of western literature, the other two being the time of the Athenian dramatists and Plato and the age of Shakespeare. In all three the western mind leapt forward into darkness by means of poetic intuition; in them was assembled much of the light that we possess on the nature of man.

Many other books have been written and will be

written about the dramatic and illustrative lives of Tolstoy and Dostoevsky, about their place in the history of the novel and the role of their politics and theology in the history of ideas. With the advent of Russia and Marxism to the threshold of empire, the prophetic character of Tolstoyan and Dostoevskyan thought, its relevance to our own destinies, has forced itself upon us. But there is need of a treatment at once narrower and more unified. Enough time has elapsed so that we may perceive the greatness of Tolstoy and of Dostoevsky in the perspective of the major traditions. Tolstoy asked that his works be compared to those of Homer. Far more precisely than Joyce's *Ulysses*, *War and Peace*, and *Anna Karenina* embody the resurgence of the epic mode, the re-entry into literature of tonalities, narrative practices, and forms of articulation that had declined from western poetics after the age of Milton. But to see why this is so, to justify to one's critical intelligence those immediate and indiscriminate recognitions of Homeric elements in *War and Peace*, requires a reading of some delicacy and closeness. In the case of Dostoevsky there is a similar need for a more exact view. It has generally been recognized that his genius was of a dramatic cast, that his was, in significant respects, the most comprehensive and natural dramatic temper since Shakespeare's (a comparison which he himself hinted at). But only with the publication and translation of a fair number of Dostoevsky's drafts and notebooks—material of which I shall largely avail myself—has it become possible to trace the manifold affinities between the Dostoevskyan conception of the novel and the techniques of drama. The idea of a theatre, as Francis Fergusson has called it, suffered a brusque decline, so far as tragedy is concerned, after Goethe's *Faust*. The chain of being which leads back, through discernible kinship, to Aeschylus, Sophocles, and Euripides seemed broken. But *The Brothers Karamazov* is firmly rooted in the world of *King Lear*; in Dostoevskyan fiction the tragic sense of life, in the old manner, is wholly renewed. Dostoevsky is one of the great tragic poets.

Too often Tolstoy's and Dostoevsky's excursions into political theory, theology, and the study of history have been dismissed as eccentricities of genius or as instances of those curious blindnesses to which great minds are heir. Where they have received serious attention, that attention has discriminated between philosopher and novelist. But in mature art techniques and metaphysics are aspects of unity. In Tolstoy and in Dostoevsky as, one would suppose, in Dante, poetry and metaphysics, the impulse towards creation and towards systematic cognition, were alternate and yet inseparable responses to the pressures of experience. Thus, Tolstoyan theology and the world view operative in his novels and tales had passed through the same crucible of conviction. *War and Peace* is a poem of history, but of history seen in the specific light or, if we prefer, in the specific obscurity of Tolstoyan determinism. The poetics of the novelist and the myth of human affairs which he propounded are equally pertinent to our understanding. Dostoevsky's metaphysics have, of late, been closely attended to; they are a seminal force in modern existentialism. But little has been observed of the crucial interplay between the novelist's messianic and apocalyptic vision of things and the actual forms of his craft. How do metaphysics enter into literature and what happens to them when they get there? The last chapter of this essay will address itself to this theme as it is exemplified in such works as *Anna Karenina, Resurrection, The Possessed,* and *The Brothers Karamazov.*

But why "Tolstoy or Dostoevsky"? Because I propose to consider their achievements and define the nature of their respective genius through contrast. The Russian philosopher Berdiaev wrote: "It would be possible to determine two patterns, two types among men's souls, the one inclined toward the spirit of Tolstoy, the other toward that of Dostoevsky." [4] Experience bears him out. A reader may regard them as the two principle masters of fiction—that is to say, he may find in their nov-

[4] N. A. Berdiaev: *L'Esprit de Dostoievski* (trans. by A. Nerville, Paris, 1946).

els the most inclusive and searching portrayal of life. But press him closely and he will choose between them. If he tells you which he prefers and why, you will, I think, have penetrated into his own nature. The choice between Tolstoy and Dostoevsky foreshadows what existentialists would call *un engagement*; it commits the imagination to one or the other of two radically opposed interpretations of man's fate, of the historical future, and of the mystery of God. To quote Berdiaev again: Tolstoy and Dostoevsky exemplify "an insoluble controversy, in which two sets of assumptions, two fundamental conceptions of existence, confront each other." This confrontation touches on some of the prevailing dualities in western thought as they reach back to the Platonic dialogues. But it is also tragically germane to the ideological warfare of our time. Soviet presses pour out literally millions of copies of the novels of Tolstoy; they have only recently and reluctantly issued *The Possessed*.

But are Tolstoy and Dostoevsky, in fact, comparable? Is it more than a critic's fable to imagine their minds engaged in dialogue and mutual awareness? The principal obstacles to such types of comparison are lack of material and disparities in magnitude. For example: we no longer possess the cartoons for "The Battle of Anghiari." Thus we cannot contrast Michelangelo and Leonardo da Vinci when they were at work in rival invention. But the documentation on Tolstoy and Dostoevsky is abundant. We know in what manner they regarded each other and what *Anna Karenina* signified to the author of *The Idiot*. I suspect, moreover, that there is in one of Dostoevsky's novels a prophetic allegory of the spiritual encounter between himself and Tolstoy. There is between them no discordance of stature; they were titans both. Readers of the late seventeenth century were probably the last who saw Shakespeare as genuinely comparable to his fellow dramatists. He now looms too large in our reverence. When judging Marlowe, Jonson, or Webster we hold up a smoked glass against the sun. This is not true of Tolstoy and Dostoevsky. They afford the historian of ideas and the literary critic a unique conjunction, as of neighbouring planets, equal in magnitude and perturbed by each other's orbit. They challenge comparison.

Moreover, there was common ground between them. Their images of God, their proposals of action, are ultimately irreconcilable. But they wrote in the same language and at the same decisive moment in history. There were a number of occasions on which they came very near to meeting; each time they drew back out of some tenacious premonition. Merezhkovsky, an erratic, untrustworthy, and yet illuminating witness, termed Tolstoy and Dostoevsky the most contrary of writers:

I say contrary, but not remote, not alien; for often they came in contact like extremes that meet.[5]

Much of this essay will be divisive in spirit, seeking to distinguish the epic poet from the dramatist, the rationalist from the visionary, the Christian from the pagan. But there were between Tolstoy and Dostoevsky areas of semblance and points of affinity which made the antagonism in their natures all the more radical. It is with these I would begin.

II

First, there is "massiveness," the vastness of dimension in which their genius laboured. *War and Peace, Anna Karenina, Resurrection, The Idiot, The Possessed,* and *The Brothers Karamazov* are novels of great length. Tolstoy's *Death of Ivan Ilych* and Dostoevsky's *Letters from the Underworld* are long stories, novellas tending towards the major form. Because it is so evident and naïve we tend to dismiss this fact as a hazard of circumstance. But the length of Tolstoyan and Dostoevskyan fiction was essential to the purpose of the two novelists. It is characteristic of their vision.

The problem of literal magnitude is elusive. But differences in sheer length between *Wuthering Heights,*

[5] D. S. Merezhkovsky: *Tolstoi as Man and Artist, with an Essay on Dostoïevski* (London, 1902).

say, and *Moby Dick*, or between *Fathers and Sons* and *Ulysses* do lead from a discussion of contrasting techniques to the realization that different aesthetics and different ideals are involved. Even if we restrict ourselves to the longer types of prose fiction, there is need for discrimination. In the novels of Thomas Wolfe length bears witness to exuberant energy and to failures of control, to dissolution amid the excessive wonders of language. *Clarissa* is long, immensely long, because Richardson was translating into the new vocabulary of psychological analysis the episodic and loose-knit structure of the picaresque tradition. In the gigantic forms of *Moby Dick* we perceive not only a perfect accord between theme and mode of treatment, but a device of narration going back to Cervantes—the art of the long digression. The *romans-fleuves*, the many-volumed chronicles of Balzac, Zola, Proust, and Jules Romains, illustrate the powers of length in two respects: as a suggestion of the epic manner and as a device for communicating a sense of history. But even within this class (so characteristically French) we must distinguish: the link between individual novels in the *Comédie humaine* is by no means the same as that between successive works in Proust's *A la recherche du temps perdu*.

Speculating on the differences between long and short poems, Poe found that the former could include dull stretches, digressions, ambivalences of tone without losing their essential virtue. In return, however, the long poem could not achieve the unflagging intensity and tightness of the short lyric. In the case of prose fiction we cannot apply the same rule. The failures of Dos Passos are, precisely, failures of inequality. On the other hand, the mesh is as finely and tightly wrought in the great cycle of Proust as it is in that brilliant miniature, Mme de La Fayette's *Princesse de Clèves*.

The massiveness of the novels of Tolstoy and Dostoevsky was noted from the start. Tolstoy was censured, and has been censured ever since, for his philosophic interpolations, for his moralizing digressions and perceptible reluctance to end a plot. Henry James spoke of "loose and baggy monsters." Russian critics tell us that the length of a Dostoevskyan novel is frequently due to its laboured and corruscated style, to the vacillations of the novelist with regard to his personages, and to the plain fact that he was being paid by the sheet. *The Idiot* and *The Possessed*, like their Victorian counterparts, reflect the economics of serialization. Among Western readers the long-windedness of the two masters has often been interpreted as peculiarly Russian, as in some manner consequent on Russia's physical immensity. This is an absurd notion: Pushkin, Lermontov, and Turgeniev are exemplary of concision.

On reflection, it becomes evident that for both Tolstoy and Dostoevsky plenitude was an essential freedom. It characterized their lives and persons as well as their view of the art of the novel. Tolstoy composed on a vast canvas commensurate to the breadth of his being and suggestive of the links between the time structure of the novel and the flow of time through history. The massiveness of Dostoevsky mirrors fidelity to detail and an encompassing grasp of the countless particularities of gesture and thought that accumulate towards the moment of drama.

The more we consider the two novelists, the more we come to realize that they and their works were hewn to the same scale.

Tolstoy's gigantic vitality, his bearish strength and feats of nervous endurance, the excess in him of every life-force are notorious. His contemporaries, such as Gorky, pictured him as a titan roaming the earth in antique majesty. There was something fantastical and obscurely blasphemous about his old age. He passed into his ninth decade every inch a king. He laboured to the end, unbent, pugnacious, rejoicing in his autocracy. Tolstoy's energies were such that he could neither imagine nor create in small dimensions. Whenever he entered into a room or a literary form he conveyed the impression of a giant stooping under a door built for ordinary men. One of his plays has six acts. There is appropriateness in the fact that the Dukhobors, a religious group whose emigration from Russia to Canada was financed by the royalties on Tolstoy's *Resurrection*, should parade naked in blizzards and burn down barns in exuberant defiance.

Everywhere in Tolstoy's life, whether in the gambling bouts and bear-hunts of his youth, in his tempestuous and fruitful marriage, or in the ninety volumes of his printed works, the might of the creative impulse is evident. T. E. Lawrence (himself a man of daemonic powers) admitted to Forster:

it is hopeless to grapple with Tolstoy. The man is like yesterday's east wind, which brought tears when you faced it and numbed you meanwhile.[6]

Ample sections of *War and Peace* were re-drafted seven times. Tolstoyan novels close reluctantly as if the pressure of creation, that occult ecstasy which comes of shaping life through language, had not yet been expended. Tolstoy knew of his immensity and gloried in the rush and pulse of his blood. Once, in a moment of patriarchal grandeur, he questioned mortality itself. He wondered whether death—clearly signifying his own physical death—was truly inevitable. Why should he die when he felt untapped resources in his body and when his presence was so urgently needed by the pilgrims and disciples flocking to Yasnaya Polyana from all over the world? Perhaps Nicholas Fedorov, the librarian of the Rumantsev Museum, was right in stressing the idea of a full and literal resurrection of the dead. Tolstoy said: "I do not share all Fedorov's views," but they obviously attracted him.

Dostoevsky is often cited in contrast, being singled out by critics and biographers as the arch-instance of creative neurosis. This view is reinforced by the images most commonly associated with his career: incarceration in Siberia, epilepsy, bitter destitution, and the thread of personal agony which appears to run through all his works and days. It is given authority by a mis-

[6] T. E. Lawrence to E. M. Forster, February 20, 1924 (*The Letters of T. E. Lawrence*, New York, 1939).

reading of Thomas Mann's distinction between the Olympian health of Goethe and Tolstoy and the sickness of Nietzsche and Dostoevsky.

In actual fact, Dostoevsky was endowed with exceptional strength and powers of endurance, with tremendous resilience and animal toughness. These sustained him through the purgatory of his personal life and the imagined hell of his creations. John Cowper Powys notes as central to Dostoevsky's nature a "mysterious and profoundly feminine enjoyment of life *even while suffering from life.*" [7] He points to that "brimming over of the life force" which enabled the novelist to maintain the furious pace of his creation while in the utmost of material want or physical discomfort. As Powys finely distinguishes, the joy which Dostoevsky attained even in moments of anguish was not masochistic (although there was masochism in his temper). It sprang, rather, from the primal, cunning pleasure that a mind will take in its own tenacity. The man lived at white heat.

He survived the agonizing experience of mock execution in front of a firing squad; indeed, he transformed the remembrance of that dread hour into a talisman of endurance and a persistent source of inspiration. He survived the Siberian *katorga* and the period of service in a penal regiment. He wrote his voluminous novels, tales, and polemic essays under financial and psychological exactions which would have worn down anyone of lesser vitality. Dostoevsky said of himself that he had the sinuous tenacity of a cat. He spent most of the days in his nine lives working at full strength—whether or not he had passed the night gambling, fighting off illness, or begging for a loan.

It is in this light that one should view his epilepsy. The pathology and origins of Dostoevsky's "holy sickness" remain obscure. What little we know of the dates makes it difficult to accept Freud's theory of a causal relation between the first seizures and the murder of Dostoevsky's father. The novelist's own conception of

[7] John Cowper Powys: *Dostoievsky* (London, 1946).

epilepsy was ambiguous and pervaded by religious over-tones: he saw in it both a cruel and demeaning trial and a mysterious gift through which a man could achieve instants of miraculous illumination and sharp-sighted-ness. Both Prince Muishkin's accounts in *The Idiot* and the dialogue between Shatov and Kirillov in *The Possessed* portray epileptic fits as realizations of total experience, as outward thrusts of the most secret and central forces of life. In the moment of seizure the soul is liberated from the constricting hold of the senses. No-where does Dostoevsky suggest that the "idiot" regrets his hallowing affliction.

It is probable that Dostoevsky's own illness was di-rectly associated with his extraordinary nervous powers. It may have acted as a release for his insurgent energies. Thomas Mann saw in it "a product of over-flowing vi-tality, an explosion and excess of enormous health." [8] Surely this is the key to Dostoevsky's nature: "enor-mous health" using illness as an instrument of percep-tion. In this respect the comparison with Nietzsche is justified. Dostoevsky is illustrative of those artists and thinkers who surround themselves with physical suffer-ing as with "a dome of many-coloured glass." Through it they see reality intensified. Thus Dostoevsky may also be compared to Proust, who built his asthma into a wall to guard the monasticism of his art, or to Joyce, who fed his ear on blindness and listened to darkness as to a sea-shell.

"Contrary, but not remote, not alien," said Merezh-kovsky: Tolstoyan health and Dostoevskyan sickness bore similar marks of creative might.

T. E. Lawrence confided to Edward Garnett:

Do you remember my telling you once that I collected a shelf of "Titanic" books (those distinguished by greatness of spirit, "sublimity" as Longinus would call it): and they were *The Karamazovs*, *Zarathustra*, and *Moby Dick*.[9]

[8] Thomas Mann: *"Dostojewski—Mit Maassen"* (*Neue Stu-dien*, Stockholm, 1948).

[9] T. E. Lawrence to Edward Garnett, August 26, 1922 (*The Letters of T. E. Lawrence*).

Five years later he extended this list to include *War and Peace*. These are "Titanic" books, and the quality which Lawrence evoked was made manifest both in their outward magnitude and in the lives of their authors.

But the characteristic magnificence of the art of Tolstoy and Dostoevsky—the manner in which it restored to literature a wholeness of conception that had passed from it with the decline of epic poetry and tragic drama—cannot be perceived in isolation. Nor can we limit our attention solely to the Russians, although Virginia Woolf was tempted to ask whether "to write of any fiction save theirs is a waste of time." [1] Before considering the works of Tolstoy and Dostoevsky in themselves, I want to pause, for a moment, on the general theme of the art of fiction and on the particular virtues of the Russian and the American novel in the nineteenth century.

III

The main tradition of the European novel arose out of the very circumstances that had brought on the dissolution of the epic and the decay of serious drama. Through the innocence of remoteness and the repeated accident of individual genius, the Russian novelists from Gogol to Gorky charged their medium with such energies, with such extremes of insight and so fierce a poetry of belief, that prose fiction, as a literary form, came to rival (and some would say, surpass) the range of the epic and of drama. But the history of the novel is not one of sustaining continuity. The Russian achievement was realized in sharp differentiation from the prevailing European mode, even in opposition to it. The Russian masters—like Hawthorne and Melville in their own, somewhat different ways—did violence to the conventions of the genre as it had been conceived from the time of Defoe to that of Flaubert. The point being this: to the eighteenth-century realists these con-

[1] Virginia Woolf: "Modern Fiction" (*The Common Reader*, New York, 1925).

ventions had been a source of strength; at the time of *Madame Bovary* they had become limitations. What were they and how did they originate?

In its natural mode an epic poem addresses itself to a rather close-knit group of listeners; the drama, where it is still alive and not merely an artifice, is intended for a collective organism—a theatrical audience. But a novel speaks to an individual reader in the anarchy of private life. It is a form of communication between a writer and an essentially fragmented society, an "imaginative creation," as Burckhardt put it, "read in solitude." [2] To inhabit a room of one's own, to read a book to oneself, is to partake in a condition rich in historical and psychological implications. These have direct bearing on the history and character of European prose fiction. They have given it its numerous and determining associations with the fortunes and world view of the middle classes. If we may say of the Homeric and Virgilian epics that they were forms of discourse between poet and aristocracy, so we may say of the novel that it has been the primary art-form of the age of the *bourgeoisie*.

The novel arose not only as the art of the housed and private man in the European cities. It was, from the time of Cervantes onward, the mirror which the imagination, in its vein of reason, held up to empirical reality. *Don Quixote* bid an ambiguous and compassionate farewell to the world of the epic; *Robinson Crusoe* staked out that of the modern novel. Like Defoe's castaway, the novelist will surround himself with a palisade of tangible facts: with Balzac's marvellously solid houses, with the smell of Dickens's puddings, with Flaubert's drug-counters . and Zola's inexhaustible inventories. Where he finds a footprint in the sand, the novelist will conclude that it is the man Friday lurking in the bushes, not a fairy spoor or, as in a Shakespearean world, the ghostly trace of "the god Hercules, whom Antony loved."

The main current of the Western novel is prosaic, in

[2] Jakob Burckhardt: *Weltgeschichtliche Betrachtungen* (*Gessamelte Werke*, IV, Basel, 1956).

the exact rather than the pejorative sense. In it neither Milton's Satan winging through the immensities of chaos nor the Weird Sisters from *Macbeth*, sailing to Aleppo in their sieve, are really at home. Windmills are no longer giants, but windmills. In exchange, fiction will tell us how windmills are built, what they earn, and precisely how they sound on a gusty night. For it is the genius of the novel to describe, analyze, explore, and accumulate the data of actuality and introspection. Of all the renditions of experience that literature attempts, of all the counter-statements to reality put forward in language, that of the novel is the most coherent and inclusive. The works of Defoe, Balzac, Dickens, Trollope, Zola, or Proust document our sense of the world and of the past. They are first cousins to history.

There are, of course, types of fiction to which this does not apply. On the confines of the governing tradition there have been persistent areas of irrationalism and myth. The great bulk of the Gothic (to which I shall return when considering Dostoevsky), Mrs. Shelley's *Frankenstein*, and *Alice in Wonderland* are representative instances of rebellion against prevailing empiricism. One need refer only to Emily Brontë, E. T. A. Hoffmann, and Poe to realize that the discredited daemonology of the "pre-scientific" era had its vigorous after-life. But in the main the European novel of the eighteenth and nineteenth centuries was secular in outlook, rational in method, and social in context.

As its technical resources and solidity increased, realism developed vast ambitions: it sought to establish through language societies as complex and substantial as those existing in the outside world. In a minor key this attempt produced Trollope's Barchester; in a major, the fantastic dream of the *Comédie humaine*. As outlined in 1845, the work was to comprise one hundred and thirty-seven distinct titles. In it the life of France was to find its total counterpart. Balzac wrote a famous letter in 1844 comparing his design with the accomplishments of Napoleon, Cuvier, and O'Connell:

Le premier a vécu de la vie de l'Europe; il s'est inoculé des armées! Le second a épousé le globe! Le troisième s'est incarné un peuple! Moi j'aurai porté une société entière dans ma tête!

(The first lived the life of Europe; he inoculated himself with armies! The second took the round earth itself in marriage! The third embodied a nation! I shall have carried an entire society in my head!)

Balzac's conquering ambition has its modern parallel: Yoknapatawpha County, "sole owner, William Faulkner."

But from the outset there was present in the doctrine and practices of the realistic novel an element of contradiction. Was the treatment of contemporary life appropriate to what Matthew Arnold called "the high seriousness" of truly great literature? Sir Walter Scott preferred historical themes, hoping to attain through them that nobility and poetic remoteness characteristic of the epic and of verse drama. It required the performances of Jane Austen and George Eliot, of Dickens and Balzac, to demonstrate that modern society and daily happenings could provide materials for artistic and moral preoccupation as enthralling as those which poets and dramatists had drawn from earlier cosmologies. But these performances, through their very thoroughness and power, confronted realism with yet another and, ultimately, more intractable dilemma. Would the sheer mass of observed fact not come to overwhelm and dissolve the artistic purpose and formal control of the novelist?

In their concern for moral discrimination, in their scrutiny of values, the mature realists of the nineteenth century were, as F. R. Leavis has shown, able to prevent the encroachment of their material on the integrity of literary form. Indeed, the keenest critical minds of the age perceived the dangers of excessive verisimilitude. Goethe and Hazlitt pointed out that in endeavouring to portray the entirety of modern life, art ran the risk of becoming journalism. And Goethe noted, in the Prologue to *Faust*, that the prevalence of newspapers had already debased the sensibilities of the literary public. Paradoxical as it may seem, reality itself had during the late eighteenth and early nineteenth centuries assumed a heightened colouring; it pressed upon ordinary men and women with mounting vivacity. Hazlitt wondered whether any one who had lived through the era of the French Revolution and the Napoleonic wars would find satisfaction in the contrived ardours of literature. Both he and Goethe saw in the vogue of melodrama and the Gothic novel direct, though misconceived, responses to this challenge.

Their fears were prophetic but, in fact, premature. They foreshadow the agony of Flaubert and the collapse of the naturalistic novel under the weight of its documentation. Prior to the 1860's European fiction flourished under the challenges and pressures of reality. To revert to an image I have used earlier: Cézanne taught the eye to see objects in what is, literally, a new light and depth. Similarly, the age of Revolution and Empire bestowed on daily life the stature and resplendency of myth. It vindicated with finality the supposition that in observing their own times artists would find themes in the grand manner. The happenings of the period from 1789 to 1820 gave to men's awareness of contemporaneity something of the freshness and vibrancy which Impressionism subsequently gave to their awareness of physical space. The assault of France upon its own past and upon Europe, the brief course of empire from the Tagus to the Vistula, heightened the pace and urgency of experience even for those who were not directly involved. What had been to Montesquieu and to Gibbon themes of philosophical inquiry, what had been to the Augustan and Neo-classical poets situations and motifs drawn from ancient history, became to the romantics the fabric of daily life.

One could assemble an anthology of crowded and passionate hours to show how the very rhythm of experience mounted. It might begin with the anecdote of how Kant was delayed in his morning walk, once and once only, on being informed of the fall of the Bastille and go on to that wonderful passage in *The Prelude* in which Wordsworth tells of hearing the news of the death of Robespierre. It would include Goethe's description of how a new world was born at the battle of Valmy and De Quincey's account of the apocalyptic and nocturnal coach rides when the mails tore out of London with bulletins from the Peninsular War. It would portray Hazlitt on the verge of suicide when hearing of Napoleon's downfall at Waterloo and Byron conspiring with Italian revolutionaries. Such an anthology could appropriately close with Berlioz's account, in his memoirs, of how he escaped from the Ecole des Beaux-Arts, joined the insurgents of 1830, and conducted them, extempore, in his arrangement of the *Marseillaise*.

The novelists of the nineteenth century inherited a heightened sense for the dramatic fitness of their own times. A world that had known Danton and Austerlitz did not think it necessary to look to mythology or the ancient past for the raw materials of poetic vision. This did not signify, however, that responsible novelists dealt directly with the events of the day. Rather, and with a subtle instinct for the range of their art, they sought to render the new tempo of life in the private experiences of men and women who were in no way historical personages. Or, like Jane Austen, they portrayed the resistances which the old-established and quieter forms of behaviour offered to the inrush of modernity. This explains the curious and important fact that the romantic and Victorian novelists of the first rank did not yield to the obvious temptations of the Napoleonic theme. As Zola pointed out, in his essay on Stendhal, the influence of Napoleon on European psychology, on the mood and tenor of consciousness, had been far-reaching:

I insist on this fact because I have never seen a study of the very real impact of Napoleon on our literature. The Empire was a time of mediocre literary achievement; but one cannot deny that Napoleon's destiny acted like a hammer-blow on the heads of his contemporaries. . . . All ambitions waxed large, all undertaking took on a gigantic air and in literature, as in all other domains, all dreams turned on universal kingship.

Balzac's dream of rule over the kingdom of words was a direct consequence.

Nevertheless, fiction did not seek to usurp the arts of the journalist and the historian. Revolution and Empire play a large role in the background of the nineteenth-century novel, but only in the background. Where they move too near the centre, as in Dickens's *Tale of Two Cities* and Anatole France's *Les Dieux ont soif*, the piece of fiction itself loses in maturity and distinction. Balzac and Stendhal were alive to the danger. Both conceived of reality as somehow illumined and ennobled by the emotions which the Revolution and Napoleon had loosed upon the lives of men. Both were fascinated by the theme of "Bonapartism" in private or commercial domains. They sought to show how the energies released by the political upheavals came to reshape the patterns of society and man's image of himself. In the *Comédie humaine* the Napoleonic legend is a centre of gravity in the narrative design and architecture. But in all except a few minor works the Emperor himself makes only fleeting and indecisive appearances. Both Stendhal's *Charterhouse of Parma* and *The Red and the Black* are variations on the theme of Bonapartism, inquiries into the anatomy of the spirit when the latter had been exposed to reality in its most violent and majestic guises. But it is richly instructive that the hero of *The Charterhouse* glimpses Napoleon only once, in a momentary and blurred vision.

Dostoevsky was a direct heir to this convention. The Russian poet and critic Vyacheslav Ivanov has traced the evolution of the Napoleonic motif from Balzac's Rastignac, through Stendhal's Julien Sorel to *Crime and Punishment*. The "Napoleon dream" found its deepest rendition in the personage of Raskolnikov, and this intensification is indicative of how greatly the art of the novel had widened its possibilities as it passed from western Europe to Russia. Tolstoy broke decisively with the previous treatments of the imperial subject. In *War and Peace* Napoleon is directly presented. Not at first: his appearance at Austerlitz bears the marks of the oblique method of Stendhal (whom Tolstoy greatly admired). But thereafter, and as the novel proceeds, he is shown, as it were, full-face. This reflects more than a change of narrative technique. It is consequent on Tolstoy's philosophy of history and on his kinship with the heroic epic. Moreover it betrays the desire of the man of letters—a desire which was particularly strong in Tolstoy—to circumscribe and thus master the man of action.

But as the events of the first two decades of the nineteenth century receded into history, glory seemed to fall from the air. When reality grew more sombre and retrenched, the dilemmas inherent in the theory and practice of realism came to the fore. As early as 1836—in *La Confession d'un enfant du siècle*—Musset argued that the period of exhilaration, the era in which Revolutionary freedom and Napoleonic heroism had reverberated in the atmosphere and fired the imagination, had faded away. In its place descended the gray, ponderous, Philistine rule of the industrial middle classes. What had once seemed the daemonic saga of money, that romance of the "financial Napoleons" which had enthralled Balzac, had turned into the inhuman routine of the counting-house and the assembly line. As Edmund Wilson shows in his essay on Dickens, Ralph Nickleby, Arthur Gride, and the Chuzzlewits were replaced by Pecksniff and, more terribly, by Murdstone. The fog which lingers on every page of *Bleak House* is symbolic of the layers of cant under which the capitalism of the mid-nineteenth century concealed its ruthlessness.

In scorn or indignation, such writers as Dickens, Heine, and Baudelaire sought to cut through the muffled hypocrisies of language. But the *bourgeoisie* took delight in their genius and shielded itself behind the theory that literature did not really pertain to practical life and could be allowed its liberties. Hence arose the image of a dissociation between the artist and society, an image which continues to haunt and alienate literature, painting, and music in our time.

But I am not concerned with the economic and social changes which began in the 1830's, with the imposition of mercenary ruthlessness through a code of rigorous morality. The classical analysis has been made by Marx, who, in Wilson's words,

was demonstrating through these middle years of the century that this system, with its falsifying of human relations and its wholesale encouragement of cant, was an inherent and irremediable feature of the economic structure itself.[3]

I am dealing only with the effect of these changes on the main current of the European novel. The transformation in the values and rhythm of actual life confronted the whole theory of realism with a bitter dilemma. Should the novelist continue to honour his commitment to verisimilitude and to the re-creation of reality when the latter was no longer worth re-creating? Would the novel itself not succumb to the monotony and moral falsehood of its subject matter?

Flaubert's genius was riven by this question. *Madame Bovary* was composed in a cold fury of heart and carries within it the limiting and ultimately insoluble paradox of realism. Flaubert escaped from it only in the flamboyant archaeology of *Salammbô* and *La Tentation de saint Antoine*. But he could not let reality be and strove, in compulsive and self-defeating labour, to gather it all into an encyclopedia of disgust, *Bouvard et Pécuchet*. The nineteenth-century world, as Flaubert saw it, had destroyed the foundations of humane culture. Lionel Trilling acutely argues that Flaubert's critique went beyond economic and social issues. *Bouvard et Pécuchet*

rejects culture. The human mind experiences the massed accumulation of its own works, those that are traditionally

3 Edmund Wilson: "Dickens: The Two Scrooges" (*Eight Essays*, New York, 1954).

held to be its greatest glories as well as those that are obviously of a contemptible sort, and arrives at the understanding that none will serve its purpose, that all are weariness and vanity, that the whole vast structure of human thought and creation are alien from the human person.[4]

The nineteenth century had come a long way since the "dawn" in which Wordsworth proclaimed that it was bliss to be alive.

In the end, "reality" overcame the novel, and the novelist shades into the reporter. The dissolution of the work of art under the pressures of fact can best be shown in the critical writings and fiction of Zola. (Here I shall follow closely on the lead given by George Lukács, one of the master critics of our time, in his essay on "The Zola Centenary.") To Zola the realism of Balzac and Stendhal was equally suspect, for both had allowed their imagination to infringe on the "scientific" principles of naturalism. He particularly deplored Balzac's attempt to re-create reality in his own image when he should have done everything in his power to give a faithful and "objective" account of contemporary life:

A naturalist writer wants to write a novel about the stage. Starting from this point without characters or data, his first concern will be to collect material, to find out what he can about this world he wishes to describe. . . . Then he will talk to the people best informed on the subject, will collect statements, anecdotes, portraits. But this is not all. He will also read the written documents available. Finally he will visit the locations, spend a few days in a theatre in order to acquaint himself with the smallest details, pass an evening in an actress' dressing-room and absorb the atmosphere as much as possible. When all this material has been gathered, the novel will take shape of its own accord. All the novelist has to do is to group the facts in a logical sequence. . . . Interest will no longer be focused on the peculiarities of the story—on the contrary, the more general and commonplace the story is, the more typical it will be.[5]

4 Lionel Trilling: "Flaubert's Last Testament" (*The Opposing Self*, New York, 1955).
5 Emile Zola, cit. by George Lukács: *"Erzählen oder Beschreiben?"* (*Probleme des Realismus*, Berlin, 1955).

27

Fortunately, Zola's genius, the strong colour of his imaginings, and the thrust of moral passion which intervened even where he thought himself most "scientific," counteracted this dreary program. *Pot-Bouille* is one of the best novels of the nineteenth century—great in its comic ferocity and tightness of design. As Henry James said,

It is in the great lusty game he plays with the shallow and the simple that Zola's mastery resides, and we see of course that when values are small it takes innumerable items and combinations to make up the sum.[6]

But the trouble was that the "mastery" was rare whereas the "shallow and the simple" abounded. In hands of lesser inspiration, the naturalistic novel became the art of the reporter, the incessant reproduction of some "slice of life" heightened with a dash of colour. As the instruments of total reproduction—the radio, photography, the cinema, and, ultimately, television—have grown more perfect and prevalent, the novel has found itself reduced either to trailing in their wake or to abandoning the canons of naturalism.

But was the dilemma of the realistic novel (and naturalism is merely its most radical aspect) wholly a consequence of the political and social *embourgeoisement* of the mid-nineteenth century? Unlike the Marxist critics, I think the roots lie deeper. The problem was inseparable from the assumptions on which the central tradition of the European novel had been founded. In committing itself to a secular interpretation of life and to a realistic portrayal of ordinary experience, eighteenth- and nineteenth-century fiction had predetermined its own limitations. This commitment had been no less operative in the art of Fielding than in that of Zola. The difference was that Zola had made of it a deliberate and rigorous method and that the spirit of the age had grown less susceptible to the ironic gallantry

[6] Henry James: "Emile Zola" (*Notes on Novelists, with Some Other Notes*, New York, 1914).

and drama with which Fielding had tempered the realism of *Tom Jones*.

In rejecting the mythical and the preternatural, all those things undreamt of in Horatio's philosophy, the modern novel had broken with the essential world view of the epic and of tragedy. It had claimed for its own what we might call the kingdom of this world. It is the vast kingdom of human psychology perceived through reason and of human behaviour in a social context. The Goncourts surveyed it when they defined fiction as ethics in action. But, for all its comprehensiveness (and there are those who would maintain that it is the only kingdom subject to our understanding), it has frontiers and they are recognizably limiting. We cross them when we pass from the world of *Bleak House* to that of *The Castle* (while noting at the same time that Kafka's principal symbol is related to Dickens's Chancery). We cross them with unmistakable enlargement when we pass from *Le Père Goriot*—Balzac's poem of father and daughters—to *King Lear*. We pass them again when we move from Zola's program for novelists to that letter of D. H. Lawrence's which I have cited earlier:

I always feel as if I stood naked for the fire of Almighty God to go through me—and it's rather an awful feeling. One has to be so terribly religious, to be an artist. I often think of my dear Saint Lawrence on his gridiron, when he said, "Turn me over, brothers, I am done enough on this side."

"One has to be so terribly religious"—there is a revolution in that phrase. For, above all else, the great tradition of the realistic novel had implied that religious feeling was not a necessary adjunct to a mature and comprehensive account of human affairs.

This revolution, which led to the achievements of Kafka and of Thomas Mann, of Joyce and of Lawrence himself, began not in Europe but in America and Russia. Lawrence declared: "Two bodies of modern literature seem to me to have come to a real verge: the Russian and the American." [7] Beyond it lay the possibility of *Moby Dick* and that of the novels of Tolstoy and Dostoevsky. But why America and Russia?

IV

The history of European fiction in the nineteenth century brings to mind the image of a nebula with wide-flung arms. At their extremities the American and the Russian novel radiate a whiter brilliance. As we move outward from the centre—and we may think of Henry James, Turgeniev, and Conrad as intermediary clusters—the stuff of realism grows more tenuous. The masters of the American and the Russian manner appear to gather something of their fierce intensity from the outer darkness, from the decayed matter of folk-lore, melodrama, and religious life.

European observers were uneasily cognizant of what lay beyond the orbit of traditional realism. They sensed that Russian and American imaginings had attained spheres of compassion and ferocity denied to a Balzac or a Dickens. French criticism, in particular, reflects the endeavours of a classical sensibility, of an intelligence attuned to measure and equilibrium, to respond justly to forms of vision that were both alien and exalting. At times, as in Flaubert's acknowledgment of *War and Peace*, this attempt to honour strange gods was tinged with scepticism or bitterness. For in defining the Russian and the American accomplishment, the European critic defined also the incompletions in his own great heritage. Even those who did most to familiarize Europeans with the stars in the eastern and western skies—Mérimée, Baudelaire, the Vicomte de Vogüé, the Goncourts, André Gide, and Valéry Larbaud—might be saddened to discover that in response to a questionnaire circulated in 1957 students at the Sorbonne set Dostoevsky high above any French writer.

In reflecting on the qualities of American and Russian fiction, European observers of the late nineteenth

[7] D. H. Lawrence: *Studies in Classic American Literature* (New York, 1923).

and early twentieth centuries sought to discover points of affinity between the United States of Hawthorne and Melville and pre-revolutionary Russia. The cold war makes this perspective seem archaic or even erroneous. But the distortion lies with us. To understand why it is (to apply Harry Levin's phrase about Joyce) that after *Moby Dick*, *Anna Karenina*, and *The Brothers Karamazov* it became far more difficult to be a novelist at all, one must consider the contrast not between Russia and America, but between Russia and America on the one hand and nineteenth-century Europe on the other. This essay is concerned with the Russians. But the psychological and material circumstances which liberated them from the dilemma of realism were present also on the American scene, and it is through American eyes that some of them may be most clearly perceived.

Obviously this is a vast topic and what follows should be regarded merely as notes towards a more adequate treatment. Four of the acutest minds of their age, Astolphe de Custine, Tocqueville, Matthew Arnold, and Henry Adams dealt with this theme. Each, from his own specific vantage point, was struck by analogies between the two emergent powers. Henry Adams went further and speculated, with extraordinary prescience, on what the fate of civilization would be once the two giants confronted each other across an enfeebled Europe.

The ambiguous yet determining nature of the relationship to Europe was, during the nineteenth century, a recurrent motif of both Russian and American intellectual life. Henry James made the classic pronouncement: "It's a complex fate, being an American, and one of the responsibilities it entails is fighting against a superstitious valuation of Europe." [8] In his tribute to George Sand, Dostoevsky said: "We Russians have two motherlands—Russia and Europe—even in cases where

---

[8] Henry James, cit. by P. Lubbock in a letter dated early 1872 (*The Letters of Henry James*, New York, 1920).

we call ourselves Slavophiles." [9] The complexity and the doubleness are equally manifest in Ivan Karamazov's celebrated declaration to his brother:

I want to travel in Europe, Alyosha, I shall set off from here. And yet I know that I am only going to a graveyard, but it's a most precious graveyard, that's what it is! Precious are the dead that lie there, every stone over them speaks of such burning life in the past, of such passionate faith in their work, their truth, their struggle and their science, that I know I shall fall on the ground and kiss those stones and weep over them; though I'm convinced in my heart that it's long been nothing but a graveyard.

Could this not be the motto of American literature from Hawthorne's *Marble Faun* to T. S. Eliot's *Four Quartets*?

In both nations the relationship to Europe assumed diverse and complex forms. Turgeniev, Henry James, and, later on, Eliot and Pound offer examples of direct acceptance, of conversion to the old world. Melville and Tolstoy were among the great refusers. But in most instances the attitudes were at once ambiguous and compulsive. Cooper noted in 1828, in his *Gleanings in Europe*: "If any man is excusable for deserting his country, it is the American artist." On this precise point the Russian intelligentsia was fiercely divided. But whether they welcomed the probability or deplored it, writers from both America and Russia tended to agree that their formative experiences would entail a necessary part of exile or "treason." Often the European pilgrimage would lead to a rediscovery and revaluation of the home country: Gogol "found" his Russia while living in Rome. But in both literatures the theme of the European voyage was the principal device for self-definition and the occasion for the normative gesture: Herzen's coach crossing the Polish frontier, Lambert Strether (the protagonist of James's *Ambassadors*) arriving in Chester. "To understand anything as vast

[9] Dostoevsky: *The Diary of a Writer* (trans. by Boris Brasol, New York, 1954).

and terrible as Russia," wrote the early Slavophile Kireevsky, "one must look on her from afar."

This confrontation with Europe gives Russian and American fiction something of its specific weight and dignity. Both civilizations were coming of age and were in search of their own image (this search being one of Henry James's essential fables). In both countries the novel helped give the mind a sense of place. Not an easy task; for whereas the European realist worked within points of reference fixed by a rich historical and literary legacy, his counterpart in the United States and in Russia either had to import a sense of continuity from abroad or to create a somewhat spurious autonomy with whatever material came to hand. It was the rare good fortune of Russian literature that Pushkin's genius was of so manifold and classical a cast. His works constituted in themselves a body of tradition. Moreover, they incorporated a large range of foreign influences and models. This is what Dostoevsky meant when he referred to Pushkin's "universal responsiveness":

Even the greatest of the European poets were never able to embody in themselves with such potency as Pushkin the genius of an alien, perhaps neighbouring people. . . . Pushkin alone—among all world poets—possesses the faculty of completely reincarnating in himself an alien nationality.[1]

In Gogol, moreover, the art of the Russian narrative found a craftsman who struck, from the first, the dominant tones and attitudes of the language and the form. The Russian novel did emerge out of his *Cloak*. American literature was less fortunate. The uncertainties of taste in Poe, Hawthorne, and Melville and the obscuring idiosyncrasies of their manner point directly to the dilemmas of individual talent producing in relative isolation.

Russia and America lacked even that sense of geo-

[1] Ibid.

graphical stability and cohesion which the European novel took for granted. Both nations combined immensity with the awareness of a romantic and vanishing frontier. What the Far West and the Red Man were to American mythology, the Caucasus and its warring tribes, or the unspoiled communities of Cossacks and Old Believers on the Don and the Volga were to Pushkin, Lermontov, and Tolstoy. Archetypal in both literatures is the theme of the hero who leaves behind the corrupt world of urban civilization and enervating passions to affront the dangers and moral purgations of the frontier. Leatherstocking and the hero of Tolstoy's *Tales from the Caucasus* are kindred as they move among the cool pine valleys and wild creatures in melancholy yet ardent pursuit of their "noble" foe.

The vastness of space brings with it exposures to natural forces at their most grandiose and ferocious; only in the Brontës and, subsequently, in D. H. Lawrence does the European novel show a comparable awareness of nature unleashed. The moody tyrannies of the sea in Dana and Melville, the archaic horrors of the ice-world in Poe's *Narrative of Arthur Gordon Pym*, the image of human nakedness in Tolstoy's *Snowstorm*—all these encounters of man with a physical setting which can destroy him in moments of wanton grandeur lie outside the repertoire of western European realism. Tolstoy's *How Much Land Does a Man Need?* (which Joyce thought the "greatest literature in the world") could have been written, in the nineteenth century, only by a Russian or an American. It is a parable on the immensity of the earth; it would have made sense neither in Dickens's Kentish landscape nor in Flaubert's Normandy.

But space isolates as much as it enlarges. Common to Russian and American literature was the theme of the artist seeking his identity and his public in a culture too new, too disorganized, and too preoccupied with the demands of material survival. Even the cities, in which the European consciousness perceived the very gathering and transcription of the past, were raw and anonymous in their Russian and American setting. From the time of Pushkin to that of Dostoevsky, St. Petersburg stands in Russian literature as a symbol of arbitrary creation; the whole structure had been conjured out of marsh and water by the cruel magic of autocracy. It was rooted neither in the earth nor in the past. Sometimes, as in Pushkin's *Bronze Horseman*, nature took vengeance on the intruder; sometimes, as when Poe perished in Baltimore, the city became a mob—that equivalent of natural catastrophe—and destroyed the artist.

But in the end, the human will triumphed over the gigantic land. Roads were cut through forests and deserts; communities gripped on to the prairie and the steppe. This achievement and the primacy of will that brought it about are reflected in the great lineage of Russian and American classics. In both mythologies what Balzac had described as "the quest for the absolute" looms large. Hester Prynne, Ahab, Gordon Pym, Dostoevsky's underground man, and Tolstoy himself assailed the will-constraining barriers of traditional morality and natural law. As epigraph to *Ligeia*, Poe chose a passage from the seventeenth-century English divine Joseph Glanvill: "Man doth not yield himself to the angels, nor unto death utterly, save only through the weakness of his feeble will." That is Ahab's secret battle-cry and it was Tolstoy's hope when he questioned the need of mortality. In both Russia and America, as Matthew Arnold remarked, life itself had about it the fanaticism of youth.

But in neither instance was it the kind of life on which European fiction drew for its material and on which it built the fabric of its conventions. This is the crux of Henry James's study of Hawthorne. The latter had written, in preface to *The Marble Faun*:

No author, without a trial, can conceive of the difficulty of writing a romance about a country where there is no shadow, no antiquity, no mystery, no picturesque and gloomy wrong, not anything but a commonplace prosperity, in broad and simple daylight, as is happily the case with my dear native land.

From the author of *The Scarlet Letter* and *The House of the Seven Gables*, one takes this to be a piece of fine-grained irony. But James chose not to do so and elaborated on Hawthorne's "difficulties." His discussion, as well as Hawthorne's text, pertain altogether to America. But what James had to say yielded perhaps the most searching analysis that we have of the main qualities of the European novel. By telling us what non-Europeans lacked he tells us also from what impediments they were free. And his treatment is, I submit, as illuminating of the differences between Flaubert and Tolstoy as it is of those between Flaubert and Hawthorne.

Noting the "thinness" and "the blankness" of the atmosphere in which Hawthorne worked, James said:

It takes so many things, as Hawthorne must have felt later in life, when he made the acquaintance of the denser, richer, warmer European spectacle—it takes such an accumulation of history and custom, such a complexity of manners and types, to form a fund of suggestion for a novelist.

Whereupon follows the famous listing of "the items of high civilization" absent from the texture of American life and, consequently, from the matrix of reference and emotion available to an American novelist:

No State, in the European sense of the word, and indeed barely a specific national name. No sovereign, no court, no personal loyalty, no aristocracy, no church, no clergy, no army, no diplomatic service, no country gentlemen, no palaces, no castles, nor manors . . . nor ivied ruins . . . no Oxford, nor Eton, nor Harrow; no literature, no novels, no museums, no pictures, no political society, no sporting class—no Epsom nor Ascot!

One cannot tell whether this list is to be taken altogether seriously. Neither the court, nor the army, nor the sporting set in James's England was very much concerned with the values of the artist. Oxford's most dramatic association with poetic genius had been the expulsion of Shelley; manors and ivied ruins were the draughty damnation of painters and musicians seeking to entertain their genteel hosts; neither Eton nor Harrow was notable for its encouragement of the gentler virtues. But James's list is relevant none the less. In sharp miniature it conveys the world picture of European realism, what Bergson would have called the *données immédiates* of the art of Dickens, Thackeray, Trollope, Balzac, Stendhal, or Flaubert.

Moreover, given the necessary qualifications and shifts in perspective, this index of deprivation applies equally to nineteenth-century Russia. That too was not a state "in the European sense of the word." Its autocratic court, with its semi-Asiatic flavour, was hostile to literature. Much of the aristocracy was steeped in feudal barbarism and only a tiny, Europeanized segment cared for art or the free play of ideas. The Russian clergy had little in common with the Anglican curates and bishops in whose panelled libraries and rook-haunted chambers James passed some of his winter evenings. They were a fanatical and uneducated host in which visionaries and saints neighboured on illiterate sensualists. Most of the other items enumerated by James—the free universities and ancient schools, the museums and political society, the ivied ruins and the literary tradition—were no more present in Russia than in the United States.

And surely in both cases the particular items point to a more general fact: in neither Russia nor America had there taken place the full evolution of a middle class "in the European sense of the word." As Marx pointed out in his later years, Russia was to provide an instance of a feudal system moving towards industrialization without the intermediary stages of political enfranchisement and without the formation of a modern *bourgeoisie*. Behind the European novel lay the stabilizing and maturing structures of constitutionality and capitalism. These did not exist in the Russia of Gogol or Dostoevsky.

James admitted that there were "fine compensations" for the thinness of the American atmosphere. He alluded to the immediacy of physical nature in its more eloquent moods, to the writer's contact with a broad range of types, and to the sense of "wonder" and "mystery" which comes with meeting men who cannot be placed in any of the distinct categories of a fixed society. But James hastened to add that this absence of hierarchies deprived an artist of "intellectual standards" and of the touchstones of manner. Instead, it committed him to a "rather chilly and isolated sense of moral responsibility."

This is a disturbing sentence even if one takes it to apply solely to Hawthorne. It goes a long way towards explaining how it was that the mature James expended time and admiration on the works of Augier, Gyp, and Dumas *fils*. It casts light on the values which led him to compare *The Scarlet Letter* with Lockhart's *Adam Blair*—not entirely to the latter's detriment. It makes plain why James hoped that American fiction would develop in the image of William Dean Howells, who had started with a "delightful volume on *Venetian Life*," rather than in that of Poe or Melville or Hawthorne with their "puerile" experiments in symbolism. Finally, it is an observation which shows why James could make nothing of the Russian contemporaries of Turgeniev.

This "isolated sense of moral responsibility" (passionate, I should have thought, rather than "chilly"), this compulsion towards what Nietzsche was to call "the revaluation of all values," carried the American and the Russian novel beyond the dwindling resources of European realism into the world of the Pequod and the Karamazovs. D. H. Lawrence remarked:

There is a "different" feeling in the old American classics. It is the shifting from the old psyche to something new, a displacement. And displacement hurt.[2]

In the American case, the displacement was spatial and cultural; the migration of the mind from Europe to the new world. In Russia it was historical and revolutionary. In both instances there were pain and unreason, but also the possibility of experiment and the

[2] D. H. Lawrence: *Studies in Classic American Literature*.

exhilarating conviction that there was at stake more than a portrayal of existing society or the provision of romantic entertainment.

It is true that by Jamesian standards Hawthorne, Melville, Gogol, Tolstoy, and Dostoevsky were isolated men. They created apart from or in opposition to the dominant literary *milieu*. James himself and Turgeniev seemed more fortunate; they were honoured and at home in the high places of civilization without sacrificing the integrity of their purpose. But, in the final analysis, it was the visionaries and the hunted who achieved the "Titanic" books.

Our imaginary discourse on Russia and America in the nineteenth century, on possible analogues in the achievement of the Russian and the American novel, and on their respective departures from European realism, might speculate on one further point. European fiction mirrors the long post-Napoleonic peace. That peace extended, save for spasmodic and indecisive interruptions in 1854 and 1870, from Waterloo to the First World War. War had been a dominant motif in epic poetry—even when it was war in heaven. It had provided the context for much of serious drama from *Antigone* to *Macbeth* and the masterpieces of Kleist. But it is significantly remote from the preoccupations and themes of the nineteenth-century European novelists. We hear the distant boom of guns in *Vanity Fair*; the approach of war gives the final pages of *Nana* their irony and their unforgettable *élan*; but not until the Zeppelin cruises over Paris, in that despairing night of debauchery which marks the end of the Proustian world, does war re-enter into the main current of European literature. Flaubert, in whom most of these problems are so intensely accentuated, wrote savage and resplendent pages about battle. But it was a battle long ago, in the museum setting of ancient Carthage. Curiously enough, it is to children's and boys' books that we must go to find convincing accounts of men at war—to Daudet and to G. A. Henty, who, like Tolstoy, was profoundly marked by his experiences in the Crimea. European realism, in the adult vein, produced neither a *War and Peace* nor a *Red Badge of Courage*.

This fact enforces a larger moral. The theatre of the European novel, its political and physical matrix from Jane Austen to Proust, was extraordinarily stable. In it, the major catastrophes were private. The art of Balzac, Dickens, and Flaubert was neither prepared nor called upon to engage those forces which can utterly dissolve the fabric of a society and overwhelm private life. Those forces were gathering inexorably towards the century of revolution and total war. But the European novelists either ignored the foreshadowings or misinterpreted them. Flaubert assured George Sand that the Commune was merely a brief reversion to the factionalism of the Middle Ages. Only two writers of fiction clearly glimpsed the impulses towards disintegration, the cracks in the wall of European stability: James in *The Princess Casamassima* and Conrad in *Under Western Eyes* and *The Secret Agent*. It is of the most obvious significance that neither novelist was native to the western European tradition.

The influence of the Civil War, or rather of its approach and aftermath, on the American atmosphere has not, to my mind, been thoroughly assessed. Harry Levin has suggested that the world view of Poe was darkened by a premonition of the impending fate of the South. It is only gradually that we are coming to realize how drastic a role the war played in the consciousness of Henry James. It accounts in part for that susceptibility to the daemonic and the crippling which deepened the Jamesian novel and carried it into areas beyond the confines of French and English realism. But more generally one may say that the instability of American social life, the mythology of violence inherent in the frontier situation, and the centrality of the war crisis were reflected in the temper of American art. They contributed to what D. H. Lawrence termed a "pitch of extreme consciousness." He addressed his observation to Poe, Hawthorne, and Melville. It applies equally to *The Jolly Corner* and *The Golden Bowl*.

But what were, in the American case, complex and at times marginal elements were, with respect to nineteenth-century Russia, the essential realities.

v

If we make exception of Gogol's *Dead Souls* (1842), of Goncharov's *Oblomov* (1859), and of Turgeniev's *On the Eve* (1859), the *anni mirabiles* of Russian fiction extend from the emancipation of the serfs in 1861 to the first revolution in 1905. In power of creation and sustained genius these forty-four years may justly be compared with the golden periods of creativity in Periclean Athens and Elizabethan and Jacobean England. They count among the finer hours of the human spirit. Unquestionably, moreover, the Russian novel was conceived under a single sign of the historical Zodiac—the sign of approaching upheaval. From *Dead Souls* to *Resurrection* (the primary image is contained in the mere juxtaposition of these two titles), Russian literature mirrors the coming of the apocalypse:

it is full of presentiments and predictions, it is constantly troubled by the expectation of approaching catastrophe. The great Russian writers of the XIXth century felt that Russia was on the edge of an abyss into which it would hurl itself; their works reflect the revolution taking place within as well as the other revolution which is on the march. . . .[3]

Consider the major novels: *Dead Souls* (1842), *Oblomov* (1859), Turgeniev's *Fathers and Sons* (1861), *Crime and Punishment* (1866), *The Idiot* (1868-9), *The Possessed* (1871-2), *Anna Karenina* (1875-7), *The Brothers Karamazov* (1879-80), and *Resurrection* (1899). They form a prophetic series. Even *War and Peace* (1867-9), which stands rather to one side of the main current, concludes with a hint of impending crisis. With an intensity of vision comparable to that of the seers of the Old Testament, the Russian novelists of

[3] N. A. Berdiaev: *Les Sources et le sens du communisme russe* (trans. by A. Nerville, Paris, 1951).

the nineteenth century perceived the gathering storm and prophesied. Often, as in the case of both Gogol and Turgeniev, they prophesied against their own political and social instincts. But their imaginings were oppressed by the certainty of disaster. In a real sense, the Russian novel is an extended gloss on the famous words which Radishchev had uttered in the eighteenth century: "My soul is overwhelmed by the weight of human suffering."

The sense of continuity and obsessive vision may be conveyed by a piece of fantasy (and it is only that). Gogol sent his emblematic troika hurtling forward through the land of dead souls; Goncharov's hero realized that he should rouse himself to grasp the reins, but yielded instead to fatalistic abandonment; in one of those villages "in N. province," so familiar to readers of Russian fiction, Turgeniev's Bazarov took the whip; in him the future was manifest, the cleansing, murderous tomorrow; the Bazarovs infected with madness and seeking to hurl the troika into the abyss form the theme of *The Possessed*; in our allegory, Levin's estate, in *Anna Karenina*, may stand for a momentary halt, a place in which problems might have been analyzed and resolved through understanding; but the journey has reached a point of no return and we are hastened towards the tragedy of the Karamazovs in which is prefigured, on a private scale, the immense parricide of revolution. Finally, we attain *Resurrection*, a strange, imperfect, and forgiving novel which looks beyond chaos to the advent of grace.

This journey led through a world too formless and tragic for the instruments of European realism. In a letter to Maikov of December 1868 (to which I shall have occasion to revert later on), Dostoevsky exclaimed:

My God! If one could but tell categorically all that we Russians have gone through during the last ten years in the way of spiritual development, all the realists would shriek that it was pure fantasy! And yet it would be pure realism! It *is* the one true, deep realism. . . .

The realities which offered themselves to the Russian writers of the nineteenth century were, indeed, fantastic: an affrighted despotism; a Church preyed upon by apocalyptic expectations; an immensely gifted but uprooted intelligentsia seeking salvation either abroad or in the tenebrous mass of the peasantry; the legion of exiles ringing their *Bell* (the name of Herzen's journal) or striking their *Spark* (the name of Lenin's) from a Europe which they both loved and despised; the raging debates between Slavophiles and Westernizers, Populists and utilitarians, reactionaries and nihilists, atheists and believers; and weighing on all spirits, like one of those oncoming summer storms which Turgeniev evokes so beautifully, the premonition of catastrophe.

In quality and modes of expression, this premonition assumed religious aspects. Belinsky stated that the question of the existence of God was the final and all-determining focus of Russian thought. As Merezhkovsky remarked, the problem of God and of His nature had "absorbed the whole Russian people from the Judaizers of the fifteenth century to the present day." [4] The iconography of the Messiah and the eschatology of Revelation gave to political debate a bizarre and feverish resonance. The shadow of millennial expectations lay across a stifled culture. In all Russian political thinking—in the pronouncements of Chaadaev, Kireevsky, Nechaiev, Tkachev, Belinsky, Pissarev, Constantine Leontiev, Soloviev, and Fedorov—the kingdom of God had moved terribly close to the declining kingdom of man. The Russian mind was, literally, God-haunted.

Hence the radical distinction between nineteenth-century fiction in western Europe and in Russia. The tradition of Balzac, Dickens, and Flaubert was secular. The art of Tolstoy and Dostoevsky was religious. It sprang from an atmosphere penetrated with religious experience and the belief that Russia was destined to play an eminent role in the impending apocalypse. No less than Aeschylus or Milton, Tolstoy and Do-

---

[4] D. S. Merezhkovsky: op. cit.

stoevsky were men whose genius had fallen into the hands of the living God. To them, as to Kierkegaard, human destiny was *Either/Or*. Thus, their works cannot be truly understood in the same key as *Middlemarch*, for example, or *The Charterhouse of Parma*. We are dealing with different techniques and different metaphysics. *Anna Karenina* and *The Brothers Karamazov* are, if you will, fictions and poems of the mind, but central to their purpose is what Berdiaev has called the "quest after the salvation of humanity."

One further point needs to be made: throughout this essay I shall be approaching the Tolstoyan and Dostoevskyan texts by way of translation. This means that the work can be of no real use to scholars of Russian and to historians of Slavic languages and literature. It is at every stage indebted to their labours and contains, I hope, nothing that will strike them as grossly erroneous. But it is not, and cannot be, intended for them. Neither were, one assumes, the writings on the Russian novel of André Gide, Thomas Mann, John Cowper Powys and R. P. Blackmur. I cite these names not in immodest precedent, but rather to exemplify a general truth: criticism is, at times, compelled to take liberties which philology and literary history must reject as fatal to their purposes. Translations are more or less flagrant modes of betrayal. But it is from them that we glean what we may, and indeed what we must, of works composed in languages not our own. In prose, at least, the mastery will often survive the treason. A criticism which is rooted in this plight and which addresses itself to it will be of restricted value, but it may be of value nevertheless.

Tolstoy and Dostoevsky, moreover, constitute a vast theme. This, as T. S. Eliot observes with respect to Dante, leaves the possibility "that one may have something to say worth saying; whereas with smaller men, only minute and special study is likely to justify writing about them at all."

TOLSTOY

CHAPTER

☼ 2 ☼

*Les poètes ont cela des hypocrites qu'ils défendent
toujours ce qu'ils font, mais que leur conscience
ne les laisse jamais en repos.*
RACINE *to* LE VASSEUR, 1659 *or* 1660

IMMEMORIALLY, literary criticism has aspired to objective canons, to principles of judgment at once rigorous and universal. But on considering its diverse history, one wonders whether such aspirations have been or indeed can be fulfilled. One wonders whether critical doctrines are ever more than the taste and sensibility of a man of genius, or a school of opinion, temporarily imposed upon the spirit of an age by force of presentation. When the work of art invades our consciousness, something within us catches flame. What we do thereafter is to refine and make articulate the original leap of recognition. The able critic is one who makes accessible to reason and to our sense of imitation an awareness which is, at the outset, tenebrous and dogmatic. This is what Matthew Arnold meant by his "touchstones" and what A. E. Housman referred to

45

when he said that a true line of poetry made his beard bristle. It is of the modern fashion to deplore such notions of intuitive and subjective judgment. But are they not profoundly honest?

There are instances in which the immediate response is so compelling and so "right" that we advance no further. Certain impressions overwhelm through their apparent simplicity. They become those dust-hallowed furnishings of the mind which we are made fully aware of only when we knock up against them in moments of speculation or disorder. A case in point is the generally accepted idea that the novels of Tolstoy are, in some way, epic. Tolstoy himself fostered this view and it has passed into the vocabulary of critical platitudes. There it is so splendidly entrenched and seemingly apposite that it has become rather difficult to see precisely what it signifies. But what are we, in fact, saying when we describe *War and Peace* and *Anna Karenina* as "prose epics"? What did Tolstoy have in mind when he referred to *Childhood, Boyhood and Youth* as a work justly comparable with the *Iliad*?

It is not difficult to understand how this use of the word "epic" first arose. Its stylistic and mythological connotations had been largely dissipated during the eighteenth century. The edges were blurring towards the range of inclusiveness which allows us to speak of an "epic landscape" or of "epic grandeur" in a musical phrase. To Tolstoy's contemporaries the notion of epic brought into focus appropriate sensations of immensity and seriousness, of temporal spaciousness and heroism, of serenity and narrative directness. The language of criticism, as it pertained to realistic fiction, had developed no term of comparable adequacy. The "epic" alone seemed clear and comprehensive enough to characterize the Tolstoyan novel or, for that matter, *Moby Dick*.

But those who spoke of Tolstoy as an "epic novelist" wrought better than they knew. They intended the epithet in rather loose tribute to the dimensions of his works and the archaic splendour of his personality. In fact, the notion is precisely and materially relevant to what Tolstoy purposed. *War and Peace, Anna Karenina, The Death of Ivan Ilych*, and *The Cossacks* call to mind epic poetry not through some vague recognition of their scope and freshness, but because Tolstoy intended definite analogies between his art and that of Homer. We have taken him so richly at his word that we rarely examine how he achieved his aim and whether it is indeed possible to trace affinities between artistic forms separated by nearly three millennia and countless revolutions of spirit. Moreover, little attention has been paid to concordances between Tolstoy's epic manner and his anarchic version of Christianity. But such concordances do exist. To say that there is much in Tolstoyan fiction related to the tone and conventions of the *Iliad*, and to cite Merezhkovsky's belief that Tolstoy possessed the soul "of a born pagan," [1] is to consider two aspects of a single unity.

It would seem natural to begin with *War and Peace*. No work of modern prose has struck more readers as belonging in some brilliant and obvious way to the epic tradition. It is commonly designated as Russia's national epic, and it abounds in episodes—such as the celebrated wolf-hunt—to which comparisons between Homer and Tolstoy inevitably refer. Tolstoy himself, moreover, conceived the work with the Homeric poems explicitly in mind. In March 1865 he came to reflect on the "poetry of the novelist." He noted in his diary that such "poetry" may spring from diverse sources. One of these is "the picture of manners based on a historical event— *Odyssey, Iliad, Year 1805*." Nevertheless, *War and Peace* is a case of particular complexity. It is penetrated with an anti-heroic philosophy of history. The multitudinous sweep of the book and the high clarity of its historical background blind us to its inner contrarieties. *War and Peace* is obviously central to my argument, but it does not offer the most straightforward approach. Rather, I propose to isolate certain of the characteristic and de-

[1] D. S. Merezhkovsky: *Tolstoi as Man and Artist, with an Essay on Dostoïevski* (London, 1902).

fining elements in Tolstoy's "epic" art by saying something about *Anna Karenina* and *Madame Bovary*.

This is a classical confrontation, and it has its history. When *Anna Karenina* first appeared, it was thought that Tolstoy had chosen the theme of adultery and suicide in challege to Flaubert's masterpiece. This is probably an oversimplification. Tolstoy knew *Madame Bovary*; he was in France at the very time when the novel was being serialized in the *Revue de Paris* (1856–7) and moved in that literary circle most passionately interested in Flaubert's work. But we do know from Tolstoy's journals that the motif of adultery and vengeance had occupied his mind as early as 1851 and that the actual impulse towards *Anna Karenina* came only in January 1872, with the suicide of Anna Stepanova Piriogova near Tolstoy's estate. All that can be said is that *Anna Karenina* was written in some awareness of its predecessor.

Both novels are masterpieces of their kind. Zola regarded *Madame Bovary* as the summation of realism, as the supreme work of genius in a tradition going back to the eighteenth-century realists and to Balzac. Romain Rolland believed it to be the only French novel which he could match against Tolstoy "by virtue of its power to convey life, and the totality of life." [2] Yet the two achievements are in no manner equal; *Anna Karenina* is incomparably the greater—greater in scope, in humanity, in technical performance. The similarity of certain main themes merely reinforces our sense of differing magnitudes.

One of the earliest systematic comparisons between the two books is Matthew Arnold's. In his essay on Tolstoy, of which the latter approved, Arnold expressed a distinction which was to receive wide currency. Seeking to characterize the contrast between the formal rigours of Flaubert and the meandering, seemingly ungoverned design of his Russian counterpart, Arnold wrote:

[2] Romain Rolland: *Mémoires et fragments du journal* (Paris, 1956).

the truth is we are not to take *Anna Karénine* as a work of art; we are to take it as a piece of life . . . and what his [Tolstoy's] novel in this way loses in art it gains in reality.

Starting from altogether different premises, Henry James argued that Tolstoyan fiction failed to give an adequate rendering of life precisely through its failure to achieve those formal virtues of which Flaubert was emblematic. With reference to Dumas and Tolstoy (a conjunction which is of itself a betrayal of responsible judgment), Henry James asks, in the Preface to the revised version of *The Tragic Muse*:

what do such large loose baggy monsters, with their queer elements of the accidental and the arbitrary, artistically *mean*? We have heard it maintained . . . that such things are "superior to art"; but we understand least of all what *that* may mean. . . . There is life and life, and as waste is only life sacrificed and thereby prevented from "counting," I delight in a deep-breathing economy of an organic form.

Both these critiques are founded on thorough misapprehensions. Arnold yielded to rank confusion when he distinguished between the "work of art" and the "piece of life." James would never have allowed this meaningless division, but he failed to perceive that *War and Peace* (to which his remarks were specifically addressed) was a supreme instance of the "deep-breathing economy of an organic form." "Organic," with its implications of aliveness, is the crucial term. It precisely qualifies that which elevates *Anna Karenina* above *Madame Bovary*; in the former, life draws the deeper breath. If we were to retain Arnold's deceptive terminology, we would have to say that Tolstoy's was the work of art and Flaubert's the piece of life—noting the overtones of deadness and fragmentation inseparable from the word "piece."

There is a famous anecdote about Flaubert and Maupassant. The master instructed his disciple to choose a given tree and to describe it with such exactitude that the reader would mistake it for no other tree in the vicinity. In this injunction we may discern the radical flaw of the naturalist tradition. For in succeeding, Maupassant would have done no more than rival a photographer. Tolstoy's use of a withering and flowering oak in *War and Peace* is a contrasting instance of how enduring realism is achieved through magic and the supreme liberties of art.

Flaubert's treatment of physical objects was central to his vision. Upon them he lavished the immense resources and stringencies of his vocabulary. At the beginning of the novel we find a depiction of Charles Bovary's cap:

It was a headgear of composite order, containing elements of an ordinary hat, a hussar's busby, a lancer's cap, a sealskin cap and a nightcap: one of those wretched things whose mute hideousness suggests unplumbed depths, like an idiot's face. Ovoid and stiffened with whalebone, it began with three convex strips; then followed alternating lozenges of velvet and rabbit's fur, separated by a red band; then came a kind of bag, terminating in a cardboard-lined polygon intricately decorated with braid. From this hung a long, excessively thin cord ending in a kind of tassel of gold netting. The cap was new; its peak was shiny.[3]

The idea for this monstrous piece of headgear came to Flaubert from a humorous drawing by Gavarni which he saw in the hotel of a certain M. Bouvaret during his journey through Egypt. The cap itself plays a momentary and insignificant role in the narrative. It has been argued by a number of critics that it symbolizes Charles Bovary's nature and prefigures his tragedy. This seems far-fetched. Observing the passage closely, one cannot escape the suspicion that it was composed for its own sake, as one of those brilliant and untiring assaults upon visible reality through which Flaubert sought to arrest life in the bonds of language. Balzac's celebrated portrayal of a house-door in *Eugénie Grandet* served a po-

[3] Quotations from *Madame Bovary* are taken from the translation by Francis Steegmuller (New York, 1957).

etic and humane end, the house being the outward and animate visage of its inhabitants. The account of Charles Bovary's cap seems in excess of intelligible purpose. It is a piece of life encroaching, by virtue of sarcasm and accumulation, on the economy of the work of art.

No comparable instance comes to mind from the vast panorama of the Tolstoyan world. The sole element Tolstoy might have retained from Flaubert's description is the final statement—"The cap was new; its peak was shiny." In the Tolstoyan novel physical objects—Anna Karenina's dresses, Bezukhov's spectacles, Ivan Ilych's bed—derive their *raison d'être* and solidity from the human context. In this, Tolstoy was profoundly Homeric. As Lessing was perhaps the first to point out, the rendering of physical objects in the *Iliad* is unvaryingly dynamic. The sword is always seen as a part of the striking arm. This pertains even to the principal set piece— Achilles' shield. We see it in the process of being forged. Reflecting on this fact, Hegel put forward a fascinating theory: he suggested that there had taken place a gradual alienation between language and the immediacies of the material world. He noted that even the minute portrayals of a bronze vessel or of a particular type of raft in the Homeric poems radiated a vitality which modern literature did not equal. Hegel wondered whether semi-industrial and industrial modes of production had estranged men from their weapons and tools and from the furnishings of their lives. It is a searching hypothesis and one which Lukács urges at great length. But, whatever the historical reason, Tolstoy did encompass outward reality with immediate kinship. In his world, as in Homer's, men's caps owe their significance and their inclusion in works of art to the fact that they cover men's heads.

The salient techniques in *Madame Bovary*—the use of rare and technical language, the prevalence of formal description, the deliberate cadences achieved within the articulations of prose, the intricately wrought structure whereby a major set piece, such as the ball, is prepared for and closed through a narrative recitative—are germane not only to Flaubert's personal genius, but to the conception of art implicit in Matthew Arnold's and Henry James's observations. They are devices through which realism endeavours to record, with relentless completion, some piece of contemporaneous life. Whether that piece was of itself significant or attractive did not really matter (witness the novels of the Goncourts). Only fidelity of rendition was decisive. In fact, the indifferent subject recommended itself through its difficulty, and we may say of Zola that he possessed the ability to make a train time-table worth re-reading. But with Flaubert the case was more uncertain. Despite its obvious mastery and the labours he had lavished upon it, *Madame Bovary* failed to satisfy him. Deep within its firm and beauteous structure there seemed to lie a principle of negation and futility. Flaubert stated that he was grievously distressed at the realization that even if the work "was executed to perfection, the achievement would only be passable and never beautiful because of its inherent subject matter [*à cause du fond même*]." [4] In saying this, Flaubert was obviously exaggerating. Perhaps he was unconsciously avenging himself on a book that had cost him rare anguish. But his point was, nevertheless, well taken. There is in this masterpiece of the realistic tradition an atmosphere of constriction and inhumanity.

Matthew Arnold described it as "a work of petrified feeling." He found that there is "not a personage in the book to rejoice or console us. . . ." He thought the reason might lie in Flaubert's attitude towards Emma: "He is cruel, with the cruelty of petrified feeling . . . he pursues her without pity or pause, as with malignity." These observations were made in contrast to the vitality and humaneness of *Anna Karenina*. But one wonders whether Arnold fully understood why it was that Flaubert harried Emma Bovary so pitilessly. It was not her morality that affronted him but rather

[4] Flaubert to Louise Colet, July 12, 1853 (*Correspondance de Gustave Flaubert*, III, Paris, 1927).

her pathetic endeavours to live the life of the imagination. In destroying Emma, Flaubert was doing violence to that part of his own genius which mutinied against realism, against the desiccating theory that a novelist is a pure chronicler of the empirical world, a camera eye dwelling with dispassionate fidelity on some matter of fact.

Even Henry James, who immensely admired *Madame Bovary*, perceived that there was something radically amiss with its perfection. Seeking to account for its "metallic" quality (James applied this epithet to Flaubert's works as a whole in his essay on Turgeniev), he suggested that Emma "in spite of the nature of her consciousness and in spite of her reflecting so much that of her creator, is really too small an affair." [5] James may be right, although Baudelaire, in his treatment of the novel, found the heroine to be "truly a great woman." But in a strict sense, both these points of view are irrelevant. The assumption of realism is that the inherent nobility of the theme has little to do with the virtues of performance. Its dogma, as Valéry defined it in his essay *La Tentation de (saint) Flaubert*, is "attentiveness to the banal."

The naturalistic writers haunted the research libraries, the museums, the lectures of archaeologists and statisticians. "Give us Facts," they said with the Dickensian schoolmaster in *Hard Times*. Many of them were, literally, enemies of fiction. *Madame Bovary* appeared with the subtitle *Mœurs de Province*. This was an echo of Balzac's famous division of the *Comédie humaine* into scenes of Parisian, provincial, and military life. But the tone had altered and there lay behind the phrase Flaubert's relentless desire to rival the sociologist and the historian on their own ground and to make of the novel a monograph in some vast compendium of reality. This desire is manifest in the very structure of his style. As Sartre notes, Flaubert's sentences "surround an object, seize it, immobilize it and break its

[5] Henry James: "Gustave Flaubert" (*Notes on Novelists, with Some Other Notes*, New York, 1914).

backbone . . . the determinism of the naturalistic novel crushes life and substitutes for human action the uniform responses of automata." [6]

If this were altogether true, *Madame Bovary* would not be the work of genius which it so obviously is. But enough of it is true to explain why there is a range of literature to which it does not, in the last analysis, belong and why Flaubert's treatment of his theme falls so short of Tolstoy's. Moreover, because Flaubert viewed himself with such castigating clarity and lacked the gifts of self-deception which preserve lesser artists from despair, *Madame Bovary* sheds a unique light on the limitations of the European novel. "The book is a picture of the middling," said Henry James. But is "the middling" not precisely that kingdom which Defoe and Fielding had staked out for their successors? And is it not highly illuminating that when he abandoned "the middling"—in the *Trois Contes*, *Salammbô*, and *La Tentation de saint Antoine*—Flaubert should have taken refuge with the saints of the golden legend and the howling daemons of irrationalism?

But the failure of *Madame Bovary* (and "failure" is here an impertinent and relative term) cannot be accounted for in respect of Arnold's distinction between works of art and pieces of life. In *Anna Karenina* we do not find pieces of life, with all the notes of decay and dissection struck by that ominous phrase. We find life itself in the plenitude and rounded glory which only works of art can convey. The revelation of it, moreover, arises out of technical mastery, out of the deliberate and controlled unfolding of poetic forms.

II

For all its wrongheadedness, Arnold's critique has been of major historical importance. It expressed the general opinion of Arnold's European contemporaries —and, in particular, of the Vicomte de Vogüé—who

[6] Jean-Paul Sartre: *"Qu'est-ce que la littérature?"* (*Situations*, II, Paris, 1948).

had first made the Russian novelists accessible to French and English readers. They conceded to the Russians a certain freshness and power of invention. But implicit in their wary admiration was the doctrine which had inspired Arnold's essay—the doctrine that European fiction was the product of deliberate and recognizable craft whereas a book such as *War and Peace* was a mysterious creation of untutored genius and formless vitality. At its crudest, this whole conception led to Bourget's attacks on Russian literature; at its subtlest, it inspired the luminous but unsteady insights of Gide's *Dostoïevsky*. It was not a new theory in European criticism, but a new version of the traditional defence of the established and the classical against achievements outside the prevailing norms. Arnold's attempts to include *Anna Karenina* within the compass of Victorian criticism by contrasting its vitality with the aesthetic sophistication of Flaubert was comparable to the efforts of Neo-classical critics to distinguish between the "natural sublimity of Shakespeare" and what they took to be the orderly, canonic perfections of Racine.

But although such distinctions were, in neither case, pertinent or founded in the texts, they are with us still. The Russian novel now casts a tremendous and accepted shadow over our sense of literary values. But it continues to do so, as it were, from outside. Its technical influence on European fiction has been restricted. Those French novelists most evidently inspired by Dostoevskyan models have been men of minor attainments, such as Edouard Rod and Charles-Louis Philippe. Stevenson's *Markheim*, some of the works of Hugh Walpole and, perhaps, of Faulkner and Graham Greene show traces of the impact of Dostoevsky. The influence of Tolstoy on Moore's *Evelyn Innes*, on Galsworthy, and on Shaw is an influence of ideas rather than of technique.[7] Among major figures, only Gide and

[7] See F. W. J. Hemmings: *The Russian Novel in France, 1884–1914* (Oxford, 1950); T. S. Lindstrom: *Tolstoï en France (1886–1910)* (Paris, 1952); and Gilbert Phelps: *The Russian Novel in English Fiction* (London, 1956).

Thomas Mann may be said to have adopted to their own ends significant aspects of Russian practice. Nor is this, primarily, a question of the linguistic barrier; Cervantes is at the heart of the European tradition and has profoundly affected writers who could not read him in his own tongue.

The reason lies in the general direction indicated by Arnold. Obscurely, but persistently, it is felt that Tolstoy and Dostoevsky fall outside the ordinary range of critical analysis. Their "sublimity" is accepted as a brute fact of nature, irresponsive to closer discrimination. Our style of praise is significantly vague. It would appear as if "works of art" could be intelligibly scrutinized whereas "pieces of life" must be gazed at in awe. Surely this is nonsense: the greatness of a great novelist must be apprehended in terms of actual form and technical realization.

The latter are in the case of Tolstoy and Dostoevsky of tremendous interest. Nothing could be more erroneous than to regard their novels as "loose baggy monsters" engendered through some mysterious or fortuitous spontaneity. In *What Is Art?* Tolstoy said plainly that excellence is achieved through detail, that it is a matter of a "wee bit" less or a "wee bit" more. *Anna Karenina* and *The Brothers Karamazov* bear out this judgment no less than does *Madame Bovary*. Indeed, their principles of design are richer and more complex than those we come upon in Flaubert or James. Compared to the problem of narrative structure and impetus resolved in the first part of *The Idiot*, so manifest a *tour de force* as the near-maintenance of a single focus of vision in *The Ambassadors* strikes one as shallow. Matched against the opening section of *Anna Karenina*, which I shall be considering in detail, the beginning of *Madame Bovary* seems heavy-handed. Yet we know that Flaubert expended on it his utmost resources. As a well-made novel, in the purely technical sense, *Crime and Punishment* has few rivals. In attending to its sense of pace and tightness of execution one calls to mind the very best of Lawrence and Conrad's *Nostromo*.

These should be critical commonplaces and propositions not worth further emphasis. But are they? Many of the "new critics" have devoted sustained insight and persuasion to the art of the novel as it was practised by Flaubert, James, Conrad, Joyce, Proust, Kafka, and Lawrence (these constituting an official pantheon). Inquiries into the use of metaphor in Faulkner, into the genesis of this or that episode in *Ulysses*, grow constantly more respectful and numerous. But many of the critics and students who justly consider such matters as vital to their interests possess only a general and indistinct awareness of the Russian masters. Involuntarily, perhaps, they follow suit on Ezra Pound's outrageously stupid dismissal of Russian fiction in *How to Read*. Part of my object in writing this essay is to counteract this tendency, and to demonstrate that C. P. Snow was right when he said: "it is the demoniac works into which we most need the technical insights, if we are to get them into any sort of proportion at all." [8]

But once this is affirmed, and if we bear steadily in view the fact that the vitality of a novel is inseparable from the technical virtues which make it a work of art, there remains a germ of truth in Matthew Arnold's contention. He was right in saying that *Madame Bovary* and *Anna Karenina* cannot be taken in quite the same way. The difference is more than one of degree. It is not merely that Tolstoy saw the human condition in a deeper and more compassionate light than Flaubert and that his genius was of a demonstrably more spacious order. It is, rather, that in a reading of *Anna Karenina*, our understanding of literary techniques, our awareness of "how the thing is done," yields only a preliminary insight. The types of formal analysis with which this chapter is mainly concerned penetrate far less deeply into the world of Tolstoy than into that of Flaubert

[8] C. P. Snow: "Dickens at Work" (*New Statesman*, July 27, 1957).

The Tolstoyan novel conveys an explicit weight of religious, moral, and philosophic preoccupations that arise out of the circumstances of the narrative but have an independent or, rather, a parallel existence and claim upon our attention. Whatever we may note regarding Tolstoyan poetics is of value principally in that it provides the necessary approach to one of the most articulate and comprehensive doctrines of experience ever put forward by a single intellect.

This may explain why it should be that the new criticism, with such distinguished exceptions as R. P. Blackmur, has generally avoided the Russian novel. Its concentration on the single image or cluster of language, its bias against extrinsic and biographical evidence, its preference for the poetic over the prosaic forms, are out of tune with the governing qualities of Tolstoyan and Dostoevskyan fiction. Hence the need for an "old criticism" equipped with the wide-ranging civilization of an Arnold, a Sainte-Beuve, and a Bradley. Hence also the need for a criticism prepared to commit itself to a study of the looser and larger modes. In his *Quintessence of Ibsenism*, Shaw observed that "there is not one of Ibsen's characters who is not, in the old phrase, the temple of the Holy Ghost, and who does not move you at moments by the sense of that mystery."

When we seek to understand *Anna Karenina*, such old phrases are in order.

III

The very first page of *Anna Karenina* transports our emotions into a world remote from that of Flaubert. The Pauline epigraph—"Vengeance is mine; I will repay"—has a tragic and ambiguous resonance. Tolstoy viewed his heroine with what Matthew Arnold called "treasures of compassion"; he condemned the society which hounds her to destruction. But at the some time he invoked the inexorable retributions of moral law. Equally striking is the fact that a Biblical citation should have been used at all in epigraph to a novel. Passages from Scripture are rarely inwoven into the fabric of nineteenth-century European fiction; they tend to destroy the substance of the surrounding prose by their sheer radiance and force of association. Henry James manages to carry it off in such moments as Lambert Strether's "Verily, verily . . ." at the climax of *The Ambassadors* or in those extraordinary evocations of Babylon in *The Golden Bowl*. But in *Madame Bovary* a Biblical text would ring false and might bring the whole deliberately prosaic structure tumbling down. With Tolstoy (and with Dostoevsky) matters are altogether different. Long citations from the Gospels are woven into *Resurrection*, for example, and into *The Possessed*. We are dealing now with a religious conception of art and a final order of seriousness. So much is at stake beyond the virtues of technical performance that the language of the Apostle seems wonderfully in place and heralds the work like a dark clarion.

Then comes the celebrated opening: "Everything was in confusion in the Oblonskys' house." Traditionally, it had been thought that Tolstoy had derived the idea for it from Pushkin's *Tales of Belkin*. The actual drafts, however, and a letter to Strakhov (published only in 1949) cast some doubt on this. In his definitive version, moreover, Tolstoy prefaced this sentence with a brief maxim: "Happy families are all alike; every unhappy family is unhappy in its own way." Whatever the exact details of composition, the broad rushing power of the beginning is unmistakable and Thomas Mann may well have been right in feeling that no other novel sets out so bravely.

As classical poetics would have it, we plunge *in medias res*—the trivial and yet harrowing infidelity of Stepan Arkadyevich Oblonsky (Stiva). In recounting Oblonsky's miniature adultery, Tolstoy sets forth in a minor key the dominant themes of the novel. Stepan Arkadyevich looks for help to his sister, Anna Karenina. She is on her way to restore peace in his distraught home. That Anna should first appear as a mender of broken marriages is a touch of thrilling irony, of the kind of Shakespearean irony which is so close to compassion. The interview between Stiva and Dolly, his outraged wife, prefigures, despite its comic brilliance, the tragic confrontations between Anna and Alexey Alexandrovich Karenin. But the Oblonsky episode is more than a prelude in which the principal motifs are stated with consummate artistry; it is the wheel which sets the multitudinous wheels of the narrative in effortless motion. For the havoc wrought in Stiva's domestic affairs leads to the encounter of Anna and Vronsky.

Oblonsky goes to his office—he owes his appointment to his formidable brother-in-law—and the true hero of the novel, Konstantin Dimitrievich Levin, "a gymnast who lifts thirteen stone [182 pounds] with one hand," joins him there. And he enters in an immensely characteristic mood. He reveals that he no longer participates in the activities of the rural *zemstvo*, he derides the sterile bureaucracy symbolized by Oblonsky's official sinecure and confesses that he has come to Moscow out of love for Oblonsky's sister-in-law, Kitty Shtcherbatsky. There we have, gathered into his first entrance, the commanding impulses of Levin's life: his quest for agronomic and rural reform, his rejection of urban culture, and his passionate love for Kitty.

There follow several episodes in which the personage of Levin is further defined. He meets with his half-brother, the well-known publicist Sergey Ivanovich Koznishev, makes inquiries about his elder brother Nicolas, and then resumes contact with Kitty. It is a profoundly Tolstoyan scene: "The old curly birches of the gardens, all their twigs laden with snow, looked as though freshly decked in sacred vestments." Kitty and Levin skate together and all about them is suffused with a fresh and brilliant light. From the point of view of strict narrative economy, Levin's conversation with Koznishev could be criticized as a digression. But I shall return to this problem, for within the structure of a Tolstoyan novel such digressions play a special role.

Levin rejoins Oblonsky and they lunch together at the Hôtel d'Angleterre. Levin is irritated by its brazen elegance and declares sourly that he would prefer "cabbage soup and porridge" to all the gastronomic splendours which the Tatar waiter lavishes before him. Though enraptured with his meal, Stiva comes back to his afflictions and asks for Levin's opinion on sexual infidelity. The brief dialogue is a masterpiece of narrative poise. Levin cannot comprehend that a man would "go straight to a baker's shop and steal a roll" when he has just dined of his own plenty. His convictions are fiercely monogamous, and when Oblonsky alludes to Mary Magdalen, Levin says bitterly that Christ would never have uttered those words "if He had known how they would be abused. . . . I have a loathing for fallen women." Yet, much later in the novel no man will approach Anna with more compassionate insight. Levin goes on to develop his conception of the uniqueness of love and refers to Plato's *Symposion*. But suddenly he breaks off; there are things in his own life out of tune with his convictions. Much of *Anna Karenina* is concentrated into this moment—the clash between monogamy and sexual freedom, the inconsistencies between personal ideals and personal behaviour, the attempt to interpret experience philosophically at first and thereafter in the image of Christ.

The setting changes to Kitty's home and we meet the fourth principal in the quadrille of love, Count Vronsky. He enters the novel as Kitty's admirer and pursuer. This is more than an example of Tolstoy's technical virtuosity, of his pleasure in refuting the conventional responses of his readers even as life refutes them. It is an expression of the "realism" and "deep-breathing economy" of great art. Vronsky's flirtation with Kitty has the same structural and psychological values as Romeo's infatuation with Rosaline. For the all-transforming impact of Romeo's adoration for Juliet and of Vronsky's passion for Anna can be poetically realized and made sensible only in contrast to a previous love. It is their discovery of the difference between this previous love and the daemonic totality of a mature passion which impels both men into unreason and disaster. Kitty's girlish infatuation with Vronsky (like Natasha's love of Bolkonsky in *War and Peace*) is similarly a prelude to self-knowledge. It is by virtue of comparison that she will recognize the authenticity of her feelings for Levin. The disenchantment which Vronsky brings about will enable Kitty to relinquish the glitter of Moscow and to follow Levin onto his estates. How subtly and yet how naturally Tolstoy winds his skein.

Kitty's mother, the Princess Shtcherbatsky, reflects on her daughter's future in one of those rambling inner monologues through which Tolstoy conveys family histories. It was all so much simpler in olden times, and once again we are confronted with the primary theme of *Anna Karenina*—the problem of marriage in a modern society. Levin appears at the Shtcherbatskys' to propose to Kitty:

> She was breathing heavily, not looking at him. She was feeling ecstasy. Her soul was flooded with happiness. She had never anticipated that the utterance of love would produce such a powerful effect on her. But it lasted only an instant. She remembered Vronsky. She lifted her clear, truthful eyes, and seeing his desperate face, she answered hastily:
> "That cannot be . . . forgive me."
> A moment ago, and how close she had been to him, of what importance in his life! And how aloof and remote from him she had become now!
> "It was bound to be so," he said, not looking at her.
> He bowed, and was meaning to retreat.

In its uncanny rightness this is the kind of passage which defies analysis. It is penetrated with tact and an inviolate grace. Yet, the vision is unswerving in its honesty and nearly in its harshness about the ways of the soul. Kitty does not really know why Levin's offer has flooded her with happiness. But the mere fact mitigates the pathos of the occasion and holds out its obscure promise for the future. In its tension and veracity the episode has something of the finest of D. H. Lawrence.

In the following chapter (XIV) Tolstoy confronts the two rivals and deepens the theme of Kitty's indiscriminate love. The ripeness and persuasion of his art are everywhere apparent. When the Countess Nordston, a loquacious busybody, goads Levin, Kitty is drawn half consciously to the latter's defence—and this despite the presence of Vronsky, to whom she looks with unfeigned joy. Vronsky is shown in the most favourable light. Levin has no difficulty in perceiving what is good and attractive in his fortunate rival. The motifs here are as delicate and ramified as in a scene in Jane Austen; a wrong touch or a misjudgment in the *tempo* would precipitate the mood towards the tragic or the artificial. But beneath the subtleties there is always the steadying vision, the Homeric sense for the reality of things. Kitty's eyes cannot help saying to Levin "I am so happy," and his cannot but answer "I hate them all, and you, and myself." But because it is conveyed without sentimentality or elaboration, his bitterness itself is humane.

The soirée ends in one of those family "interiors" which make the Rostovs and the Shtcherbatskys so incomparably "real." Kitty's father prefers Levin and instinctively feels that the Vronsky match may not come off. Listening to her husband, the Princess is no longer confident:

And returning to her own room, in terror before the unknown future, she, too, like Kitty, repeated several times in her heart, "Lord, have pity; Lord, have pity; Lord, have pity."

It is a sudden and sombre note and marks, very aptly, the transition to the main plot.

Vronsky goes to the railway station to await his mother's arrival from St. Petersburg. He meets Oblonsky, for Anna Karenina is coming on the same train. The tragedy begins, as it will end, on a railway platform (an essay could be written on the role of such platforms in the lives and novels of Tolstoy and Dostoevsky). Vronsky's mother and the charming Madame Karenina have travelled together, and as Anna is introduced to the Count she tells him "Yes, the countess and I have been talking all the time, I of my son and she of hers." This remark is one of the saddest and most perceptive touches in the entire novel. It is the comment of an older woman to the son of a friend, to a younger man not really of her own generation. Therein lies the catastrophe of the Anna-Vronsky relationship and its essential duplicity. The subsequent tragedy is contracted into a single phrase, and in his genius for bringing this about Tolstoy is of a measure with Homer and Shakespeare.

As the Vronskys and Anna and Stiva move towards the exit, there is an accident: "A guard, either drunk or too much muffled up in the bitter frost, had not heard the train moving back, and had been crushed." (The quiet statement of the two alternatives is characteristically Tolstoyan.) Oblonsky reports on the terrible appearance of the man, and voices are heard debating whether or not he suffered much pain. Half surreptitiously, Vronsky gives two hundred rubles to help the widow. But his gesture is not altogether pure; it is made in the probably ill-defined hope of impressing Madame Karenina. Though it is quickly forgotten, the accident darkens the air. It acts somewhat like the death motif in the overture to *Carmen*, which seems to reverberate softly long after the curtain has risen. It is instructive to compare Tolstoy's handling of this thematic device with Flaubert's allusions to arsenic in the early stages of *Madame Bovary*. The Tolstoyan version is less subtle but more authoritative.

Anna arrives at the Oblonskys' and we are plunged into the warm, comical whirl of Dolly's indignation and growing forgiveness. Anyone doubting that Tolstoy has a sense of humour should watch Anna as she sends her repentant but embarrassed brother to his wife: "'Stiva,' she said to him, winking gaily, crossing him, and glancing toward the door, 'go, and God help you.'" Anna and Kitty are left together and they speak of Vronsky. Anna praises him in the tone of an older woman encouraging a young girl in love: "But she did not tell Kitty about the two hundred roubles. For some reason it was disagreeable to her to think of it. She felt that there was something that had to do with her in it, and something that ought not have been." Of course, she is right.

Throughout these preliminary chapters two kinds of material are treated with equal mastery. The nuances and shadings of individual psychology are rendered with great precision. The treatment is close and not radically dissimilar from the psychological mosaic-work which we associate with Henry James and Proust. But at the same time the pulse of physical energy and gesture beats loud. The physicality of experience is strongly conveyed and it surrounds, and somehow humanizes, the life of the mind. This can best be shown in the final moments of Chapter XX. The intricate and tightly meshed conversation between Anna and Kitty is trailing off on a vague note of malaise. Kitty fancies that Anna Karenina is "displeased with something." In that instant the room is invaded:

"No, I'm first! No, I!" screamed the children, who had finished tea, running up to their Aunt Anna.

"All together," said Anna, and she ran laughing to meet them, and embraced and swung around all the throng of swarming children, shrieking with delight.

The motifs here are evident; Tolstoy once again focuses attention on Anna's relative age and mature status, as well as on her radiant charm. But one marvels at the ease of transition between the rich, inward play of the preceding dialogue and the bright leap of physical action.

Vronsky passes by, but declines to join the family circle. Kitty believes that he has come for her sake but would not show himself "because he thought it late, and Anna's here." She is vaguely troubled, as is Anna herself. On this minor and oblique note begins the tragedy of deceit in which Anna is destined to become enmeshed and which will, at the last, destroy her.

Chapter XXII takes us to the ball, where Kitty, like another Natasha, expects Count Vronsky to declare his love. The affair is wonderfully described and makes the dance at La Vaubyessard, in *Madame Bovary*, seem rather ponderous. This is not because Kitty is gifted with a greater wealth of consciousness than Emma; at this stage in the novel she is a very ordinary young woman indeed. The difference lies altogether in the perspective of the two writers. Flaubert steps back from his canvas and paints at arm's length with cool malignity. Even in translation we can sense that he is striving after special effects of lighting and cadence:

the chink of gold pieces came clearly from the gaming tables in the next room; then everything was in full swing again; the cornet blared, once again feet tramped in rhythm, skirts ballooned and brushed together, hands joined and separated; eyes lowered one moment looked intently into yours the next.

The ironic distance is preserved, but the vision as a whole is impoverished and made artificial. In *Anna Karenina*, with its omniscient narrator, there is no single point of view. The ball is seen through Kitty's sudden grief, through Anna's dazed enchantment, in the light of Vronsky's nascent passion, and from the point of view of Korsunsky, "the first star in the hierarchy of the ballroom." Setting and personages are indivisible; each detail—and this is where Tolstoy differs trenchantly from Flaubert—is given not for its own sake or for atmosphere but as dramatically pertinent. Through Kitty's anguished observation we watch Vronsky falling under Madame Karenina's spell. It is the young Princess, in her bewilderment and shame, who conveys to us the full quality of Anna's fascination. During the mazurka the latter looks at Kitty with "drooping eyelids." It is a minute touch, but it concentrates, with utter precision, the sense of Anna's cunning and of her potential cruelty. A lesser artist would have shown Anna through Vronsky's eyes. But Tolstoy does what Homer did when he let a chorus of old men catalogue and exalt the splendours of Helen. In both instances we are persuaded through indirection.

The ensuing chapters deepen the portrayal of Levin and we catch a brief glimpse of him on his estate, in his proper element, amid the dark fields, the birch thickets, the problems in agronomy, and the brooding quiet of the land. The contrast with the ball is intended and points to the foremost thematic duality in the novel: Anna, Vronsky, and the social life of the city; Levin, Kitty, and the natural universe. Subsequently these two *leitmotifs* will harmonize and develop in complex patterns. But the prelude as such is completed, and in the last five chapters of Book I the actual conflict—the tragic *agon*—is begun.

Anna prepares to rejoin her husband in St. Petersburg. She settles down in her compartment and reads an English novel, identifying herself wistfully with its heroine. This, together with a famous episode in the following chapter, seems to derive directly from Tolstoy's remembrance of *Madame Bovary*. The train stops at a station in the middle of a snow-storm, and Anna, who is already in a state of exalted tension, steps out into "the frozen, snowy air." Vronsky has followed her and confesses his passion: "All the awfulness of the storm seemed to her more splendid now. He had said what her soul longed to hear, though she feared it with her reason." How simply and even archaically Tolstoy divides the human spirit into soul and reason. Flaubert would not have written that sentence; but in his sophistication lay his narrowness.

The train pulls into St. Petersburg; Anna at once catches sight of Alexey Alexandrovich Karenin: " 'Oh, mercy! why do his ears look like that?' she thought, looking at his frigid and imposing figure, and especially the ears that struck her at the moment as propping up the rim of his round hat." Is this not Tolstoy's version of Emma Bovary's discovery that Charles makes uncouth noises while eating? When Anna comes home she finds that her little son is less entrancing than she had anticipated. Already her capacities for discrimination and the habits of her moral life are being distorted by a passion of which she is, as yet, only partially aware. To sharpen the dissociation between Anna and the *milieu* to which she has returned, Tolstoy introduces the Countess Lidia, one of Karenin's unctuous and bigoted friends. But at the very moment when we expect Anna to reveal herself, to awaken to her new life, the fever subsides. She grows calm and wonders why her emotions have run riot over so banal and trivial a matter as a momentary flirtation with an elegant young officer.

In the quiet of the evening the Karenins are together. Alexey admits, with his brutal honesty, that he finds Oblonsky's escapade unpardonable. His words are like a flash of lightning on the horizon, but Anna accepts them and rejoices in his candour. At midnight Karenin bids Anna come to bed. The small touches, the slippers, the book under his arm, the precision of the hour tell us that there is in the physical relations of the Karenins a central monotony. As Anna enters the bedroom "the fire seemed quenched in her, hidden somewhere far away." The image acquires, from the given moment, an extraordinary force; but even when bearing most steadfastly on a sexual theme, Tolstoy's genius was chaste. As Gorky observed, the grossest and most concrete erotic language assumed, in Tolstoy's mouth, a natural purity. The sense of erotic incompletion in Anna's marriage is fully realized; but there is nothing here of the corset string which "hissed" around Emma Bovary's hips "like a gliding snake." This is a point of some importance, for it was in his luminous treatment of physical passion that Tolstoy was, at least until his later years, closest to the Homeric mood.

Book I of the novel concludes on a buoyant note. Vronsky returns to his quarters and plunges into the life of revelry and ambition of a young officer in imperial St. Petersburg. It is a life which Tolstoy utterly repudiates, but he is too fine an artist not to show how admirably it suits Vronsky. Only the very last sentences carry us back to the tragic theme. The Count plans to "go into that society where he might meet Madame Karenina. As he always did in Petersburg, he left home not meaning to return till late at night." That seemingly casual remark has a prophetic exactitude. For what lies ahead is darkness.

Much more could be said about the first part of *Anna Karenina*. But even a cursory examination of how the dominant themes are stated and developed should make untenable the myth that the novels of Flaubert or Henry James are works of art whereas the novels of Tolstoy are pieces of life transmuted into masterpieces by some daemonic and artless necromancy. R. P. Blackmur points out that *War and Peace* "does have every quality" which James prescribed when he called for the "deep-breathing economy of an organic form." [9] This is even truer of *Anna Karenina*, in which the integrity of Tolstoy's poetic gift was less imperilled by the demands of his philosophy.

When pursuing this notion of the organic in the initial sections of *Anna Karenina*, one is led time and again to a sense of musical analogy. There are effects of counterpoint and harmony in the development of the two principal plots out of the "Oblonsky prelude." There is the use of motifs which will recur with increasing amplitude at later stages in the novel (the accident at the railway station, the bantering discussion on divorce between Vronsky and Baroness Shilton, the "dazzle of red fire" before Anna's eyes). Above all, there is the impression of a multiplicity of themes subordinated to the forward impulse of a grand design. Tolstoy's method is polyphonic; but the major harmonies unfold with tremendous directness and breadth. Musical and linguistic techniques cannot be compared with any degree of precision. But how else is one to elucidate the feeling that the novels of Tolstoy grow out of some inward principle of order and vitality whereas those of lesser writers are stitched together?

But because a novel such as *Anna Karenina* is so massive in its dimensions and because it exercises an immediate control over our emotions, the deliberateness and

[9] R. P. Blackmur: "The Loose and Baggy Monsters of Henry James" (*The Lion and the Honeycomb*, New York, 1955).

sophistication of the individual detail tend to escape us. In epic poetry and verse drama the metrical form particularizes our attention and focuses it on the given passage, on the single line or recurrent metaphor. When reading an extended piece of prose (particularly in translation) we submit to the total effect. Hence the belief that the Russian novelists can be grasped in their generality and that little is to be gained from the kind of close study we apply to Conrad, say, or to Proust.

As is shown by his drafts and revisions, Tolstoy laboured over particular problems of narration and presentment with minute attention. But he never forgot that beyond technical virtuosity, beyond "doing the thing beautifully," there lay the thing to be done. He condemned *l'art pour l'art* for being the aesthetics of frivolity. And it is precisely because there is such a large and central world view in Tolstoyan fiction, such a complex humanity and so clear an assumption that great art touches on experience philosophically and religiously, that it is difficult to single out the particular element, the specific *tableau* or metaphor and say "here is Tolstoy the technician."

There are set pieces in Tolstoy: the famous mowing scene in *Anna Karenina*, the wolf-hunt in *War and Peace*, the church service in *Resurrection*. There are similes and tropes as carefully wrought as any that we find in Flaubert. Consider, for example, the antinomy of light and darkness which inspired the titles of Tolstoy's two principal dramas and which pervades *Anna Karenina*. In the last sentence of Book VII, Anna's death is communicated through the image of a light kindled into momentary radiance and then quenched for ever; the final sentence of Chapter XI in Book VIII portrays Levin blinded with light as he recognizes the way of God. The echo is deliberate; it resolves the ambiguity latent in the Pauline epigraph and brings towards reconciliation the two major plots. As always in Tolstoy, the technical device is the conveyor of a philosophy. All the great sum of invention in *Anna Karenina* points towards the moral which Levin receives from an old peasant: "We must live not for ourselves but for God."

Without seeking to give a precise definition, Matthew Arnold spoke of the "high seriousness" which distinguishes a small number of works from the greater mass of literary achievement. He found this quality in Dante, for instance, rather than in Chaucer. Perhaps that is as near as we can come to contrasting *Madame Bovary* with *Anna Karenina*. *Madame Bovary* is a very great novel indeed; it persuades us through its miraculous skill and through the manner in which it exhausts all the potentialities of its theme. But the theme itself and our identification with it remain, at the last, "too small an affair." In *Anna Karenina* we pass beyond technical mastery to the sense of life itself. The work belongs (in a way in which *Madame Bovary* does not) with the Homeric epics, the plays of Shakespeare, and the novels of Dostoevsky.

IV

Hugo von Hofmannsthal once remarked that he could not read a page of Tolstoy's *Cossacks* without being reminded of Homer. His experience has been shared by readers not only of *The Cossacks* but of Tolstoy's works as a whole. According to Gorky, Tolstoy himself said of *War and Peace*: "Without false modesty, it is like the *Iliad*," and he made precisely the same observation with regard to *Childhood, Boyhood and Youth*. Moreover, Homer and the Homeric atmosphere appear to have played a fascinating role in Tolstoy's image of his own personality and creative stature. His brother-in-law, S. A. Bers, tells in his *Reminiscences* of a feast which took place on Tolstoy's estate in Samara:

a steeplechase of fifty versts. Prizes were got ready, a bull, a horse, a rifle, a watch, a dressing-gown and the like. A level stretch was chosen, a huge course four miles long was made and marked out, and posts were put up on it. Roast sheep, and even a horse, were prepared for the entertainment. On the appointed day, some thousands of people assembled, Ural Cossacks, Russian peasants, Bashkirs and

Khirgizes, with their dwellings, koumiss-kettles, and even their flocks. . . . On a cone-shaped rise, called in the local dialect "Shishka" (the Wen), carpets and felt were spread, and on these the Bashkirs seated themselves in a ring, with their legs tucked under them. . . . The feast lasted for two days and was merry, but at the same time dignified and decorous. . . .[1]

It is a fantastic scene; the millennia dividing the plains of Troy from nineteenth-century Russia are bridged and Book XXIII of the *Iliad* springs to life. In Richmond Lattimore's version:

> But Achilleus
> held the people there, and made them sit down in a wide assembly,
> and brought prizes for games out of his ships, cauldrons and tripods,
> and horses and mules and the powerful high heads of cattle
> and fair-girdled women and grey iron.

Like Agamemnon, Tolstoy thrones upon the hillock; the steppe is dotted with tents and fires; Bashkirs and Khirgizes, like Achaeans, race the four-mile course and take their prizes from the hands of the bearded king. But there is nothing here of archaeology, of contrived reconstruction. The Homeric element was native to Tolstoy; it was rooted in his own genius. Read his polemics against Shakespeare and you will find that his sense of kinship with the poet, or poets, of the *Iliad* and *Odyssey* was palpable and immediate. Tolstoy spoke of Homer as equal of equal; between them the ages had counted for little.

What was it that struck Tolstoy as peculiarly Homeric in his collection of early memories? Both the setting, I think, and the kind of life he recalled to mind. Take the account of "The Hunt" in the volume on *Childhood*:

Harvesting was in full swing. The limitless, brilliantly yellow field was bounded only on one side by the tall, bluish

[1] Quoted in D. S. Merezhkovsky: op. cit.

forest, which then seemed to me a most distant, mysterious place beyond which either the world came to an end or uninhabited countries began. The whole field was full of sheaves and peasants. . . . The little roan papa rode went with a light, playful step, sometimes bending his head to his chest, pulling at the reins, and brushing off with his thick tail the gadflies and gnats that settled greedily on him. Two borzois with tense tails raised sickle-wise, and lifting their feet high, leapt gracefully over the tall stubble, behind the horse's feet. Milka ran in front, and with head lifted awaited the quarry. The peasants' voices, the tramp of horses and creaking of carts, the merry whistle of quail, the hum of insects hovering in the air in steady swarms, the odour of wormwood, straw, and horses' sweat, the thousands of different colours and shadows with which the burning sun flooded the light yellow stubble, the dark blue of the forest, the light lilac clouds, and the white cobwebs that floated in the air or stretched across the stubble—all this I saw, heard, and felt.

There is nothing here that would have been incongruous on the plains of Argos. It is from our own modern setting that the scene is oddly remote. It is a patriarchal world of huntsmen and peasants; the bond between master and hounds and the earth runs native and true. The description itself combines a sense of forward motion with an impression of repose; the total effect, as in the friezes of the Parthenon, is one of dynamic equilibrium. And beyond the familiar horizon, as beyond the Pillars of Hercules, lie the mysterious seas and the untrodden forests.

The world of Tolstoy's recollections, no less than that of Homer, is charged with sensuous energies. Touch and sight and smell fill it at every moment with rich intensity:

In the passage a samovár, into which Mítka, the postilion, flushed red as a lobster, is blowing, is already on the boil. It is damp and misty outside, as if steam were rising from the odorous manure heap; the sun lights with its bright gay beams the eastern part of the sky and the thatched roofs, shiny with dew, of the roomy pent-houses that surround the yard. Under these one can see our horses tethered to the mangers and hear their steady chewing. A shaggy mongrel that had had a nap before dawn on a dry heap of manure, stretches itself lazily, and wagging its tail, starts at a jog-trot for the opposite side of the yard. An active peasant-woman opens some creaking gates and drives the dreamy cows into the street, where the tramping, the low-ing and the bleating of the herd is already audible. . . .

So it was when "rosy-fingered Dawn" came to Ithaca twenty-seven hundred years ago. So it should be, pro-claims Tolstoy, if man is to endure in communion with the earth. Even the storm, with its animate fury, be-longs to the rhythm of things:

The lightning flashes become wider and paler, and the roll-ing of the thunder is now less startling amid the regular patter of the rain. . . . .

. . . an aspen grove with hazel and wild cherry under-growth stands motionless as if in an excess of joy, and slowly sheds bright raindrops from its clean-washed branches on to last year's leaves. On all sides crested sky-larks circle with glad songs and swoop swiftly down. . . . The delicious scent of the wood after the spring storm, the odour of the birches, of the violets, the rotting leaves, the mushrooms, and the wild cherry, is so enthralling that I cannot stay in the brichka. . . .

Schiller wrote in his essay *Ueber naïve und sentimen-talische Dichtung* that certain poets "are Nature" while others only "seek her." In that sense, Tolstoy is Nature; between him and the natural world language stood not as a mirror or a magnifying glass, but as a window through which all light passes and yet is gathered and given permanence.

It is impossible to concentrate within a single for-mula or demonstration the affinities between the Ho-meric and the Tolstoyan points of view. So much is pertinent: the archaic and pastoral setting; the poetry of war and agriculture; the primacy of the senses and of physical gesture; the luminous, all-reconciling back-ground of the cycle of the year; the recognition that en-ergy and aliveness are, of themselves, holy; the accept-ance of a chain of being extending from brute matter to the stars and along which men have their apportioned places; deepest of all, an essential sanity, a determination to follow what Coleridge called "the high road of life," rather than those dark obliquities in which the genius of a Dostoevsky was most thoroughly at home.

In both the Homeric epics and the novels of Tolstoy the relationship between author and characters is paradoxical. Maritain gives a Thomistic analogue for it in his study of *Creative Intuition in Art and Poetry*. He speaks "of the relationship between the transcendent creative eternity of God and the free creatures who are both acting in liberty and firmly embraced by his purpose." The creator is at once omniscient and everywhere present, but at the same time he is detached, impassive, and relentlessly objective in his vision. The Homeric Zeus presides over the battle from his mountain fastness, holding the scales of destiny but not intervening. Or, rather, intervening solely to restore equilibrium, to safeguard the mutability of man's life against miraculous aid or the excessive achievements of heroism. As in the detachment of the god, so there is in the clear-sightedness of Homer and Tolstoy both cruelty and compassion.

They saw with those blank, ardent, unswerving eyes which look upon us through the helmet-slits of archaic Greek statues. Their vision was terribly sober. Schiller marvelled at Homer's impassiveness, at his ability to communicate the utmost of grief and terror in perfect evenness of tone. He believed that this quality—this "naïveté"—belonged to an earlier age and would be unrecapturable in the sophisticated and analytic temper of modern literature. From it Homer derived his most poignant effects. Take, for example, Achilles' slaying of Lykaon in Book XXI of the *Iliad*:

"So, friend, you die also. Why all this clamour about it?
Patroklos also is dead, who was better by far than you are.
Do you not see what a man I am, how huge, how splendid
and born of a great father, and the mother who bore me
immortal?

Yet even I have also my death and my strong destiny,
and there shall be a dawn or an afternoon or a noontime
when some man in the fighting will take the life from me
also
either with a spearcast or an arrow flown from the bow-
string."
So he spoke, and in the other the knees and the inward
heart went slack. He let go of the spear and sat back,
spreading
wide both hands; but Achilleus drawing his sharp sword
struck him
beside the neck at the collar-bone, and the double-edged
sword
plunged full length inside. He dropped to the ground, face
downward,
and lay at length, and the black blood flowed, and the
ground was soaked with it.

The calm of the narrative is nearly inhuman; but in
consequence the horror speaks naked and moves us unutterably. Moreover, Homer never sacrifices the steadiness of his vision to the needs of pathos. Priam and
Achilles have met and given vent to their great griefs.
But then they bethink themselves of meat and wine.
For, as Achilles says of Niobe:

"She remembered to eat when she was worn out with
weeping."

Again, it is the dry fidelity to the facts, the poet's refusal to be outwardly moved, which communicate the
bitterness of his soul.

In this respect, no one in the western tradition is
more akin to Homer than is Tolstoy. As Romain Rolland noted in his journal for 1887, "in the art of Tolstoy a given scene is not perceived from two points of
view, but from only one: things are as they are, not otherwise." In *Childhood*, Tolstoy tells of the death of his
mother: "I was in great distress at that moment but involuntarily noticed every detail," including the fact that
the nurse was "very fair, young, and remarkably handsome." When his mother dies, the boy experiences "a
kind of enjoyment," at knowing himself to be unhappy.

That night he sleeps "soundly and calmly," as is always the case after great distress. The following day he becomes aware of the smell of decomposition:

It was only then that I understood what the strong, oppressive smell was that mingling with the incense filled the whole room; and the thought that the face that but a few days before had been so full of beauty and tenderness, the face of her I loved more than anything on earth, could evoke horror, seemed to reveal the bitter truth to me for the first time, and filled my soul with despair.

"Keep your eyes steadfastly to the light," says Tolstoy, "this is how things are."

But in the unflinching clarity of the Homeric and Tolstoyan attitude there is far more than resignation. There is joy, the joy that burns in the "ancient glittering eyes" of the sages in Yeats's *Lapis Lazuli*. For they loved and revered the "humanness" of man; they delighted in the life of the body coolly perceived but ardently narrated. Moreover, it was their instinct to close the gap between spirit and gesture, to relate the hand to the sword, the keel to the brine, and the wheel-rim to the singing cobblestones. Both the Homer of the *Iliad* and Tolstoy saw action whole; the air vibrates around their personages and the force of their being electrifies insensate nature. Achilles' horses weep at his impending doom and the oak flowers to persuade Bolkonsky that his heart will live again. This consonance between man and the surrounding world extends even to the cups in which Nestor looks for wisdom when the sun is down and to the birch-leaves that glitter like a sudden riot of jewels after the storm has swept over Levin's estate. The barriers between mind and object, the ambiguities which metaphysicians discern in the very notion of reality and perception, impeded neither Homer nor Tolstoy. Life flooded in upon them like the sea.

And they rejoiced at it. When Simone Weil called the *Iliad* "The Poem of Force" and saw in it a commentary on the tragic futility of war, she was only partially right. The *Iliad* is far removed from the despairing nihilism of Euripides' *Trojan Women*. In the Homeric poem,

77

war is valorous and ultimately ennobling. And even in the midst of carnage, life surges high. Around the burial mound of Patroklus the Greek chieftains wrestle, race, and throw the javelin in celebration of their strength and aliveness. Achilles knows that he is foredoomed, but "bright cheeked Briseis" comes to him each night. War and mortality cry havoc in the Homeric and Tolstoyan worlds, but the centre holds: it is the affirmation that life is, of itself, a thing of beauty, that the works and days of men are worth recording, and that no catastrophe—not even the burning of Troy or of Moscow—is ultimate. For beyond the charred towers and beyond the battle rolls the wine-dark sea, and when Austerlitz is forgotten the harvest shall, in Pope's image, once again "embrown the slope."

This entire cosmology is gathered into Bosola's reminder to the Duchess of Malfi when she curses nature in agonized rebellion: "Look you, the stars shine still." These are terrible words, full of detachment and the harsh reckoning that the physical world contemplates our afflictions with impassiveness. But go beyond their cruel impact and they convey an assurance that life and star-light endure beyond the momentary chaos.

The Homer of the *Iliad* and Tolstoy are akin in yet another respect. Their image of reality is anthropomorphic; man is the measure and pivot of experience. Moreover, the atmosphere in which the personages of the *Iliad* and of Tolstoyan fiction are shown to us is profoundly humanistic and even secular. What matters is the kingdom of *this* world, here and now. In a sense, that is a paradox; on the plains of Troy mortal and divine affairs are incessantly confounded. But the very descent of the gods among men and their brazen involvement in all-too-human passions give the work its ironic overtones. Musset invoked this paradoxical attitude in his account of archaic Greece in the opening lines of *Rolla*:

> *Où tout était divin, jusqu'aux douleurs humaines;*
> *Où le monde adorait ce qu'il tue aujourd'hui;*
> *Où quatre mille dieux n'avaient pas un athée. . . .*

Precisely; with four thousand deities warring in men's quarrels, dallying with mortal women, and behaving in a manner apt to scandalize even liberal codes of morality, there was no need for atheism. Atheism arises in contrariety to the conception of a living and credible God; it is not a response to a partially comic mythology. In the *Iliad* divinity is quintessentially human. The gods are mortals magnified, and often magnified in a satiric vein. When wounded they howl louder than men, when they are enamoured their lusts are more consuming, when they flee before human spears their speed exceeds that of earthly chariots. But morally and intellectually the deities of the *Iliad* resemble giant brutes or malevolent children endowed with an excess of power. The actions of gods and goddesses in the Trojan War enhance the stature of man, for when odds are equal mortal heroes more than hold their own and when the scales are against them a Hector and an Achilles demonstrate that mortality has its own splendours. In lowering the gods to human values, the "first" Homer achieved not only an effect of comedy, though such an effect obviously contributes to the freshness and "fairy-tale" quality of the poem. Rather, he emphasized the excellence and dignity of heroic man. And this, above all, was his theme.

The pantheon in the *Odyssey* plays a subtler and more awesome role, and the *Aeneid* is an epic penetrated with a feeling for religious values and religious practice. But the *Iliad*, while accepting the mythology of the supernatural, treats it ironically and humanizes its material. The true centre of belief lies not on Olympus but in the recognition of *Moira*, of unyielding destiny which maintains through its apparently blind decimations an ultimate principle of justice and equilibrium. The religiosity of Agamemnon and Hector consists in an acceptance of fate, in a belief that certain impulses towards hospitality are sacred, in reverence for sanctified hours or hallowed places, and in a vague but potent realization that there are daemonic forces in the motion of the stars or the obstinacies of the wind. But beyond that, reality is immanent in the world of man and of his senses. I know of no better word to express the non-transcendence and ultimate physicality of the *Iliad*. No poem runs more strongly counter to the belief that "we are such stuff as dreams are made on."

And this is where it touches significantly on the art of Tolstoy. His also is an immanent realism, a world rooted in the veracity of our senses. From it God is strangely absent. In Chapter IV, I shall attempt to show that this absence can not only be reconciled to the religious purpose of Tolstoy's novels but that it is a hidden axiom of Tolstoyan Christianity. All that needs saying here is that there lies behind the literary techniques of the *Iliad* and of Tolstoy a comparable belief in the centrality of the human personage and in the enduring beauty of the natural world. In the case of *War and Peace* the analogy is even more decisive; where the *Iliad* evokes the laws of *Moira*, Tolstoy expounds his philosophy of history. In both works the chaotic individuality of battle stands for the larger randomness in men's lives. And if we consider *War and Peace* as being, in a genuine sense, a heroic epic it is because in it, as in the *Iliad*, war is portrayed in its glitter and joyous ferocity as well as in its pathos. No measure of Tolstoyan pacifism can negate the ecstasy which young Rostov experiences as he charges down on the French stragglers. Finally, there is the fact that *War and Peace* tells of two nations, or rather of two worlds, engaged in mortal combat. This alone has led many of its readers, and led Tolstoy himself, to compare it with the *Iliad*.

But neither the martial theme nor the portrayal of national destinies should blind us to the fact that the philosophy of the novel is anti-heroic. There are moments in the book in which Tolstoy is emphatically preaching that war is wanton carnage and the result of vainglory and stupidity in high places. There are also times at which Tolstoy is concerned solely with seeking to discover "the real truth" in opposition to the alleged truths of official historians and mythographers. Neither the latent pacifism nor this concern with the evidence of history can be compared to the Homeric attitude.

War and Peace is most genuinely akin to the *Iliad* where its philosophy is least engaged, where, in Isaiah Berlin's terms, the fox is least busy trying to be a hedgehog. Actually, Tolstoy is closest to Homer in less manifold works, in *The Cossacks*, the *Tales from the Caucasus*, the sketches of the Crimean War and in the dread sobriety of *The Death of Ivan Ilych*.

But it cannot be emphasized too strongly that the affinity between the poet of the *Iliad* and the Russian novelist was one of temper and vision; there is no question here (or only in the minute instance) of a Tolstoyan imitation of Homer. Rather, it is that when Tolstoy turned to the Homeric epics in the original Greek, in his early forties, he must have felt wondrously at home.

v

Until now we have been concerned with generalities, with attempting to express along broad lines what is meant when the works of Tolstoy are qualified as "epic" and more precisely as Homeric. But if these generalities are to be of value they must be founded on matters of detail. The major effects and qualities which give the writings of Tolstoy their particular tone arise from a mosaic of technical practices. It is to some of these that I want to turn.

The stock epithet, the recurrent simile and repeated metaphor are a well-known characteristic of the Homeric style. Probably their origin was mnemonic; in oral poetry recurrent phrases assist the memory of both the singer and his audience; they act like interior echoes recalling to mind earlier incidents in the saga. But such tags as "rosy-fingered Dawn" or the "wine-dark sea," and the stock similes in which wrath is compared with the irruption of a savage lion into a herd of sheep or cattle, appeal to more than memory. They form a tapestry of normal life before which the heroic action unfolds. They create a backdrop of stable reality which gives the personages in the poem both their roundedness and their dimensions. For in evoking the pastoral mood or the daily routine of husbandry and fishing, Homer is saying that the Trojan War has not encroached upon the lives of all men. Elsewhere the dolphin leap and the shepherds drowse in the peace of the mountains. In the midst of carnage and the swift revolutions in human fortunes, these unchanging phrases proclaim that dawn will follow on the night, that the tides will surge inland when the location of Troy is a disputed memory, and that mountain lions will assail flocks when the last descendants of Nestor are in their dotage.

Homer juxtaposes the elements in his similes and metaphors to achieve a particular effect. The eye is borne away from an image of vivid and clamorous action and as the angle of vision widens, a scene of tranquil normality comes into focus. The picture of helmeted warriors scattering before Hector grows dim and now we see the grass bending before a storm. By their juxtaposition, both terms in the comparison are made subtler and more immediately a part of our consciousness. There are Flemish painters who handle this effect magnificently; think of Brueghel's Icarus plummeting into the calm sea as the ploughman walks his furrow in the foreground, or of the Passions and massacres painted against the background of an opulent and impassive landscape of walled cities, unruffled meadows, and fantastic alps. This "double awareness" is perhaps the essential device of pathos and serenity in Homer. It is the tragedy of the doomed heroes to recollect that other world of autumnal hunts, harvests, and domestic revels which they have left irremediably behind. But at the same time the clarity of their remembrance and the constant intrusion of a more stable plane of experience into the sound and fury of battle give the poem its strong repose.

There are moments in art (and they strike one as among the summits of the imagination) in which this "double awareness" is itself made the theme of formal rendition. Consider the performance of an air from *Figaro* in the last act of Mozart's *Don Giovanni* or the allusion to *La Belle Dame sans Merci* in Keats's *Eve of St. Agnes*. There is such a moment, also, in Homer. It comes in Book VIII of the *Odyssey* when Demodocus sings a portion of the Trojan saga and Odysseus weeps. In this poignant episode the two planes of reality, the two terms in the metaphor, have been reversed. Troy is now the distant memory and Odysseus is once again in the normal world.

Like Homer, Tolstoy uses stock epithets and recurrent phrases both to assist our memory over the vast stretches of his narrative and to create a dual vision of experience. The massiveness and complexity of such works as *War and Peace* and *Anna Karenina*, together with the fact that they were published in successive fragments and over considerable lapses of time, created problems comparable to those of oral poetry. Throughout the opening sections of *War and Peace*, Tolstoy seeks to aid the reader to keep the multitude of characters distinctly in mind. Princess Mary is shown ever and again walking "with her heavy tread." Pierre is firmly associated with his spectacles. Even before Natasha has loomed large in our mind's eye, her lightness of step and vivacity of motion have been emphasized. As a modern poet has written of an altogether different young lady,

> There was such speed in her little body
> And such lightness in her footfall. . . .

The defect in Denisov's speech is introduced not only for purposes of verbal comedy but to distinguish him at once from a host of other military figures. Tolstoy, moreover, continues this practice in later stages of the novel. Napoleon's hands are the subject of constant allusion, and, as Merezhkovsky remarks, Vereshchagin's "thin neck" is noted five times during his brief but harrowing appearance.

It is an important element of Tolstoy's genius that he gradually complicates his portrayals without effacing the broad strokes. Although we come to know Natasha more closely than we do many a woman whom we meet in our own lives, the initial image, the vision of celerity and gracious impulse, remains with us. In fact, one finds it difficult to believe Tolstoy's statement in the First Epilogue that Natasha had "abandoned all her witchery" and grown "stouter and broader." Would we believe Homer if he told us that Odysseus had grown dull-witted?

More significantly, Tolstoy's use of imagery and metaphor seeks to relate and contrast the two planes of experience with which he is most concerned—the rural and the urban. We touch here on what may well be the centre of his art; for the distinction between life on the land and in the city is illustrative, to Tolstoy, of the primordial distinction between good and evil, between the unnatural and inhuman codes of urbanity on the one hand, and the golden age of pastoral life on the other. This fundamental dualism is one of the motives for the double- and triple-plot structure in the Tolstoyan novel and was ultimately systematized in Tolstoy's ethics. For if Tolstoy's thought is indebted to Socrates, Confucius, and Buddha, it is penetrated also with the pastoralism of Rousseau.

As in Homer, so we find in Tolstoy the juxtaposition of the immediate scene with a recollection of rural impressions. The unchanging and finally meaningful level of experience is set, in criticism and illumination, behind the momentary episode. There is a beautiful example of this technique in *Childhood, Boyhood and Youth*. The little boy has failed dismally in his attempts to dance the mazurka and retreats covered with humiliation:

". . . Oh, it is terrible! Now if mamma had been here, she would not have blushed for her Nicholas . . ." And my imagination carried me far away after that dear vision. I recalled the meadow in front of the house, the tall lime-trees in the garden, the clear pond over which the swallows circled, the azure sky with motionless transparent clouds, the fragrant heaps of new-mown hay, and many other peaceful and bright memories floated through my distracted imagination.

Thus the narrator is restored to a sense of harmony with what Henry James called, in *The Portrait of a Lady*, "the deeper rhythms of life."

Another instance, in which the technique and the metaphysics are no longer separable, occurs in that formidable sketch, *After the Ball*. (In Tolstoy's vocabulary, a ball has ambiguous overtones; it is both an occasion of grace and elegance and a symbol of consummate artificiality.) In this brief tale, the narrator is enraptured with love and cannot go to sleep after having danced all night. Seeking to release his joyous tension, he walks through the village at dawn: "It was regular carnival weather—foggy, and the road full of water-soaked snow just melting, and water dripping from the eaves." He comes, by chance, upon a horrible spectacle —a soldier being flogged through the ranks for his attempt to desert. The father of the young woman with whom the narrator is in love is presiding over the affair with pedantic savagery. At the ball, only an hour before, he was a model of decorum and affection. Which, now, is the natural man? And the fact that the flogging takes place under the open sky and amid the tranquil routine of an awakening village makes it all the more bestial.

There are two brilliant examples of Tolstoy's divided consciousness in Book IV of *War and Peace*. Chapter III describes the gala dinner held in honour of Bagration at the English Club in Moscow on March 3, 1806. Count Ilya Rostov is in charge of the lavish arrangements and has put aside the financial perplexities which are beginning to gather about his household. Tolstoy portrays, in glittering strokes, the scurrying servants, the members of the club, the young heroes back from their first war. He is enthralled by the artistic "chances" of the scene; he knows how fine a chronicler he is of high society. But the undercurrent of disapproval is manifest. The luxury, the waste, and the inequality of servant and master stick in Tolstoy's throat.

A footman scurries in with a frightened mien to announce that the guest of honour is arriving:

Bells rang, the stewards rushed forward, and—like rye shaken together in a shovel—the guests who had been scattered about in different rooms came together and crowded in the large drawing-room by the door of the ball-room.

The simile acts in three ways: it gives a precise equivalent for the movement of the guests; it shocks the imagination into alertness because it derives from an area of experience so different from the one before our eyes; and it conveys a subtle but lucid commentary on the values of the entire episode. By identifying the elegant members of the English Club with grains of rye unceremoniously shaken together, Tolstoy reduces them to something automatic and faintly comical. The simile pierces at one stroke to the heart of their frivolity. Moreover, in its deliberate reversion to pastoral life, it contrasts the world of the English Club—the "false" social world—with that of the land and of the harvest cycle.

In Chapter VI of the same Book we find Pierre on the verge of a new existence. He has fought his duel with Dolokhov and has no more illusions regarding his wife, the Countess Helen. He contemplates the degradation which has come about through his marriage and seeks the experience of grace that will transform his soul. Helen enters with "imperturbable calm" to mock at Pierre's jealousy. He looks at her "timidly over his spectacles" and tries to continue reading—

like a hare surrounded by hounds who lays back her ears and continues to crouch motionless before her enemies. . . .

Again, we have here a comparison which moves us in various and conflicting ways. There is an immediate impression of pity, mingled, however, with amusement. Pictorially, Pierre with his spectacles on his nose and his ears laid back is both pathetic and comical. But in reference to the actual situation, the simile strikes one as ironic: it is Helen, despite her brazen advance, who is the much weaker personage. In a moment Pierre will explode to his full stature and nearly kill her with the marble top of a table. The hare will turn and rout the hunters. Once again, moreover, we have an image taken from rural life. It acts like a burst of wind and sunlight in a scene of stifling urban intrigue. But, at the same time, the picture of the crouching hare shatters the surface of social propriety and says clearly that what we are witnessing is a consequence of elementary lusts. High society hunts in packs.

The examples I have cited embody in miniature the major design in Tolstoy's creation. Two ways of life, two primordially disparate forms of experience are presented in contrast. This duality is not always a simple emblem for good and evil; in *War and Peace* urban life is shown in some of its most attractive colours and *The Power of Darkness* depicts the bestiality which can prevail on the land. But, in the main, Tolstoy saw experience morally and aesthetically divided. There is the life of the city with its social injustices, its artificial sexual conventions, its cruel display of wealth, and its power to alienate man from the essential patterns of physical vitality. On the other hand, there is life in the fields and forests with its alliance of mind and body, its acceptance of sexuality as hallowed and creative, and its instinct for the chain of being which relates the phases of the moon to the phases of conception and which associates the coming of the seed-time with the resurrection of the soul. As Lukács observes, nature was to Tolstoy "the effective guarantee that beyond the world of conventionalities there exists a 'real' Life." [2]

This double vision characterized Tolstoy's thought and aesthetics from the start. His later doctrines, the evolution of his instinctive preferences into a coherent philosophic and social discipline, were not a result of sudden changes but rather a maturing of ideas first set

[2] George Lukács: *Die Theorie des Romans* (Berlin, 1920).

forth in adolescence. The young landowner who attempted to improve the lot of his serfs in 1847 and who founded a school for their children in 1849 was the same Tolstoy who conceived "the immense idea" of a rational and fundamentalist Christianity in 1855 and who finally abandoned the imperfections of worldly life and fled from his home in October of 1910. There was no brusque conversion, no sudden renunciation of art in favour of the higher good. As a very young man, Tolstoy knelt and wept before a prostitute and noted in his diaries that the way of the world was the way of damnation. This conviction burned in him always, and the relentless energy of his literary works reflects the fact that each was a victory of his poetic genius over the gnawing belief that it profits a man nothing to gain the high places of artistic renown if he lose his own soul. Even in his most imaginative achievements, Tolstoy reveals the inner struggle and gives it form in an ever recurrent theme—the passage from the city to the land, from moral myopia to self-discovery and salvation.

The most articulate version of this theme is the departure of the hero or principal personage from St. Petersburg and Moscow towards his estates or some remote province of Russia. Both Tolstoy and Dostoevsky experienced in their personal lives this symbolic departure, Tolstoy when he left St. Petersburg for the Caucasus in April 1851, Dostoevsky when he was escorted out of the city in irons on Christmas night 1849 to begin the terrible journey to Omsk and penal servitude. One would have supposed that there could be few moments more charged with anguish. But on the contrary:

My heart beat with a peculiar flutter, and that numbed its pain. Still, the fresh air was reviving in its effect, and, since it is usual before all new experiences to be aware of a curious vivacity and eagerness, so I was at bottom quite tranquil. I looked attentively at all the festively-lit houses of Petersburg, and said good-bye to each. They drove us past your abode, and at Krayevsky's the windows were brilliantly lit. You had told me that he was giving a Christmas party and tree, and that your children were going to it, with Emilie Fyodorovna; I did feel dreadfully sad as we passed that house. . . . After the eight months' captivity, sixty versts in a sledge gave us appetites of which, even today, I think with pleasure. I was in a good temper.[3]

It is an extraordinary reminiscence. In atrocious personal circumstances, at the parting of the ways between ordinary life, family affections, and physical comfort on the one hand and probable death after long degradation on the other, Dostoevsky—like Raskolnikov under similar circumstances—experiences a sense of physical liberation. The sounds of revelry by night fade behind him and he seems to possess already some insight into the resurrection which lies beyond the term in purgatory. Even where the journey leads toward the house of the dead or, as in the case of Bezukhov in *War and Peace*, to probable execution before a French firing squad, the mere fact of transition from the city to the open land brings with it an element of joy.

Tolstoy may have been exploring this theme as early as 1852 when he worked on a translation of Sterne's *Sentimental Journey*. But it is in *The Cossacks*, sketched later the same year, that Tolstoy fully realized and mastered a situation which was to become a recurrent parable of his philosophy. After a night of drunken farewells, Olenin sets out for military service against the warring tribes in the distant Caucasus. What he leaves behind is unpaid gambling debts and the stale memories of time wasted in the idle pleasures of high society. Though the night is cold and full of snow,

The departing man felt warm, even hot, in his fur coat. He sat down in the bed of the sleigh and stretched himself; and the shaggy stage-horses flew from one dark street into another, past houses he had never seen. It appeared to Olenin that only those who departed travelled through these streets. Around him it was dark, speechless, gloomy,

[3] Dostoevsky to his brother, Michael, February 22, 1854 (*Letters of Fyodor Michailovitch Dostoevsky*, trans. by E. C. Mayne, London, 1914).

and his soul was full of recollections, love, regrets, and of pleasurable tears that choked him.

But soon he is out of the city, gazing at the snow-covered fields and rejoicing. All the mundane concerns which have beset his mind fade away into insignificance. "The farther Olenin travelled from the centre of Russia, the more distant his memories seemed to him; and the nearer he approached the Caucasus, the happier he felt." At last he comes to the mountains, "with their delicate contours and the fantastic and sharply defined outline of their summits, against the distant sky." His new life has begun.

In *War and Peace*, Pierre makes premature departures—such as when he abandons the false existence of the wealthy young aristocrat for the equally false haven of Freemasonry. His purgatorial journey really begins when he is led from the charred ruins of Moscow with other prisoners and sets out on the cruel march across the frozen plains. Like Dostoevsky, Pierre has survived the shock of near-execution and sudden reprieve. But "the mainspring of his life" has been wrenched out and "his faith in the right ordering of the universe, in humanity, in his own soul and in God, had been destroyed." A few moments later, however, he meets with Platon Karataev, the "natural man." Karataev offers him a baked potato. It is a trivial gesture, easily intended; but through it is initiated Pierre's pilgrimage and his sufferance of grace. As Tolstoy emphasizes, the strength of Karataev, his acquiescence in life even where it seems most destructive, derives from the fact that, having let his beard grow (a symbol laden with Scriptural associations), "he seemed to have thrown off all that had been forced upon him—everything military and alien to himself—and had returned to his former peasant habits." So he becomes to Pierre an "eternal personification of the spirit of simplicity and truth," a new Virgil conducting him out of the inferno of the burnt city.

Tolstoy suggests that the great fire has broken down

the barriers between Moscow and the open country. Pierre sees "the hoar frost on the dusty grass, the Sparrow Hills, and the wooded banks above the winding river vanishing in the purple distance"; he hears the noise of the crows and he feels "a new joy and strength in life such as he had never before known." Moreover, this feeling grows in intensity as the physical hardships of his position increase. As Natasha observes subsequently, he emerges from captivity as from "a moral bath." Pierre is cleansed of his former vices and has discovered the essential Tolstoyan dogma: "While there is life there is happiness."

The First Epilogue of *War and Peace* confirms this equation of life in the country with "the good life." It is a light-hearted stroke of irony that, in one of our last glimpses of Bald Hills, we should see the Countess Mary's children pretending that they are "going to Moscow" in a carriage made of chairs.

In *Anna Karenina* the contrast between the city and the land is, quite obviously, the axis around which the moral and technical structure of the novel revolves. The whole of Levin's salvation is prefigured in his arrival in the country after the unsuccessful proposal to Kitty:

But when he got out at his own station, when he saw his one-eyed coachman, Ignat, with the collar of his coat turned up; when, in the dim light reflected by the station fires, he saw his own sledge, his own horses with their tails tied up, in their harness trimmed with rings and tassels; when the coachman Ignat, as he put in his luggage, told him the village news, that the contractor had arrived, and that Pava had calved,—he felt that little by little the confusion was clearing up, and the shame and self-dissatisfaction were passing away.

On the land even the relations between Anna and Vronsky, which are already haunted with dissolution, take on an idyllic and sanctified quality. No novel (unless it be Lawrence's *White Peacock*) brings language closer to the sensuous actualities of farm life, to the sweet smell of a cow shed on frosty nights or the rustle of the fox through the high grass.

When Tolstoy came to write *Resurrection*, the teacher and prophet in him did violence to the artist. The sense of equilibrium and design which had previously controlled his invention was sacrificed to the urgencies of rhetoric. In this novel the juxtaposition of two ways of life and the theme of the pilgrimage from falsehood to salvation are set forth with the nakedness of a tract. And yet, *Resurrection* marks the ultimate reaalization of motifs which Tolstoy had announced in his very first stories. Nekhlioudov is the Prince Nekhlioudov of the early unfinished *Morning of a Landed Proprietor*. Between the two works lie thirty-seven years of thought and creation; but the fragment already contains, in recognizable outline, many of the elements of the last novel. Nekhlioudov is also the protagonist of a strange short story, *Lucerne*, which Tolstoy wrote in 1857. Indeed, this character appears to have served the novelist as a kind of self-portrait whose traits he could alter as his own experience deepened.

In *Resurrection*, moreover, the return to the land, as the physical correlative to the rebirth of the soul, is beautifully rendered. Before following Maslova to Siberia, Nekhlioudov resolves to visit his domains and sell the estate to the peasants. His wearied senses spring to life; he sees himself once more as he was before his "fall." The sun glimmers on the river, the colt nuzzles, and the pastoral scene enforces on Nekhlioudov the full realization that the morality of urban life is founded on injustice. For in the Tolstoyan dialectic, rural life heals the spirit of man not only through its tranquil beauties but also in that it opens his eyes to the frivolity and exploitations inherent in a class society. This emerges clearly from the drafts for *Resurrection*:

In town we do not fully understand why the tailor, the coachman, the baker work for us, but in the country we see very plainly why the share-croppers work in their green house and gardens, why they bring in the wheat and thresh it and abandon to the landowner half the produce of their labour.

The land is the awakener of the Tolstoyan hero as well as his reward.

I have dwelt on this topic at some length, but it would be difficult to exaggerate its importance towards an understanding of Tolstoy and of our general theme. The contrast between urban and rural pervades both the major groupings and designs in Tolstoy's novels and the particular resources of his style. Moreover, it is the element which binds into essential unity the literary, the moralistic, and the religious aspects of Tolstoy's genius. The dilemmas which first beset Nekhlioudov in 1852 perplex Prince Andrew, Pierre, Levin, Ivan Ilych, and the narrator of the *Kreutzer Sonata*. Tl e question, which Tolstoy used as the title for one of his tracts, is always the same: *What Then Must We Do?* What one can say is that in the end the portrait overcame the painter and seized upon his soul; Nekhlioudov abandoned his worldly possessions and set out on a final pilgrimage in the guise of Tolstoy.

The polarity of city and land is one of the main aspects of any comparison between Tolstoy and Dostoevsky. The motif of departure toward salvation was common to the lives and imaginings of both men, and *Resurrection* is, in many respects, an epilogue to *Crime and Punishment*. But in Dostoevsky we do not actually see the promised land (except for a momentary, shadowy glimpse of Raskolnikov's Siberia). The Dostoevskyan inferno is the *Grosstadt*, the modern metropolis, and more specifically the Petersburg of the "white nights." There are purgatorial departures, but the reconciliation and grace which Tolstoy's protagonists find on the land, the "great sinners" of Dostoevsky will find only in the Kingdom of God. And to Dostoevsky—in utter contrariety to Tolstoy—that Kingdom is not, and cannot be, of this world. It is in this context that one must weigh the often noticed fact that Dostoevsky, who excels in describing city life, nearly never attempts to describe a rural landscape or the open country.

Finally, the twofold plane of experience in the Tolstoyan novel is one of the traits which make a comparison between Homer and Tolstoy possible and illuminating. The point of view in the *Iliad* and the *Odyssey* (the latter can now be pertinently referred to) arises from an association of *bas-relief* with deep perspective. As Erich Auerbach noted in *Mimesis*, the contemporaneity of events in the Homeric narrative gives an impression of "flatness." But behind the surface, and shimmering through it, is the great vista of the marine and pastoral world. It is from this background that the Homeric poems derive their power of suggesting depth and pathos. Only thus, I think, can one understand why certain scenes in Homer and Tolstoy are so uncannily alike in composition and effect. Thomas Mann considered the chapters which tell of Levin mowing with his peasants as archetypal of Tolstoy's philosophy and technique. So they are. Many strands are interwoven: Levin's triumphant return to his own kind of life, his unspoken concord with the land and those who till it, the test of his bodily strength against that of the peasants, the physical exhaustion which revitalizes the mind and which orders past experience in the cleansed and forgiving memory. All this is, in Mann's phrase, *echt tolstoïsch.* But we find a close parallel in Book XVIII of the *Odyssey*. Odysseus, in beggar's rags, sits unrecognized at his own hearth, scorned by Penelope's serving women and mocked by Eurymachus. He replies (in T. E. Lawrence's translation):

Ah, Eurymachus, if only there might be a working match just between us two during the late springtide when the days are long: in a hay meadow, perhaps; me with a well-curved scythe and you with one like mine; our match to last all day, foodless, and far into the gloaming, with grass yet to spare! Or draught oxen of the finest, great flaming beasts lusty with feed, well matched in age and pulling-power, and fresh: also a four-team field of loam that turns cleanly from the coulter. Then should you see what a long straight furrow I would drive.

The words are uttered in a context of grief and sordid spoliation and Odysseus is evoking memories of the

94

time before he set out for Troy, twenty years earlier. But their poignancy springs also from our knowledge that the suitors shall never again mow in the gloaming.

Set the two passages side by side; compare their tonality and the world image they convey. You may not find a third to match them. From such comparison derives the force of the idea that *War and Peace* and *Anna Karenina* can, in some crucial manner, be qualified as Homeric.

It is tempting to speculate whether the motif of a journey towards material or spiritual resurrection and the sense of two worlds which is so strongly marked in Tolstoy are not typical elements of epic poetry as such. This question raises fascinating and difficult issues. There are voyages, in the actual and allegoric sense, in the *Odyssey*, the *Aeneid*, and the *Divine Comedy*. In many of the major epics, most evidently in *Paradise Lost* and *Paradise Regained*, we find the theme of the blessed realm, of the pastoral vision or the golden Atlantis. Amid such variety of instance one can hardly generalize. But something of this idea of the voyage and the divided world lies behind the fact that it should be *Don Quixote, Pilgrim's Progress*, and *Moby Dick* to which the mind turns most readily when we think of the notion of "epic novels."

VI

Tolstoyan fiction raises an ancient problem in the theory of literary forms—that of the multiple plot or divided centre. Here again, a technique directs our attention to a metaphysic, or at least to philosophic implications. Despite the view of many of Tolstoy's critics and exasperated readers, the double and triple plots of the Tolstoyan novel are essential components of Tolstoy's art, not symptoms of stylistic disorder or self-indulgence. Writing to the novelist in 1877, Strakhov spoke contemptuously of "a critic who wonders why you should dwell . . . on a certain Levin, when you should be dealing with Anna Karenina alone." The critic may have been naïve in his reading, but the reasons behind the Tolstoyan method are not as obvious as Strakhov seems to suppose.

From the outset, Tolstoy intended to distribute the narrative weight in *Anna Karenina* between two principal plots, and there is a suggestive duality in his search for a title. *Two Marriages* and *Two Couples*, as Tolstoy successively planned to name the book, reflect both an early draft in which Anna obtains a divorce and marries Vronsky and the fundamental purpose of inquiring into the nature of marriage from two contrasting points of view. At the outset, Tolstoy did not know precisely how the secondary plot could best be interwoven with the story of Anna. Initially he conceived of Levin (who was successively called Ordynstev and Lenin) as being a friend of Vronsky's. It was only gradually, and through explorations of the material which can be followed in fascinating detail in the drafts, that Tolstoy found the situations and plot lines which now strike us as organic and inevitable. In the midst of writing *Anna Karenina*, moreover, Tolstoy turned to the problem of popular education. For a time he found work on the novel repellent.

As Empson and other critics have pointed out, a double plot is a complex device capable of operating in a number of ways. It can be used to generalize a particular idea, to enforce by a sense of recurrence or universality some insight which the spectator or reader could evade by thinking it applicable to only one exceptional instance. This is what comes to pass in *King Lear*. The double plot conveys the universality of horror, lechery, and treason. It prevents the mind from protesting against the singularity of Lear's fate. There are indications in the play that Shakespeare was ill at ease with the double structure but felt some inner compulsion to express his terrible vision twice and make assertion doubly strong.

A double plot is a traditional medium for irony. Shakespeare's *Henry IV* illustrates both usages: it generalizes the material so as to create a mosaic, a portrait of a whole nation and period, and in it the two main plots are juxtaposed ironically. Personages and virtues are reflected between two mirrors set at different angles; heroism stands midway between Shrewsbury and Gadshill.

Lastly, a double or multiple plot can act to render the atmosphere more dense and to reproduce the meshed complications of reality. We see a sophisticated example of this in *Ulysses*, where the divisions of narrative focus and consciousness communicate the teeming thickness and multiplicity of a day in a modern metropolis.

The double plot in *Anna Karenina* works in each of these directions. The novel is a *Physiologie du mariage* more searching than Balzac's. Tolstoy's treatment derives its broad authority from the fact that he portrays three separate marriages; the richness and maturity of his argument would be less clear to us if he had chosen, like Flaubert, to dwell exclusively on the single case. *Anna Karenina* expounds some of Tolstoy's doctrines on pedagogy; Strakhov assured him that even the most enlightened teachers found in the chapters dealing with Anna's son "important hints for a theory of education." The multiple plot enables the novel to carry the weight of polemic and abstraction. Some of Dickens's "programmatic" novels impress one as rhetorical and flat precisely because the part of fiction in them is too restricted to absorb and dramatize the social polemic.

The confrontation of the two couples, Anna-Vronsky and Kitty-Levin, is the main device whereby Tolstoy conveys his meaning. The sense of contrast, the juxtaposition of the two stories, concentrates the morality of the fable. There is something of Hogarth here—something of the parallel sets of engravings depicting a virtuous and a licentious marriage or career. But light and shade are more subtly apportioned; Anna's nobility of heart is indestructible, and at the close of the novel Levin is shown at the beginning of a very difficult road. This, precisely is the distinction between satire and irony. Tolstoy was not a satirist; Flaubert, as *Bouvard et Pécuchet* shows, was nearly so.

But it is the third function of a double or multiple plot—its capacity to suggest realness by making the design of a work dense, jagged, and complex—which counts most heavily in the Tolstoyan novel. It is often said that Tolstoy is a more "classical" writer than Dickens, Balzac, or Dostoevsky because he relies less than they do on the mechanics of a plot, on the accidents of chance encounter, on the lost letter or the sudden thunder-storm. In a Tolstoyan narrative, events happen naturally and without the aid of those coincidences on which novelists of the nineteenth century so frankly depended. This is true only in part. Tolstoy was far less influenced than such masters as Dostoevsky or Dickens by the techniques of contemporary melodrama and he attached somewhat less importance than a Balzac or a James to the intricacies of his story. But in fact there are as many improbabilities in a Tolstoyan plot as in any other. And often Tolstoy contrived his major scenes with as fine a gusto for the unlikely hazard as was displayed notoriously by a Dumas and an Eugène Sue. In both *War and Peace* and *Anna Karenina* chance meetings, timely exits, and the long arm of coincidence play an important role. All of *Resurrection* is founded on a stroke of purest chance—Nekhlioudov's recognition of Maslova and his appointment to the jury dealing with her case. The fact that this should have happened in "real life"—the event was reported to Tolstoy by A. F. Kony, a St. Petersburg official, in the autumn of 1877, and the unfortunate heroine bore the name of Rosalie Onv—does not alter its improbable and melodramatic quality.

Tolstoy's use of what James called the *ficelles* of a novel pertains to both the major situations and the episodic moments in his plots. Prince Andrew's sudden reappearance at Bald Hills in a splendidly Victorian storm and precisely when his wife is in labour; Natasha's reunion with him during the evacuation of Moscow; Rostov's chance ride to Bogucharovo and his consequent meeting with Princess Mary; Vronsky's fall in the presence of Anna and her huband—all these are no less contrived than the trap-doors and overheard conversations around which lesser novelists construct their works. Then where is the difference? What is it that creates the sense of naturalness and organic coherence in a Tolstoyan narrative? The answer lies in the effect of the multiple plot and in Tolstoy's deliberate avoidance of formal neatness.

The strands of narrative in *War and Peace* and *Anna Karenina* are so numerous and so constantly interwoven that they form a thick mesh within which all the coincidences and artifices necessary to a novel lose their edge and come to be accepted as probable. Certain theories about the origins of the solar system postulate a "necessary density" of matter in space so that creative collisions could occur. Tolstoy's divided plots engender such density and by it he communicates a marvellous illusion of life, of reality in all its bustling friction. So very much happens in a Tolstoyan novel, so many personages are involved in such various situations and over such massive stretches of time, that they are bound to meet, to act upon one another, and to experience those improbable collisions which would irritate us in a thinner medium.

There are in *War and Peace* scores of accidental confrontations; they are demonstrably part of the machinery of the plot, but we accept them as natural because Tolstoyan "space" is so dense with life. For example, when Pierre comes to the bridge across the Kolocha in the midst of the exits and alarums of Borodino, angry soldiers order him to keep out of their line of fire: "Pierre went to the right, and unexpectedly encountered one of Raevski's adjutants whom he knew." We accept this fact, for Pierre has been with us so long and in such a multiplicity of contexts that we feel as if we too had met the adjutant in some earlier chapter. A few moments later, Prince Andrew is wounded and borne to the operating tent. A man's leg is being amputated next to him; it is Anatole Kuragin, and this despite the obvious objection that tens of thousands of men are being crowded into operating tents at the same moment all over the rear lines. Tolstoy transforms the momentary improbability into something which is at once essential to his story and convincing in itself:

"Yes, it is he! Yes, that man is somehow closely and painfully connected with me," thought Prince Andrew, not yet clearly grasping what he saw before him. "What is the connexion of that man with my childhood and my life?" he asked himself, without finding an answer. And suddenly a new unexpected memory from that realm of pure and loving childhood presented itself to him. He remembered Natasha as he had seen her for the first time at the ball in 1810. . . . He now remembered the connexion that existed between himself and this man who was dimly gazing at him through tears that filled his swollen eyes. He remembered everything, and ecstatic pity and love for that man overflowed his happy heart.

The process of gradual recollection in the Prince's mind evokes a similar process in the mind of the reader. The allusion to Natasha at her first ball spans a long stretch in the novel and assembles its various themes into a coherent memory. The association that comes first to Prince Andrew's consciousness is not the evil done by Kuragin—it is the beauty of Natasha. Through his recollection of it, Prince Andrew is moved, in turn, towards love for Kuragin, towards a recognition of the ways of God and peace with himself.

The psychological treatment is of such conviction and obvious significance that the melodramatic and improbable character of the actual circumstances is forgotten.

The mesh of parallel and interwoven plots in a Tolstoyan novel necessitates an immense roll of characters many of whom are bound to be minor and momentary props. And yet, even the smallest part is given an intense humanity. It is difficult to forget altogether any of the personages who crowd *War and Peace*. This applies even to the humblest servant. Who can forget

Gabriel, Marya Dimitrievna's "gigantic footman," or Old Michael, or Prokofy, "who was so strong that he could lift the back of the carriage from behind" and who sits in the hall plaiting slippers when Nicholas Rostov returns from the wars? Tolstoy never mentions a human being in namelessness or isolation. Each character, however minor, has the nobility of a past. When preparing the dinner for Bagration, Count Ilya Rostov says: "go on to Rasgulyay—the coachman Ipatka knows —and look up the gipsy Ilyushka, the one who danced at Count Orlov's, you remember, in a white Cossack coat. . . ." Stop the sentence after the name Ilyushka and you have lost a profoundly Tolstoyan touch. The gipsy makes only a fleeting and indirect appearance in the novel. But he has his integral life and we realize that he will dance at other parties in his white Cossack coat.

The technique of giving even minor characters proper names and of saying something about the lives they lead outside their brief appearance in the novel is simple enough; but the effect is far-reaching. The art of Tolstoy is humanistic; there is in it none of that transformation of human beings into animals or inert objects through which fables, satires, comedies, and naturalistic novels achieve their purposes. Tolstoy reverenced the integrity of the human person and would not reduce it to a mere implement even in fiction. The methods of Proust offer an illuminating contrast; in the world of Proust minor personages are often left anonymous and they are used in the literal and metaphoric sense. In *Albertine Disparue*, for example, the narrator summons two laundresses to a *maison de passe*. He bids them make love and scrutinizes their every reaction in order to reconstruct imaginatively Albertine's lesbian past. I know of few scenes in modern literature of comparable cruelty. But the horror lies not so much in the action of the two girls or in the *voyeurisme* of the narrator as in the namelessness of the two women, in their metamorphosis into objects deprived of privacy and inherent value. The narrator is totally impassive. He remarks that the two creatures "were unable, by the way, to give me any information; they did not know who Albertine was." Tolstoy could not have written this sentence, and in that incapacity lay much of his greatness.

Ultimately, the Tolstoyan approach is the more persuasive. We trust and delight in the reality of Count Ilya Rostov, of his coachman, of Count Orlov and Ilyushka the gipsy dancer. The insubstantiality and degradation of the two laundresses, on the other hand, infect the entire scene with a macabre automatism. We are brought dangerously close to either laughter or disbelief. Like Adam, Tolstoy named the things which passed before him; they live for us still because his own imagination could not think of them as lifeless.

The vitality of a Tolstoyan novel is achieved not only by the dense interweaving of various plots but also by a disregard of architectural finish and neatness. The major novels of Tolstoy do not "end" as *Pride and Prejudice, Bleak House,* or *Madame Bovary* can be said to end. They must be compared not to a skein which is unravelled and rewound, but to a river, incessantly in motion and flowing beyond our sight. Tolstoy is the Heraclitus among novelists.

The problem of how he would conclude *Anna Karenina* intrigued his contemporaries. The earliest outlines and drafts show that Anna's suicide was to be followed by some kind of epilogue. But it was only the outbreak of the Russo-Turkish War, in April 1877, when Tolstoy had already completed Book VII, that inspired him to write the last section of the novel as we now have it. As he first drafted it, Book VIII was a strident denunciation of Russia's attitude towards the war, of the false sentiments lavished on the Serbs and Montenegrins, of the lies spread by an autocratic regime in order to whip up martial enthusiasm, and of the false Christianity of the rich who raised money to buy bullets or cheerily sent men off to slaughter other men in a trumped-up cause. Into this tract for the times (to which Dostoevsky took bitter exception) Tolstoy wove the strands of his novel.

Once again we encounter Vronsky on a railway platform; but this time he is bound for the wars. On his estate, at Pokrovskoie, Levin is feeling his tormented way towards a *vita nuova*, a new understanding of life. The polemic and the psychological motifs are brought into collision; Levin, Koznishev, and Katavasov argue about the events of the day. Levin expounds the Tolstoyan thesis that the war is a fraud imposed by an autocratic clique on an ignorant populace. On the level of debate he is bested by his brother's oratorical skill. This merely convinces him that he must find his own moral code and pursue his pilgrimage without regard to the ridicule which he may incur at the hands of the intelligentsia and of fashionable society. Levin and his guests hasten towards the house under gathering storm clouds. As the tempest bursts, Levin discovers that Kitty and his son are out on the estate ("Chance," said Balzac, "is the world's greatest novelist.") He rushes out and finds them unharmed in the shelter of the lime trees. Fear and relief wrench him away from the world of sophistic arguments and restore him to that of nature and family love. The novel ends in a pastoral mood and on a dawning of revelation. But it is only a dawning, for the questions which Levin asks himself as he stares into the serene depths of the night are precisely those to which neither he nor, at that time, Tolstoy knew an adequate answer. Here, as at the close of Goethe's *Faust*, salvation lies all in the striving.

The eighth Book of *Anna Karenina* impressed contemporaries most forcibly through its polemic against the war. Although Tolstoy softened his tone in two successive versions, Katkov refused to publish either in *The Russian Messenger*, where the rest of the novel had been serialized. Instead, he printed a brief editorial note summarizing the story.

As an expression of Tolstoyan pacifism and a relatively early version of his critique of the czarist regime, the account of the "gentlemen volunteers" and the debate at Pokrovskoie retain considerable interest. More fascinating, however, is the light which these final chapters throw on the structure of the novel as a whole. The injection of a massive political theme into a network of private lives—what Stendhal referred to as "the pistol shot during the concert"—is not restricted to *Anna Karenina*; one need think only of the close of *Nana* or of the epilogue to *The Magic Mountain* in which we find Hans Castrop on the western front. What is remarkable is the fact that Tolstoy should have founded the concluding portion of his novel on events which took place when seven eighths of the work had already been composed and published. Some critics have seen in this a definite failing and believe that the last Book of *Anna Karenina* marks the triumph of the reformer and pamphleteer over the artist.

I think not. The most stringent test of the aliveness of an imagined character—of its mysterious acquisition of a life of its own outside the book or play in which it has been created and far exceeding the mortality of its creator—is whether or not it can grow with time and preserve its coherent individuality in an altered setting. Place Odysseus in Dante's *Inferno* or in Joyce's Dublin and he is Odysseus still, though barnacled from his long voyage through those imaginings and remembrances of civilization which we call myths. How a writer imparts this germ of life to his personages is a mystery; but it is clear that Vronsky and Levin possess it. They live with the times and beyond them.

Vronsky's departure is a gesture of some heroism and abnegation; but Tolstoy's view of the Russo-Turkish War is such that Vronsky's action strikes us as yet another surrender to impulses which are, at bottom, frivolous. This surrender underscores the principal tragedy in the novel. To Levin the war is one of those irritants which exasperate his mind to self-scrutiny. It compels him to make articulate his rejection of prevailing moral codes and prepares him for Tolstoyan Christianity.

Thus, Book VIII of *Anna Karenina*, with its unpremeditated polemic and its tractarian intent, is not an accretion adhering clumsily to the main structure of the novel. It expands and clarifies that structure. The characters respond to the new atmosphere as they would to a change of circumstances in "real life." There are many mansions in a Tolstoyan edifice and in them the novelist and the preacher are equally present. This is possible solely because Tolstoy builds in sovereign disregard of the more formal canons of design. He does not aim at the kind of radial symmetry which we find wonderfully carried through in James's *Ambassadors* or at the self-enclosedness of *Madame Bovary*, in which either addition or retrenchment would be a mutilation. There could well be a Book IX in *Anna Karenina*, recounting Vronsky's search for martial expiation or the beginnings of Levin's new life. Indeed, *A Confession*, on which Tolstoy began work in the fall of 1878, takes up precisely where *Anna Karenina* ends. Or would it be more accurate to say, where it breaks off?

The ultimate paragraph of *Resurrection* is an even clearer example of the lack of a final curtain in the Tolstoyan novel; the effect being that of a live continuum in which the individual narrative had marked a brief and artificial segment:

That night was the beginning of a new existence for Nekhlioudov. Not that he adopted a different mode of life, but rather that everything which happened to him from that time on appeared to him in an entirely different light. The future will show what will be the conclusion of this new period in his life.

Tolstoy wrote these lines on December 16, 1899, and shortly thereafter, when he undertook his essay *The Slavery of Our Times*, the saga of Nekhlioudov was, in a very real sense, being carried forward.

The history of the composition of *War and Peace* and of the incessant transformations in its designs, emphasis, and poetic intent is well known. The French scholar Pierre Pascal says of the work:

first a domestic novel within the framework of the war, then an historical novel, finally a poem with philosophic tendencies; first a depiction of life among the aristocracy, then a national epic; published in serial form over the course of four to five years and revised in the process; then transformed by its author but without much conviction that the transformation was necessary; brought back to its original state, but without the direct participation of the novelist—this work is not really finished.[4]

It is finished neither in the sense of being a definitive version nor in the sense of having exhausted its themes. The two ample epilogues and the postscript convey the impression that Tolstoy had marshalled creative energies too great to be confined even within the fantastic dimensions of a *War and Peace*. He declared in the postscript: "It is not a novel, even less is it a poem, and still less an historical chronicle. *War and Peace* is what the author wished and was able to express in the form in which it is expressed. Such an announcement of disregard of conventional form in an artistic production might seem presumptuous were it premeditated, and were there no precedents for it." Whereupon Tolstoy cites *Dead Souls* and the *House of the Dead* as examples of fiction which cannot be strictly classified as novels. Though his apologia is disingenuous—Gogol's work survives only as a fragment and Dostoevsky's is plainly an autobiography—Tolstoy's assertion is obviously justified. In the immensities of the book, in its "disregard of conventional form" lie much of its magic and enduring fascination. It embraces a whole group of novels, a work of history, a dogmatic philosophy, and a treatise on the nature of war. In the end the released pressures of imagined life and the dynamics of the material become so powerful that *War and Peace* brims over into an epilogue that is the beginning of a new novel, into a second epilogue seeking to organize the Tolstoyan philosophy of history, and into a postscript which reads like the preface to an autobiography.

The role of these epilogues in relation to Tolstoy's practices as a novelist has received scant attention. Isaiah Berlin has brilliantly shown the origins and significance of the meditation on historical necessity in

---

[4] Preface to *La Guerre et la paix* (trans. by H. Mongault, Bibliothèque de la Pléiade, Paris, 1944).

the Second Epilogue. What he says of the implicit antagonism between Tolstoy's poetic vision and philosophic program throws light on the book as a whole. We can now see plainly how the "mosaic" technique of Tolstoyan battle scenes—the whole rendered through splinters and fragments of detail—accords with the belief that military actions are an unsurveyable and uncontrollable aggregate of individual gestures. We see also how directly the novel was conceived as a refutation of official historiography.

But my immediate concern is different. The seeming shapelessness of *War and Peace*—more exactly, the lack of an absolute ending—contributes powerfully to our feeling that here is a piece of work which, though obviously fiction, does embody the teeming wealth of life and comes to possess our recollections as do the most intense of personal experiences. Seen from this point of view, it is the First Epilogue which counts most heavily.

Many readers have found this epilogue disconcerting and even repellent. The first four chapters are a brief treatise on the nature of history in the Napoleonic era. The actual opening sentence—"Seven years had passed" —is probably a later addition designed to relate the historical analysis to the events of the novel. Tolstoy had long proposed to conclude *War and Peace* with a categorical expression of his views on the "movement of the mass of the European peoples from west to east and afterwards from east to west," and on the significance of "chance" and "genius" in a philosophy of history. But after four chapters he broke off to resume the fictional narrative. The argument on historiography was carried over into a Second Epilogue. Why? Was it out of some compelling instinct for verisimilitude, out of a desire to play the role of time in the lives of his personages? Was Tolstoy loath to part from his creation, from a gallery of characters who had held his spirit in their strong grasp? We can only conjecture. In May 1869 he wrote to the poet Fet that the epilogue to *War and Peace* had not been "invented" but "torn from his entrails." Demonstrably, he expended upon it immense energies and thought. The effect of all these partial endings is like that of the long codas in Beethoven symphonies—rebellious against silence.

The main body of the novel ends on a note of resurrection. Even the charred ruins of Moscow move Pierre through their "beauty." The cabmen, the "carpenters cutting the timber for new houses," the hawkers and shopkeepers "all looked at him with cheerful beaming eyes." In the exquisite closing dialogue between Natasha and Princess Mary the two marriages towards which the plot has been moving are clearly foretold. "Think what fun it will be when I am his [Pierre's] wife and you marry Nicholas!" exclaims Natasha in a moment of sheer joy.

In the First Epilogue, however, "brightness falls from the air." The sense of rapture and the mood of that year of dawn 1813 are wholly extinguished. The opening sentence of Chapter V sets the tone: "Natasha's wedding to Bezukhov, which took place in 1813, was the last happy event in the family of the old Rostovs." The old Count dies and leaves debts amounting to twice the value of his property. Out of filial piety and a sense of honour, Nicholas assumes this tremendous burden: "He wished for nothing and hoped for nothing, and deep in his heart experienced a gloomy and stern satisfaction in an uncomplaining endurance of his position." This sombre rectitude, with its nuance of intolerance and pomposity, will mark Nicholas's character even after his marriage with Princess Mary and his own labours have restored him to wealth.

In 1820 the Rostovs and the Bezukhovs are gathered at Bald Hills. Natasha has grown "stouter and broader" and "the old fire very rarely kindled in her face." Moreover, "to her other defects . . . of untidiness and neglect of herself, she now added stinginess." She is dangerously jealous and when questioning Pierre about his trip to St. Petersburg she remembers the quarrels which disfigured their honeymoon. Tolstoy writes: "her eyes glittered coldly and vindictively." When we last saw Natasha, "A bright questioning light shone in her eyes, and on her face was a friendly and strangely roguish expression." Tolstoy's iconoclasm is relentless; each character in turn is seen corroded. The old Countess is in her dotage: "Her face had shrivelled, her upper lip had sunk in, and her eyes were dim." She is now a miserable old woman who cries "as a child does, because her nose had to be cleared." Sonya sits "weary but resolute at the samovar," idling away her sterile existence, kindling an occasional spark of jealousy in Princess Mary and reminding Nicholas of a braver innocence in times past.

The saddest metamorphosis is that of Pierre. With marriage to Natasha he has suffered a sea-change into something neither rich nor strange:

Pierre's subjection consisted in the fact that he not only dared not flirt with, but dared not even speak smilingly to, any other woman; did not dare to dine at the Club as a pastime, did not dare spend money on a whim, and did not dare absent himself for any length of time, except on business—in which his wife included his intellectual pursuits, which she did not in the least understand but to which she attributed great importance.

This is a portrait which could derive from one of Balzac's more sombre and cynical inquiries into the physiology of marriage. Natasha's incomprehension of Pierre's disorderly enthusiasms and perennial youth is tragic. She is punished for it by the inherent smallness of their relationship, by its tyrannical domesticity. Pierre has surrendered to her demand "that every moment of his life" should belong to her and to the family. As Tolstoy penetratingly tells us, her exactions flatter him. And this is the Pierre whom Platon Karataev had guided through the inferno of 1812.

Tolstoy darkens our image of his characters with an excessive honesty. The effect is nearly macabre, as on one of those Spanish *retablos* which portray the same personage passing from splendour to dust by every stage of dissolution. Throughout these eleven chapters the fantasy of the novelist is in retreat before the memories of the man and the beliefs of the reformer. Much of the narrative reads like an earlier version of the *Recollec-*

tions which Tolstoy set down between 1902 and 1908. Nicholas Rostov's acceptance of Count Ilya's debts parallels the biography of Tolstoy's father. He too spent difficult years with "an old mother accustomed to luxury, as well as a sister and another relative." In his memoirs Tolstoy speaks of his grandmother who would "sit on the divan and lay out the cards, occasionally taking a pinch of snuff from her gold snuff-box." The cards and the very box—"with the count's portrait on the lid"—reappear in Chapter XIII of the epilogue. The children's game at Bald Hills is a direct reminiscence of the "game of travellers" played at Yasnaya Polyana. In this First Epilogue, Tolstoy was paying tribute to the family history on which he had drawn with such inventive grace throughout the main body of the novel.

As in all Tolstoyan fiction, moreover, the element of doctrine plays its part. In his account of Nicholas's administration of Bald Hills, in Princess Mary's diary, in the portrayal of Pierre's and Natasha's marriage, Tolstoy dramatized his theses on agronomy, pedagogy, and the proper relationship between man and wife. Hence the ambiguous light in which he placed the new Natasha. He notes her parsimony, untidiness, and querulous jealousy with the hard irony of a poet; but through her are proclaimed essential Tolstoyan doctrines. We are to endorse Natasha's utter disregard of the elegance and *galanteries* which conventional women in high society carry over into their marriages; we are to assent in her ferocious standards of monogamy and to applaud her utter absorption in the details of childbearing and family life. Tolstoy proclaims: "If the purpose of marriage is the family, the person who wishes to have many wives or husbands may perhaps obtain much pleasure, but in that case will not have a family." The Natasha of the epilogue incarnates this belief, and the entire portrayal of Bald Hills is one of those studies for the picture of the good life which Tolstoy detailed in *Anna Karenina* and so many of his later writings.

But the elements of autobiography and of ethics, though they explain the character of the First Epilogue, account neither for its existence nor for its full effect. Behind this effect lies a deliberate pursuit of veracity at the expense of form. The epilogues and postscripts to *War and Peace* express Tolstoy's conviction that life is continuous, fragmented, and in a state of incessant renewal; the conventions of a final curtain or an ending in which all the threads are neatly ravelled do violence to reality. The First Epilogue imitates the ravages of time. Only fairy tales end in the imagined artifice of eternal youth and eternal passion. By blurring our luminous recollection of Pierre and Natasha, by bringing us close to the smells and monotony of "the unbroken routine" at Bald Hills, Tolstoy is exemplifying his commanding realism. There are types of fiction essentially subject to canons of symmetry and controlling dimension. Actions end in a peal of ordnance. It is a conception realized in the last paragraph of *Vanity Fair* when Thackeray puts his puppets back in their box. Of necessity, the dramatist must have a formal close and an assurance that "now our tale is ended." But not Tolstoy; his characters grow old and dismal and do not live happily ever after. Obviously he knew that even the longest novel must have its last chapter, but he saw in that inevitability a distortion and sought to obscure it by building into his endings the preludes to his next work. In the frame of each picture, in the immobility of each statue, in the cover of each book, there is a measure of defeat and an admission that in imitating life we fragment it. But we are less conscious of this fact in Tolstoy than, perhaps, in any other novelist.

It is possible to trace the beginnings of *Anna Karenina* in the final sections of *War and Peace*. Nicholas's life at Bald Hills and his relationship with Princess Mary are a preliminary sketch for the portrayal of Levin and Kitty. Already there are rough notations for later motifs: Princess Mary is puzzled that Nicholas should be so "particularly animated and happy when, after getting up at daybreak and spending the whole morning in the fields or on the threshing floor, he returned from the sowing, or mowing, or reaping, to have tea with her." Moreover, the children whom we meet in the First Epilogue give back to us some of the sense of freshness which Tolstoy has methodically destroyed in their elders. Nicholas's three-year-old daughter, Natasha, is a reincarnation of her aunt as we once knew her. She is dark-eyed, saucy, and quick on her feet. There has been a transmigration of souls; ten years hence this second Natasha will burst into men's lives with the radiant impetuosity which marked the heroine of *War and Peace*. Nicholas Bolkonsky is also a figure in whom a new novel is gathering its forces. We are shown his difficult relationship with Nicholas Rostov and his love of Pierre. Through him Prince Andrew re-enters the novel and it is young Nicholas who will bring it to an apparent close.

Rostov, Pierre, and Denisov quarrel over politics in a scene which is similar to the acrimonious debate in the final section of *Anna Karenina*. But thematically the episode is like a bridge spanning a long period in Tolstoy's work. There are allusions in it to the Decembrist conspiracy about which Tolstoy had proposed to write a novel before he undertook *War and Peace*. But I would guess also that this chapter embodies the first impulses towards the historical and political novel on the age of Peter the Great which occupied Tolstoy's mind between the conclusion of *War and Peace* in 1869 and the beginning of *Anna Karenina* in 1873.

This epilogue can, therefore, be considered in two ways. In its corrosive account of the Rostov and Bezukhov marriages there is expressed Tolstoy's nearly pathological realism, his preoccupation with the processes of time, and his dislike of those narrative graces and evasions which the French call *de la littérature*. But the First Epilogue also proclaims the Tolstoyan conviction that a narrative form must endeavour to rival the infinity—literally, the unfinishedness—of actual experience. The last sentence in the fictional part of *War and Peace* is left incomplete. Thinking of his dead father, Nicholas Bolkonsky says to himself: "Yes, I will do something with which even he could be satisfied . . ." The three dots are apt. That novel which supremely matches the flow and variousness of reality cannot end with a period.

The Russian literary historian Prince Mirsky observed that here again a comparison between *War and Peace* and the *Iliad* is illuminating. For in the novel, as in the epic poem, "nothing is finished, the stream of life flows on." It is, naturally, extremely difficult to discuss the "end" of the Homeric poems.[5] Aristarchus maintained that the *Odyssey* concluded with line 296 of Book XXIII, and a great many modern scholars agree that the rest is a more or less spurious addition. There is also much doubt about the ending of the *Iliad* as we presently have it. I am not equipped to enter into these highly technical controversies; but some of the implications and effects of works which end with action suspended in mid-air are manifest. Lukács puts it this way:

The "in-the-middle" beginning of the Homeric epics and their "not-at-the-conclusion" endings are motivated by the indifference of the genuine epic temper toward formal architectural structures; the intrusion of alien materials will not impair the equilibrium [of the true epic]: for in the epic all things live their own life and create their proper "finish" and roundedness out of their own integral significance.[6]

The incompletion reverberates in our minds and creates a sense of energies moving outward from the work. The effect is musical, as E. M. Forster notes precisely with reference to *War and Peace*: "Such an untidy book. Yet, as we read it, do not great chords begin to sound behind us, and when we have finished does not every item—even the catalogue of strategies—lead a larger existence than was possible at the time? "[7]

Probably the most mysterious passage in the *Odyssey* is the one in which we learn of Odysseus' pre-

---

[5] One of the most lucid discussions of this vexed question is to be found in Denys Page: *The Homeric Odyssey* (Oxford, 1955).

[6] George Lukács: op cit.

[7] E. M. Forster: *Aspects of the Novel* (New York, 1950).

destined voyage to a land where men know nothing of the sea and have never tasted salt. This final argosy is foretold by Tiresias speaking out of death, and the hero reveals it to Penelope a few moments after their reunion and even before they sleep together. Some have taken this revelation to be textually spurious; others have seen in it a clear instance of that unimaginative and cold-blooded egotism with which T. E. Lawrence charges Odysseus. I prefer to view it as an example of the characteristically Homeric acquiescence in fate and levelness of vision which control the poem even in moments of great pathos. The theme itself has an aura of archaic magic. Scholars have, until now, failed to elucidate its origins and precise meaning; Gabriel Germain suggests that the Homeric motif embodies memories of an Asiatic myth about a landlocked and supernatural kingdom. But, whatever its genesis or its exact place in the poem as a whole, the impact of the passage is unmistakable. It throws open to uncharted seas the doors of Odysseus' palace and transforms the end of a poem from that of a fairy tale into that of a saga of which we have heard only a part. At the close of the second movement in Beethoven's "Emperor" Concerto we suddenly hear, in a veiled and remote form, the upward surging theme of the *rondo*. So at the end of the *Odyssey* the singer's voice trails off into a new beginning. The story of Odysseus' final voyage to a mysterious reconciliation with Poseidon echoed through the centuries, through pseudo-Homeric literature and Seneca until it reached Dante. If there is an ending to the *Odyssey*, it can be found in that tragic voyage past the Pillars of Hercules which is recounted in Canto XXVI of the *Inferno*.

The *Iliad* and the *Odyssey*, as the general reader knows them, both terminate abruptly in the midst of action. After the Trojans will have lamented Hector's bones, war shall resume, and as Book XXIV ends, scouts are sent out to prevent a surprise attack. The *Odyssey* concludes with an unconvincing *deus ex machina* and a truce between the clan of Odysseus and those who would avenge the suitors. These may not be the "authentic" endings, but all the available evidence does suggest that each epic poem or cycle of poems should be understood as one element in a larger saga. For both the Greek epic poets and Tolstoy, the destiny shaping the ends of their characters might well lie beyond the knowledge or prophecy of the artist. This is a mythical notion, but it is also supremely realistic. In both the Homeric poems and the novels of Tolstoy the rough-hewn edges are similarly convincing.

Thus all the elements in the art of Tolstoy conspire towards diminishing the irremediable barrier between the reality of the world of language and that of the world of fact. To many it has seemed that Tolstoy succeeds beyond any other novelist. Hugh Walpole wrote in his well-known introduction to the Centenary Edition of *War and Peace*:

Pierre and Prince Andrew, Nicholas and Natasha carried me away with them into their living world—a world more truly real than the uneasy one in which I was myself living. . . . It is that reality which is the final incommunicable secret. . . .

It is this reality, also, which possessed Keats when he imagined himself shouting in the trenches with Achilles.

VII

In his later writings on art, in those stubborn, self-destructive, and yet strangely moving essays, Tolstoy looked on Homer as a talisman. To the end, the Homeric poems stood between Tolstoy and total iconoclasm. In particular, he sought to distinguish between a false portrayal of reality which he associated with Shakespeare and a true rendering exemplified in the *Iliad* and the *Odyssey*. With an assured majesty which goes beyond arrogance, Tolstoy implied that his own place in the history of the novel was comparable to that of Shakespeare in the history of the drama and to that of Homer in the epic. He strove to demonstrate that Shakespeare did not merit such a position, but the very vehemence of his attack betrays the regard of a duelist for an equal opponent.

Tolstoy contrasts Shakespeare and Homer at the crucial point in his essay on *Shakespeare and the Drama*. This is a rather famous tract, but it has been more read than understood.[8] Among the few serious treatments of it are G. Wilson Knight's lecture "Shakespeare and Tolstoy" and George Orwell's paper on "Lear, Tolstoy and the Fool." Neither is wholly satisfactory. Knight's reading, for all its acuteness, depends on his highly personal interpretation of Shakespeare's meaning and symbolism. He is not really concerned with Tolstoy's motives and does not allude to the role of Homeric poetry in the Tolstoyan argument. Orwell, on the other hand, oversimplifies the case in the interest of his social polemic.

The crux of the essay is Tolstoy's assertion that "when one compares Shakespeare with Homer . . . the infinite distance separating true poetry from its imitation emerges with special vividness." A lifetime of prejudice and experience went into that statement. We cannot judge it if we fail to realize how directly it bears on Tolstoy's image of his own achievement. Moreover, it concentrates into a single expression what I take to be the inherent antagonism between the art of Tolstoy and that of Dostoevsky.

What must be understood first is Tolstoy's attitude towards the theatre. In it there was a strain of puritanism. He saw in the physical structure of the playhouses a brazen symbol of the social snobbery and frivolous elegance of the urban upper classes. More radically, Tolstoy found in the discipline of pretence, which is the core of theatrical acting, a deliberate distortion of men's capacity to distinguish between truth and falsehood, between illusion and reality. He argued in *Varenka, a Tale for Children* that children—who are by nature truthful and who have not yet been corrupted by

8 George Gibian's essay *Tolstoj and Shakespeare* (Gravenhage, 1957) reached me as this book was going into print.

society—find the theatre ridiculous and implausible. But although he condemned the stage, Tolstoy was also fascinated by it. In a number of letters to his wife written in the winter of 1864, he betrayed his perplexity: "I went to the theatre. I got there at the end of the second act. Fresh from the country it always seems to me bizzare, forced and false; but when one gets accustomed to it, it again pleases one." And on another occasion he wrote of a visit to the opera, "where I experienced much pleasure both at the music and at seeing the different men and women in the audience all of whom strike me as types."

But throughout his novels Tolstoy's point of view is clear; the theatre is associated with a loss in moral perception. In both *War and Peace* and *Anna Karenina* the opera house serves as a setting for moral and psychological crises in the lives of the heroines. It is in their boxes at the opera that Natasha and Anna (like Emma Bovary) are shown to us in a troubling and ambiguous light. The danger arises, in the Tolstoyan analysis, from the fact that spectators forget the contrived and artificial nature of the performance and transfer to their own lives the false emotions and tinsel of the stage. The account of Natasha's visit to the opera in Book VIII of *War and Peace* is a satire in miniature:

The floor of the stage consisted of smooth boards, at the sides was some painted cardboard representing trees, and at the back was a cloth stretched over boards. In the centre of the stage sat some girls in red bodices and white skirts. One very fat girl in a white silk dress sat apart on a low bench, to the back of which a piece of green cardboard was glued. They all sang something. When they had finished their song the girl in white went up to the prompter's box, and a man with tight silk trousers over his stout legs, and holding a plume and a dagger, went up to her and began singing, waving his arms about.

The intended ridicule is obvious; the tone is that of a half-wit recounting a silent film. Natasha's initial response is the "right" one: "She knew what it was all meant to represent, but it was so pretentiously false and unnatural that she first felt ashamed for the actors and then amused at them." But gradually the black magic of the theatre seduces her "into a state of intoxication. . . . She did not realize who or where she was, nor what was going on before her." At that moment Anatole Kuragin appears, "his sword and spurs slightly jingling and his handsome perfumed beard held high." The ludicrous personages on the stage "began dragging away the maiden who had been in white and was now in light blue." Thus the action of the opera travesties Anatole's intended abduction of Natasha. Later on in the spectacle there is a solo dance in which a man "with bare legs jumped very high and waved his feet about very rapidly. (He was Duport, who received sixty thousand roubles a year for his art.)" Tolstoy is outraged both by the expense and the irreality. But Natasha "no longer thought this strange. She looked about with pleasure, smiling joyfully." Towards the end of the performance her sense of discrimination has been radically impaired:

All that was going on before her now seemed quite natural, but on the other hand all her previous thoughts of her betrothed, of Princess Mary, or of life in the country, did not once recur to her mind. . . .

The word "natural" is crucial here. Natasha no longer distinguishes real nature, "life in the country" and the moral saneness which it implies, from the false nature shown on the stage. Her failure to do so coincides with the beginnings of her surrender to Kuragin.

The second act in this near-tragedy is also associated with the art of the drama. Anatole presses his suit during a soirée at Princess Helen's. It is being given in honour of the celebrated tragic actress Mademoiselle Georges. The latter recites "some French verses describing her guilty love for her son." The allusion to Racine's *Phèdre* is inaccurate, but the tone is plain. Because of its stylized form and its incestuous theme, *Phèdre* appeared to Tolstoy as deeply "unnatural." But as Natasha listens, she is borne away "into this strange senseless world . . . in which it was impossible to know what was good or bad. . . ." The dramatic illusion destroys our sense of moral distinctions.

The situation in *Anna Karenina* is different. By going to Patti's benefit at the opera, Anna is challenging society on its own most hallowed ground. Vronsky disapproves of her action and for the first time we notice that his love has lost its freshness and its sense of mystery. Indeed, he looks upon her through the very glass of fashion and conventionality which she is seeking to challenge. Anna is cruelly snubbed by Madame Kartasova, and though the evening ends in the lovers' reconciliation, the tragic future is clearly foreshadowed. The ironic intensity of the scene springs from the setting; society condemns Anna Karenina precisely in that place where society is most frivolous, ostentatious, and steeped in illusion.

It was the element of illusion in the theatre that obsessed Tolstoy. The essay on *Shakespeare and the Drama* is only one among his several attempts to grapple with the problem. He sought to understand the origins and nature of theatrical illusion and to distinguish among various orders of illusion. Secondly, he wished to ensure that the powers of dramatic *mimesis* should be devoted to fostering a vision of life which is realistic, moral, and ultimately religious. Much of what he wrote on this topic is dry and acrimonious; but it throws light on Tolstoy's own novels and on contrasts between the epic and the dramatic temper.

In the first part of his critique, Tolstoy set out to show that Shakespeare's plays are a tissue of absurdities, that they fly in the face of reason and good sense and have "absolutely nothing in common with art or poetry." Tolstoy's dialectic hinges on the notion of what is "natural." Shakespeare's plots are "unnatural" and his characters speak in an "unnatural language, which not only they could not speak, but which no real people could ever have spoken anywhere." The situations in which Shakespeare's personages "are quite arbitrarily placed are so unnatural that the reader or spectator is unable either to sympathize with their sufferings or even be interested in what he reads or hears." All this is underlined by the fact that Shakespearean characters "live, think, speak, and act, quite out of accord with the given period and place." To document his thesis, Tolstoy points to the absence of coherent motivation in the conduct of Iago and undertakes an extended analysis of *King Lear*.

Why *King Lear*? In part, no doubt, because the actual plot of the tragedy is among Shakespeare's most fantastic and because there are episodes in it—such as the leap from Dover Cliff—which strain even the most willing suspension of disbelief. But there were other reasons and they take us very close to the most private and opaque elements in Tolstoy's genius. In his *Lettre sur les spectacles*, Rousseau concentrated his strongest fire on Molière's *Le Misanthrope* precisely because he saw in Alceste someone disturbingly close to the image which he, Rousseau, treasured of himself. A similar sense of kinship appears to have existed between Tolstoy and the figure of Lear. It came to influence even his distant memories. There is a description of a storm in the second chapter of *Boyhood*. When the elements are at their pitch of fury,

a human creature suddenly appears in a dirty tattered shirt, with a swollen meaningless countenance, with a shaking, close-cropped, bare head, crooked muscleless legs and in place of a hand a red shiny stump, which he thrusts straight into the brichka.

"Ma-a-ster! Give something to a cripple for Christ's sake!" he says in a suffering voice, and at each word crosses himself and bows down to his waist.

. . . .

But we have hardly started before a blinding flash of lightning, that for an instant fills the whole hollow with fiery light, causes the horses to stop, and is immediately followed by such a deafening clap of thunder that it seems as if the whole vault of heaven will crash down upon us.

Between the incident and the recollection stands Act III of *King Lear*.

This sense of identification, which Orwell noted, is strengthened by numerous references to Lear in Tolstoy's correspondence; and there are, in actual history, few moments closer to the world of *King Lear* than that in which the aged, yet regal Tolstoy abandoned his home and set out into the night in quest of justice. I cannot, therefore, escape the impression that there was in Tolstoy's attacks on *King Lear* an obscure and elemental anger—the anger of a man who finds his own shadow cast for him through some black art of foresight. In his moments of gesture and self-definition, Tolstoy felt drawn towards the figure of Lear, and he must have been troubled—he, the arch-imaginer of lives —at finding in his own mirror the creation of a rival genius. There is here something of Amphytrion's baffled and tenacious fury at discovering that some essential part of his own life is being lived outside himself— albeit by a god.

Whatever his precise motives, Tolstoy did hammer with insistence at the obvious point that there are in *King Lear* preposterous and even inexplicable events. Had he persevered in this line of argument, Wilson Knight would be justified in saying that the novelist "suffered from clear thinking." But Tolstoy did not repudiate Shakespearean drama merely on the ground that it was not "naturalistic." He was far too great and subtle a writer himself not to perceive that Shakespeare's vision went beyond criteria of common-sense realism. His crucial charge was that Shakespeare "cannot produce on the reader that illusion which constitutes the chief condition of art." This is an obscure statement if only because "that illusion" is left undefined. Behind this obscurity lies a complex chapter in the history of aesthetics during the eighteenth and nineteenth centuries. Minds as acute and diverse as Hume's, Schiller's, Schelling's, Coleridge's, and De Quincey's had wrestled with the origins and nature of dramatic illusion. Many of the turgid aestheticians whom Tolstoy examines in *What Is Art?* sought to determine the "laws" which govern our psychological responses to the theatre. They produced little of value, and despite all the forays of modern psychology into the problem of games and fantasy we are not much further along. What makes us "believe" in the reality of a Shakespearean play? What is it that makes *Oedipus* or *Hamlet* as exciting to us after we have seen ten performances as when we saw the play for the first time? How can there be suspense without surprise? We do not know; and by invoking some undefined notion of "true illusion" Tolstoy betrayed his argument.

The entire essay on *Shakespeare and the Drama* results in paradox. To Tolstoy the plays of Shakespeare were demonstrably absurd and amoral. Yet their power of seduction was a fact and Tolstoy testified to his awareness of it by the very vehemence of his protest. Thus he was compelled to postulate two different types of illusion: the one a false illusion such as obscures Natasha's sense of values at the opera, the second a "true illusion." It is the latter which "constitutes the chief condition of art." How do we distinguish between them? By determining the "sincerity" of the artist, the degree of belief which he attaches to the actions and ideas presented in his works. Tolstoy was explicitly engaged in what certain modern critics call "the intentional fallacy." He refused to separate artist from creation and creation from intent. Tolstoy condemned the plays of Shakespeare because he perceived in them a genius that was morally neutral.

Not unlike Matthew Arnold, Tolstoy insisted that the distinctive quality of great art was its "high seriousness" and an elevation of tone in which ethical values are reflected or dramatized. But whereas Arnold tended to limit his judgment to the actual work before him, Tolstoy sought to determine the beliefs of the author. An act of literary criticism, in the Tolstoyan sense, is an act of moral judgment embracing the artist, his works, and the effect of those works on the public. From the point of view of the literary critic or historian of taste, the results are often bizarre or downright indefensible. But considered as a statement of

Tolstoy's doctrines about his own craft and as a reflection of the temperament which produced *War and Peace* or *Anna Karenina*, the essay on Shakespeare is revealing. It cannot be dismissed as merely another example of an aging man's ferocious iconoclasm. Tolstoy's hatred of Shakespeare can be traced all the way back to 1855. Though complicated by a sense of the evil of his own works which dogged the later Tolstoy, the essay embodies instincts and reflections of a lifetime.

Its central passage contrasts Homer and Shakespeare:

However distant Homer is from us, we can without the slightest effort transport ourselves into the life he describes. And we are thus transported chiefly because, however alien to us may be the events which Homer describes, he believes in what he says and speaks seriously of what he is describing, and therefore he never exaggerates and the sense of measure never deserts him. And therefore it happens that, not to speak of the wonderfully distinct characters of Achilles, Hector, Priam, Odysseus, and the eternally touching scenes of Hector's farewell, of Priam's embassy, of the return of Odysseus, and so forth, the whole of the *Iliad* and still more the *Odyssey*, is as naturally close to us as if we had lived and were now living among the gods and heroes. But it is not so with Shakespeare. . . . It is at once evident that he does not believe in what he is saying, that he has no need to say it, is inventing the occurrences . . . and so we do not believe either in the events or in the actions, or in the sufferings of his characters. Nothing so clearly shows the absence of aesthetic feeling in Shakespeare as a comparison between him and Homer.

The argument is fraught with prejudice and emphatic blindness. In what way was Homer less of a contriver of occurrences than Shakespeare? What did Tolstoy know of the latter's beliefs and "sincerity"? But it is futile to contest Tolstoy's essay on grounds of reason or historical evidence. In the unclear manifesto of *Shakespeare and the Drama* we see concentrated one of Tolstoy's insights into the characteristics of his own genius. What we must retain is its positive element—the affirmation of kinship with Homer.

To say, with Lukács, that Tolstoy's cast of mind was "truly epic and that it was alien to the forms of the novel," [9] is to suppose a far greater knowledge of the types and structure of the creative imagination than we actually possess. Aristotle's *Poetics* suggests that although Greek theory recognized numerous practical distinctions between the epic and the drama, it did not assume some radical difference of mind between the epic poet and the dramatist. The first to do so with conviction was Hegel; his distinction between the "totality of objects" in the world of the epic and the "totality of action" in that of the drama is a critical idea of great subtlety and implication. It tells us a good deal about the failure of such mixed forms as Hölderlin's *Empedokles* or Hardy's *Dynasts* and suggests how the dramatic technician in Victor Hugo encroached continuously on the would-be epic poet. But beyond that we are on precarious ground.

What we can say is that in considering his own art, Tolstoy invited comparison with epic poetry and especially with Homer. His novels—in essential contrast to those of Dostoevsky—range over wide tracts of time. Through some curious optical illusion, we associate temporal breadth with the notion of the epic. In actual fact, the events directly related in the Homeric epics or the *Divine Comedy* are contracted into a brief span of days or weeks. Thus, it is the method of narration rather than the time encompassed which accounts for our sense of analogy between Tolstoy and the epic mode. Both perceive action along a central narrative axis; around it, like a spiral, we find the passages of recollection, the forward-leaping prophecies, and the digressions. For all the intricacy of detail, the dynamic forms in the *Iliad*, in the *Odyssey*, and in *War and Peace* are simple and rely heavily upon our unconscious belief in the reality and forward motion of time.

Homer and Tolstoy are omniscient narrators. They employ neither the independent and fictional voice

9 George Lukács: op. cit.

which novelists such as Dostoevsky or Conrad interpose between themselves and their readers, nor the deliberately limited "point of view" of the mature James. The major works of Tolstoy (with the important exception of *The Kreutzer Sonata*) are recounted in the ancient third-person style of the story-teller. Plainly, Tolstoy regarded the relations between himself and his personages as those of omniscient creator to created being:

I myself, when I write, suddenly feel pity for some character, and then I give him some good quality or take a good quality away from some one else, so that in comparison with the others he may not appear too black.[1]

And yet, there is nothing of Thackeray's puppets and puppet-show in the art of Tolstoy. Both a Shakespearean and a Tolstoyan personage "live" apart from their creators. Natasha is no less "alive" than Hamlet. No less, but differently. She stands somehow closer to our knowledge of Tolstoy than the Prince of Denmark does to Shakespeare. The difference lies not, I think, in the fact that we know more about the Russian novelist than we do about the Elizabethan playwright, but rather in the nature and conventions of their respective literary forms. But neither criticism nor psychology can wholly account for it.

In Hegelian language, there is in the novels of Tolstoy, as in the major epics, a "totality of objects." The drama—and Dostoevsky—isolate human personages into an essential nakedness; the room is stripped of furniture so that nothing will muffle the clash of action. But in the epic genre the ordinary impediments of life, the tools and the houses and the food, play an important part; hence the nearly comical solidity of the Miltonic Heaven, with its tangible artillery and its provisions for the digestion of the angels. The Tolstoyan canvas is laden with teeming detail, particularly in what Henry James called, through some hostile lapse of

---

[1] Tolstoy to Gorky, in Gorky: *Reminiscences of Tolstoy, Chekhov and Andreev* (trans. by Katherine Mansfield, S. S. Koteliansky, and Leonard Woolf, London, 1934).

mind, *Peace and War*. An entire society, an entire age is portrayed no less than in the time-rooted vision of Dante. Both Tolstoy and Dante evidence the frequently asserted and yet little understood paradox that there are works of art which achieve timelessness, precisely by being anchored in a specific moment of time.

But this entire approach—the attempt to relate the novels of Tolstoy to epic poetry and primarily to Homer —encounters two very real difficulties. Whatever the final outcome of his thinking, Tolstoy was involved, passionately and throughout his entire life, with the figure of Christ and the values of Christianity. How could he write, as late as 1906, that he felt more at home "among the gods and heroes" of Homeric polytheism than in the world of Shakespeare, which, for all its religious neutrality, does abound in habits of Christian symbolism and awareness? There is a complex problem here which Merezhkovsky touched upon in the remark which I quoted earlier, that Tolstoy "has the soul of 'a born Pagan.'" I shall return to it in the last chapter.

The second difficulty is more obvious. Given Tolstoy's profound scepticism about the value of the theatre, his condemnation of Shakespeare, and the clear affinities between his novels and the epic, how shall we account for Tolstoy the dramatist? What makes this question even more perplexing is the fact that Tolstoy's case is nearly unparalleled. Outside Goethe and Victor Hugo, one can hardly cite another instance of a writer who produced masterpieces in both the novel and the drama. And neither case is rigorously comparable with Tolstoy; Goethe's novels are of interest mainly through their philosophic content, and it can be said of Victor Hugo's that, for all their festive glory, they do not really lay claim to adult attention. We do not think of *Les Miserables* and *Notre-Dame de Paris* as we do, say, of *Madame Bovary* or *Sons and Lovers*. Tolstoy is the exception, and this exception is made bewildering by virtue of his own literary and ethical doctrines.

For the first point to be emphasized is that Tolstoy would have had a place in literary history had he written only his dramas. They are not an eccentric off-shoot from his main works as are, for example, the plays of Balzac and Flaubert or Joyce's *Exiles*. Several of the plays of Tolstoy are of the first rank. This fact has been obscured both through the eminence of his novels and through the kinship of such works as *The Power of Darkness* and *The Living Corpse* with the whole naturalistic movement. When thinking of the kind of dramas which Tolstoy wrote, we tend to think first of Hauptmann, Ibsen, Galsworthy, Gorky, and Shaw. Regarded in that light, the significance of Tolstoy's plays seems to lie mainly in their subject matter, in their presentation of the "lower depths" and their vehement social protest. But in fact their interest goes much beyond the polemics of naturalism; the plays of Tolstoy are genuinely experimental, like those of the later Ibsen. As Shaw wrote in 1921, Tolstoy "is a tragi-comedian, pending the invention of a better term." [2]

There have been few satisfactory studies of Tolstoy the dramatist. Perhaps the most thorough is a recent work by the Soviet critic K. N. Lomunov. I can only refer briefly to some of the main points. Tolstoy's interest in drama extended over most of his creative life; he wrote two comedies in 1863, shortly after his marriage, and there are dramatic projects among his posthumous papers. When it came to learning the techniques of drama, Tolstoy's attitude toward Shakespeare was strikingly different from that which we have seen in his essay. With Goethe, Pushkin, Gogol, and Molière, Shakespeare was one of the masters whom Tolstoy studied with close attention. As he wrote to Fet, in February of 1870, "I very much want to talk about Shakespeare and Goethe, and the drama in general. This whole winter I am occupied only with the drama. . . ."

The Power of Darkness was composed when Tolstoy was nearly sixty and when the conflict within him of art and morality had grown fierce. Of all his plays it is, probably, the best known. Zola, who was instrumental

[2] George Bernard Shaw: "Tolstoy: Tragedian or Comedian" (*The Works of Bernard Shaw*, Vol. 29, London, 1930–8).

in its first production in Paris in 1886, saw in it the triumph of the new drama, the proof that "social realism" could achieve effects of high tragedy. And, curiously enough, it was precisely as tragic drama in the Aristotelian sense that the play impressed as romantic a sensibility as Arthur Symons's. *The Power of Darkness* is a tremendous piece of work; in it, like Nietzsche, Tolstoy "philosophizes with a hammer." The play exemplifies Tolstoy's massive concreteness, his power to overwhelm through an aggregate of exact observations. Its true subjects are the Russian peasants: "There are many millions of the likes of you in Russia, and all as blind as moles—knowing nothing!" And out of their ignorance grows bestiality. The five acts march forward with the naked energy of an indictment. The art lies all in the unity of tone, and I know of no other drama in western literature which gives as authoritative a re-creation of rural life. It came as a grievous disappointment to Tolstoy that the peasants to whom he actually read *The Power of Darkness* did not recognize themselves in it. As Marxist critics point out, however, if they had done so, the revolution would have been considerably nearer.

The climax moves beyond realism into a mood of tragic ritual. The grotesque and yet lyric scene between Nikita and Mitrich (which Shaw so greatly admired) prepares us for the moment of expiation. Like Raskolnikov in *Crime and Punishment*, Nikita bows to the ground, confesses his crimes, and begs forgiveness "in Christ's name," from the astounded bystanders. Only his father, Akim, comprehends the full intent of the gesture: "Here God's work is being done. . . ." And with a characteristically Tolstoyan insight he bids the Police Officer stand aside until the real law has burned its mark into the soul.

To find anything comparable to *The Power of Darkness* we must look to the plays of Synge. The *Fruits of Enlightenment*, written only three years later for a Christmas celebration at Yasnaya Polyana, reflects Tolstoy's reading of Molière, of Gogol, and perhaps of

Beaumarchais. It is Tolstoy's *Meistersinger*, his one major excursion into gaiety. With its teeming cast, its bustle of intrigue and stage-business, and its joyous satire on spiritualism, the play could pass for a straightforward comedy by Ostrovsky or Shaw. We know from Aylmer Maude that Tolstoy wished the part of the peasants to be acted with seriousness; but the general laughter is infectious and for once the voice of the truth-seeker is subdued. Like *Twelfth Night*, the work reflects the merriment of the season and the sense of having been conceived for a close-knit group of spectators. After its first production on Tolstoy's estate, *Fruits of Enlightenment* achieved great popularity and was brilliantly performed before the Czar by a troupe of aristocratic amateurs.

I would have liked to speak in some detail of *The Living Corpse*, a grimly fascinating drama which, as so many of the writings of Tolstoy and Dostoevsky, was founded on an actual court case. Shaw said about Tolstoy: "Of all the dramatic poets he has the most withering touch when he wants to destroy. . . ." It is in *The Living Corpse* that we can clearly see what Shaw meant. The mood, and even the technique, are Strindbergian. But to discuss the work adequately one would have to undertake a separate essay on Tolstoy the dramatist.

Finally, we come to that colossal fragment, *The Light That Shines in Darkness*. Legend has it that Molière satirized his own infirmities in *Le Malade imaginaire* and parodied his approaching death in an ironic and macabre mingling of fact and fancy. Tolstoy did something crueller; in his last, unfinished tragedy he held up to public ridicule and indictment his own most hallowed beliefs. In Shaw's words, he turned "his deadly touch suicidally on himself." Nicholas Ivanovich Sarintsev destroys his own life and the lives of those who love him best by seeking to realize a program of Tolstoyan Christianity and anarchy. Nor is he portrayed as a martyred saint. With pitiless veracity Tolstoy shows the man's blindness, his egotism, and the ruthlessness which can inspire a prophet who believes himself entrusted with revelation. There are scenes Tolstoy must have written in sheer agony of spirit. Princess Cheremshanov demands of Sarintsev that he save her son, who is about to be flogged for adopting Sarintsev's doctrine of pacifism and non-violence:

Princess: What I want of you is this: they are sending him to the disciplinary battalion, and I cannot bear that. And it is you who have done it—you —you—you!

Sarintsev: Not I—God has done it. And God knows how I pity you. Do not set yourself in opposition to the will of God. He is testing you. Bear it humbly.

Princess: I cannot bear it humbly. My son is all the world to me, and you have taken him from me and have ruined him. I cannot accept it quietly.

In the end the Princess kills Sarintsev and the dying reformer is uncertain whether God in fact wanted him to be His servant.

It is Tolstoy's equity which gives the play its immense force. He presented the anti-Tolstoyan case with uncanny persuasiveness. In dialogues between Sarintsev and his wife (which seem to echo, word for word, similar debates between the writer and Countess Tolstoy), Marie is the more convincing. And yet, it is precisely through their "absurdity" that Tolstoy's doctrines must be understood. In *The Light That Shines in Darkness*, as in Rembrandt's last self-portraits, we see artists attempting to be totally true unto themselves. Nowhere was Tolstoy more naked.

But how do Tolstoy's achievements as a playwright accord with the image of the epic and essentially anti-dramatic novelist? There is no clear and completely satisfactory answer, but something of a hint lies in the very confusion of the argument in *Shakespeare and the Drama*. In that late essay, Tolstoy declared that the drama "is the most important sphere of art." It is likely that this assertion reflects Tolstoy's repudiation of his own past as a novelist; but it is not certain. To merit this exalted rank, the theatre "should serve the elucidation of religious consciousness" and reaffirm its Greek and medieval origins. In Tolstoy's view, the "essence" of drama is "religious." If we expand this word to include the advocacy of a better life and a truer morality, we can see that the definition closely fits Tolstoy's own practice. For he made his plays the undisguised conveyors of his religious and social program. In Tolstoy's novels this program is implicit, but it is partially submerged in the work of art. In the plays—as on those placards and billboards with which Brecht, one of Tolstoy's heirs, decorated his stage—the "message" is trumpeted to the deaf world.

What is involved is not, as Orwell would have it, "the quarrel between the religious and the humanistic attitudes towards life," [3] but rather a quarrel between Tolstoy's mature doctrines and his view of his own past creations. He had denied his novels in the belief that didacticism must come before all else. But he knew that *War and Peace*, *Anna Karenina*, and the great tales would endure triumphantly. Thus Tolstoy took comfort in the obviously moralistic character of his principal plays and went on to argue that Shakespeare had distorted and betrayed the proper functions of the drama. Why morality and "guidance for life" should be the special responsibility of the playwright is a question which Tolstoy refuses to explore. In his stubborn endeavour to impose upon his own life a principle of unity, to claim that he had been a hedgehog all along, too much was at stake.

But let us not fall into his trap. No single anatomy of Tolstoy's genius can wholly reconcile the man who detested Shakespeare and characterized playhouses as settings for corruption with the author of one brilliant comedy and at least two first-rate tragic dramas in all of which there are traces of a close study of dramatic technique. What we can say is that when he chose Homer

---

[3] George Orwell: "Lear, Tolstoy, and the Fool" (*Polemic*, VII, London, 1947).

against Shakespeare, Tolstoy did express the predominant spirit of his own life and art.

Unlike Dostoevsky, who learned enormously from the theatre but wrote no plays (except for a number of verse fragments composed in adolescence), Tolstoy wrote both novels and drama but kept the two genres strictly apart. His, however, was the subtlest and most comprehensive attempt ever made to introduce into prose fiction elements of the epic. The confrontation of Homer and Shakespeare in his late essay was both a defence of the Tolstoyan novel and the incantation of a daemonic old magician trying to stake out his piece of salvation and to exorcise at the same time the enchantments wrought in the past by his own incomparable spells.

DOSTOEVSKY

CHAPTER

 3

Il faut en venir au théâtre. . . .
BALZAC *to* MME HANSKA, *August 23–24,* 1835

IT was in music that the nineteenth century fulfilled
its dream of creating tragic forms comparable in nobility and coherence to those of classical and renaissance
drama: in the ceremonies and griefs of the Beethoven
quartets, in the C major quintet of Schubert, in Verdi's
Otello, and, consummately, in *Tristan und Isolde.* The
great ambition of "reviving" poetic tragedy, which obsessed the romantic movement, went unrealized. When
the theatre once again took life, with Ibsen and Chekhov, the old modes of heroism had been irremediably
altered. And yet, the century brought forth, in the person of Dostoevsky, one of the great masters of tragic
drama. As the mind moves, via chronology, onward
from *King Lear* and from *Phèdre,* it pauses in immediacy of recognition when, and only when, it reaches
The Idiot, The Possessed, and *The Brothers Karamazov.* As Vyacheslav Ivanov said, in his search for a defining image, Dostoevsky is "the Russian Shakespeare."

Though eminent in lyric poetry and prose fiction, the nineteenth century regarded drama as the supreme literary genre. There were historical reasons for this view. In England, Coleridge, Hazlitt, Lamb, and Keats had formulated the canons of romanticism in the name of Elizabethan drama; led by Vigny and Victor Hugo, the French romantics looked to Shakespeare as their titular saint and chose the theatre as their chief battle-ground against Neo-classicism; the theory and practice of German romanticism, from Lessing to Kleist, was haunted by the belief that Sophoclean and Shakespearean tragedy could be welded into a new and total form. The state of dramatic literature was deemed by the romantics to be a touchstone for the health of both language and the body politic. Shelley wrote in his *Defense of Poetry*:

it is indisputable that the highest perfection of human society has ever corresponded with the highest dramatic excellence: and that the corruption or the extinction of drama in a nation where it has once flourished, is a mark of a corruption of manners, and an extinction of the energies which sustain the soul of social life.

At the close of the century, we find the same idea expounded in the essays of Wagner and incarnate in the very conception of Bayreuth.

These historical and philosophic tenets were mirrored in the sociology and economics of literature. The theatre was regarded by poets and novelists alike as the principal access to respectability and material gain. In September 1819, Keats wrote to his brother, with reference to *Otho the Great*:

At Covent Garden there is a great chance of its being damn'd. Were it to succeed even there it would lift me out of the mire. I mean the mire of a bad reputation which is continually rising against me. My name with the literary fashionables is vulgar—I am a weaver boy to them—a Tragedy would lift me out of this mess. And mess it is as far as it regards our pockets.[1]

[1] *The Letters of John Keats* (ed. by M. B. Forman, Oxford, 1947).

Working too close to their Elizabethan models, the English romantics failed altogether to create a living drama. *The Cenci* and Byron's Venetian tragedies survive as imperfect monuments to an obstinate endeavour. In France, only thirteen years elapsed between the hard-fought victory of *Hernani* and the fiasco of *Les Burgraves*. The brusque flowering of German drama did not extend beyond the death of Goethe. After 1830, the theatre and *belles lettres* drew apart across a deepening gulf. Despite Macready's productions of Browning and Musset's gradual penetration of the Comédie Française, and despite the lone genius of Büchner, this gulf was not to be bridged until the age of Ibsen.

The consequences were far-reaching. The principles of the dramatic—primacy of dialogue and gesture, the strategies of conflict whereby characters are revealed in moments of extreme pronouncement, the notion of the tragic *agon*—were adapted to literary forms not intended for the theatre. Much of the history of romantic poetry is a history of the dramatization of the lyric mode (Browning's dramatic monologues being merely the most trenchant example). Similarly, the values and techniques of the drama played a major role in the development of the novel. Balzac argued that the very survival of fiction depended on whether or not the novelist could master "the dramatic element," and Henry James found in the "divine principle" of the scenario the key to his craft.

The ranges of the dramatic are wide and disparate, and fiction drew upon them variously. Balzac and Dickens were artisans of theatrical light and shadow; they play on our nerves in the fashion of melodrama. *The Awkward Age* and *The Ambassadors*, on the other hand, are "well-made plays" retarded by the complicating rhythms of narrative. They reach back to the day artistry of Dumas *fils*, Augier, and the whole Comédie Française tradition of which James was so assiduous a student.

Tragedy, however, proved stubborn gold to the alchemists of the nineteenth century. We find in a good many poets and philosophers fragments of a coherent tragic vision. Baudelaire and Nietzsche are obvious instances. But only twice, I believe, do we come upon a realization through literary forms—a "making concrete" —of a mature and articulate tragic reading of life. In both cases we are dealing with novelists. They are Melville and Dostoevsky. And we must add at once that it is necessary to distinguish between them on grounds of method—Melville being a dramatist only in the exceptional instance—and on grounds of centrality. Melville's rendering of the human condition is marvellously intense, and few writers have evolved symbolic equivalents and settings more appropriate to their purpose. But the vision is eccentric and severed from the more general currents of existence as a ship is severed from the land on a three years' voyage. In Melville's cosmology, men are very nearly islands and vessels unto themselves. Dostoevsky's range is much greater; it encompasses not only the archipelagos of human affairs—the extremes and solitudes of unreason—but also the continents. Nowhere, in language, did the nineteenth century come nearer to holding up to experience the great mirror of tragedy than in *Moby Dick* and *The Brothers Karamazov*. But the amount and quality of light gathered are very different, the difference being of the kind we invoke when we distinguish between the accomplishments of Webster and of Shakespeare.

In this chapter I want to set forth those aspects of Dostoevsky's genius which enable us to recognize in *Crime and Punishment*, in *The Idiot*, in *The Possessed*, and in *The Brothers Karamazov* the architecture and substance of drama. Here, as in the case of the Tolstoyan epic, inquiries into technique lead directly and rationally to a discussion of the writer's metaphysics. The given text is the necessary beginning.

Among Dostoevsky's earliest writings there appear to have been two dramas or dramatic fragments. To my knowledge neither has survived. But we do know that he was working on a *Boris Godounov* and a *Mary Stu-*

art in the course of 1841. The Boris theme was a staple of Russian dramatic literature and Dostoevsky doubtless knew both Alexander Sumarokov's *Demetrius the Pretender* and Pushkin's *Boris Godounov*. But the juxtaposition of Boris and the Queen of Scotland points to the influence of Schiller. The latter was one of the "guardian spirits" of Dostoevsky's genius; the novelist confided to his brother that Schiller's very name was "a beloved and intimate password, which awakens countless memories and dreams." Certainly he knew both *Maria Stuart* and the unfinished *Demetrius*—a magnificent fragment which might well have become Schiller's masterpiece. We cannot tell how far Dostoevsky advanced in his attempt to dramatize the story of czar and pretender; but echoes of both Schiller and the Demetrius motif resound in *The Possessed*.

That the idea of the theatre continued to occupy Dostoevsky's mind, and that he may, in fact, have had some kind of manuscript in hand, is proved by a remark in a letter to his brother dated September 30, 1844:

You say that my salvation lies in my drama. But it will be a long time before it's played, and longer still before I get any money for it.

By this time, moreover, Dostoevsky had translated Balzac's *Eugénie Grandet* and had nearly completed *Poor Folk*. But his fascination with the stage never ceased entirely; we hear of plans for a tragedy and a comedy in the winter of 1859, and at the very close of his creative life, while working on the eleventh Book of *The Brothers Karamazov* in the summer of 1880, Dostoevsky wondered whether he might not turn one of the main episodes in the novel into a play.

His knowledge of dramatic literature was intimate and wide-ranging. He was steeped in the works of Shakespeare and Schiller, for these were the traditional deities in the romantic pantheon. But Dostoevsky also knew and valued the French theatre of the seventeenth century. He wrote a fascinating letter to his brother in January 1840:

But do tell me how, when you were talking about forms, you could advance the proposition that neither Racine nor Corneille could please us, because their forms were bad? You miserable wretch! And then you add with such effrontery: "Do you think, then, that they were both bad poets?" Racine no poet—Racine the ardent, the passionate, the idealist Racine, no poet! Do you dare to ask that? Have you read his "Andromaque"—eh? Have you read his "Iphigénie"? Will you by any chance maintain that it is not splendid? And isn't Racine's Achilles of the same race as Homer's? I grant you, Racine stole from Homer, but in what a fashion! How marvellous are his women! Do try to apprehend him. . . . Brother, if you won't agree that "Phèdre" is the highest and purest poetry, I don't know what I shall think of you. Why, there's the force of a Shakespeare in it, if the medium *is* plaster of Paris instead of marble.

Now about Corneille. . . . Why, don't you know that Corneille, with his titanic figures and his romantic spirit, nearly approaches Shakespeare? You miserable wretch! Do you happen to know that it was not until fifty years later than the inept miserable Jodelle (author of that disgusting "Cléopâtre") and Ronsard, who was a fore-warning of our own Trediakovsky, that Corneille made his appearance, and that he was almost a contemporary of the insipid poetaster Malherbe? How can you demand form from him? It was as much as one could expect that he should borrow his form from Seneca. Have you read his "Cinna"? What, before the divine figure of Octavius, becomes of Karl Moor, of Fiesco, of Tell, of Don Carlos? That work would have done honour to Shakespeare. . . . Have you read "Le Cid"? Read it, unhappy man, and fall in the dust before Corneille. You have blasphemed him. Anyhow, read him. What does the romantic stand for, if it doesn't reach its highest development in the "Cid"? [2]

This is a remarkable document composed—one must remind oneself—by a passionate admirer of Byron and Hoffmann. Note the choice of epithets for Racine: "ardent," "passionate," "idealist." The judgment regarding the supremacy of *Phèdre* is obviously well founded

[2] *Letters of Fyodor Michailovitch Dostoevsky* (trans. by E. C. Mayne, London, 1914)

(the fact that Schiller had translated the play may have strengthened Dostoevsky's conviction). The paragraph on Corneille is even more revealing. That Dostoevsky should have known Jodelle's *Cléopâtre* is astounding enough; what is extraordinarily impressive is his reference to it in defence of the archaic and rough-hewn elements in Corneille's technique. He perceived, moreover, that the early Corneille could be related more satisfactorily to Seneca than to Attic tragedy and that this makes a comparison with Shakespeare possible. Finally, it is of the greatest interest that Dostoevsky should have associated Corneille, and particularly *Le Cid*, with the notion of romanticism. This view accords with such modern readings of Corneille as Brasillach's and the contemporary notion that there were "romantic" strains in the heroics, in the Spanish colouring, and in the rhetorical exuberance of French pre-classicism.

Although Dostoevsky never lost touch with Racine— "he is a great poet whether we will or not" says the hero of *The Gambler*—Corneille's was the more penetrating influence. In the drafts and jotting for the last part of *The Brothers Karamazov*, for instance, we find the following: "Grushenka *Svetlova*. Katya: *Rome unique objet de mon ressentiment.*" The reference is, of course, to the opening line of Camille's imprecations against Rome in Corneille's *Horace*. Perhaps Dostoevsky concentrated around this phrase the raw material for the encounter between Grushenka and Katya in Dimitri's prison ward. The line from *Horace* strikes the apposite note of relentlessness:

Katya moved swiftly to the door, but when she reached Grushenka, she stopped suddenly, turned as white as chalk and moaned softly, almost in a whisper: "Forgive me!"

Grushenka stared at her and, pausing for an instant, in a vindictive, venomous voice answered: "We are full of hatred, my girl, you and I! We are both full of hatred. As though we could forgive one another! Save him, and I'll worship you all my life."

"You won't forgive her!" cried Mitya, with frantic reproach.

But it may also be that Dostoevsky's cryptic note refers to Katya's sudden impulse towards vengeance and to her damning testimony at the trial. In either case, the novelist was drawing on his memories of Corneille to crystallize and record a stage in his own creation. The Corneillian text had, quite literally, entered into the fabric of Dostoevsky's mind.

Let us take this as one of many particular illustrations of the primary argument: more, perhaps, than those of any novelist of comparable dimension, Dostoevsky's sensibility, his modes of imagination, and his linguistic strategies were saturated by the drama. Dostoevsky's relationship to the dramatic is analogous, in centrality and ramification, to Tolstoy's relationship to the epic. It characterized his particular genius as strongly as it contrasted it with Tolstoy's. Dostoevsky's habit of miming his characters as he wrote—like Dickens's—was the outward gesture of a dramatist's temper. His mastery of the tragic mood, his "tragic philosophy," were the specific expressions of a sensibility which experienced and transmuted its material dramatically. This was true of Dostoevsky's whole life, from adolescence and the theatrical performance recounted in *The House of the Dead* to his deliberate and detailed use of *Hamlet* and Schiller's *Räuber* to control the dynamics of *The Brothers Karamazov*. Thomas Mann said of Dostoevsky's novels that they are "colossal dramas, scenic in nearly their whole structure; in them an action which dislocates the depth of the human soul and which is often packed into a few days, is represented in surrealistic and feverish dialogue. . . ." [3] It was recognized early that these "colossal dramas" could be adapted to actual performance; the first dramatization of *Crime and Punishment* was produced in London in 1910. And, referring to the Karamazovs, Gide remarked that "of all imaginative creations and of all protagonists in history none had better claims to being presented on a stage." [4]

[3] Thomas Mann: *"Dostojewski—Mit Maassen"* (*Neue Studien*, Stockholm, 1948).

With each year, the list of dramatic adaptations of Dostoevskyan novels grows longer. During the winter of 1956–7 alone, nine "Dostoevsky plays" were being performed in Moscow. There are operas set to Dostoevskyan librettos: among them, Prokofiev's *Gambler*, Otakar Jeremiáš's *Brothers Karamazov*, and Janáček's bizarre but deeply moving *From the House of the Dead*.

Readers as different from each other as Suarès and Berdiaev, Shestov and Stefan Zweig, have resorted to the vocabulary of the drama in their responses to Dostoevsky. But it is only with the publication (and partial translation) of the Dostoevsky archives that it has become possible for the general reader to observe the constancy of the dramatic element in the Dostoevskyan method. It can now be shown in detail that *Crime and Punishment, The Idiot, The Possessed,* and *The Brothers Karamazov* were conceived according to the Jamesian "principle of the scenario," that they are instances of the kind of vision F. R. Leavis refers to when he speaks of "the novel as drama." Often, in examining these tunings and preliminaries of creation, one receives the impression that Dostoevsky wrote plays, retained the essential structure of dialogue, and then expanded the stage-directions (which are plainly recognizable in the drafts) into what we now know as his narrative prose. Where his techniques of fiction do betray insufficiencies, we shall usually find that the material or momentary context is of a type intractable to dramatic treatment.

This does not mean that the completed and published work should be judged in the light of preliminary and essentially private exercises. Such evidence bears not on judgment but on understanding. "The main ideal of criticism," says Kenneth Burke, "is to use all that is there to use." [5]

[4] André Gide: *Dostoïevsky* (Paris, 1923).
[5] Kenneth Burke: *The Philosophy of Literary Form* (New York, 1957).

Dostoevsky's choice of subject matter was unvaryingly expressive of his dramatic bias. Turgeniev began with the image of a character or small group of personages; the relevant plot would arise out of their posture and confrontation. Dostoevsky, on the contrary, saw action first; at the root of his invention lay the *agon*, the dramatic event. Always, he began with some brief cataclysm or gust of violence in which the dislocation of ordinary human affairs yields a "moment of truth." Each of Dostoevsky's four major novels is centred around or climaxes in an act of murder.

One thinks—in the obvious light of the *Oresteia*, of *Oedipus*, of *Hamlet* and *Macbeth*—of the ancient and persistent concordance between murder and the tragic form. Perhaps there are, as anthropologists have supposed, shadowy but indelible recollections of sacrificial rites in the very origins of drama. Perhaps the pendulous motion from murder to retribution is uniquely emblematic of that progress from the act of disorder to the state of reconciliation and equipoise which we associate with our very notions of the tragic. Murder, moreover, terminates privacy; by definition the doors may at any time be forced open in the house of an assassin. He has only three walls left, and this is another way of saying that he lives "scenically."

Dostoevsky did not dramatize murders out of past history or legend. He drew his material, even to the point of minute detail, from contemporary crimes, from the kind of *fait divers* on which Stendhal founded *The Red and the Black*. Dostoevsky was a devourer of newspapers, and the difficulty of obtaining Russian papers abroad is a recurrent theme in his letters. What the art of the historian was to Tolstoy, journalism was to Dostoevsky. He found in newspapers a confirmation for his own strained vision of reality. Writing to Strakhov in 1869, he remarked:

In any newspaper one takes up, one comes across reports of wholly authentic facts, which nevertheless strike one as extraordinary. Our writers regard them as fantastic, and take no account of them; and yet they are the truth, for they are facts. But who troubles to observe, record, describe, them?

The link between *Crime and Punishment* and actual fact is paradoxical and rather terrifying. The general theme of the novel appears to have evolved in Dostoevsky's mind during the period of Siberian captivity. The first instalment was published in the *Russian Messenger* for January 1866. Immediately thereupon, on January 14, a student in Moscow murdered a usurer and his servant under circumstances undeniably similar to those which Dostoevsky had imagined. Nature rarely imitates art with such swift precision.

The assassination of the jeweler Kalmykov by a young man named Mazurin in March 1867 provided material for Rogojin's murder of Nastasia Philipovna in *The Idiot*. Several of Dostoevsky's famous touches— the oil-cloth, the disinfectant, the fly buzzing above Nastasia's body—are paralleled exactly in the accounts of the crime in the newspapers. This does not mean, however, that Allen Tate's luminous explorations of their symbolic functions are unfounded. For again, the connections between the brute matter of actuality and the work of art are complex and curiously bilateral. A buzzing fly appears in Raskolnikov's dream-image of the murderer's room in *Crime and Punishment*; when Raskolnikov awakens, a large fly is, in fact, drumming against his window-panes. In other words, the authentic circumstances of the Kalmykov case matched Dostoevsky's previous imaginings; as in Raskolnikov's dream, the fly buzzed simultaneously in "exterior reality" and in the symbolic complex of the novel. Pushkin celebrated this order of coincidence in *The Prophet* (a poem to which Dostoevsky frequently referred) and Dostoevsky speculated about such parallelisms in his search for links between epilepsy and clairvoyance. One thinks also of the buzzing fly which hovers above Prince Andrew in Book XI of *War and Peace* and which recalls the dying man to a sense of reality.

The part of fact in the genesis of *The Possessed* is even more diverse. As we know it, the structure of the novel represents an unstable compromise between fragments from the projected cycle on *The Life of a Great Sinner* and the dramatization of a political crime. Karakozov's attempt on the life of the Czar in April 1866 figured among the first impulses towards *The Possessed*; but it was the murder of a student, Ivanov, at the orders of the nihilist leader Nechaiev, on November 21, 1869, which gave Dostoevsky his narrative focus. Combing through all the Russian newspapers obtainable in Dresden, Dostoevsky followed the Nechaiev affair with enthralled attention. Once again he experienced the odd sensation of having foreseen the crime, of having anticipated through intuition and by virtue of his political philosophy the necessary progression from nihilism to murder. Throughout major portions of the drafts for *The Possessed*, the personage who was to become Pyotr Stepanovich Verkhovensky is designated simply as "Nechaiev." Writing to Katkov in October 1870, the novelist maintained that he was not copying the actual crime and that his imagined character might not, after all, resemble the brilliant and cruel nihilist. But the notes and sketches show clearly that Dostoevsky envisioned and developed his theme in the context of Ivanov's death and Nechaiev's reputed philosophy. While the work was in progress, moreover, reality added yet another important motif: the fires set in Paris during the Commune, in May 1871, profoundly excited Dostoevsky and recalled to his mind the great St. Petersburg fire of 1862. Hence the conflagration which destroys a part of the town and leads to Liza's death in the novel.

The trial of Nechaiev began in July 1871, and Dostoevsky drew on the court records for significant details in the final sections of *The Possessed*. Even in the last stages of composition he was able to incorporate exterior and essentially fortuitous material into his narrative. The drafts reveal, for instance, that Virginsky's famous outcry after the murder of Shatov—"It's not the right thing; it's not, it's not at all!"—stems from a letter written by the conservative pamphleteer T. I. Philippov. Indeed, the critique to be made regarding the design of *The Possessed* is that it was too "open," too vulnerable to the impact of contemporaneous happenings. Dostoevsky's vision of the whole became fragmented and some of the narrative outline is blurred. Rarely, on the other hand, do a prophet's intuitions and fears become melodramatically realized before his own eyes; in the case of *The Possessed* this is precisely what happened.

If there are in *The Possessed* strains of prophecy, there is in *The Brothers Karamazov* a germ of recollection. Dostoevsky's father was murdered by three serfs under circumstances which a number of critics and psychologists have judged comparable to those depicted in the novel. But there are in Dostoevsky's treatment of parricide philosophic and factual elements which lay closer at hand. To him, as to Turgeniev and Tolstoy—whose *Two Hussars* was originally entitled "Father and Son"—the struggle between the generations, between the liberals of the 1840's and their radical heirs, was the dominant Russian theme. In this struggle parricide was symbolic of the absolute. When composing his novel, moreover, Dostoevsky went back to a *fait divers* recorded in *The House of the Dead*. One of his fellow inmates was a nobleman, Ilinsky, falsely convicted of having murdered his father in the town of Tobolsk. Ilinsky was cleared after some twenty years of captivity, and Tobolsk does, in fact, figure in some of the early notes for the novel.

Two contemporary criminal affairs also contributed to Dostoevsky's treatment of the murder of Fyodor Pavlovich Karamazov. Preliminary drafts refer repeatedly to the assassination of a certain Von Zon by a gang of criminals in November 1869. In March 1878 Dostoevsky attended the trial of Vera Zasulich, who had sought to assassinate the notorious police prefect Trepov. From it, Dostoevsky gathered material for the trial of Dimitri Karamazov; in his view, there were spiritual links between a private act of parricide and the attempt of a terrorist on the life of the Czar—the father—or one of his chosen representatives. Another theme of major importance in the novel is that of criminal behaviour against small children—a symbolic reversal of parricide. I shall return to its literary sources and implications in detail, but it is worth noting at the outset how many of the bestialities cited by Ivan Karamazov in his indictment of God were taken from contemporary newspapers and judicial dossiers. Some were first related by Dostoevsky in his *Diary of a Writer*; others came to his attention when parts of *The Brothers Karamazov* had already been completed. Two specific inhumanities, the Kroneberg affair and the Brunst case, which was tried in Kharkov in March 1879, furnished Dostoevsky with some of his most harrowing details. The ninth Book, "The Preliminary Investigation," had not been anticipated in Dostoevsky's outlines. It resulted from his encounter with A. F. Kony. This meeting complicated and deepened the novelist's understanding of legal proceedings. It is one of the curious hazards of contact between Tolstoy and Dostoevsky that it should have been Kony who, in the autumn of 1887, suggested to Tolstoy the plot of *Resurrection*.

Schematic and abridged, these are some of the principal elements of factual background to Dostoevsky's major novels. They point an obvious moral: Dostoevsky's imagination crystallized around a core of violent action, around incidents very much alike in nature and stylistic potential. The thematic movement from crime to punishment through the intervening and exploratory rhetoric of detection contains inherently—in *Oedipus* or *Hamlet* or *The Brothers Karamazov*—the forms of drama. The contrast with Tolstoy's choice of material and modes of treatment is radical and instructive.

Dostoevsky's techniques and the characteristic mannerisms of his craft arise out of the demands of a dramatic form. Dialogues culminate in gesture; all superfluity of narrative is stripped away in order to render the conflict of personages naked and exemplary; the law of composition is one of maximum energy, released over the smallest possible extent of space and time. A Dostoevskyan novel is a supreme instance of the "totality of motion" in the Hegelian definition of drama. Dostoevsky's drafts and notebooks demonstrate, beyond doubt, that he imagined and composed theatrically. Consider, for example, two entries from the preliminary sketches for *The Possessed*:

Explanation between Lisa and Shatov—
and apparition of Nechaiev in the style of
Khlestakov
and dramatic form.—
AND THE START BY MEANS OF DIFFERENT SCENES ALL INTER-
CONNECTED IN A SINGLE KNOT.

The reference to Khlestakov—the hero of Gogol's *Inspector General*—is of obvious significance. As he set down his material in rough outline, Dostoevsky imagined his characters and situations as if they were on stage. The proper note for the entry of Nechaiev-Verkhovensky is achieved through a process of resonance; Gogol's comedy acts as a tuning fork. Or take this jotting in which Dostoevsky—like Henry James—engaged in dialogue with himself:

Does the difficulty not arise from the manner of the narrative? After "prepare yourself for your anniversary at the Drozdovs and Lisa," should one not continue *dramatically?*

And within the reaches of narrative prose this is precisely what Dostoevsky proceeded to do.

As we shall see in more detail, the temper of the dramatist is implicit in the unmistakable tone and idiosyncrasies of the Dostoevskyan narrator. The voice speaks in direct address, and in what is probably the most Dostoevskyan of books, the *Letters from the Underworld*, the relations between the "I" and the audience are clothed in the rhetoric of drama. Writing to Schiller in December 1797, Goethe observed that epistolary novels are, by their very nature, "totally dramatic." The point is germane to Dostoevsky's first novel. *Poor Folk* is narrated in the form of letters and may represent a transition between Dostoevsky's hopes of writing for the theatre and his later adaption of the scenario to prose fiction. Seeking to refine the distinctions between literary genres, Goethe added in the same letter: "One could not condone narrative [*erzählende*] novels mingled with dialogue" (and it is dramatic dialogue which he has in mind). *Crime and Punishment, The Idiot, The Possessed,* and *The Brothers Karamazov* were to prove him wrong. These novels are, in the literal sense, "imitations" of tragic action. In them dialogue is charged with the utmost significance; it becomes what R. P. Blackmur calls "language as gesture." The connecting prose complicates, but never entirely conceals, the scenic design; rather, it serves as a kind of stage-direction focused inward.

Evidence for such a reading of Dostoevsky abounds in all of his major works. But nowhere can it be marshalled more clearly—can narrative be seen more totally penetrated with the conventions and values of the drama—than in the opening chapters of *The Idiot*. These chapters, it will be remembered, span a period of twenty-four hours.

III

The problems of time in literature are intricate. Epic poetry conveys a sense of long duration. In fact, the action in both the *Iliad* and the *Odyssey* takes only about fifty days, and though the precise chronology of the *Divine Comedy* is a matter of dispute, it is fairly clear that the poem encompasses no more than a week. But the epic uses retarding conventions—the formal saga or recitation incorporated in the main narrative, the long parenthesis in which the previous history of some object or personage is recorded, the dream or the descent into the underworld—which momentarily suspend the forward motion of the plot. These motifs which, in Goethe's words, "separate the action from its goal" were already recognized in Greek theory as being essentially epic. They characterize a literary genre whose principal instruments are remembrance and prophecy.

The opposite holds true of the drama. But an understanding of why this should be so has been obscured by the gloss which the renaissance and Neo-classicism put on Aristotle's celebrated observations concerning "unity of time." The actual remark in the *Poetics*—"tragedy endeavours to keep as far as possible within a single circuit of the sun, or something near that"—was intended, as Humphry House emphasized in his searching commentary, to enforce "the elementary comparison between the physical length of the two different kinds of work, an epic being several thousand lines, and a tragedy hardly ever more than about 1600." [6] Contrary to certain Neo-classical theories, there is no hint in Greek practice that the duration of the performance was to equate that of the imaginary events. In the *Eumenides*, in Euripides' *Suppliants* and probably in *Oedipus at Colonus* there are substantial time-gaps between successive episodes. What Aristotle intended to express by the notion of unities—"unity of action" being all-embracing—was the recognition that the drama concentrates, compresses, and isolates from the diffuse matter of normal experience a rigorously defined and artificially "totalitarian" conflict. Manzoni saw this clearly when he rejected the interpretation of Aristotle which had originated with Castelvetro. He pointed out, in his *Lettre à M. C.—sur l'unité de temps et de lieu dans la tragédie*, that the "three unities" stood for a way of saying that drama contracts and intensifies the spatial and temporal co-ordinates of reality even to the point of distortion in order to achieve its total effects. It transforms into a rectilinear action what is ordinarily discontinuous and intermingled with irrelevancies. The dramatist works with Occam's razor; nothing is preserved beyond strict necessity and pertinence (where is Lear's wife?). As Dr. Johnson argues in his *Preface to Shakespeare*, "nothing is essential to the fa-

[6] Humphry House: *Aristotle's Poetics* (London, 1956).

ble, but unity of action." If the latter is maintained, even substantial lapses of chronological time will not impair the dramatic illusion. Indeed, Shakespeare's chronicle plays suggest that the juxtaposition of the length of time portrayed in the plot with the length of time needed for performance is rich in dramatic consequences.

The novel inherited these complexities and misunderstandings, and it is possible to distinguish between those novelists whose sense of time inclines them towards epic conventions and those who perceive time in the dramatic mode. For although prose fiction is read, rather than recited or performed, "a play read," as Dr. Johnson says, "affects the mind like a play acted." Conversely, a novel read affects the imagination like an action seen. Thus for the writer of prose fiction, no less than for the dramatist, the problem of real and imagined time is a constant one. The most ingenious and deliberate solution has been that of *Ulysses*, in which a diurnal—and hence dramatic—temporal scheme is imposed on material whose structure and associations are explicitly epic.

Dostoevsky perceived time from the point of view of a dramatist. He asked in the notebooks for *Crime and Punishment*: "What is time?" And answered: "Time does not exist; time is a series of numbers, time is the relation of the existing to the non-existent." Instinctive to him was the concentration of tangled and multitudinous actions into the briefest time span that could be reconciled with plausibility. This concentration contributes signally to a sense of nightmare, of gesture and language stripped of all that softens and delays. Whereas Tolstoy moves tide-like and gradual, Dostoevsky twists time into narrowness and contortion. He empties it of those spells of leisure which can qualify or reconcile. Deliberately, he crowds the night as thickly as the day lest sleep muffle the exasperations or dissipate the hatreds bred by the clash of characters. Dostoevsky's are the contracted, hallucinatory days and the "white nights" of St. Petersburg; not the ample noon under which Prince Andrew lies at Austerlitz or the deep star-spaces in which Levin finds peace.

The fact that a major part of *The Idiot* transpires in twenty-four hours, that the bulk of the incidents narrated in *The Possessed* covers only forty-eight hours, and that everything but the trial in *The Brothers Karamazov* comes to pass in five days is as central to Dostoevsky's vision and intent as is the terrifying brevity of time which separates King Oedipus from Oedipus the beggar. The speed with which Dostoevsky occasionally wrote—the first part of *The Idiot* was set down in twenty-three days—was like a physical counterpart to the hurtling rhythm of his plots.

The opening sentence of *The Idiot* sets the pace: "Toward the end of November, during a thaw, at nine o'clock one morning, a train on the Warsaw and Petersburg railway was approaching the latter city at full speed." By one of those coincidences essential to the Dostoevskyan scheme of things, Prince Muishkin and Rogojin are sitting opposite each other in the same third-class carriage. It is a defining proximity, for they are aspects of what was originally a single complex figure. This use of "doubles" is more sophisticated than in Dostoevsky's early Hoffmannesque story *Goliadkin*, but these men are doubles nevertheless. The separation of Muishkin from Rogojin can be followed through successive stages of uncertainty in the drafts for the novel. Initially, Muishkin is an ambiguous, Byronic figure—a sketch for the Stavrogin of *The Possessed*. In him (as in the very heart of Dostoevskyan metaphysics) good and evil are indissolubly entangled, and associated with his name we find such phrases as "murder," "rape," "suicide," "incest." In what is, in effect, a seventh outline for *The Idiot*, Dostoevsky asks: "Who is he? A fearful scoundrel or a mysterious ideal?" Then the great insight flashes across the page of the notebook: "He is a *prince*." And a few lines below: "Prince, innocent (with the children)?!" [7]

[7] The editors of the notebooks in the Pléiade edition point out that the word "Prince" is written in a manner suggesting

This would appear decisive. Yet the case of Stavrogin and of Alyosha Karamazov shows that in the language of Dostoevsky this princely title carries rather ambiguous overtones.

Muishkin is a composite figure; we come to discern in him the parts of Christ, of Don Quixote, of Pickwick, and of the saintly fools from the Orthodox tradition. But his relations to Rogojin are unequivocal. Rogojin is Muishkin's original sin. To the extent that the Prince is human, and thus heir to the Fall, the two men must remain inseparable companions. They enter the novel together and leave it to a common doom. In Rogojin's attempt to murder Muishkin there is the strident bitterness of suicide. Their inextricable nearness is a Dostoevskyan parable on the necessary presence of evil at the gates of knowledge. When Rogojin is taken away from him, the Prince collapses once again into idiocy. Without darkness, how should we apprehend the nature of light?

Also in the railway compartment is "a shabbily dressed man of about forty, who looked like a clerk, and possessed a red nose and a very blotchy face." Lebedev is one of that host of grotesque yet sharply individualized minor characters with which Dostoevsky surrounds his protagonists. Spawned by the city, they gather at the merest scent of violence or scandal and are both audience and chorus. Lebedev is descended from the pathetic clerk in Gogol's *Cloak* and from Mr. Micawber—a personage who profoundly impressed Dostoevsky. Like Marmeladov in *Crime and Punishment*, Lebyadkin in *The Possessed*, and Captain Snegiryov in *The Brothers Karamazov* (their very names speak volumes of abasement), Lebedev scurries about, courting reward or degradation at the hands of the rich

---

Dostoevsky's recognition that he had hit upon a central motif. But the princely title does not yet pertain to Muishkin; rather, it seems to belong to a secondary character in the original conception of the novel. Only gradually did Dostoevsky come to realize that the Prince was none other than the "idiot" himself.

and the powerful. He and his tribe live like parasites nesting in lions' manes.

Lebedev's sole real property is a vast fund of gossip, which he pours out, during the opening moments of *The Idiot*, in a clattering, jerking rhythm suggesting that of the train. He tells us all we need to know about the Epanchins to whom Muishkin is tenuously related. He elicits from the Prince a hint that the house of the Muishkins is ancient and of high nobility (a muffled allusion, I take it, to Christ's royal lineage). Lebedev is acquainted with the fact that Rogojin has inherited a fortune. He is bursting with gossip about the beautiful Nastasia Philipovna. He even knows of her association with Totski and of the latter's friendship with General Epanchin. Exasperated by the little man's indiscretions, Rogojin reveals his own furious ardour for Nastasia. The speed of the dialogue and its unadorned vehemence carry us through what is, in essence, a rather crude mode of exposition. We are literally jolted into accepting the primary convention of the dramatic—the "publication" through dialogue of the most private knowledge and emotions.

As the train arrives in St. Petersburg, Lebedev attaches himself to Rogojin's followers—a troupe of buffoons, derelicts, and bullies living off the daemonic vitality and largesse of their master. That Lebedev should have nothing better to do and that Muishkin should be homeless and nearly without baggage are traits characteristic of the Dostoevskyan manner. Lionel Trilling remarks that "every situation in Dostoevsky, no matter how spiritual, starts with a point of social pride and a certain number of rubles." [8] This is misleading so far as it suggests that determining core of economics and stable social relations which we find, notably, in the novels of Balzac. Raskolnikov desperately needs a certain number of rubles, as does Dimitri Karamazov; and it is perfectly true that Rogojin's fortune plays a vital role in *The Idiot*. But the money involved is never

[8] Lionel Trilling: "Manners, Morals, and the Novel" (*The Liberal Imagination*, New York, 1950).

earned in any clearly definable manner; it does not entail the attenuating routine of a profession or the disciplines of usury upon which Balzac's financiers expend their powers. Dostoevsky's characters—even the neediest among them—always have leisure for chaos or an unpremeditated total involvement. They are available day and night; no one need go and ferret them out of a factory or an established business. Above all, their use of money is strangely symbolic and oblique—like that of kings. They burn it or wear it over their hearts.

Homer and Tolstoy circumscribe their personages with a "totality of objects," with daily pursuits and the enveloping norms of habitual experience. Dostoevsky reduces them to a bare absolute; for in drama the naked confront the naked. "From the dramatic point of view," writes Lukács, "any character, and psychological trait of character, which are not strictly requisite to the living dynamics of collision, must be judged superfluous." [9] This principle governs Dostoevsky's craft. Muishkin and Rogojin part at the station and set off in different directions. But the "dynamics of collision" will compel them to move in narrowing orbits until they clash and reunite in a final catastrophe.

Muishkin arrives at General Epanchin's door at "about eleven o'clock." The recurrent time-references are worth watching; through them the novelist exercises a measure of control over the hallucinatory pace of his narrative. In the waiting-room the Prince—who now begins to reveal the innocence of his wisdom—pours out his soul to an astounded footman. If there is a mood in which comedy moves us to unutterable sadness and yet remains comedy, Dostevsky in this scene shows himself a master of it. Muishkin has an angel's immediacy of perception. Before him the furniture of life—reticence, gradualness of acquaintance, the delaying and obscuring tactics of discourse—is brushed aside. Whatever the Prince touches turns not to gold but to transparency.

He is conducted to General Epanchin by the latter's

[9] George Lukács: *Die Theorie des Romans* (Berlin, 1920).

secretary, Gavrila Ardalionovich, or "Gania." By yet another one of those coincidences inherent in the dramatic method, this day happens to be Nastasia's twenty-fifth birthday and she has promised to announce whether she will accept Gania in marriage. For reasons of his own, the General favours the match. Nastasia has given Gania a large photograph of herself and he has brought it to his patron. The picture—an identical device prepares Catherina Nicolaevna's entrance in *Raw Youth*—is one of those physical "properties" (Muishkin's cross, Rogojin's knife) which connect the bewilderingly diverse strands of narrative and give them coherence.

Muishkin gazes at the portrait and finds it "wonderfully beautiful." He seems to perceive in it more than those who actually know the lady. Interrogated by his host, he recounts what he has heard from Rogojin in the railway compartment earlier that morning. Again, the scaffolding of Dostoevsky's exposition strikes one as rather obvious and laboured; but the tension of the dialogue and the constant play of dramatic intelligence over material with which our responses are by now fairly heavily involved prevents this impression from gathering force.

Gania's feelings towards the proposed marriage are ambiguous. He knows that the scheme has been devised by Totski and the General for sinister and even repellent motives. But he hungers after the wealth which will be heaped on Nastasia by her protectors. Shortly after half past twelve Epanchin leaves the room. He has promised to assist Muishkin towards earning a living and has urged him to take lodgings with Gania's family. The secretary and the "idiot" are left with the portrait:

"It's a proud face too, terribly proud! And I—I can't say whether she is good and kind or not. Oh, if she be but good! That would make all well!"

"And would *you* marry a woman like that, now?" continued Gania, never taking his excited eyes off the Prince's face.

"I cannot marry at all," said the latter. "I am an invalid."

"Would Rogojin marry her, do you think?"

"Why not? Certainly he would, I should think. He will marry her tomorrow!—marry her tomorrow and murder her in a week!"

Hardly had the Prince uttered the last word when Gania gave such a fearful shudder that the Prince almost cried out.

The whole of *The Idiot* is latent in that exchange. Muishkin has glimpsed Nastasia's morbid, self-lacerating pride and is seeking to unriddle the enigma of her beauty. "All" would indeed be well if she were "good" (a word which we must take here in its theological totality); for it is Nastasia's moral qualities that finally determine the lives of the other characters. Gania has sensed the enormous and unconventional force of the Prince's sympathies for her; obscurely he makes out that innocence moves with untrammelled directness towards radical solutions. The thought of a marriage between Muishkin and Nastasia hovers on the edge of his mind. The Prince has spoken truly in asserting that he cannot marry; but, being only a material truth—a contingency from the world of fact—it need not bind him. What makes Gania shudder is not fear for Nastasia's life. It is his confrontation with final clearsightedness, with effortless prophecy. The "idiot" foretells the murder of Nastasia, for he has perceived realities of character and situation which Gania—who is remarkably intelligent—had either failed to see altogether or had suppressed from his affrighted consciousness. That his single gesture—the "fearful shudder"—should compel us to so explicit and detailed a response points to the level of drama achieved in the dialogue.

We are told next of Nastasia's childhood and of her early liaison with Totski. At the risk of being tedious, I note once more that the transmission of complicated "background knowledge" creates particular difficulties for the dramatic method. The dilemma of exposition in *The Idiot* is obtrusive precisely because, as Allen

Tate observes, "the development of the plot is almost exclusively 'scenic.' " [1]

Totski is planning to marry one of the Epanchin daughters, and Nastasia's marriage to Gania would facilitate matters. There is, moreover, "a strange rumour" that General Epanchin is himself fascinated by Nastasia and that he is counting on the discreet complaisance of his secretary. With this hint we are possessed of all but one major circumstance in a tight and even melodramatic situation.

Around lunch time Muishkin is introduced to Madame Epanchin and her three daughters, Alexandra, Adelaida, and Aglaya. The ladies are charmed by his lucid innocence. Drawn out by their questions, the Prince narrates, under a thin veil of fiction, the famous and harrowing story of Dostoevsky's mock execution on December 22, 1849. A similar recital is inserted in several of Dostoevsky's novels and tales. It seems to act as a kind of signature which gives Dostoevsky's style, in the particular moment, its requisite key. Like Cassandra's animal cries in the *Agamemnon*, it proclaims that a dread and experienced truth lies at the heart of the poem. As Muishkin concludes his monologue, Aglaya challenges him: "And why did you tell us this?" It is a fair question foreshadowing her subsequent assaults upon the mystery of his "simple-mindedness."

But instead of answering, the Prince launches into two further narratives. He relates his impressions of a capital execution (which he had already communicated to the footman, and thus to the reader, in the Epanchin foyer). Lastly, he tells a frankly Dickensian tale of seduction and forgiveness which he claims to have enacted during his stay in Switzerland. Dostoevsky's motives in presenting these successive stories are somewhat obscure. It could be argued that the theme of the fallen woman and of children converted to insight and love prepares us both for the association of Christ with the figure of Muishkin and for the latter's special under-

[1] Allen Tate: "The Hovering Fly" (*The Man of Letters in the Modern World*, New York, 1955).

standing of Nastasia. But Aglaya insists (rightly, I think) that there is some particular "motive" behind the Prince's behaviour and behind his choice of themes. Dostoevsky fails to convey it, and one wonders whether the rhetorical urgency with which the material is handled in these three "set pieces" does not stem from the author rather than from the character. This becomes more plausible if we bear in mind how radically each of the motifs touched upon by Muishkin implicated Dostoevsky's personal memories and obsessions.

Looking at Aglaya, the Prince calls her "almost as lovely as Nastasia Philipovna." He has drawn the names of the two women into dangerous proximity and is forced to tell Madame Epanchin about the photograph. This indiscretion puts Gania into a frenzy; for the first time he pronounces the word "idiot." It flashes on us— and the revelation is made entirely through the dramatic context—that Gania is tormented not only by his ambiguous feelings towards Nastasia, whom his family despises, but also by his love for Aglaya. Gania begs Muishkin to convey a note to her. In it he pleads for some faint encouragement; if Aglaya will only look upon him he is prepared to renounce Nastasia and his feverish expectations of wealth. Aglaya promptly shows the note to Muishkin and humiliates the secretary in Muishkin's presence. That she should do so suggests her nascent interest in the "idiot" and the strain of hysterical cruelty which runs darkly through her temper.

Flaring up out of his own abasement, Gania turns on the Prince and reviles his alleged idiocy. But when Muishkin courteously reproves him, Gania's fury vanishes and he invites the Prince to his home. Their dialogue has in it those brusque reversals of mood in which Dostoevsky delighted. He tended to omit narrative transitions, moving directly from hatred to affection or truth to concealment, because he composed theatrically and saw the facial expressions and gestures of his characters as if they were speaking their lines on a stage. As they walk together, Gania glances savagely at Muishkin. His amiable invitation is meant to gain time. The "idiot" may still be of use. The whole physical interplay is there, surrounding the language. Dostoevsky is an example of a novelist who must be read with a constant commitment of our visual imagination.

It is now afternoon. Gania's house is one of those Dostoevskyan towers of Babel from whose dank rooms an army of characters pours forth like dazzled bats. The drunken clerks, penniless students, starving seamstresses, virtuous but imperilled maidens, and wide-eyed children have a familiar air. They are the descendants of Little Nell and of the whole Dickensian gallery. They haunt the European and Russian novel from *Oliver Twist* to Gorky. They sleep on "an old sofa . . . with a torn rug over it," eat thin gruel, live in terror of landlords and pawnbrokers, earn a pittance by washing clothes or copying legal documents, and breed dismayingly large families in the crowded gloom. They are the minor damned in the inferno of the great cities through which Dickens and Eugène Sue led their many disciples. What Dostoevsky added to the convention was the rather ferocious comedy which springs from abasement and the notion that in fiction, as well as in Scripture, the truth can be heard most plainly from the mouths of children.

Muishkin is thrust into a hive of new characters: Gania's mother, his sister Varvara, his brother Colia—one of those weirdly perceptive Dostoevskyan adolescents—Ptitsin (Varvara's admirer), one Ferdishenko (a drunken Micawber), and Gania's father, General Ivolgin. This latter figure is among the most humane and beautifully rounded in *The Idiot*. His self-introduction as "retired and unfortunate" sets the mock-heroic tone. His memoirs, which he relates to all and sundry, range from pure fabrication to the leavings of yesterday's newspapers. When found out or driven to the wall by the discomforts of fact, this Falstaff of the tenements refers pathetically to the siege of Kars and the bullets in his breast. Muishkin's presence acts like a catalyst; at his touch the various characters kindle into a kind of luminous intensity. His nature—and this is its wholly dramatized magic—is open to every influence and is defined by the Prince's relations to other human beings; yet it possesses a demonstrable and inviolate identity.

Gania and his family erupt over the question of the marriage to Nastasia. Muishkin leaves the room and hears the door-bell:

The Prince took down the chain and opened the door. He started back in amazement—for there stood Nastasia Philipovna. He knew her at once from her photograph. Her eyes blazed with anger and she looked at him.

This is the first of the *coups de théâtre* around which the novel is built.

Dostoevsky has assembled his cast for a "big scene" (compare the gathering at Stavrogin's house in *The Possessed* and the conference in Father Zossima's cell in *The Brothers Karamazov*). The dialogue is interrupted only by sparse stage-directions: "Gania was motionless with horror"; Varia and Nastasia exchange "looks of strange import."

Gania is torn between detestation and embarrassment. His distress reaches a paroxysm as his father enters in evening clothes and proceeds to recount as his own an adventure reported in the papers. Nastasia draws him on cruelly and exposes the fraud. Like Aglaya, she is impelled by the hysteria and insecurity in her own nature to reveal the derelictions in men's souls. "At this moment there was a terrific bang at the front door, almost enough to break it down." Second major entrance. Rogojin marches in, attended by a dozen ruffians and hangers-on whom Dostoevsky designates as a "chorus." Rogojin calls Gania "Judas" (we are meant to settle firmly in our minds the symbolic values associated with Muishkin). Rogojin has come to exploit Gania's avarice, to "buy" Nastasia from him. And it is part of the subtle texture of the plot that if Gania "sells" Nastasia for Rogojin's silver, he will have betrayed Muishkin. It should be noted that our difficulties in perceiving all the levels of action at a first reading are strictly comparable to the difficulties we experience when first hearing a complex piece of dramatic dialogue in the theatre.

Rogojin's tone alternates spasmodically between animal pride and a kind of sensuous humility. "Oh, Nastasia Philipovna! don't turn me out!" She assures him "with a haughty, ironical expression" that she has no intention of marrying Gania, but goads him nevertheless into offering one hundred thousand rubles for her. Horrified at this "auction," Gania's sister denounces Nastasia as a "shameless creature." Gania loses his head and is about to strike Varvara (Varia):

but suddenly another hand caught his. Between him and Varia stood the Prince.

"Enough—enough!" said the latter, with insistence, but all of a tremble with excitement.

"Are you going to cross my path for ever, damn you!" cried Gania; and loosening his hold on Varia, he slapped the Prince's face with all his force.

Exclamations of horror arose on all sides. The Prince grew pale as death; he gazed into Gania's eyes with a strange, wild, reproachful look; his lips trembled and vainly endeavoured to form some words; then his mouth twisted into an incongruous smile.

"Very well—never mind about me; but I shall not allow you to strike her!" he said, at last, quietly. Then, suddenly he could bear it no longer, turned to the wall and murmured in broken accents: "Oh! how ashamed you will be of this afterwards!"

This is one of the very great passages in *The Idiot*—indeed, in the history of the novel. But how closely can particular effects be scrutinized when they depend, as in a poem or a piece of music, on no less than the work as a whole?

With the instinct of a tortured animal, Gania has seen that his real adversary is the "idiot" and not Rogojin. What is involved in the clash between them—though neither Gania nor Muishkin may be fully conscious of it—is not Nastasia but Aglaya. The Prince accepts the slap as Christ would, and Rogojin makes the symbol articulate by referring to him, a few moments later, as "a sheep." But although the Prince forgives, he cannot bear his own involvement in Gania's pain and humiliation. For through his insight into Aglaya he *is* involved. His possession of so much truth is like a touch of sin, and once more we note how the nearness of Rogojin sharpens Muishkin's intelligence. The misery that pushes him to the wall is subtly compounded of foresight into his own future agonies and of his feelings towards Gania. Nor should we miss the hint of epilepsy in his "strange, wild look" and trembling lips.

Nastasia has witnessed the incident. "New feelings" possess her (is Dostoevsky forcing our hand just a little?). Referring to the Prince, she exclaims: "I really think I must have seen him somewhere!" This is a wonderful touch: it points to the "idiot's" mysterious kinship with that other Prince whom Nastasia has seen gazing from the ikons. Muishkin asks her whether she is really the sort of woman she is pretending to be. Nastasia whispers to him that she is not and turns to go. In that instant she is probably saying the truth. But it is only part of the truth. Rogojin knows the rest—in the dialectics of his relationship to Muishkin it is necessarily true that each of the two men arrives at contrary halves of wisdom. He knows what else there is in Nastasia and values it at one hundred thousand rubles. Accompanied by his minions, he storms out to get the money.

Remembering the urgency and pressure under which this first part of *The Idiot* was composed, one marvels at the precision and surety of Dostoevsky's treatment. The sudden gesture—Gania slapping the Prince, Shatov slapping Stavrogin, Zossima bowing to Dimitri Karamazov—is language made irrevocable. After the gesture comes the momentary silence, and when the dialogue resumes, the tone-values and our sense of the relations between the characters have altered. The tension is so great that there is always the risk that speech will exceed itself and pass into motion—that it will become the blow, the kiss, or the epileptic fit. Words charge their context with energy and latent violence. The gestures, in turn, are so startling that they reverberate inside the language, not like a physical reality narrated at some remove, but like an explosive image or metaphor unleashed by the force of syntax (and I take syntax in its largest implications). Hence the equivocal and hallucinatory air of Dostoevsky's rendering of physical action. Are we confronted with matters spoken or performed? Our hesitations confirm the extent to which a Dostoevskyan dialogue is made dramatically concrete. It is of the essence of drama that speech should move and motion speak.

I pass over further incidents and complications involving Gania's family. Towards half past nine in the evening, Prince Muishkin arrives at Nastasia's soirée. Though uninvited, he is drawn to the maelstrom. General Epanchin, Totski, Gania, Ferdishenko, and other guests are waiting tensely for Nastasia's decision regarding the marriage. Somewhere in the city Rogojin is prowling about and drumming up a small fortune. Nastasia's house is characteristically Dostoevskyan and "on stage": it seems to have only three walls and is literally open to the riotous assault of Rogojin or the silent invasion of the Prince. To pass the heavy time, Ferdishenko proposes "a new and most delightful game" (which was, in fact, played occasionally during the 1860's). Each guest must, in turn, relate "the very worst action" of his life. Totski shrewdly notes that this curious idea—Dostoevsky used it again in his Gothic tale, *Bobok*—is "only a new way of boasting." Ferdishenko draws the first lot and recollects a petty theft for which he allowed the blame to be put on an unfortunate housemaid. This theme haunted the novelist; it reappears, in a more odious guise, in *The Possessed*. Excited by Nastasia's promise that she will reveal "a certain page" out of her own life, Epanchin tells his story. It derives fairly obviously from Pushkin's *The Queen of Spades*, which had influenced Dostoevsky's previous novel, *The Gambler*. Totski then confesses to a cruel practical joke that led, indirectly, to the death of a young friend.

The three stories thicken the atmosphere of hysterical candour in which Dostoevsky can render the approaching climax believable; they are allegories and speculations in miniature on the larger treatment of good and evil in the novel as a whole; and they bridge what is, unavoidably, a tense moment of inaction. But when Totski has concluded, Nastasia, instead of taking her turn in the game, interrogates Muishkin point-blank:

"Shall I marry or not? As you decide, so shall it be." Totski grew white as a sheet. The general was struck dumb. All present started and listened intently. Gania sat rooted in his chair.

The prose between the lines of dialogue is a kind of scenic short-hand. It merely fixes the actors in position. As Merezhkovsky says: "The story is not quite a text, but, as it were, small writing in brackets, notes on the drama . . . it is the setting up of the scenery, the indispensable theatrical paraphernalia—when the characters come on and begin to speak then at length the piece begins." [2]

"Marry whom?" asked the Prince, faintly.

"Gavrila Ardalionovich Ivolgin," said Nastasia, firmly and evenly. There were a few seconds of dead silence. The Prince tried to speak, but could not form his words; a great weight seemed to lie upon his breast and suffocate him.

"N-no! don't marry him!" he whispered at last, drawing his breath with an effort.

Nastasia explains that she is submitting her fate to the "idiot" because he is the first man she has ever encountered endowed "with real truthfulness of spirit." Though essential to the paradox of the novel—the equation between innocence and wisdom—her pronouncement is unjust. Rogojin's integrity is the counterpart of Muishkin's, and it is nearly as absolute. His

[2] D. S. Merezhkovsky: *Tolstoi as Man and Artist, with an Essay on Dostoïevski* (London, 1902).

Christian name, Parfen, signifies "virginal." On hearing the Prince's injunction, Nastasia throws off her bonds. She will not take Totski's money, she will not accept General Epanchin's pearls—let him give them to his wife! Tomorrow she will start on a new existence:

At this moment there was a furious ring at the bell, and a great knock at the door—exactly similar to the one which had startled the company at Gania's house in the afternoon. "Ah, ah! here's the climax at last, at half-past twelve!" cried Nastasia Philipovna. "Sit down, gentlemen, I beg you. Something is about to happen."

The events which began at nine o'clock that morning are moving towards a melodramatic *dénouement*. What follows (it justifies one further stretch of close reading) is among the most theatrical episodes in modern fiction.

Rogojin enters, "wild" and "dazed." He has brought the hundred thousand rubles, but quails before Nastasia "as though awaiting his sentence." To her mind his crude offer has the virtue of sincerity. It is the naked statement of a sexual code which Totski and Epanchin live by but seek to gloss over with polished manners. Dostoevsky's social critique here is the more telling for being implicit. Nastasia turns on Gania. His servility, marked by the fact that he sits paralysed in his chair, infuriates her. To make Gania's acquiescence in the proposed marriage even more abject, she calls herself "Rogojin's mistress." "Why even Ferdishenko wouldn't have me!" she exclaims. But that Micawber has a piercing eye. He tells her quietly that Muishkin would. He is right. The Prince proposes:

". . . I consider that you would be honouring me, and not I you. I am a nobody. You have suffered, you have passed through hell and emerged pure, and that is very much."

Nastasia's retort that such ideas come "out of novels" and that Muishkin needs "a nurse, not a wife," is accurate and should be decisive. But it passes unnoticed in the mounting tumult. To substantiate the Prince's offer, Dostoevsky resorts to a device which has become stale even in the popular melodrama of the day. Pulling a letter out of his pocket, the "idiot," who in the morning had to borrow twenty-five rubles from the Epanchins, discloses that he is heir to a vast fortune. Indefensible on thematic or rational grounds, the stroke is nevertheless "brought off" by the sheer intensity of the surrounding medium. The atmosphere is so extreme, chaos has drawn so near the limits of behaviour, that we accept the metamorphosis of pauper into prince as we would a turn in a revolving stage.

Nastasia kindles into a blaze of laughter, pride, and hysterics—the discriminations between nuances of feeling being maintained throughout. She is beside herself with apparent delight at becoming a princess who can avenge herself on Totski or have General Epanchin shown to the door. Dostoevsky is unmatched in this kind of half-delirious monologue during which a human being dances around its own soul. At last Rogojin understands, and the sincerity of his lust is unmistakable:

He wrung his hands; a groan made its way up from the depth of his soul.
"Surrender her, for God's sake!" he said to the Prince.

Muishkin knows that Rogojin's passion is stronger and, in a physical sense, more authentic than his. But once again he addresses Nastasia:

"You are proud, Nastasia Philipovna, and perhaps you have really suffered so much that you imagine yourself to be a desperately guilty woman."

But perhaps not. Her sense of abjection seems in excess of the facts. The Prince wonders whether pride does not achieve its most refined pleasures in self-damnation and thus touches on one of the leitmotifs in Dostoevskyan psychology. The tranquil clarity of his remark brings Nastasia out of her ecstatic unreason. She leaps up from the sofa:

". . . You thought I should accept this good child's invitation to ruin him, did you?" she cried. "That's Totski's way, not mine. He's fond of children."

She is referring, with cruel malice, to the fact that Totski first showed erotic interest in her when she was a young girl. Proclaiming that she has no sense of shame left, that she has been "Totski's concubine," Nastasia bids the Prince marry Aglaya. Dostoevsky does not tell us how she could have arrived at this idea. Is she yielding, in blind lucidity, to her loathing of Gania? Has she heard anything about the impression which the "idiot" made on the Epanchin household? We do not know. We accept the fact that in the rage of action the characters experience moments of total insight. Language itself is pouring out its secrets.

Rogojin is convinced that he has won the bout and parades around his "queen" breathless with weariness and desire. Muishkin is weeping and Nastasia seeks to comfort him by dramatizing her own vileness. But she has yet to settle with Gania and his patrons. She has crawled through such foulness of spirit this night that she must compel another human being to crawl bodily. She will throw Rogojin's hundred thousand rubles in the fire. If Gania retrieves them they are his.

Dostoevsky conjured up the ultimate powers of darkness, and the scene makes harrowing reading. Perhaps the germ of it lay in Schiller's ballad *The Glove*. Curiously enough, it had its analogue in an incident which actually took place in the house of a *demi-monde* in Paris in the 1860's. This lady received an admirer, whom she despised, bade him form a circle of thousand-franc bills, and allowed him to make love to her only as long as the blaze lasted.

Nastasia's guests are mesmerized by the ordeal. Lebedev cannot control himself. He will thrust his whole head into the fire. He cries: "I have a poor lame wife and thirteen children. My father died of starvation last week." He is lying; but his voice is like the wail of the damned. Gania stands motionless, with an imbecile smile on his "white, death-like lips." Only Rogojin exults; he sees in this torture proof of Nastasia's wild spirit and eccentric sovereignty. Ferdishenko offers to pull the money out of the fire with his teeth. Through its strong suggestion of animalism, this proposal enforces the moral and psychological bestiality of the scene. Ferdishenko seeks to draw Gania towards the fire, but Gania thrusts him aside and starts to leave the room. After taking a few steps he faints. Nastasia retrieves the pack of rubles and proclaims that they are his. The act and the agony (our theories of drama are founded on the radical kinship of the two words) draw to a close. Nastasia cries out: "Off we go, Rogojin! Good-bye, Prince. I have seen man for the first time in my life."

I cite this phrase in challenge to my own purpose. Nowhere in the novel is an attempt to work through translations shown to be more inadequate. Both the Constance Garnett version and the French text prepared by Mousset, Schloezer, and Luneau read: "I have seen *a* man for the first time in my life." This yields a satisfactory meaning: Nastasia is paying homage to Prince Muishkin; compared to him, other human beings strike her as brutish and incomplete. The alternative reading (suggested to me by a Russian scholar) offers richer and more pertinent implications. In this lurid night, Nastasia has literally seen *man* for the first time. She has witnessed extremes of nobility and corruption; the range of potentialities in human nature has been defined for her.

Nastasia and Rogojin rush out amid clamorous farewells. Muishkin hurries after them, leaps into a sledge, and starts in pursuit of the fleeing troikas. Epanchin, whose crafty spirit is beginning to ponder the Prince's wealth and Nastasia's imperious hint that he should marry Aglaya, seeks in vain to hold him back. The tumult and the chaos recede. In one of those epilogues in early dawn characteristic of romantic stagecraft, Totski and Ptitsin wander home discoursing on Nastasia's extravagant behaviour. As the curtain falls, Gania is seen lying on the floor with the charred money beside him. The three protagonists in the drama are racing on the road to Ekaterinhof and the troika bells fade in the distance.

Such are Prince Muishkin's first twenty-four hours in St. Petersburg. I add, without seeking to judge whether the fact is relevant, that this part of *The Idiot* was written while the novelist was suffering under two particularly violent attacks of epilepsy.

Even a partial study of the text demonstrates that Dostoevsky thought the dramatic mode to be the closest to the realities of the human condition. I shall try, subsequently, to narrow this postulate by showing how he realized his tragic point of view through the strategies and conventions of melodrama. But the main tenets are apparent in this first portion of *The Idiot*. The primacy of dialogue is established. The "episodic climaxes" (to use Allen Tate's expression) are similarly arrived at: in both Gania's house and at Nastasia's soirée the elements of action and rhetoric are identically disposed. We find a chorus, two major entrances, a culminating gesture—the slap and the ordeal by fire —and an exit contrived to arrest the momentum of the drama with the utmost finality. In its directness and fulness of energy (which, as Russian critics would have us bear in mind, is not the same thing as verbal grace) the Dostoevskyan dialogue corresponds to the sensibilities and traditions of the theatre. "At times," notes Merezhkovsky, "it seems as if he did not write tragedy only because the outward form of epic narration, that of the novel, was by chance the prevailing one in the literature of his day, and also because there was no tragic stage worthy of him, and what is more, because there were no spectators worthy of him." [3] I would quarrel only with the term "epic narration."

Dostoevsky's use and mastery of dramatic means lead to the comparison between his genius and Shakespeare's. It is a difficult comparison to sustain unless

[3] Ibid.

one works backward from the effect and concedes, at the outset, the immense difference in specific media. What one implies, I take it, is that Dostoevsky achieved through his special handling of dramatic modes concrete tragic situations and degrees of insight into human motives which recall to our minds Shakespearean achievements more than they do those of other novelists. And, keeping in focus the strict incomparability of Shakespearean verse and Dostoevskyan prose, one can maintain that to both writers dialogue was the essential medium of realization. The comparison with Shakespeare is one which the novelist would have valued. He wrote in the notebooks for *The Possessed* that Shakespeare's "realism"—like his own—was not restricted to mere imitations of daily life: "Shakespeare is a prophet, sent by God, to proclaim to us the mystery of man and of the human soul." Doubtless, this judgment hints at Dostoevsky's image of himself. The contrast with Tolstoy's condemnation of Shakespeare is, in every respect, illuminating.

Similarly apt—but no more so—are the analogies proposed between Dostoevsky and Racine. It is true of both writers that they expressed through dramatic action and dramatic rhetoric a comparable acuity of insight into the shadings and multiplicities of consciousness. Racine and Dostoevsky gave concrete dramatic embodiment to their rare science of the mind and were able to project through clashes of reason and argument their suppositions about the masks of the unconscious.

Such comparisons derive their imperfect authority from a recognition that there are in the novels of Dostoevsky values, conceptions, proceedings of action of a type that had declined from western literature after the passing of Elizabethan and Neo-classical tragedy. Dostoevsky can be regarded as a "dramatist" in the eminent tradition. He possessed an unfailing instinct for the dramatic theme. He sacrificed to unity of action the minor claims of verisimilitude. He advanced in sovereign disregard of melodramatic improbabilities, coincidences, grossness of device. All that mattered was the truth and splendour of human experience in the ardent light of conflict. And direct utterance, spirit to spirit or soul to self, was his constant medium.

IV

Structurally, *The Idiot* is the simplest of Dostoevsky's novels. It proceeds with diagrammatic clarity from the prologue and from Muishkin's prophecy of doom to the actual murder. The novel poses, in exemplary directness, the ancient riddle of the tragic hero. The Prince is both innocent and guilty. He confesses to Evgenie Pavlovich: "I am guilty and I know it—I know it! Probably I am at fault all around—I don't quite know how—but I am at fault no doubt." Muishkin's "crime" is the excess of compassion over love, for even as there is a blindness of love (*King Lear*), so there is a blindness of pity. The Prince "loves" both Aglaya and Nastasia, yet his love encompasses neither. As symbolic of the tragic drift of things, this theme of the dispersion of love among three personages fascinated Dostoevsky. It is set forth in the central plot of *The Insulted and the Injured* (a book which is in many ways a preliminary sketch for *The Idiot*) and it is explored more fully in *The Eternal Husband*, in *The Possessed*, and *The Brothers Karamazov*. Dostoevsky believed that it was possible to love two human beings with tremendous force and in a way which excluded neither. He perceived in this not a perversion but a heightening of the capacity for love. But if the quality of mercy is not strained through breadth of application, the quality of love is.

The presentation of these matters in a dramatic form, in a form in which direct speech and physical action are sole agents, creates obvious difficulties. In seeking to objectify the nature of Muishkin's love, in plotting for it appropriate dramatic enactments, Dostoevsky severed that love from its physical roots. The "idiot" is love incarnate, but in him love itself is not made flesh. At several points in the novel Dostoevsky comes very near to telling us straight out that Muishkin is an invalid in-

171

capable of sexual passion in any ordinary sense. Yet the implications are allowed to lapse from our awareness and from that of the other characters. Aglaya and Nastasia are, at various moments, conscious of the Prince's limitations; but at other times they are not and consider the possibility of marriage as self-evident. The ambiguity is complicated by the association of Muishkin with Christ. To that association the motif of immaculateness is essential. But if it were to be fully realized, we could not suspend disbelief in our reading of the plot. As Henri Troyat argues in his *Dostoïevski*, the Prince's impotence is rendered not so much through its specifically erotic implications as through a general incapacity for action: "When he tries to act he goes wrong. . . . He has not known how to adapt himself to the human condition. He has not succeeded in becoming a man."

This situation poses technical and formal problems which *The Idiot* does not wholly resolve. Cervantes came much nearer to a really convincing solution: the platonic nature of Don Quixote's love is an instance not of privation but of virtue in action; the "irreality" which qualifies Don Quixote's relations with other human beings is the positive medium of the fable and not, as in *The Idiot*, an occult principle which enters into the structure of the novel at arbitrary moments. Dostoevsky himself returned to the challenge in *The Brothers Karamazov*. Alyosha's transition from monkhood to the world is the counterpart in gesture to his psychological transformation; he moves from chastity to potential involvement. Having been both monk and man, he signifies to us a total humanity.

For a long time Dostoevsky could not decide on a proper conclusion to *The Idiot*. In one version Nastasia does marry Muishkin; in another she escapes to a brothel on the eve of the marriage; in a third she marries Rogojin; in yet another variant she befriends Aglaya and furthers her marriage to the Prince; there are even indications that Dostoevsky explored the possibility of making Aglaya Muishkin's mistress. These indecisions point to the profound liberality of his imagination. In contrast to Tolstoy, whose relentless and omniscient control over his personages is metaphoric of God's governance of man, Dostoevsky, like all genuine dramatists, seemed to listen with an inward ear to the independent and unforeseeable dynamics of action. As we follow him through his notebooks, we observe Dostoevsky allowing his dialogues and confrontations to evolve out of their own integral laws and potentialities. Michelangelo spoke of liberating form out of the marble in which it perfectly inhered. What were to him the grain and imperceptible convolutions of matter, the energies and affirmations latent in a dramatic character were to Dostoevsky. At times the play of forces is so free that we feel a certain ambiguity of intent (are the half-finished backs of the reclining figures in the Medici Chapel those of men or of women?). In rereading a novel by Dostoevsky, as in seeing a long-familiar play freshly produced, the sense of the unexpected renews itself.

Thus, the tension in a Dostoevskyan scene derives from the fact that alternative resolutions and the interplay between them literally surround the text. The characters seem admirably free from their creator's will and our own previsions. Let us consider the episode in Nastasia's house in which the four "principals" are crucially gathered and compare it with the great quartet at the climax of Henry James's *The Golden Bowl*.

In his distinguished reading of that novel, Marius Bewley points to the explicitly theatrical organization of the encounter between Maggie and Charlotte on the terrace at Fawns. Rightly, he adduces the superb economy of the thing and cites the undertones of formal ritual which James deepens by his covert reference to the betrayal of Christ in another garden. There are fascinating areas of comparison with *The Idiot*. In both instances two women engage in a duel whose issue must, in effect, determine their lives. In both scenes the two men at stake are tremendously present and yet immobile. They define the terrain on which the match is fought. They are like armed seconds desperately involved but momentarily neutral. Both novelists set their stage with great care. James characterizes Maggie's state of mind as that "of a tired actress"; he refers to the personages as "figures rehearsing some play" and gives the scene its mimetic intensity by having the two women meet outside a lit window through which they observe the two men. The chapter is organized around the duality of light and dark; Charlotte's advance—"the splendid shining supple creature was out of the cage"—is marked by her transition from streaks of illumination to zones of shadow. Dostoevsky hints at the same polarity: Aglaya is clad "in a light mantle" whereas Nastasia is all in black. (A similar clash between "raven" and "blond" defines the conflict in the climactic scene of Melville's *Pierre*—and there, too, we see a quartet of characters in crucial juxtaposition.) James comments:

There reigned . . . during these vertiginous moments that fascination of the monstrous, that temptation of the horribly possible, which we so often trace by its breaking out suddenly, lest it should go further, in unexplained retreats and reactions.

But whereas Maggie, by not deflecting "by a hair's breadth" into sincerity, avoids "the monstrous," Nastasia and Aglaya yield to "that temptation of the horribly possible." They taunt each other into the kind of half-truths out of which there is no retreat but to disaster.

Nastasia's mood varies abruptly throughout the scene: it moves from asperity to amusement and from pathos to insane rage. Dostoevsky conveys the enormous wealth of possibilities latent in the encounter. We come to realize that it could turn in a number of totally different directions and that the violences of rhetoric which lead to catastrophe could—but for a final twist—have led to reconciliation. In the complex of energies, the dialogue acts as a dominant; but above and below it we should hear those other notes which Dostoevsky struck in his successive drafts and which the characters continue to strike in their integral freedom. (We speak, do we not, of a "living text"?)

Aglaya has come to tell Nastasia that Muishkin is attached to her solely out of compassion:

"When I asked him about you, he told me that he had long since ceased to love you, that the very recollection of you was a torture to him, but that he was sorry for you; and that when he thought of you his heart was pierced. I ought to tell you that I never in my life met a man anything like him for noble simplicity of mind and for boundless trustfulness. I guessed that anyone who liked could deceive him, and that he would immediately forgive anyone who did deceive him; and it was for this that I grew to love him. . . ."

Though her love for the Prince had shown itself during his epileptic fit at the Epanchins', this is the first time she has formally declared it. The echo from Othello's address to the Senators is deliberate; in his drafts Dostoevsky records that Aglaya's declaration should convey something of the Moor's serene simplicity. But in both instances simplicity borders on blindness. Muishkin is more greatly deceived by himself than by others; the separation in him of love from pity is too unstable to support Aglaya's lucid portrayal. Being the riper woman, Nastasia knows this and will exploit it brilliantly. Hence her insistence that Aglaya should continue speaking. She divines that the young girl will literally "talk herself" into an obscuring frenzy. Aglaya plunges into the trap laid for her by Nastasia's silence. She assaults Nastasia's private life and charges her with living in idleness. This irrelevant thrust, like a sudden imprecision of swordsmanship, allows Nastasia her revenge. She ripostes: "And do you not live in idleness?"

This brings to the fore the social critique latent but undeveloped in *The Idiot*. Nastasia suggests that Aglaya's purity is dependent on her wealth and caste. She implies that her own degradation arose out of social circumstance. Driven by mounting anger and by awareness that she is no longer on firm ground, Aglaya hurls the name of Totski at her rival. Nastasia now blazes into fury, but it is the fury of reason and she swiftly masters the debate. Aglaya shouts: "If you had cared to be an honest woman, you would have gone out as a laundress." The overtones of "laundress" in colloquial Russian and Dostoevsky's handling of the phrase in his notebooks suggest that Aglaya's onslaught is specific and savage. She seems to be equivocating on the idea of a brothel; if Nastasia were honest she would live out her role to the full. The stroke is sharpened when we recollect that Nastasia herself had predicted she might become a "laundress" in the wild gaiety of her flight with Rogojin.

But Aglaya has exceeded measure. Muishkin cries out in deep distress: "Aglaya, don't! This is unfair." His cry is the signal for Nastasia's victory. With that completeness of realization which always leaves one awestruck, Dostoevsky adds in the next sentence that "Rogojin was not smiling now; he sat and listened with folded arms, and lips tight compressed." Goaded by Aglaya, Nastasia is impelled towards a triumph which she did not foresee and may not even have desired. She will tear Muishkin from General Epanchin's daughter. In so doing, she signs her own death warrant. Here again a tragic philosophy of experience predominates: in the great duels of tragedy there are no victories, only diverse orders of defeat.

Nastasia passes to the attack. She tells Aglaya why this whole intolerable scene has come about:

"You wished to satisfy yourself with your own eyes as to which he loves best, myself or you, because you are fearfully jealous."

"He has told me already that he hates you," murmured Aglaya, scarcely audibly.

"Perhaps, perhaps! I am not worthy of him. I know. But I think you are lying all the same. He *cannot* hate me, and he cannot have said so."

She is right, and Aglaya's falsehood (in which weakness is so manifest) prompts Nastasia to exhibit her powers. Momentarily, she bids the girl take Muishkin and leave. But vengeance and a kind of desperate caprice prevail. She commands the Prince to choose between them:

> Both she and Aglaya stood and waited as though in expectation, and both looked at the Prince like mad women.
> But he, perhaps, did not understand the full force of this challenge; in fact, it is certain he did not. All he could see was the poor despairing face which, as he had said to Aglaya, "had pierced his heart for ever." He could bear it no longer, and with a look of entreaty, mingled with reproach, he addressed Aglaya, pointing to Nastasia the while:
> "How can you?" he murmured; "she is *so* unhappy."
> But he had no time to say another word before Aglaya's terrible look bereft him of speech. In that look was embodied so dreadful a suffering and so deadly a hatred, that he gave a cry and flew to her; but it was too late.

For sharpness of crisis and totality of resolution, there is little to choose between James and Dostoevsky. But the effect of the two scenes is entirely different. When Maggie and Charlotte move back into the light and are joined by the two men, it is James's resistance to melodrama which achieves a sense of persuasive reality. Pressures long accumulated and detailed for us in the course of minute analysis have been released through the narrowest of channels. We hold our breath lest either of the two women should deviate, even for an instant, into one of the modes of rhetoric or gesture lying outside the exact range of the Jamesian manner. Nothing of the kind occurs, and our response is of a musical or architectural order; a series of harmonic patterns have been resolved within the strict dictates of the form; an area in space and light has been defined by the expected arch.

Dostoevsky, in contrast, yields to every temptation of melodrama. We do not know, until the last moment, whether Nastasia will surrender the Prince to her rival, whether Rogojin will intervene, whether the Prince will choose between the two women. There is warrant for each of these alternatives in the nature of the characters. And we are, I submit, meant to bear all these possibilities in mind as we read the text. In *The Golden Bowl* the impact depends on the exclusion of anything tangential; our satisfaction derives from realizing that "things could not have been otherwise." The climactic moments in *The Idiot* are moments of shock. Predestined (they exist only in the medium of language once set down), the characters nevertheless convey that sense of spontaneous life which is the particular miracle of drama.

The end of the scene is pure theatre. Nastasia is left mistress of the field:

"Mine, mine!" she cried. "Has the proud young lady gone? Ha, ha, ha!" she laughed hysterically. "And I had given him up to her! Why—why did I? Mad—mad! Get away, Rogojin! Ha, ha, ha!"

Aglaya has fled and Rogojin departs without uttering a word. The Prince and his "fallen angel" are left together in chaotic bliss. He is stroking Nastasia's face and hair as he would "a little child's." The image is that of a *pietà* reversed. It is now Nastasia, the incarnation of will and intelligence, who lies incoherent whereas the "idiot" watches over her in silent wisdom. As is often the case in tragedy, there is an interlude of peace—an armistice with disaster—between the events which have made disaster inevitable and the tragic end. Thus, Lear and Cordelia sit together joyfully among their murderous foes. No scene in fiction conveys more beautifully a sense of transitory calm after fury. Perhaps one should add that Dostoevsky preferred *The Idiot* to all his other works.

V

A study of the notes and drafts for the novel is profoundly revealing. In them we can trace the first shadowy impulses of memory and imagination. We can see the lists of names and places that novelists appear to use as formulas of incantation to conjure up the tentative daemons from whom characters evolve. We can follow the false directions, the premature solutions, and the process of laborious abandonment which precedes insight. In the notebooks of Henry James, the self and the critical awareness pursue a fascinating dialogue; but it is a dialogue which already shows the stamp and finish of art. In the dossiers of papers, notebooks, and fragments published by Soviet libraries and archives, the raw materials of creation lie brute in the crucible. Like the letters and drafts of Keats or the corrected proof sheets of Balzac, these documents allow us to come nearer the mystery of invention.

The drafts for *The Idiot* are enlightening in many ways. Poised between abstraction and the jet of creative life, to use a phrase from D. H. Lawrence, Dostoevsky chanced on aphorisms of extraordinary power. In the first sketches towards the double figure of Muishkin-Stavrogin, we find this haunting remark: "Daemons have faith, but they tremble." It is here, or in the aphorismic statement "Christ did not understand women" (from the notebooks for *The Possessed*), that the comparison between Dostoevsky and Nietzsche is most apt. At times, Dostoevsky set down in the margin of his scenario affirmations of belief: "There is only one thing in the world: direct compassion. As to justice, that comes second." The notes for *The Idiot* are a constant reminder that the motifs and themes of Dostoevskyan fiction are ever recurrent (Proust maintained that all of Dostoevsky's novels could be entitled *Crime and Punishment*). As originally conceived, the "idiot" did not only have many of Stavrogin's qualities, but was secretly married and publicly insulted precisely as the hero of *The Possessed* would be. Even in some of the late versions, Muishkin is attended by a "club" of children. They play an important role in the plot and lead him to reveal his true nature. This is the story of Alyosha in the epilogue to *The Brothers Karamazov*. There appears to be a law of the conservation of matter in the poetics of creation as well as in nature.

Of particular interest are the glimpses we are allowed into the unconscious or semi-conscious stages of literary composition. For instance, we find Dostoevsky repeatedly jotting down the phrase "King of the Jews" or "Kings of Judea." We know that Petrashevsky, to whose circle the novelist had loosely adhered in 1848–9, designated James de Rothschild as "King of the Jews," and that it was to be the explicit ambition of the hero of *Raw Youth* to become "a Rothschild." In the context of the early drafts of *The Idiot* the words seem to refer to the usurers with whom Gania is involved. In the novel itself, Gania uses the expression only once, as symbolic of his financial ambitions. But, recurring as it did under Dostoevsky's pen, it probably led, by degrees below consciousness, to his recognition of the Christ motif.

It is through the drafts, moreover, that we can come to grips with the paradox of the "independent character." "Characters," writes Blackmur,

are an end-product, an objective form, of imaginative composition, and their creation depends on the deepest-seated of human convictions, so humanly full of error, by the occasion of genius so superhumanly right.[4]

The end-product and its objectivity are consequent upon a creative effort of great complexity. What appears, in final rendition, "so superhumanly right" is the result of a process of exploration and counter-attack engaging the genius of the writer and the nascent freedom or "resistance" of his material. Not only was the initial conception of *The Idiot*—the notes inspired by the crime of Olga Umetzky in September 1867—entirely different from subsequent versions, but the novel continued to alter in focus even after its first instalments had appeared in Katkov's *Russian Messenger*. The changes seem to have come from within. Dostoevsky was quite literally unprepared for the role assumed by Aglaya and struggled, through numerous drafts and re-examinations, against the fatality of Rogojin's crime.

[4] R. P. Blackmur: "The Everlasting Effort" (*The Lion and the Honeycomb*, New York, 1955).

In his inquiry *What Is Literature?* Sartre rejects the notion that an imagined character possesses, in any rational sense, "a life of its own":

Thus a writer never encounters anything save *his* knowledge, *his* will, *his* projects, in short himself; he grasps only his own subjectivity. . . . Proust at no time "discovered" the homosexuality of Charlus, as he had resolved upon the fact even before undertaking his book.

What evidence we have of the workings of imagination does not bear out Sartre's logic. Though a character is, indeed, a creation of a writer's subjectivity, he appears to represent that part of himself of which the writer lacks complete knowledge. Sartre is saying that the formulation of a problem—an algebraic equation with unknowns—necessarily entails its solution and the nature of that solution. But the process is none the less creative; the discovery of the "answer" is only in an ideal sense a tautology. "All things that surround us, and all things that happen to us," wrote Coleridge in an appendix to *The Statesman's Manual*, "have but one common final cause, namely the increase of consciousness in such wise that whatever part of the terra incognita of our nature the increased consciousness discovers, our will may conquer and bring into subjection to itself under the sovereignty of reason." Don Quixote, Falstaff, and Emma Bovary represent such discoveries of consciousness; it was in creating them, and in the reciprocal illumination of the creative act and the growth of the thing wrought, that Cervantes, Shakespeare, and Flaubert literally came to know "parts" of themselves previously unrealized. The German dramatist Hebbel asked how far any personage invented by a poet could be thought "objective." He gave his own reply: "So far as man is free in his relations to God."

The degree of Muishkin's objectivity, the extent to which he resisted Dostoevsky's total control, can be documented in the drafts. The problem of the Prince's impotence is one of indistinct perception on Dostoevsky's part. When we find him asking in the notebooks whether or not Aglaya is the "idiot's" mistress, the novelist is, in one mode of operation, asking a question of himself, but in another, and no less legitimate mode, he is interrogating his material. The unclarity of Muishkin's answer points to the necessary limitations of the dramatic method. A dramatist can know only "so much" about his personages.

With reference to Tolstoy, Henry James spoke of characters surrounded by "a wonderful mass of life." This mass both reflects and absorbs their vitality; it reduces the incursions of "the horribly possible." The dramatist works without this enveloping plenitude; he makes the air thin and narrows reality to an atmosphere of conflict in which language and gesture cry havoc. The very shapes of matter become insubstantial; all the fences are either low enough for the Karamazovs to leap over or have loose boards through which Pyotr Verkhovensky can steal on his sinister errands. To combine such primacy of action with a detailed and cogent presentation of complex personalities is difficult enough in the drama (witness what Eliot terms the "artistic failure" of *Hamlet*). It is even more difficult through the medium, however "dramatized," of narrative prose. Constantly, the leisures of prose, the fact that we *read* a novel, put it aside, and pick it up in a different mood (none of which occurs in the theatre), imperil the sense of continuous action and unflagging tension on which a dramatic formula such as Dostoevsky's relies.

To show how he resolved some of the difficulties, I propose to look at the sixty culminating hours in *The Possessed*. "All that night, with its almost grotesque incidents and the terrible dénouement that followed in the early morning, still seems to me like a hideous nightmare," observes the narrator. (In this novel we have an individualized narrator by whom the action is perceived and recollected. This further complicates the task of dramatic presentation.) Throughout the wild and confused happenings which follow on this opening statement, Dostoevsky will maintain a tone of nightmarish intensity. He must parry our sense of the implausible and do so over sixty pages of prose without the material aids to illusion available to a playwright.

Dostoevsky uses two exterior occurrences to condition our responses for the descent into chaos. They are the "literary quadrille" which concludes the Governor's miserable soirée and the fire in the riverside quarter. Both are integral to the narrative, but they also carry symbolic values. The quadrille is a *figura* (the old rhetoric had terms which we forgo at our peril) of the intellectual nihilism and irreverence of soul in which Dostoevsky discerned the principal cause of the coming upheavals. The fire is the herald of insurrection, a malignant, mysterious offence to the normality of life. Flaubert saw in the incendiarism of the Commune a delayed spasm of the Middle Ages; more perceptively, Dostoevsky recognized in the conflagrations symptons of vast social insurrections which would seek to raze the old cities and found instead the new city of justice. He linked the fires raging in Paris with the traditional Russian theme of a fiery apocalypse. Lembke, the Governor, rushes to the fire and exclaims to his terrified entourage: "It's all incendiarism! It's nihilism! If anything is burning, it's nihilism!" His "madness" fills the narrator with horror and pity; but it is, in fact, clairvoyance exaggerated to the point of hysteria. Lembke is right when he shouts in his delirious panic that "The fire is in the minds of men and not in the roofs of houses." That could stand in epigraph to *The Possessed*. The actions of the novel are gestures of the soul when it is in dissolution. The devils have entered into it, and by some obscure accident the sparks have leapt from men to mere buildings.

As the flames die down, Lebyadkin, his sister Marya, and their old servant are found murdered (murder being once again the conveyor of the tragic vision). There is every indication that at least one of the fires has been set to cover the crime. Using the flames as a beacon, at the centre of his space of action, Dostoevsky takes us to one of the windows of Stavrogin's house, Skvoreshniki. It is dawn and Liza is watching the fading glow. Stavrogin joins her. We are told only that some of the hooks on her dress are undone, but the whole night is in that detail. Dostoevsky's imagination is significantly chaste; like D. H. Lawrence, he saw erotic experience too intensely, too integrally not to realize that means more stringent than a portrayal of the thing itself must be used to evoke its meanings. It is when realism becomes brute depiction, as in much of Zola, that the direct representation of the erotic once again assumes importance. The result is an impoverishment of technique and sensibility.

The night has been disastrous. It has revealed to Liza Stavrogin's crippling inhumanity. Dostoevsky does not communicate the precise nature of the sexual failure, but the impact of utter sterility is drastically conveyed. This impact does violence to Liza; she confuses the motives which made her leap into Stavrogin's carriage the day before. She mocks his present gentleness, his intimations of decorous rapture: "And this is Stavrogin, 'the vampire Stavrogin,' as you are called. . . ." The taunt is double-edged; Liza has been bled of the will to live. But she has penetrated also to the core of Stavrogin. She knows that there is some appalling and yet ridiculous secret staining and corroding his mind:

"I always fancied that you would take me to some place where there was a huge wicked spider, big as a man, and we should spend our lives looking at it and being afraid of it. That's how our love would spend itself."

The dialogue is composed in semi-tones and fragments. But a great shrillness hangs in the air.

Pyotr Verkhovensky enters and Stavrogin says: "If you hear anything directly, Liza, let me tell you I am to blame for it." Pyotr seeks to refute Stavrogin's assumption of guilt. He launches into a monologue in which lies, dangerous half-truths, and malignant foresight are inextricably confounded. It is he who has "unwittingly" set the scene for the murders. But the fires are premature. Could some of his minions have taken matters into their own clumsy hands? And out tumbles one of Pyotr's hidden dogmas:

"No, this democratic rabble with its cells of five members is a poor foundation; what we want is one magnificent, despotic will, like an idol, resting on something fundamental and external."

Pyotr is endeavouring now to prevent that idol from self-destruction. Stavrogin cannot be allowed to take the murder upon himself; yet he must share the guilt. Thus he and Pyotr shall be entangled even more closely. The priest remains essential to his god (has he not created him?), but that god must endure in outward intactness. The nihilist's strategy toward Stavrogin is developed in one of the most astounding monologues in the novel, a *tour de force* of divided intent and duplicity of meaning. Pyotr shifts, through modulations of rhetoric, from the moral to the legal realities of innocence:

"A stupid rumour is soon set going. But you really have nothing to be afraid of. From the legal point of view you are all right, and with your conscience also. For you didn't want it done, did you? There's no clue, nothing but the coincidence. . . . But I am glad, anyway, that you are so calm . . . for though you are not in any way to blame, even in thought, but all the same. . . . And you must admit that all this settles your difficulties capitally: you are suddenly free and a widower and can marry a charming girl this minute with a lot of money, who is already yours, into the bargain. See what can be done by crude, simple coincidences—eh?"

"Are you threatening me, you fool?"

The agony in Stavrogin's question stems not from fear of blackmail; the threat lies in Pyotr's power to destroy the remnants of Stavrogin's self-awareness. The man is threatening to reshape the god after his own vile image. Stavrogin's fear of encroaching darkness—the metaphor of madness—is beautifully countered by Pyotr's rapid answer: "You are the light and the sun. . . ."

185

I would like to quote at greater length, but the essential point can, I think, be clearly made. The dialogue here operates through the same modes as in poetic drama. The "stichomythia" of Greek tragedy, the dialectic in the *Phaedo*, the Shakespearean soliloquy, the *tirade* of the Neo-classical theatre, are consummate strategies of rhetoric, dramatizations of discourse in which one cannot separate actual forms of expression from the entirety of meaning. Tragic drama is perhaps the most lasting and comprehensive statement of human affairs yet achieved by essentially verbal means. The modes of rhetoric which it employs are conditioned by the idea and material circumstances of the theatre. But they may be translated into settings that are not dramatic in the technical or physical sense. This happens in oratory, in the Platonic dialogues, in the dramatic poem. Dostoevsky translated the languages and grammars of drama into prose fiction. This is what we mean when we speak of Dostoevskyan tragedy.

Stavrogin tells Pyotr that "Liza guessed somehow during this night that I don't love her . . . which she knew all along indeed." The little Iago regards it all as "horribly shabby":

> Stavrogin suddenly laughed.
> "I am laughing at my monkey," he explained at once.

The phrase places the two men with cruel precision. Pyotr is Stavrogin's sordid familiar; he "apes" Stavrogin so as to sully or destroy the latter's image of himself (we may think of the role of the baboon in Picasso's famous series of drawings of artists and models). Pyotr pretends to have known all along that the night was a "complete fiasco." It delights him. His sadism— the sadism of the watcher—dwells on Liza's humiliation. Stavrogin's apparent impotence will make him more vulnerable to abjection. But Verkhovensky has underestimated the sheer weariness of his god. Stavrogin tells Liza the truth: "I did not kill them, and I was against it, but I knew they were going to be killed and I did not stop the murderers." His assumption of indirect guilt—a motif explored more fully in *The Brothers Karamazov*—enrages Pyotr. He turns upon his idol "muttering incoherently . . . and foaming at the mouth." He draws a revolver, but cannot kill his "prince." Out of his frenzy bursts a hidden truth: "I am a buffoon, but I don't want you, my better half, to be one! Do you understand me?" Stavrogin does, perhaps alone of all the characters. Pyotr's tragedy is that of any priest who has erected a deity in his own image, and it is a stroke of dramatic irony that Stavrogin should dismiss him with the words "Go to the devil now. . . . Go to hell. Go to hell." Instead, the buffoon avenges himself on Liza. She is rescued from his taunts by Mavriky Nicolaevich, her faithful admirer who has waited out the night in Stavrogin's garden. She goes with him to the scene of the murder.

They arrive when a large crowd is milling about and when suppositions about Stavrogin's role in the crime are at their fiercest. The scene is based on an actual mob demonstration—the first organized strike in modern Russian history. Liza is struck down and killed. The narrator comments that it "all happened entirely accidentally through the action of men moved by ill feeling yet scarcely conscious of what they were doing—drunk and irresponsible." But the vagueness of it merely strengthens our impression that Liza has sought death in a ritual act of expiation. She dies near the smouldering flames in which three other human beings had been sacrificed to Stavrogin's inhumanity.

From that harrowing dawn until nightfall, Pyotr rushes about seeking to persuade everyone that he has played a noble part in these events. At two o'clock news of Stavrogin's departure for St. Petersburg flashes through the town. Five hours later, Pyotr meets with his cell of conspirators. No one has slept for two nights, and Dostoevsky admirably suggests the consequent blurring of reason. Once more this small-town Robespierre cows his mutinous agents into obedience and compels upon them the necessity of murdering Shatov. But, inwardly, Pyotr is a hollow vessel; Stavrogin's flight has destroyed the pivot of his cold, mad logic. Pyotr leaves with one of his followers, and the manner of his going is a symbolic image of his state of mind. Literally, in the language of Kenneth Burke, it is the "dancing of an attitude":

Pyotr Stepanovich walked in the middle of the pavement, taking up the whole of it, utterly regardless of Liputin. . . . He suddenly remembered how he had lately splashed through the mud to keep pace with Stavrogin, who had walked, as he was doing now, taking up the whole pavement. He recalled the whole scene, and rage choked him.

Exasperated by Pyotr's contempt, Liputin blurts out his belief that "instead of many hundreds of secret cells in Russia we are the only one that exists, and there is no network at all." But Pyotr's tyranny has destroyed the will in lesser men and Liputin tags along like an angry dog.

The thirty-six hours remaining before Pyotr's departure witness the murder of Shatov, the suicide of Kirillov, the birth of Stavrogin's son, Lyamshin's access of folly, and the disintegration of the revolutionary group. This section of *The Possessed* contains some of Dostoevsky's highest achievements: the two encounters between Pyotr and Kirillov culminating in the latter's nightmarish death, Shatov's reunion with Marya and the reawakening of their love after the birth of her child, the actual assassination in the nocturnal park, and Poytr's hypocritical farewell to the most pathetic of the murderers, young Erkel. I shall consider some of these episodes in greater detail when dealing with the Gothic in Dostoevsky and when comparing Tolstoy's and Dostoevsky's images of God.

I want to draw attention now mainly to the feat of dramatic control and temporal organization which allows Dostoevsky to conduct his plot without causing confusion or disbelief. Lacking the traditional mirror for man which the rhythm of the seasons and the coordinates of normal life provide in the Tolstoyan epic, Dostoevsky makes a virtue of disorder. The frenzied happenings in the novel trace onto the surface of reality the patterns of chaos in the mind. In Yeats's terms, "the centre cannot hold" and the Dostoevskyan plot incarnates the forms of experience when "mere anarchy is loosed upon the world." The failure of tragedy took place, as Fergusson notes in his *Idea of a Theater*, when it became increasingly difficult for "artists, or anyone else, to make sense out of the human life they could actually see around them." Dostoevsky made of this difficulty a new focus of understanding. If there is no sense in experience, then that style of art which conveys the tragedy of disorder and of the absurd will come nearest to realism. To reject coincidences and extremes of tone would be to read into life a kind of harmony and respect for the probable which it simply does not have. Hence Dostoevsky unworriedly accumulates the unlikely on the fantastic. It is bizarre that Marya should return and bear Stavrogin's son on the eve of Shatov's death; it is implausible that none of Pyotr's terrified accomplices should have betrayed himself or his secret, or that Kirillov should not warn Shatov that there is something afoot. It is nearly incredible that Virginsky and his wife—it is she who delivers Marya's child—do not stop the crime once they both realize that Pyotr is lying about Shatov's alleged treason. Finally, it is difficult to believe in Kirillov's suicide after his experience of "illumination" and after Pyotr has told him of the intended murder.

But we do accept all these things as we accept the Ghost in *Hamlet*, the binding force of prophecy in *Oedipus*, *Macbeth*, and *Phèdre*, and the series of interlocking accidents and chance revelations in *Hedda Gabler*. For as Aristotle, Huizinga, and Freud have said (in very diverse contexts), the drama is related to the notion of games. Like a game it sets its own rules, and the determining canon is internal coherence. The validity of the rules can only be tested in the playing. Moreover, games and dramas are arbitrary delimitations of experience, and in so far as they delimit they conventionalize and stylize reality. Dostoevsky believed that his "true, deep realism" would, by virtue of contraction and intensification, portray the authentic meaning and temper of a historical era in which he saw the coming of the apocalypse.

Dryly, Dostoevsky records the chronology of pandemonium: Shatov is murdered at about seven o'clock; Pyotr arrives at Kirillov's at about one in the morning and his host kills himself at around two thirty; at five fifty Pyotr and Erkel arrive at the station; ten minutes later the nihilist enters a first-class compartment. It has been, in the words of the novelist, "a busy night." Possibly things could have happened at such a pace; probably not. But no matter; the sense of fatality and forward motion is maintained to the last—the train pulls out and gathers speed.

Any comprehensive view of the dramatic elements in Dostoevskyan fiction would have to deal also with the structure of *The Brothers Karamazov*. Indeed, that novel can be shown to have been conceived with articulate reference to *Hamlet*, *King Lear*, and Schiller's *Die Räuber*. At certain moments—for example, in Grushenka's cry that she will go to a nunnery—the Dostoevskyan text is a variation on a theme previously set out in drama. But these points have been examined in various studies on Dostoevsky and I prefer to come back to them, from a somewhat different angle, when discussing the Legend of the Grand Inquisitor.

What kind of dramatic vision most strongly influenced Dostoevsky? For if he is a "dramatist," he is also a dramatist of a certain school and period, and many of the motifs which strike us as arch-Dostoevskyan were, in fact, commonplaces of contemporary literary practice. Dostoevsky's "surrealism" ("I am called a psychologist," he observed in 1881. "That is erroneous. I am merely a realist in the higher sense") arose in part out of the matrix of his private experience. In part it was a necessary medium for his interpretation of God and of history. But it also embodied a major literary tradition with which many of us are no longer familiar.

In Dostoevsky's harrowed life, with its Siberian chapters, its epilepsy, its spells of destitution and excess, the world image of his novels was latent. Much of what appears strained and garish in the loves of Dostoevskyan characters portrays, with little embellishment, his own relations with Maria Issaïeva and Paulina Suslova. Episodes in the novels bearing all the marks of heightening and invention often turn out to be severely autobiographical: Dostoevsky suffered all those illuminations and partial deaths of the soul before a firing squad of which he later told and retold in the key of fiction. Or in another vein: Dostoevsky did faint in the drawing-room of the Vyelgorskys, in January 1846, under the bare impression of first meeting the famous beauty Seniavina. Even the Dostoevskyan dialogue—which is so expressly an enactment of dramatic purpose—was related to his personal habits, somewhat in the manner in which Coleridge's style and metaphysics were, according to Hazlitt, related to his meandering walk. Sophia Kovalevsky, the eminent mathematician, recorded an exchange between the novelist and her sister, whom he was wooing at the time:

"Where were you last night?" asks Dostoevsky crossly.
"At a ball," says my sister carelessly.
"And did you dance?"
"Naturally."
"With your cousin?"
"With him and others."
"And that amuses you?" Dostoevsky further inquires.
"For want of anything better, it does," she answers, and begins to sew again.
Dostoevsky regards her in silence for some moments.
"You are a shallow, silly creature," he suddenly declares.[5]

This "was the tone of most of their conversations," many of which ended up with Dostoevsky storming out of the house.

But the autobiographical strains in Dostoevskyan fiction should not, for all their importance, be exagger-

[5] "The Reminiscences of Sophie Kovalevsky" as cited in *Letters of Fyodor Michailovitch Dostoevsky*.

ated. Writing to Strakhov in February 1869, the novelist declared: "I have my own idea about art and it is this: What most people regard as fantastic and lacking in universality, *I* hold to be the inmost essence of truth." And he added: "is not my fantastic 'Idiot' the very dailiest truth?" Dostoevsky was a metaphysician of the extreme. No doubt, personal experience confirmed and sharpened his sense of the fantastic. But we must not identify a poetic method and a philosophy as tenacious and subtle as Dostoevsky's with the more restricted domain of biographical fact. To do so would be to fall into the bias of Freud's study of *The Brothers Karamazov*, in which the theme of parricide, which is an objective reality charged with dramatic and ideological content, is reduced to the shadowy level of personal obsession. Yeats asked: "How can we know the dancer from the dance?" We can do so only in part, but without this part no rational criticism would be possible.

Let us, for a moment, retain the Yeatsian image. The dancer brings to the dance his own specific individuality; no two dancers perform the same dance in exactly the same way. But beyond this diversity lies the stable and communicable element of choreography. In literature there are also choreographies—traditions of style and agreed convention, temporal fashions, values that penetrate the general atmosphere in which the particular writer is at work. Neither Dostoevsky's millennial eschatology nor the history of his life could wholly account for the technical manner of his performance. The novels of Dostoevsky would not have been conceived and written in the way they were had it not been for a literary tradition, for a highly articulate body of convention which arose in France and England in the 1760's, subsequently encompassed all of Europe, and finally reached the outermost frontiers of Russian literacy. *Crime and Punishment, The Idiot, The Possessed, Raw Youth, The Brothers Karamazov*, and the principal tales were heir to the Gothic tradition. From it derives the Dostoevskyan setting, the countenance and flavour of the Dostoevskyan world with its murders in garrets and nocturnal streets, its destitute innocence and rapacious lechery, its mysterious crimes and magnetic influences corroding the soul in the great night of the city. But because the Gothic is so pervasive, and because it has passed so readily into the conventions of modern *kitsch*, we have lost sight of its special tenor and of the tremendous role it played in determining the climate of nineteenth-century literature.

We realize that Victor Hugo's *Han d'Islande* (Stavrogin will visit Iceland), Balzac's *Peau de chagrin*, Dickens's *Bleak House*, the novels of the Brontës, the tales of Hawthorne and Poe, Schiller's *Räuber*, and Pushkin's *Queen of Spades* are Gothic in theme and treatment. We know that the novel of terror, refind and "psychologized," is alive in the art of Maupassant, in the ghostly tales of Henry James and Walter de la Mare. Literary historians tell us that, after the decline of formal tragedy, melodrama conquered the theatres of the nineteenth century and ultimately created the world picture of the film, of the radio play, and of popular fiction. In his essay on Wilkie Collins and Dickens, T. S. Eliot comments on "the replacement of dramatic melodrama by cinematographic melodrama"; in either instance the foundations are Gothic. We know, moreover, that the cosmology of melodrama —the world of daemonic heroes in ample capes, of maidens poised between torment and dishonour, of beggared virtue and malignant wealth, of gas lamps casting their sinister sheen over fog-bound alleys, of sewers from which underground men emerge in decisive moments, of philters and moonstones, of Svengali and the lost Stradivarius—represented the adaptation of the Gothic mode to the surroundings of the industrial metropolis.

In works as diverse as *Oliver Twist* and the tales of Hoffmann, in *The House of the Seven Gables* and Kafka's *Trial*, we can discern the Gothic substance. But only specialists are aware that works and authors now consigned to footnotes in literary history or to yellowing playbills in museums were the models of sensibility to which a Balzac, a Dickens, and a Dostoevsky looked for guidance. We have altogether lost the feel for a criterion of values by which Balzac—seeking to distinguish with high praise an episode in *The Charterhouse of Parma*—compared Stendhal's achievement to that of "Monk" Lewis and to "the last volumes of Ann Radcliffe." We forget that the "horrific romances" of Lewis and Mrs. Radcliffe were more universally read and did more to colour European taste in the nineteenth century than any other books with the probable exception of Rousseau's *Confessions* and Goethe's *Werther*. Dostoevsky recalled that during his childhood he "used to spend the long winter evenings before going to bed listening (for I could not yet read), agape with ecstasy and terror, as my parents read aloud to me from the novels of Ann Radcliffe. Then I would rave deliriously about them in my sleep." We have only to think of the heroine of Pushkin's tale *Dubrovsky* to document the fact that *The Romance of the Forest* and *The Mysteries of Udolpho* were well known on the frontiers of Russian Asia. Who today, reads Eugène Sue, whom Sainte-Beuve matched with Balzac "in fecundity and composition," or remembers that his *Wandering Jew* and his *Mystères de Paris* were translated into a dozen languages and devoured by literally millions of admirers from Madrid to St. Petersburg? Who, at present, could name the volumes of horror and romance that set Emma Bovary to mortal dreaming?

And yet, it was precisely these artisans of the horrible and the necromantic, these false antiquarians and revivers of a medieval world that had never existed, who scattered abroad the material out of which Coleridge wrought *The Ancient Mariner* and *Christabel*, who enabled Byron to compose *Manfred*, Shelley to write *The Cenci*, and Victor Hugo his *Notre-Dame de Paris*. The captains of today's literary industry, moreover, the purveyors of historical fiction and of the novel of crime, are the lineal descendants of Horace Walpole, Matthew Gregory Lewis, Ann Radcliffe, and Charles Maturin (the author of the immensely influential *Melmoth*).

Even the special genre of science fiction originated in the Gothic impulse of Mrs. Shelley's *Frankenstein* and in the Gothic imaginings of Poe.

Within the general tradition of Gothicism and melodrama there were distinct forms of sensibility. One of the major aspects has been examined in Mario Praz's *The Romantic Agony*. It originated with Sade and the eroticists of the eighteenth century and shaped a vast body of literature and graphic art to the time of Flaubert, Wilde, and d'Annunzio. Gothicism of this order is evident in Keats's *La Belle Dame sans Merci* and *Otho the Great*, in Flaubert's *Salammbô*, in the poetry of Baudelaire, in the more sombre moods of Proust, and, by virtue of travesty, in *The Penal Colony* of Kafka. Dostoevsky knew the works of Sade and such classics of lechery as *Thérèse Philosophe* (Montigny's book is referred to several times in the notes for *The Idiot* and *The Possessed*). He dwelt on themes which are "decadent" in the historical and technical sense. His "proud women" are related to the *femmes fatales* and vampires cited in *The Romantic Agony*. And there are sadistic elements in Dostoevsky's treatment of sexual crime. But we must be careful to distinguish his very special handling of the Gothic conventions and to understand the part of Dostoevskyan metaphysics behind the techniques of melodrama. If we do so, it becomes difficult to accept Praz's assertion that "from Gilles de Rais to Dostoevsky the parabola of vice is always identical."

Before looking, however, at these extreme and hermetic forms of Gothicism in the novels of Dostoevsky, I want to consider briefly the more "open" Gothic of nineteenth-century melodrama. In its eighteenth-century beginnings, the Gothic mode had been medieval and pastoral. It began, as Coleridge informed William Lisle Bowles in a letter written in March 1797, with

dungeons, and old castles, and solitary Houses by the Sea Side, and Caverns, and Woods, and extraordinary characters, and all the tribe of Horror and Mystery. . . .

But after the initial delight in exoticism and the archaic had worn thin, the setting shifted. What readers and spectators of the mid-nineteenth century knew and feared was the encroaching vastness of the city—particularly when the recurrent crises of the industrial revolution had filled it with dark slums and the visage of hunger. Nowhere did man's fall from the garden of grace seem more desperate and irremediable. Balzac's nocturnal Paris, the "sinister sunset" of the Victorian penny-dreadfuls, the Edinburgh of Mr. Hyde, the world of labyrinthine streets and tenements through which Kafka's K. is hurried to his doom—they are images of the same night-shrouded Babylon. But of all the chroniclers of the metropolis in its spectral and savage guises, Dostoevsky was pre-eminent.

The masters from whom he sought inspiration form a fascinating gallery. Even before the flowering of the Gothic, Restif de la Bretonne, a man neglected and difficult to value because the anger and variousness in him brought talent so near the pitch of genius, had realized that the city after sundown would be the *terra incognita* of modern society. In *Les Nuits de Paris* (1788) the principal elements of the new mythology are clearly set forth: the underworld and the prostitutes, the frozen garrets and the miasma of the cellars, the melodramatic contrariety between the faces at the window and the luxurious revels in the mansions of the rich. Restif, very much like Blake, saw concentrated in the nocturnal metropolis the symbols of financial and judicial inhumanity. He seized upon the paradox that the poor and the hunted are nowhere more "unhoused" than amid a huge armada of houses. In his wake came the night wanderers of Victor Hugo and Poe, the Opium Eater and Sherlock Holmes, the personages of Gissing and Zola, Leopold Bloom and the Baron de Charlus. In the opening pages of Dostoevsky's *White Nights of St. Petersburg*, Restif's influence seems to run strong.

Among Dostoevsky's forerunners was De Quincey. De Quincey had shown that even amid tenements and factories a poet's eye would chance upon moments of hallucination and fiery vision as authentic as any to be found in Gothic forests and the fabled Orient of romanticism. Together with Baudelaire, he resorted to the image of a city a fierce strangeness such as it once possessed in the imprecations of the apocalyptics against Nineveh and Bablyon. Dimitri Grigorovich's reminiscences tell us that *The Confessions of an English Opium Eater* was one of the favourite books of the young Dostoevsky. It left its mark on his early writings and on *Crime and Punishment*. Behind the figure of Sonia we may discern that of the "little Ann" of Oxford Street.

The influence of Balzac and Dickens is too obvious and far-reaching to require detailed proof. The Paris and London which Dostoevsky portrayed in his *Winter Notes on Summer Impressions* of 1863 (a book particularly favoured by Soviet commentators) were cities seen in the light of *Le Père Goriot*, *Les Illusions perdues*, and *Bleak House*.

But it was in Eugène Sue's *Les Mystères de Paris* (1842–3) that the urban Gothic reached its fullest expression. The work was praised by Belinsky and read as avidly in Russia as throughout Europe. In *Childhood, Boyhood and Youth*, Tolstoy recollects how he revelled in Sue's oddly powerful pot-boilers. Dostoevsky knew both *Les Mystères* and *The Wandering Jew*. Though he wrote to his brother, in May 1845, that Sue was "very limited in range," he learnt a good deal from him. This is particularly true of a number of episodes in Part I of *Raw Youth*—though it is difficult at times to distinguish parody from imitation. Sue carried to a new pathos that mingling of melodrama with philanthropy which characterizes the descent of nineteenth-century fiction into the lower depths. A brief quotation from the famous chapter "*Misère*" in *Les Mystères de Paris* conveys the prevailing tone:

The second of the two daughters . . . wracked with consumption, languidly leans her wretched little face, of a livid and morbid hue, against the frozen breast of her sister, aged five.

We shall find her languishing still in the house of Marmeladov and in the hovels among which Alyosha Karamazov pursues his ministry. Some of Sue's revolutionary statements are echoed nearly verbatim in Dostoevsky. Thus we see reproduced in *The Brothers Karamazov* the remark "Idle wealth . . . nothing distracts it from boredom . . . nothing guards it against anguished bitterness." There are analogies in subject matter and presentation between Fleur-de-Marie (in *Les Mystères*) and Dostoevsky's meek heroines, between Eugène Sue's account of the Marquis d'Harville's epilepsy and the dilemma of marriage in *The Idiot*.

But the Dostoevskyan inheritance went beyond instances of specific inspiration. It pertained to his entire career as a novelist. He was more profoundly versed in European literature and more immediately an heir to it than any of his major Russian contemporaries. It is difficult to imagine the kind of writer Dostoevsky might have become had he not known the works of Dickens and Balzac, of Eugène Sue and George Sand. They laid the indispensable groundwork for his conception of the infernal city; he took over from them the conventions of melodrama which he mastered and deepened in his turn. *Poor Folk*, *Crime and Punishment*, *Raw Youth*, *The White Nights of St. Petersburg*, and *The Insulted and the Injured* are part of a lineage that began with Restif de la Bretonne and with Le Sage's scrutiny of urban life in *Le Diable boiteux* (1707), and which persists in the American slum novel of our own day.

Tolstoy was most thoroughly at home in a city when it was being burnt down. Dostoevsky moved with purposeful familiarity amid a labyrinth of tenements, garrets, railway yards, and tentacular suburbs. The dominant note is sounded on the first page of *The Insulted and the Injured*: "All that day I had been walking about the town trying to find a lodging. My old one was very damp. . . ." Where Dostoevsky invokes natural beauty, the setting is urban:

I love the March sun in Petersburg. . . . The whole
street suddenly glitters, bathed in brilliant light. All the
houses seem suddenly, as it were, to sparkle. Their grey,
yellow and dirty-green hues for an instant lose all their
gloominess.

There are very few landscapes in Dostoevskyan fiction.
As Professor Simmons notes, a unique "bright out-of-
doors atmosphere" prevails in *The Little Hero*; significantly, Dostoevsky composed this story during his incarceration in St. Petersburg. Merezhkovsky is not
convincing when he argues that the novelist failed to
depict nature because he loved her too passionately.
Quite plainly, the pastoral lay to one side of Dostoevsky's range. When he does write a formal piece of natural description, in *Poor Folk*, the scene promptly turns
into one of Gothic terror:

Yes, truly I love autumn-tide—the late autumn when
the crops are garnered, and field-work is ended, and the
evening gatherings in the huts have begun, and every one
is awaiting winter. Then does everything become more
mysterious, the sky frowns with clouds, yellow leaves strew
the paths at the edge of the naked forest, and the forest
itself turns black and blue—more especially at eventide
when damp fog is spreading and the trees glimmer in the
depths like giants, like formless, weird phantoms. . . . Oh
horrors! Suddenly one starts and trembles as one seems to
see a strange looking being peering from out of the darkness of a hollow tree. . . . Then a strange feeling comes
over one, until one seems to hear the voice of some one
whispering: "Run, run, little child! Do not be out late,
for this place will soon have become dreadful! Run, little
child! Run!"

In the phrase "this place will soon have become dreadful" the Gothic mood and the techniques of melodrama are concentrated. Bearing in mind Dostoevsky's
indebtedness to both, let us turn to what is usually
taken to be a leitmotif in his writings—the enactment
of violence against children.

VII

It used to be thought that the nineteenth-century novel, at least until Zola, had avoided the more scabrous and pathological aspects of erotic experience. Dostoevsky was cited as a pioneer in the revelation of that underworld of repression and "unnatural" lust which Freud has so richly opened to our awareness. But the facts are different. Even in the "high" novel we find masterpieces such as Balzac's *Cousine Bette* and Henry James's *Bostonians* treating precarious sexual themes with free intelligence. Stendhal's *Armance* and Turgeniev's *Rudin* are tragedies of impotence; Balzac's Vautrin predates the Proustian *invertis* by nearly three quarters of a century and Melville's *Pierre* is an extraordinary, though unrealized, foray into the indirections of love.

All this is doubly true of the "lower" novel, of the Gothic *romans noirs* and the immense outpouring of serialized horror and romance. Sadism, perversion, unnatural guilt, incest, the attendant machinery of abduction and mesmerism, were hackneyed motifs. The bookseller's injunction to Balzac's Lucien de Rubempré, when the latter first arrives in Paris, "write something in the manner of Mrs. Radcliffe," was graven on the tables of literary law. Set plots involving distressed maidens, licentious oppressors, assassinations by gaslight, and redemption through love were held in readiness for the aspiring novelist. With genius he could turn them into *The Old Curiosity Shop* and *La Fille aux yeux d'or*; with talent, into *Trilby* and *Les Mystères de Paris*; with bare craft he could make of them one of the hundred thousand *romans feuilletons* now forgotten even by bibliographers. And it is because we have forgotten them that certain of Dostoevsky's recurrent themes and dramatic situations appear to us as unique and pathological. In fact, his plots—considered purely as raw material or as stories that can be summarized— were no less dependent on a body of contemporary tradition and practice than were those of Shakespeare.

To read into them matters of private obsession may be illuminating; but such a reading should follow, not precede, awareness of the public material at hand.

In many writers there are certain images or type-situations which recur openly or masked in most of their works. In the poems and dramas of Byron, for example, it is the hint of incest. As is well known, Dostoevsky alludes time and again to the sexual assault of an older man on a young girl or woman. To trace this theme through all of his writings and to show where it is present in covert symbolic forms would require a separate essay. It appears in Dostoevsky's first novel, *Poor Folk*, where the orphaned Varvara is persecuted by Monsieur Buikov. It is hinted at in *The Landlady*, a tale in which the relations between Murin and Katerina are shadowed by a mysterious sin. In *A Christmas Tree and a Wedding* it takes the transparent guise of an old man's attentions to an eleven-year-old girl whom he proposes to marry when she is sixteen. A similar motif is at work in that magnificent *nouvelle, The Eternal Husband*. The heroine of *Netochka Nezvanova*, a fragmentary novel, is morbidly attracted to her drunken stepfather. In *The Insulted and the Injured* the theme becomes dominant: Nellie (the Dickensian original being close by) is rescued melodramatically from violation, and Valkovsky is rumoured to have indulged in "secret debauchery" and "loathsome and mysterious vices." In the drafts for *Crime and Punishment*, Svidrigailov's confessions of assaults on young girls are lurid and repetitive:

Rape committed by chance. Tells suddenly as if nothing unusual were happening anecdotes in the manner of those about Reisler. About violating children, impassibly. . . . [Says about the boarder that her daughter had been raped and drowned, but does not say who, only later explains it is he.]
N.B. He had whipped her to death. . . .

In the definitive version, these details are obscured. Svidrigailov tells of his lesser debauches, and the theme of sexual assault is translated into Luzhin's courtship of

Dunia and Svidrigailov's attempt to seduce her. As we have seen, the early relations between Nastasia and Totski in *The Idiot* are founded on the erotic corruption of a young girl by a mature lover. This motif was to occupy a major place in *The Life of a Great Sinner*— the novel in five parts first projected at the end of 1868 and of which *The Possessed* and *The Brothers Karamazov* are fragments. In it, the hero was to torment a crippled girl and pass through a period of cruelty and perversion. Stavrogin's "Confession" embodies these ideas and is Dostoevsky's most famous rendering of sadistic sensuality. But even after he had so terribly portrayed the thing, it continued to haunt him. Acts of violence against children are catalogued and detailed in *The Diary of a Writer*. Versilov, in *Raw Youth*, is involved in secret inhumanities. Before turning to *The Brothers Karamazov*, Dostoevsky composed two tales in the pure Gothic manner: *Bobok* and *The Dream of a Ridiculous Man*. On the verge of suicide, the "ridiculous man" recalls his foul treatment of a little girl. Finally, we see the theme scattered throughout the last novel. Ivan Karamazov declares that bestialities committed upon children are the supreme charge against God. It is hinted that Grushenka was outraged when she was a young girl. Liza Hohlakova tells Alyosha that she dreams of crucifying a little child:

He would hang there moaning and I would sit opposite him eating pineapple *compote*. I am awfully fond of pineapple *compote*.

(A similar scene is actually described in Pierre Louÿs's *Aphrodite*.) Moreover, the notion of erotic submission and enforced sexuality is implicit in the narrative of Katya's visit to Dimitri Karamazov when the latter is rescuing her father from public disgrace.

Even during Dostoevsky's lifetime, it was rumoured that this recurrent motif sprang from some dark wildness in his own past. But there is not a shred of solid evidence to support such a contention. Later on, psychologists were drawn to the scent. Their findings may or may not throw light on the personality of the novelist; with respect to his works they are essentially irrelevant. The latter constitute an objective reality; they are conditioned by technique and historical circumstance. In plumbing the depths we might mar the surface; and to the precise degree that it is made formal and public, a work of art is a surface. The theme of erotic and sadistic persecution of children in Dostoevskyan fiction has articulate and generalized significance; and it is supported by a literary tradition whose influence on Dostoevsky can be amply documented.

Dostoevsky regarded the torment of children, and especially their sexual degradation, as a symbol of evil in pure and irreparable action. He saw in it the incarnation—some critics would call it "the concrete universal"—of unforgivable sin. To torture or violate a child is to desecrate in man the image of God where that image is most luminous. But even more dreadfully, it is to put in doubt the possibility of God, or, rigorously stated, the possibility that God retains some sense of affinity to His creation. Ivan Karamazov makes all this perfectly clear:

Can you understand why a little creature, who can't even understand what's done to her, should beat her little aching heart with her tiny fist in the dark and the cold, and weep her meek unresentful tears to dear kind God to protect her? . . . I say nothing of the sufferings of grown-up people, they have eaten the apple, damn them, and the devil take them all! But these little ones! . . . What good can hell do, since those children have already been tortured?

The doctrine that man falls from grace through the mere process of adulthood is strange theology; but Dostoevsky's meaning is explicit and we cannot respond to it adequately by seeking to ferret out the private obsessions which might lie entangled in its roots. What is at stake—as in the *Oresteia*, in the "storms" and "music" of Shakespeare's last plays, in *Paradise Lost*, and, so differently, in *Anna Karenina*—is the problem of theodicy. Tolstoy cites the promise that vengeance is the Lord's. Dostoevsky inquires whether such vengeance has any equity or meaning "since those children have already been tortured." We debase the great terror and compassion of his challenge by ascribing it to some unconscious rite of expiation.

As I have already mentioned, moreover, crimes against children are the actual and symbolic counterpart to parricide. Dostoevsky saw in this duality the image of the struggle between fathers and sons in the Russia of the 1860's. Shakespeare employs the identical device in Part Three of *Henry VI* to convey the internecine totality of the War of the Roses.

In choosing motifs of erotic cruelty to objectify his philosophic and moral vision, Dostoevsky was not yielding to some autonomous and eccentric impulse. He was working in the main of contemporary practice. In fact, by the time he began publishing his novels and tales, the persecution of children and the seduction of women through money or blackmail were commonplaces of European fiction. At the very outset of Gothicism, in *The Mysteries of Udolpho*, we find a virtuous and beautiful young woman being tormented and incarcerated in a dungeon. The Gothic panoply alters; dungeons become lonely manors, as in the melodramas of the Brontës, or hidden apartments, as in Balzac's *Duchesse de Langeais*. Equally widespread, as Praz points out, was the fable of the crippled child and the penniless orphan. Baudelaire's *mendiante rousse* and Tiny Tim, in the *Christmas Carol*, are distant cousins. Long before Dostoevsky, artisans of suspense and pathos had exploited the psychological truth that mutilation and helplessness can tempt depravity. If we seek for a rendering of this insight comparable to Dostoevsky's in tragic scope, we need only look to the etchings and late canvases of Goya.

Dostoevsky's persecuted maidens—Varvara, Katerina, Dunia, Katya—are variations, often fresh and subtle, on a hackneyed theme. Nellie, in *The Insulted and the Injured*, clearly reflects her Dickensian model. When

Raskolnikov protects Sonia and Prince Rodolphe rescues *la Goualeuse* (in *Les Mystères de Paris*), they are acting out a plot which universality had turned into ritual. Even where his purposes were most complex and radical, Dostoevsky adhered to the stock situations of contemporary melodrama. Old lechers wooing improvident girls, sons corrupted by debauchery, daemonic heroes haunted by the devil, "fallen women" with hearts of gold—these were the conventional cast in the melodramatic repertoire. Under the sorcery of genius, they became the *dramatis personae* of *The Brothers Karamazov*. And those who insist that the confessions of Svidrigailov and Stavrogin are unprecedented in literature and must stem from the nakedness of Dostoevsky's soul probably have not read Balzac's *La Rabouilleuse* (1842), in which an aged man's desires for a twelve-year-old girl are rather plainly set forth.

The same awareness of tradition should guide our understanding of Dostoevskyan heroes—those defeated angels in whom memories of salvation alternate with infernal malice. Their ancestry includes the Miltonic Satan, the fiery lovers of the Gothic novel and the romantic ballad, Balzac's "men of power" such as Rastignac and Marsan, Pushkin's Onegin, and Lermontov's Pechorin. Dostoevsky himself, it is interesting to note, considered Prince Andrew in *War and Peace* to be typical of the "dark heroes" of romantic mythology.

The early sketches of Svidrigailov read like a pastiche of Byron or Victor Hugo:

N.B. THE ESSENTIAL.—Svidrigailov is conscious of certain mysterious atrocities which he discloses to no one, but reveals through actions: his is a convulsive, bestial need to tear apart, to kill in cold passion. A wild beast. A tiger.

Valkovsky, in *The Insulted and the Injured*, marks a deepening of the Gothic tone. In him there is the clash of bestiality with self-contempt which Byron dramatized in Manfred, and Eugène Sue in his Wandering Jew:

I was a philanthropist. Well, I nearly flogged the peasant to death on his wife's account. . . . I did that when I was in my romantic stage.

. . . .

I'm even fond of secret, hidden vice, a bit more strange and original, even a little filthy for variety, ha ha ha!

Gothic villainy often broke out into wild laughter.

In one of the jottings of Thomas Lovell Beddoes, a purist of the Gothic mood, we find a formula which is exactly pertinent to Svidrigailov, Valkovsky, Stavrogin, and Ivan Karamazov:

their words should be dark, deep, and treacherous: with an occasional simulation of candour; varied by bursts of venomous sarcasm and unholy ridicule; with a roughness of phrase.

Rogojin is also very much a part of the Byronic legacy. He is a dark, melancholy youth who sacrifices all worldly goods to the absoluteness of his passion and who kills the thing he loves in a moment of adoration and hatred. His eyes possess magnetic virtues and haunt Muishkin during the latter's wanderings through St. Petersburg. This is a trait in the approved Gothic manner; even before Coleridge, the gift of mesmerizing sight—the glittering eye of the Ancient Mariner—had become one of the conventional marks of the romantic Cain.

But unquestionably it is in Stavrogin that we see traditional materials utilized with the greatest skill. Like all his tribe, he is preceded by rumours linking him with unspeakable crimes. And here Dostoevsky uses a very curious, though prevalent, motif. It is hinted that Stavrogin at one time belonged to a secret society of thirteen men who participated in satanic orgies. Such secret associations, usually numbering twelve or thirteen, reappear in Dostoevsky's work. Alyosha, in *The Insulted and the Injured*, for example, refers enthusiastically to a group of "about twelve fellows" gathered to discuss the questions of the day. The notion would have attracted the novelist through its religious symbolism—Christ and the apostles—and through its links with the Russian schismatic tradition. But again Dostoevsky's handling of the theme must not obscure its literary background. The Gothic novel abounds in tales of satanic covens and occult associations practising the black arts and exerting power over political and personal affairs. Kleist's *Kätchen von Heilbronn* is a famous example. Balzac devoted three melodramatic novels to the workings of such a league compacted to secrecy and mutual aid. United under the title *Histoire des Treize*, these books are landmarks for the penetration of Gothic sensibility into the fabric of "high" fiction. To obtain a contrasting and essentially classical perspective, one need merely recall the ironic treatment of Freemasonry in *War and Peace*.

Though he is accorded the title only once in the final text of *The Possessed*, the drafts show plainly that Dostoevsky conceived of Stavrogin as "a prince." The overtones and implications are exceedingly subtle: the double figure Muishkin-Rogojin was a prince, and Grushenka bestows the same title on Alyosha Karamazov. For Dostoevsky the term carried ritual and poetic values of a specific but perhaps rather private order. In all three characters aspects of the messianic Christ are latent. Stavrogin is, as I shall try to show in the next chapter, an instrument both of grace and of damnation. To Marya he was, at some point in the action, the princely redeemer and falcon-like chevalier. But to envision Stavrogin on this plane of meaning should not—and this is the burden of my argument—prevent us from realizing that there are in him borrowings from the figure of Steerforth in *David Copperfield* or from supposing that his title may be a distant echo of that of Prince Rodolphe in *Les Mystères de Paris*. There was a "King Leir" before Shakespeare.

Dostoevsky would have been the last to deny the range of his indebtedness. The reference to Mrs. Radcliffe's *Mysteries of Udolpho* in *The Brothers Karamazov* is like a salute, offered in irony and recognition, to a remote but undeniable ancestor. He made no secret of the influence which Balzac, Dickens, and George Sand, at their most sentimental and melodramatic, had exerted on his own craft. He prized Schiller's *Räuber* beyond the poet's mature achievements for the frenzy and the terror in it. Dostoevsky's notebooks (some as yet unpublished) are said to be filled with pen-and-ink drawings of Gothic casements and towers, and we know from the memoirs of his wife that he was fascinated by such arch-themes of melodrama as the practices of the Inquisition. This is only one of the affinities between the Gothic imaginations of Dostoevsky and of Poe—a writer whom Dostoevsky helped introduce to the Russian public.

There have always been those who recognized the special, contemporaneous quality in Dostoevsky's vision and who deplore it. Writing to Edward Garnett, Conrad condemned this whole image of experience as one of "strange beasts in a menagerie, or damned souls knocking themselves to pieces." Henry James informed Stevenson that he had found himself unable to read *Crime and Punishment* to its finish. The author of *Dr. Jekyll and Mr. Hyde* countered by saying that it was he—Stevenson—who had been nearly "finished" by Dostoevsky's novel. D. H. Lawrence's dislike of the Dostoevskyan manner is notorious; he hated the strident, rat-like confinement of it.

Others have sought to minimize the extent to which Dostoevsky's genius can, in fact, be related to the Gothic tradition. One recalls the commentary of the narrator in Proust's *La Prisonnière*:

"Dostoevsky's unique contribution is the new and terrible beauty with which he can show a house, the new and ambiguous beauty in a woman's countenance. Literary critics point to affinities between Dostoevsky and Gogol or between Dostoevsky and Paul de Kock. But such affinities are devoid of interest, being, as they are, exterior to this secret beauty."

These "affinities" are the commonly held conventions and responses of the Gothic and melodramatic world view. By "secret beauty" Proust appears to mean the transfiguration of Dostoevskyan reality through a tragic sense of life. I submit that the one could not have been realized without the other.

Dostoevsky's problem was this: to apprehend and make concrete the realities of the human condition in a series of extreme and defining crises; to translate experience into the mode of tragic drama—the only mode that Dostoevsky regarded as verifiable—and yet to remain within the naturalistic setting of modern urban life. Unable to rely upon the possession by his readers of the habits and discriminations appropriate to tragedy—habits sufficiently diffuse and traditional to have been depended upon by the Elizabethan dramatists, for example—and unable to present the whole of his meaning in one of the historical and mythological settings formerly available to tragic poets, Dostoevsky had to bend to his own uses the existing conventions of melodrama. Clearly, melodrama is anti-tragic; its root formula calls for four acts of apparent tragedy followed by a fifth act of rescue or redemption. The compulsion of the genre was such that in two of Dostoevsky's masterpieces, in *Crime and Punishment* and in *The Brothers Karamazov*, action terminates on the "upward swing" characteristic of the happy endings of melodrama. *The Idiot* and *The Possessed*, on the contrary, close in that twilight limbo of bleakness and veracity, of calm arrived at through despair, which we recognize as generically tragic.

Think of some of the fables, episodes, and confrontations through which Dostoevsky communicates his tragic view—Rogojin's pursuit and near-murder of the Prince, the meeting of Stavrogin and Fedka by the storm-lashed bridge, the dialogues between Ivan Karamazov and the Devil. Each, in its own manner, falls outside the dimensions of a rationalistic or wholly secular convention. But each could be justified to the reader in terms of responses drilled into his sensibility by Gothic novelists and melodramatists. A reader moving from *Bleak House* or *Wuthering Heights* to *Crime and Punishment* would experience that initial familiarity without which the vital *rapport* between author and audience cannot be established.

In brief: Dostoevsky accepted Belinsky's injunction that it was the signal duty of Russian fiction to be realistic and to portray authentically the social and philosophic dilemmas of Russian life. But Dostoevsky insisted that his realism differed from that of Goncharov, Turgeniev, and Tolstoy. In Goncharov and Turgeniev he saw mere painters of the superficial or typical; their vision did not penetrate to the chaotic but essential depths of contemporary experience. The realities conveyed by Tolstoy, on the other hand, struck Dostoevsky as archaic and irrelevant to the anguish of the day. Dostoevskyan realism—to use a phrase which he used himself in the drafts for *The Idiot*—was "tragico-fantastic." It sought to give a total and true picture by concentrating the nascent elements of the Russian crisis into moments of drama and extreme revelation. The techniques through which Dostoevsky achieved this concentration were translated, in significant measure, from a rather shopworn and hysterical literary tradition. But through the uses to which his genius put Gothicism and melodrama, he was able to answer affirmatively a question raised by both Goethe and Hegel: would it be possible to create or present a tragic vision of experience in a post-Voltairean era? Could the tragic note be sounded in a world in which the market place, the temple porches, and the castle walls of Greek and renaissance drama had lost their actuality?

Not since the platform at Elsinore and the marbled, vibrant spaces in which the personages of Racine act their solemn destinies had there been anything nearer the locus and arena of tragic drama than the Dostoevskyan city. Rilke wrote in *Malte Laurids Brigge*:

The city strove against me, intent upon my life; it was like an exam which I did not pass. The scream of the city, the endless scream, broke into my silence; the terribleness of the city pursued me to my dreary room. . . .

The terribleness of the city and its "scream" (one thinks of Edvard Munch's famous painting) had rung through the art of Balzac, Dickens, Hoffmann, and Gogol. Dostoevsky scrupulously acknowledged his debt when he remarked at the beginning of *The Insulted and the Injured* that the setting had "stepped out of some page of Hoffmann illustrated by Gavarni." But he gave that "scream of the city" its choral significance; in his hands the city became tragic rather than merely melodramatic. The difference can be seen if one compares *Bleak House* or *Hard Times* with the effects achieved by Rilke and Kafka—both of whom were explicit followers of the Dostoevskyan manner.

In Dostoevsky's novels we cannot separate "the tragic" from "the fantastic." Indeed, the tragic ritual is presented and lifted above the current flatness of experience by means of the fantastic. There are moments in which we can clearly make out how the tragic *agon* penetrates and ultimately transforms the gestures of melodrama. But even transformed, the latter have been no less of an essential medium to Dostoevsky than the established myths were to Greek dramatists or the *opera seria* was to the early Mozart.

The episode of the death of Kirillov in *The Possessed* illustrates in perfect detail how Gothic fantasy and the machinery of horror lead us into the tragic effect. The presuppositions are blatant melodrama: Pyotr must see to it that Kirillov commits suicide after signing a paper charging himself with Shatov's murder. But the engineer, who moves between states of metaphysical ecstasy and raw contempt, may not go through with it. Both Mephistopheles and his equivocating Faust are armed. Pyotr is too astute not to realize that if he goads Kirillov too far, their devil's bargain will collapse. After a passionate dialogue, Kirillov yields to the temptation of despair. He takes his revolver and rushes into the next room, shutting the door. What ensues is strictly comparable—in terms of literary technique—to the climactic moments in the House of Usher or the frenzied death of the hero in Balzac's *Peau de chagrin*. After ten minutes of tortured expectancy, Pyotr seizes a dying candle:

he did not hear the slightest sound. He suddenly opened the door and lifted up the candle: something uttered a roar and rushed at him. He slammed the door with all his might and pressed his weight against it; but all sounds died away and again there was deathlike stillness.

Pyotr reckons he will have to shoot it out with the reluctant metaphysician and flings the door open, revolver in hand. A horrible sight greets him. Kirillov is standing against the wall, motionless, unnaturally pale. With blind fury Pyotr longs to scorch the man's face and make sure that he is alive:

Then something happened so hideous and so soon over that Pyotr Stepanovich could never afterwards recover a coherent impression of it. He had hardly touched Kirillov when the latter bent down quickly and with his head knocked the candle out of Pyotr Stepanovich's hand; the candlestick fell with a clang on the ground and the candle went out. At the same moment he was conscious of a fearful pain in the little finger of his left hand. He cried out, and all that he could remember was that, beside himself, he hit out with all his might and struck three blows with the revolver on the head of Kirillov, who had bent down to him and had bitten his finger. At last he tore away his finger and rushed headlong to get out of the house, feeling his way in the dark. He was pursued by terrible shouts from the room.

"Directly, directly, directly, directly." Ten times. But he still ran on, and was running into the porch when he suddenly heard a loud shot.

The motif of the bite is a curious one. It was probably derived from *David Copperfield*, and we find it in the early sketches for the figure of Razumihin in *Crime and Punishment*. It appears three times in *The Possessed*: Stavrogin bites the Governor's ear; we are told of a young officer who bit his superior; and we see Pyotr being bitten by Kirillov. The latter instance is one of peculiar horror. The engineer seems to be drained of human consciousness. The part of reason in him is frozen to the thought of self-destruction. Death, in the form of an animal which "roars" and uses its savage teeth, is master of him. When the human voice erupts, it is with a single cry ten times repeated. Kirillov's insane "directly" is a counterpart to Lear's five-fold repetition of "never." In the case of Lear, a man's spirit refuses annihilation and clings to a single word as to the gates of life; in the other, it is shown embracing darkness. Kirillov kills himself in abject despair, because he could not kill himself in an affirmation of freedom. Both cries move us unutterably though arising out of circumstances which are wholly fantastic.

Pyotr crawls back and finds "splashes of blood and brains" on the floor. The guttering candle, the dead engineer, Pyotr with his bleeding finger and inhuman visage—we have here as set a piece of melodrama as Fagin's appearance at the window or the awesome scene of torture in Conrad's *Nostromo*. But the conventions do not blunt or deflect the tragic purpose; they serve it. The episode confirms a distinction proposed in Aristotle's *Poetics*: "Those who employ spectacular means to create a sense not of the terrible but only of the monstrous, are strangers to the purpose of tragedy." The Dostoevskyan novel is a "novel of terror"; but it expounds the term in the sense in which Joyce defined it in A *Portrait of the Artist*:

Terror is the feeling which arrests the mind in the presence of whatsoever is grave and constant in human sufferings and unites it with the secret cause.

Dostoevsky's "tragico-fantastic" realism and its Gothic implements distinguish his conception of the art of the novel irreconcilably from that of Tolstoy. There are in the writings of Tolstoy, especially in the late tales, elements of daemonism and obsession which thrust the narrative to the edges of melodrama. In a posthumous fragment, *Memoirs of a Lunatic*, we find effects of sheer horror:

"Life and death were flowing into one another. An unknown power was trying to tear my soul into pieces, but could not rend it. Once more I went out into the passage to look at the two men asleep; once more I tried to go to sleep. The horror was always the same—now red, now white and square."

But this tone, with its hint of how Gothicism will later pass into surrealism, is exceedingly rare in Tolstoy. Seen as a whole, the atmosphere of his novels is filled with a sense of normality and health. It is penetrated with a clear hard light. Allowing for obvious differences the perspective is like that intended by D. H. Lawrence when he asserted in *The Rainbow* that "The cycle of creation still wheeled in the Christian year." If we except *The Kreutzer Sonata* and *Father Sergius*, we can say that Tolstoy deliberately avoided the motifs of evil and perversion proper to the Gothic. Sometimes he did so at the expense of richness. We see an example in *War and Peace*. In the early drafts there are strong hints that Anatole and Helen Kuragin have had incestuous relations. But as he proceeded, Tolstoy began effacing all traces of this theme, and in the final version only a few oblique allusions remain. Thinking back on his ruined marriage, Pierre recalls how "Anatole used to come to borrow money from her and used to kiss her naked shoulders. She did not give him the money but let herself be kissed."

Tolstoy's "pastoralism" was obviously related to his rejection of contemporary melodrama. It is under an open, frosty sky, or when it is in ruins, that Pierre finds Moscow beautiful. Arriving in Moscow, Levin hastens to that part of the city—the frozen pond—which is closest to a rural setting. Tolstoy was intensely conscious of urban misery and darkness; he spent long hours in the depths of slums and charity wards. But he did not associate this awareness with the materials of his art—particularly when that art was in its flowering. Whether the epic mode inevitably relates to a pastoral background is, as I have mentioned before, a very complex question. But a number of critics, such as Philip

Rahv, have argued that the distinctions between the art of Tolstoy and Dostoevsky—distinctions of technique as well as of world image—can be resolved, finally, to the timeless contrast between the city and the land.

VIII

Of all the creatures that inhabit what Professor Poggioli has called Dostoevsky's "monads of bricks and lime," [6] the most famous is the "underground man." His symbolic role and the significance of his various guises have been examined in numerous critiques. He is *l'étranger, l'homme révolté, der unbehauste Mensch*, the outcast, the outsider. Dostoevsky regarded him as the most poignant of his creations. He proclamied in the notebooks for *Raw Youth*:

I alone have evoked the tragic condition of the underground man, the tragic of his sufferings, of his self-punishment, of his aspirations towards the ideal and of his incapacity to attain it; I alone have evoked the lucid insight these wretched beings possess into the fatality of their condition, a fatality such that it would be useless to react against it.

In the drama of the city, the underground man is at once the experiencer of humiliation and the necessary chorus whose ironic commentary lays naked the hypocrisies of convention. Immure him among casks of amontillado; his stifled whisperings shall bring down the house. The man from the lower depths possesses intelligence without power, desire without means. The industrial revolution has taught him how to read and given him a minimum of leisure; but the concomitant triumph of capital and bureaucracy has left him without an overcoat. He perches at his clerk's desk—Bartleby in Wall Street or Joseph K. in his office—drudges in acrimonious servility, dreams of richer worlds, and shuffles home in the evening. He lives in

[6] R. Poggioli: "Kafka and Dostoyevsky" (*The Kafka Problem*, New York, 1946).

what Marx characterized as a bitter limbo between proletariat and genuine bourgeoisie. Gogol recounts what happens to him when he at last acquires an overcoat; and the ghost of Akaky Akakievich Bashmatskin will haunt not only officials and night watchmen in St. Petersburg but the imaginations of European and Russian novelists to the time of Kafka and Camus.

Despite the importance of Gogol's archetype and Dostoevsky's just claims for the originality of his *Letters from the Underworld*, the underground man has roots in remotest antiquity. If we think of him as the *ewig verneinende Geist*, as the thorn of contempt in the side of creation, he is as old as Cain. Indeed, he is with the first Adam, for after the Fall a part of every man descended into the underground. The mien, the jeering tone, the mingling of abjection and arrogance, which are emblematic of the Dostoevskyan figure, can be observed in the Homeric Thersites, in the parasites of Roman satire and comedy, in the legendary Diogenes, and in Lucan's dialogues.

The type is represented twice in Shakespeare: in Apemantus and Thersites. To Timon's bounteous welcome, the "churlish philosopher" replies:

> No;
> You shall not make me welcome.
> I come to have thee thrust me out of doors.

Like the Dostoevskyan narrator, Apemantus comes "to observe" and rages at having to feed off a richer man's meat. He prizes the truth where it wounds and carries honesty writ large across his spite. As to Thersites: Trousotsky in *The Eternal Husband* designates himself as such and refers to the famous distich from Schiller's *Siegesfest*:

> For Patroclus lies buried
> And Thersites sails for home.

Whether Dostoevsky knew the Shakespearean version is not certain, though it is probable. There are monologues of Thersites in *Troilus and Cressida* that might aptly stand in epigraph to the *Letters from the Under-world*:

How now, Thersites! What, lost in the labyrinth of thy fury! Shall the elephant Ajax carry it thus? He beats me, and I rail at him. O, worthy satisfaction! Would it were otherwise; that I could beat him, whilst he rail'd at me. 'Sfoot, I'll learn to conjure and raise devils, but I'll see some issue of my spiteful execrations.

Like Thersites, the underground man incessantly talks to himself. His sense of alienation is such that he sees "otherness" even in his mirror. He is the contrary to Narcissus and reviles creation precisely because he cannot believe that so abject a thing as himself should have been formed in the image of God. He envies the wealth and power of the rich; irony will not keep out the cold of winter. But in his cellar, in the "labyrinth of fury," he schemes vengeance. He will "raise devils" and one day the petty bureaucrats who lord it over him, the coachmen who splatter him with mud, the majestic footmen who close doors in his face, the ladies who snigger at his torn vest, the landlords who ambush him on the unlit stairs—all of them shall crawl at his conquering feet. This is Rastignac's dream and Julien Sorel's and the sustaining fantasy of that host of starved clerks and unemployed tutors who gaze from the outside into the festive windows of the nineteenth-century novel.

But the underground man is necessary to his betters. He is a reminder of mortality in moments of *hubris*, a buffoon who speaks the truth and a confidant who saps illusion. There is something of him in Sancho Panza, in Don Juan's Leporello calling for his wages even in the face of hell, in Faust's Wagner. By echoing or contradicting or questioning his masters, he assists in the process of self-definition, and this process —we see it in the role of the Fool in *King Lear*—is one of the principal dynamics of tragedy. Through the canons of decorum inherent in Neo-classism, the underground man became a respectful courtier. But his essential function was preserved: he laid bare the hypocrisies of high rhetoric and compelled the grand personages to live their moments of truth (consider the Nurse in *Phèdre*). Thus the confidants in Corneille and Racine mark an advance from the view that "the outsider" is literally a separate individual to the recognition that he is one of the *personae* of the psyche.

This recognition was latent in the outward presentation of Good and Bad Conscience wrestling for the soul of Everyman or Faust in medieval morality plays. It had been hinted at in the allegoric discourses between "reason" and "passion" in the amorous and philosophic poetry of the renaissance and the baroque. But the assertion that there are within individual men several conflicting personalities, and that baser, ironic, irrational strains of consciousness may be more authentic than the semblance of coherence and reason offered to the outside world, was put forward only in the eighteenth century. It was then, as Berdiaev writes in his study of Dostoevsky, that "a chasm opened in the depths of man himself, and therein God and Heaven, the Devil and Hell were revealed anew." The first "modern" character, as Hegel pointed out, was Rameau's nephew in Diderot's imaginary dialogue. He was, moreover, a direct ancestor of the underground man.

Musician, mime, parasite, philosopher, Rameau's nephew is at once arrogant and obsequious, energetic and slothful, cynical and candid. He harkens to himself as a fiddler harkens to his instrument. Outwardly, he typifies the underground species:

I, poor blighter, lie shrivelled under my blanket when I have made it back to my garret in the evening and have crawled on to my straw pallet. I have a sunken chest and a strained breath; it comes out with a kind of feeble lament which is scarcely audible. A financier, on the contrary, makes his apartment resound with his breathing and amazes the whole street with the clamour of it.

In the architecture of symbolism, garrets are cellars reversed. Cellars, or in the Dostoevskyan phrase, the space immediately beneath the floor boards, give the stronger image. We tend to picture the soul in tiers and have formed habits of language suggesting that the forces of protest and unreason mount "from below."

Rameau's nephew was prophetic in his divisive self-awareness, but also in his proclamation of the kind of intimate truths that earlier literary conventions had disguised or suppressed. He was one of the first confessors in the modern sense, and stands at the fountainhead of a long tradition. In the *Letters from the Underworld* this tradition is explicitly invoked. But Dostoevsky maintained that his forerunners including Rousseau, had been less than honest. Some had draped themselves in rags; none had gone truly naked.

According to Nisard's famous quip, romanticism proved that the language of the nobility was not necessarily equivalent to the nobility of language. The underground men went further. They declared that literature which dealt only with public acts and drawing-rooms —drawing-rooms in the soul and in the house—was an adjunct to hypocrisy. There was more darkness in man than had been dreamt of in the psychology of rationalism. They gloried in the mind's descent into its own depths—an adventure so great that it made exterior reality seem insubstantial. Writing in 1799, in a book significantly entitled *Cataractes de l'imagination*, J.-M. Chassaignon exclaimed:

I prefer myself to everything which exists; it is with this self alone that I have passed the choicest moments of my life; this "I" in isolation, surrounded with graves and invoking the Great Being, would suffice to content me amid the ruins of the universe.

The final image is prophetic of the extremes to which solipsism can attain. It anticipates, exactly, the assertion of Dostoevsky's narrator:

Indeed, if I were given the choice between the world coming to an end and my retaining my liberty to drink tea, I tell you that the universe might go to the devil so long as I could go on drinking tea.

But although Diderot's successors, and Dostoevsky himself, had arrived at a multiple image of the individual soul and had advanced far into the vocabulary of the unconscious, the figure of the underground man went through a bizarre intermediary stage. The "double" of Gothic literature was an attempt to make the new psychology articulate and concrete. One half of the "double" embodies the habitual, rationalistic, social parts of man. The other half incarnates that in him which is daemonic, subconscious, antagonistic to reason, and potentially criminal. At times—as in the tales of Poe and Musset, in Ahab and Fedallah, in Muishkin and Rogojin—the "double" actually connotes the fatal coexistence of two dependent but distinct beings. At other times, the "double" is fused into one agent, into Jekyll-Hyde or Dorian Gray. Even where he used the less sophisticated versions of the myth, as in *Goliadkin* or in Ivan Karamazov's colloquies with the Devil, Dostoevsky stands out as one of the foremost students of the schizophrenic. But it was in the *Letters from the Underworld* that he resolved most decisively the problem of dramatizing through a single voice the many-tongued chaos of human consciousness.

I will not attempt to deal with the technical philosophic implications of the work. Had Dostoevsky written nothing else, he would have been remembered as one of the master builders of modern thought. As is well known, the *Letters* fall into two parts, of which the first is primarily a monologue on the paradox of free will and natural law. Reinhard Lauth discusses the epistemological significance of this text in his massive treatise, *Die Philosophie Dostojewskis*. He suggests that much of the argument was meant to refute the utilitarian and empirical optimism of Bentham and Buckle (Dostoevsky repeatedly took issue with Buckle in the drafts for *The Brothers Karamazov*). Lauth further argues that the existentialist reading of the *Letters* —Shestov's, for example—is mistaken in that it neglects the irony of Dostoevsky's tone and the conservatism of his personal opinions.

There is also a substantial literature concerning the psychological and psychoanalytic material in the *Letters from the Underworld*. Of all of Dostoevsky's "surfaces," none yields less resistance to this style of approach. It is lent cogency, moreover, by the fact that the work was composed at a time when its author was suffering grievous emotional upheavals.

But while allowing the eminent fascination of the *Letters* from the points of view of metaphysics and psychology, one should not overlook the way in which Dostoevsky converted prevailing literary devices and conventions to his particular ends. Live burial, descents into caverns, maelstroms or sewers, and the figure of the redeeming prostitute were commonplace of romantic melodrama. The underworld which the narrator "carries within him" has specific literary and historical intonations; it was not necessarily that of Dostoevsky himself. Indeed, in the brief prefatory note, the novelist says that he is depicting a character "peculiar to the present age," and that his personality is "due to the *milieu* which all of us share in Russia." In that respect, the whole work belongs with other Dostoevskyan polemics against spiritual nihilism.

At the end of Part I, Dostoevsky considers the problem of literary form. The narrator proposes to set down a manual of total candour: "I wish, in particular, to try whether one can *ever* be really open with oneself—*ever* be really fearless of any item of truth." The sentence echoes the celebrated opening paragraph of Rousseau's *Confessions*, and the Dostoevskyan narrator promptly observes that Heine thought Rousseau a liar "partly out of set purpose, and partly out of vanity." He adds: "I believe that Heine is right." Heine's presence in this context is illustrative of how the symbolic imagination works: by virtue of his long and cruel entombment in the *Matratzengruft*—literally in a burial vault of illness —Heine had become an archetype of the underground man. Contrary to Montaigne or Cellini or Rousseau,

though I may seem to be writing for the eye of a reader, I do so out of mere show, and because I find that that kind of writing comes easier. It is all mere form—all a mere empty form, for which I shall never have a reader.

This fiction is conveyed through a traditional device which Poe used to similar effects; we are asked to believe that a manuscript never intended for publication has been anonymously "transcribed."

Such claims to privacy are, of course, rhetorical. But a real problem is at issue. With the irruption of the unconscious into poetics, with the endeavour to portray characters in their divided entirety, classical methods of narrative and discourse became inadequate. Dostoevsky believed that the dilemma of inadequate form— Rousseau's *Confessions*—entailed the more significant dilemma of inadequate truth. Modern literature has sought to resolve this problem in various ways, but neither the alternate use of "public" and "private" speech in O'Neill's *Strange Interlude* nor the stream of consciousness perfected by Joyce and Hermann Broch has proved wholly satisfactory. What we can hear of the language of the unconscious falls too readily into our own syntax. Perhaps we do not yet know how to listen.

The *Letters from the Underworld* are experimental in range of content rather than in dislocation or deepening of narrative form. Once again, the primary mode is dramatic: by compressing the course of outward happenings into a series of crises, Dostoevsky caused the narrator to speak with a frenzied candour which human beings, under less final circumstances, reserve for their unavowed thoughts. In the *Letters*, soul and unreason confront each other in extremity, and the reader overhears truths as awesome as the truths Dante overheard in hell.

The setting is arch-Dostoevskyan: "a mean, shabby room" on the fringes of St. Petersburg—"the most abstract, the most deviously-minded city on this terrestrial sphere of ours." The weather is in the appropriate key:

Today half-melted, yellow, dirty snow is falling. It was falling yesterday, and it does so nearly every day. I believe that it is the wet snow which has reminded me of the episode of which I cannot rid my thoughts; so here goes for my confession *àpropos* of the fall of sleet.

The next sentence, which opens Part II, reads:

At that time I was only twenty-four and, so far, had lived a dull ill-regulated existence that was well-nigh as solitary as that of a savage.

One is reminded of Villon—the first great voice from the underground of the European metropolis. In him, also, meditation followed on *les neiges d'antan* and the attainment of *l'an de mon trentiesme aage* (and is it not a fine coincidence that the old saint's legend of Mary the Egyptian, to which Villon refers in several poems, should reappear in *Raw Youth*?).

The "I" of the *Letters* says repeatedly that his philosophy "is the fruit of forty years in the underworld," of forty years spent in the isolation of self-scrutiny. It is difficult to dismiss the echo of the forty years passed by Israel in the desert or of Christ's forty days in the wilderness. For the *Letters from the Underworld* cannot be considered in isolation. They are closely related to the symbolic values and thematic material of Dostoevsky's major fictions. Thus, the prostitute is called Liza. In the final tableau she sits on the floor, sobbing:

By this time she knew all. She knew that I had outraged her to the core, and that (how am I to express it?) my short-lived passion had sprung only from a desire for vengeance, from a yearning to subject her to a new indignity. . . .

The lines are a gloss on the scene between Liza and Stavrogin in *The Possessed* and prefigure Dostoevsky's treatment of the relations between Raskolnikov and Sonia in *Crime and Punishment*. Nor is the Dostoevskyan emblem of primordial evil lacking in the narrator's tale. When he asks Liza why she left her father's house to come to a brothel, she hints at some mysterious infamy: "But what if things were *worse* there than here?" Unconsciously—the dramatization being as subtle and open to every shift of value as it is in Shakespeare—the underground man seizes on her hint. He confesses that if he had a daughter, "I should love her even more than I did my sons." He tells of a father who kisses his girl's hands and feet "and folds her in his arms as she lies asleep." The immediate reference would seem to be to Balzac's *Père Goriot*. Beyond it lies the motif of father-daughter incest which, in the guise of the Cenci affair, had fascinated Shelley, Stendhal, Landor, Swinburne, Hawthorne, and even Melville. The narrator makes a revealing admission; he would not have his daughter marry:

Because, by heavens, I should have been jealous. What? She to kiss another man—to love a stranger more than she did her father? It hurts me even to think of it!

And he concludes with the classical Freudian insight that "the man whom the daughter loves is generally the man who cuts the worst figure in her father's eyes."

In the *Letters* we even find traces of the myth of the "double" which Dostoevsky's conception of the human soul had, in fact, rendered archaic. The surly Apollon is both the underground man's servant and his inseparable shadow:

My present tenement was an isolated one, and therefore my sheath, my box into which I could withdraw from all humanity; and for some infernal reason or another Apollon always seemed to form part of it. Consequently for seven whole years I found myself unable to make up my mind to dismiss him.

And yet, when the traditional literary elements in the *Letters* have been set aside, and when close affinities to Dostoevsky's other works have been noted, the profound originality of the thing continues to assert itself. Chords previously unheard had been struck with admirable precision. No other text by Dostoevsky has exerted more influence on twentieth-century thought or technique.

The portrayal of the narrator is an achievement for which one does not find a genuine precedent:

I wish to tell you, gentlemen (no matter whether you care to hear it or not), why I have never been able to become an insect. I solemnly declare to you that I have often *wished* to become an insect, but could never attain my desire.

This notion, which obviously contains the germ for Kafka's *Metamorphosis*, is pursued throughout the narrative. Other personages look upon the speaker "as some kind of ordinary fly." He describes himself as "the foulest . . . the most ill-gained worm upon earth." In themselves, these images are not new. The source of Dostoevsky's insect symbolism has, indeed, been traced to Balzac.[7] What is new and terrifying is the sustained methodic use of such imagery to "inhumanize" and dehumanize man. The narrator "crouches" in his lair and waits "in his cranny." The sense of animality infects his consciousness. The ancient metaphors linking man to worms and vermin, the representation of man's death, in *King Lear*, as a wanton massacre of flies, are transformed by Dostoevsky into psychological realities, into actual conditions of the mind. The tragedy of the underground man is, literally, his retreat from manhood. This retreat is made explicit through the cruel impotence of his assault on Liza. In the end, he sees matters plainly:

We grow weary of being human beings at all—of possessing real, individual flesh and blood. We are ashamed of being human—we account it beneath our dignity.

If there is one main element contributed by modern literature to our world view, it is precisely this sense of dehumanization.

What has brought it on? Perhaps it is a result of the industrialization of life, of the downgrading of the human person through the blank, nameless monotony of industrial processes. In the *Letters*, Dostoevsky describes "the throng of hurrying workmen and artisans

[7] This aspect of Dostoevskyan imagery has been thoroughly dealt with bv R. E. Matlaw: "Recurrent Images in Dostoevskij" (*Harvard Slavic Studies*, III, 1957).

(their faces worn almost to brutality).'' With Engels and Zola, he was one of the first to realize what factory labour can do to eradicate individual traits or the play of intelligence in a man's face. But, whatever its origins, the "shame of being human" has, in our century, assumed proportions grimmer than those foreseen by Dostoevsky. In his parable *Les Bêtes*, Pierre Gascar tells how the kingdom of the beasts supplants that of men in the world of concentration camps and gas chambers. And in a minor, yet grave key, James Thurber has shown the waking of the animals behind the imperfect, rent covering of the human skin. For since the *Letters from the Underworld* we know that the insect is gaining on the part of man. Ancient mythology dealt with men who were half-gods; post-Dostoevskyan mythology depicts roaches who are half-man.

The *Letters* carried to a new finality the conception of the non-heroic. Mario Praz has shown that the abandonment of the heroic type was one of the major currents in Victorian fiction. Gogol and Goncharov had made of the non-heroic protagonist a figure symbolic of contemporaneous Russia. But Dostoevsky went further. His narrator not only affects a sense of degradation and self-loathing; he is genuinely odious. He recounts his abject experiences "as a well-merited punishment" and does so with hysterical malevolence. Consider Gogol's terrifying *Diary of a Madman* and Turgeniev's *Journal of a Superfluous Man*; both are essays in the non-heroic, but both move us to compassion through grace and irony of presentment. Tolstoy's Ivan Ilych, a truly mediocre and selfish creature, is, at the last, ennobled by the tenacity of his despair. In the *Letters*, however, Dostoevsky treats his material with a withering touch. The "transcriber" indicates in the postscript that this "dealer in paradoxes" wrote further notes but that these were not worth preserving. We are left with an intended nothingness.

In his portrayal of the "anti-hero" Dostoevsky has had a legion of disciples. Add to his method the more ancient tradition of the picaresque and you find the sinful confessor of Gide's novels. Camus's *The Fall* is a palpable imitation of the tone and structure of the *Letters*; in Genet the logic of avowal and degradation is carried to the excremental.

Finally, the *Letters from the Underworld* are of tremendous importance in that they formulated, with utmost clarity, a critique of pure reason which had been gathering impetus in much of romantic art. Some of the passages in which the narrator mutinies against natural law have become touchstones of twentieth-century metaphysics:

> Good Lord! What have *I* to do with the laws of Nature, or with arithmetic, when all the time those laws and the formula that twice two make four do not meet with my acceptance! Of course, I am not going to beat my head against a wall if I have not the requisite strength to do so; yet I am not going to *accept* that wall merely because I have run up against it, and have no means to knock it down.

How can man's will attain total freedom "except by thrusting through the wall," asked Ahab. Non-Euclidean geometry and the more abstruse reveries of modern algebra were to breach some of these walls of axiom. But the rebellion of the Dostoevskyan narrator is all-encompassing. With his derisive rejection of the *savants*, the Hegelian idealists and the believers in rational progress, he offered a declaration of independence from reason. Long before his existentialist followers, the man from the underground proclaimed the majesty of the absurd. This is why Dostoevsky is so often cited in the pantheon of modern metaphysics with other mutineers against liberal empiricism—Pascal, Blake, Kierkegaard, and Nietzsche.

It would be fascinating to inquire into the sources of the Dostoevskyan dialectic. Condorcet asserted that if men said *calculemus*—if they grasped the tools of reason in a Newtonian world—nature would yield her answers. Dostoevsky said "No." He said "No" to Spencerian faith in progress and to the rational physiology of Claude Bernard (a man of genius whom Dimitri

Karamazov refers to with particular rage). One might examine the elements of Rousseauism in the underground man's contempt for formal authority and in his obsession with the primacy of will. For between Rousseau's pronouncement that the private conscience is an "infallible judge of good and evil, making man similar to God," and the narrator's conviction that he can dismiss natural law and the categories of conventional logic, there is a complex but authentic link. These matters pertain, however, to a more technical study.

What needs emphasizing is the fact that the *Letters from the Underworld* were a brilliant solution to the problem of philosophic content within the literary form. Unlike the *contes philosophiques* of the enlightenment or the novels of Goethe, in which the part of speculation is so deliberately exterior to the fiction, the *Letters* coalesce the abstract with the dramatized—or in Aristotelian terminology, they fuse "thought" with "plot." In point of genre, neither Nietzsche's *Zarathustra* nor the theological allegories of Kierkegaard impress one as equally successful. Together with Schiller, to whom he looked as a constant model, Dostoevsky achieved a rare instance of creative equilibrium between poetic and philosophic powers.

The *Letters from the Underworld* are, indeed, a Dostoevskyan *summa*—even if we grant that the narrator's views cannot be identified with the novelist's political program and official Orthodoxy. It is appropriate that the contrast with Tolstoy should nowhere be more final. Even in abjection, a Tolstoyan personage remains man; if anything, his humanity deepens and grows lustrous with disgrace. As Isaiah Berlin puts it, Tolstoy saw men "in natural, unaltering daylight." The hallucinatory collapse of the human into the bestial was alien to his view. Even at its most brutal, Tolstoyan pessimism was amended by a central belief that human beings would not merely "endure," to use Faulkner's distinction, but also "prevail."

Tolstoy's "non-heroes"—as, for example, the narrator of the *Kreutzer Sonata*—have a humaneness in suffering and a moral assertiveness which set them worlds apart from the bilious masochism of the underground man. The difference flashes through beautifully in a dialogue between Shakespeare's Apemantus and the fallen Timon. Even when the latter is reduced to hatred and self-mockery, it appears as if the "bleak air" were still his "boisterous chamberlain."

Tolstoy's philosophy, for all its rejection of the schoolmen and the idealists, is profoundly rationalistic. During his whole life he sought for a unifying principle through which the multitudinous individuality of observed experience could be reconciled to an apprehension of order. Dostoevsky's homage to the absurd, his assault on the ordinary mechanics of tautology and definition, would have seemed to Tolstoy a peevish madness. Tolstoy was, in Vyazemsky's phrase, a "negativist." But his negations were axe-strokes to carve a clearing for the light. His portrayal of life culminates in humanism, in that final "Yes" of Molly Bloom's soliloquy. In his journal for July 19, 1896, Tolstoy recorded seeing a clump of burdock in the midst of a ploughed field; one shoot was alive.

black from dust, but still alive and red in the centre. . . . It makes me want to write. It asserts life to the end, and alone in the midst of the whole field, somehow or other has asserted it.

The narrator of the *Letters from the Underworld* expresses through his acts and language a final "No." When Tolstoy remarked to Gorky that Dostoevsky "ought to have made himself acquainted with the teachings of Confucius or the Buddhists; that would have calmed him down," the underground man must have howled derisively from his lair. Our times have given substance to his derision. The *univers concentrationnaire*—the world of the death camps—confirms beyond denial Dostoevsky's insights into the savagery of men, into their inclination, both as individuals and as hordes, to stamp out within themselves the embers of humanity. The subterranean narrator defines his species as "A creature which walks on two legs and is devoid of gratitude." Tolstoy also realized that there was no abundance of gratitude, but instead of "creature" he would always have written "man."

That we should, at times, think him old-fashioned marks the desecration of our estate.

CHAPTER

 4 ✸

To judge a work of art by artistic or by religious standards, to judge a religion by religious or artistic standards should come in the end to the same thing: though it is an end at which no individual can arrive.

T. S. ELIOT,
Notes Towards the Definition of Culture

✸

AS anthropologists and art historians know, myths become statues and statues give rise to new myths. Mythologies, creeds, images of the world enter into language or marble; the inward movements of the soul, what Dante called the *moto spiral*, are realized in the shapes of art. But in the act of realization, the mythology will be altered or re-created. When Sartre said that the techniques of a novel refer us back to a metaphysical system, to an underlying philosophy of experience, he pointed to only one direction in a double-rhythm. The metaphysics of the artist refer us forward to the techniques of his art. It is with techniques that we have, so far, been principally concerned—with the epic mode in the novels of Tolstoy and the elements of drama in Dostoevsky. In this final chapter, I shall consider the beliefs and mythologies behind these outward shapes.

But in saying "behind," in suggesting that a novel may be a façade or a mask for a philosophic doctrine, we involve ourselves in error. The relationship between thought and expression is at all times reciprocal and dynamic. The least inadequate image for it may be found in the dance (and this is why the renaissance saw in the dance an allegory of creation): the dancer translates into the speech of motion a meditation on passion or reality—metaphysics are translated into techniques by choreography. But at each instant of the dance, the forms and eloquence of gesture engender new insights, new mythologies. Delight, born of the mind, passes into the upward surge of the body; but the formal style, the never-to-be-repeated particularities of the gesture, are in themselves creators of myth and ecstasy. When Hazlitt tells us that Coleridge shifted continually from one side of the foot-path to the other whereas Wordsworth composed while walking in straight evenness, he is giving us a parable of how form and content act upon each other in continuous reciprocity.

Mythologies are the shapes which we seek to impose, through will or desire or in the shadow of our fears, on the otherwise uncontrollable chaos of experience. They are not, as I. A. Richards reminds us in *Coleridge on Imagination*, mere fancies, but

the utterance of the whole soul of man, and as such, inexhaustible to meditation. . . . Without his mythologies man is only a cruel animal without a soul . . . a congeries of possibilities without order and without aim.

These mythologies ("metaphysics" in Sartre's vocabulary, *Weltanschauungen* in that of German criticism) can be of diverse orders: political, philosophic, psychological, economic, historical, or religious.

The novels of Aragon and the plays of Brecht, for example, are representations, through imaginary happenings, of the political and economic mythology of Marxism. From the Marxist point of view, their virtues lie in the explicitness and fidelity with which they re-enact the official myths. Likewise, there are mythologies of *élitisme* (as, for instance, in the fictions and dramas of Montherlant). Lionel Trilling's novel, *The Middle of the Journey*, actualizes a liberal mythology. Part of the strategy of this delicate fable lies in its title: together with the echo from Dante, we are to remember that liberalism claims the "middle ground."

Lucretius' *De Rerum Natura*, Pope's *Essay on Man*, and Shelley's *Alastor* are embodiments in poetry and re-creations through poetry of particular metaphysics. In judging them we dwell less upon the specific merits of atomism or romantic Neo-Platonism than we do on the propriety with which the abstract world view has been accorded to the poetic instrument. A comparable response is called for by the treatment of Schopenhauer's philosophy in the early novels and tales of Thomas Mann.

Various myths of psychology play an important role in modern art. We speak of "Freudian" novels; there are poets who evoke in their prosody the dislocated immediacies of the subconscious; in their own medium, painters have sought to visualize the symbol-world of the crippled or naked mind. Mythologies of this order are nothing new; they began with men's earliest attempts to rationalize their apprehensions of the soul. The mythology of "humours" and astral influence is powerfully at work in the characterizations of Elizabethan drama. Ben Jonson's *Alchemist* and Webster's *Duchess of Malfi* are presentations, through the techniques of the theatre, of particular images of human consciousness. Different images—alternate myths—are implicit in the comedies of Molière or the "Proverbs" of Goya.

One further distinction should be noted: there are mythologies whose conceptual content and symbolic forms are private and unique. Blake and Yeats developed highly complex and idiosyncratic bodies of myths.

In contrast, there are the great mythologies that have been assembled and codified over long periods of history and that are a part of the poet's formative inheritance. Thus, Dante worked within the established mythologies of the Latin Middle Ages.

But every mythology, however traditional, is transmuted through the alchemy of the particular artist and by the materials and techniques of the particular artform. Brecht was charged with formalism by his censors precisely because his personal dramatic style tended to question, through laughter, or liberalize, through pathos, the official proletarian "message." According to Marxist precepts, an artist should convey, with unswerving precision, the reigning mythology; the steps of the dance, or at least its precise limits, are traced on the floor of the stage. Whether great art can flourish in this manner is very much of a question, for the real poet is always a changer and contriver of myths. Dante's Thomism was, in notable regards, Dante's. The Thomistic mythology entered into the poem but was refracted by the special medium of Dante's language and poetic practice. Even as the "line" of a particular draughtsman models the shapes of perception, so prosody—*terza rima*, the heroic couplet, the alexandrine—gives particular contours to the shapes of reason.

The purest example, in the realm of language, of the interplay between mythologies and techniques of expression is to be found in the Platonic dialogues. These dialogues are poems of the mind when the mind is in the condition of drama. In the *Republic*, the *Phaedo* or the *Symposion*, the dialectical proceeding, the clash and trial of argument, is directed over each given stretch of inquiry by the dramatics of human encounter. Philosophic content and dramatic realization are inseparable. By accomplishing this degree of unity, Plato brought his metaphysics very near to the oneness of music, for in music content and form (mythology and technique) are identical.

In a work of art several mythologies may be realized

concurrently. The *Letters from the Underworld* embody both a philosophic myth—the rebellion against positivism—and a psychological myth, the descent of man into the dark places of the soul. In *War and Peace* we find a conflict of mythologies: one voice proclaims the myth of impersonal and uncontrollable history, the other, with its Homeric cadence, invokes a classical, heroic mythology of personal valour and of the impact of individuals on the course of events.

The central mythologies in the works and personal lives of Tolstoy and Dostoevsky were religious. All their lives long the two novelists wrestled with the angel, demanding of him a coherent myth of God and a verifiable account of God's role in the destiny of man. The answers which they obtained in their passionate inquiry are, if I understand them rightly, irreconcilable. The metaphysics of Tolstoy and Dostoevsky are opposed to each other like death and the sun in Pascal's famous image of eternal antagonism. Moreover, they prefigure that radical division of purpose which underlies the ideological and quasi-religious wars of the twentieth century. The contrariety between the Tolstoyan and Dostoveskyan interpretations of the world and of the condition of man are incarnate in, and expressed through, their contrasting methods as writers of fiction. Irreconcilable mythologies point to contrasting forms of art.

In his valuable book *Le Dieu caché*, Lucien Goldmann establishes a sustained concordance between a Jansenist image of God and the conception of tragedy in the plays of Racine. I cannot hope to be as rigorous. My evidence, particularly with respect to the enigmatic affinities between Tolstoyan theology and the world image of the Tolstoyan novel, is of a tentative and preliminary nature. With Dostoevsky we are, I think, on sure ground. But even there, correspondences between tragic metaphysics and tragic art must be interpreted with the utmost caution.

Contemporaneously, we find it difficult to respond fully to religious art. Our age welcomes the banal and diffuse religiosity of pseudo-theologians, and great masses flock to hear the comforting trivialities of matinée prophets and salvation-peddlers. But our minds balk at the subtle asperities of traditional doctrine, at the harsh and demanding science of God practised in a disciplined theology. As Professor Kitto says:

Neither today nor for some centuries past have we been in immediate and imaginative contact with a religious culture —with its habits of mind, its natural means of expression. We may reflect on what has happened to us since the Elizabethan Age. This was one which had by no means lost contact with the late Middle Age; and the drama of this age was played, literally, not on two levels but on three: Heaven, Earth and Hell, side by side. It was a drama with the very widest reference. But the succeeding Age of Reason was entirely out of touch with this. . . .[1]

Romanticism reacted against this alienation. But instead of returning to an organic grasp of religious experience, the nineteenth century gave rise to confused, and at times wholly erroneous, theories of the relations between religion and art. On the Age of Reason followed an age in which at least one great poet could equate truth with beauty. The gist of the confusion is contained in Matthew Arnold's famous pronouncement in *The Study of Poetry*:

Our religion has materialized itself in the fact, in the supposed fact; it has attached its emotions to the fact, and now the fact is failing it. But for poetry the idea is everything; the rest is a world of illusion, of divine illusion. Poetry attaches its emotion to the idea; the idea *is* the fact. The strongest part of our religion today is its unconscious poetry.

Inevitably, this identification between doctrine and aesthetics led to the "art-religions" of the later nineteenth century. Arnold's theory was carried to its final consequences by Wagner. In his essay on *Religion and Art*, Wagner declared that the artists would save religion by their sensuous re-creation of ancient religious sym-

[1] H. D. F. Kitto: *Form and Meaning in Drama* (London, 1956).

bols which had lost their hold over the modern spirit. Conveyed to the dizzied mind by the magic of *Parsifal*, the root emblems of Christianity would, once again, reveal "their hidden truth."

Arnold's "unconscious poetry" and Wagner's *"ideale Darstellung"* (both of which are representative instances from a dominant intellectual current) have little in common with religion as Dante and Milton understood it. They could in no way contribute towards a coherent structure of faith and gnosis. In spite of *Parsifal*, opera houses did not become temples. The consecrated character of the Athenian and medieval stage was unrecapturable even at Bayreuth.

In our time attempts have been made to re-establish an "immediate and imaginative contact" with the genuine religious cultures of the past. Through anthropology and the study of ritual, Frazer and his disciples have confirmed the notion that drama arose out of sacred rites calculated to ensure the rebirth of the dead year. Scholars have carried over into their study of Shakespeare the quest for "ritual forms" which "haunt and shadow the play, whatever its plot, like ancient traditional ghosts." [2] This kind of inquiry has enriched our feeling for Greek and medieval drama; it has given us clues towards the more riddling aspects of Shakespeare's late plays. But the anthropological approach is limited in scope and pertinence; it does not throw much light on non-dramatic genres and it is truly relevant only where drama is archaic in date or in style.

Exiled from prevailing habits of mind by rationalism and the "scientific philosophies" of materialism, religious sensibility has assumed oblique and subterranean forms. Psychology and psychiatry follow its spoors to the threshold of the unconscious. Armed with psychological probes, modern critics read in depth and often make brilliant soundings. But again, this kind of insight applies only to certain schools and traditions of literature. Melville, Kafka, and Joyce, for example,

[2] J. E. Harrison: *Ancient Art and Ritual* (New York, 1913).

were cabbalists. Their practices of rhetoric retreat inward to a guarded meaning, and much of that meaning may be qualified as religious. But it would be wrong to approach in this manner—to "decode," as it were—works in which the shaping powers of religious feeling or the materials of theology are explicit and have been formulated in traditional terms.

In short: anthropology and the black arts of the psychiatrist enable us to recognize allusions to fertility cults in *The Waste Land* or ambiguous versions of *rites de passage* in the hunting stories of Faulkner. But they do not assist us in the least towards comprehending the theological structure of *Paradise Lost*; they tell us nothing of the gradations of light through which Beatrice approaches Dante in Canto XXX of the *Purgatorio*. In fact—and this is the crucial point—the comparative study of ritual and twentieth-century anatomies of the mind make it ever more difficult for us to respond to a religious sensibility in its open and natural modes of expression. Ideas around which literature and the life of the intellect gravitated from Aeschylus to Dryden —theodicy, grace, damnation, foreknowledge, and the paradox of free will—have, to the major part of a contemporary audience, become an indifferent mystery or the relics of a dead language.

Confronted with this legacy of confusion and ignorance, modern critical theory has developed what one might call a technique of detachment. The crucial statement occurs in I. A. Richards's *Practical Criticism*: "the question of belief or disbelief, in the intellectual sense, never arises when we are reading well. If unfortunately it does arise, either through the poet's fault or our own, we have for the moment ceased to be reading and have become astronomers, or theologians, or moralists, persons engaged in quite a different type of activity."

But can we, in fact, preserve such neutrality? As Cleanth Brooks points out, the poem or the novel is never autonomous. We approach a text from outside and carry with us a baggage of previous beliefs. The act of reading implicates our memories and the totality of our consciousness. In his commentary on Dante, T. S. Eliot concedes that a Catholic might grasp the poem more easily than an agnostic, but argues, as Richards would, that this is "a matter of knowledge and ignorance, not of belief or scepticism." Can we dissociate knowledge from belief? A Marxist will read a play by Brecht differently from a non-Marxist though they may be equally familiar with the material and the dialectical process. Knowledge is the prelude to belief and draws the latter after it. A genuinely neutral mind, moreover, would be closed to that order of literature in which direct appeal is made to our convictions. Neither the *Phaedo* nor the *Divine Comedy* is intended to leave us impartial. They woo our souls with their argument. Much of great art exacts belief. What we must aim for is to render our imaginations as liberal as possible so that we may respond with scrupulous knowledge and charity of insight to the widest range of persuasions.

But are these problems of art and religion relevant to the modern novel?

It has often and justly been said that the world view of the novel is predominantly secular. The upsurge of European prose fiction during the eighteenth century cannot be divorced from the concurrent decline in religious feeling. The novel prevailed in concert with a rationalistic and essentially social interpretation of reality. When submitting to Napoleon his treatise on celestial mechanics, Laplace observed that there was no need in it for "the hypothesis of God." There was no real need for it either in the world of Moll Flanders and Manon Lescaut. Balzac, who together with Sir Walter Scott staked out a territory for the craft of modern fiction, defined the proper subject of a novel as "the history and critique of Society, the analysis of its ills and the discussion of its principles." In doing so, he realized that significant areas had been omitted. Repeatedly, he sought to bring religious and transcendent experience into the *Comédie humaine*. But his achievements in the secular vein greatly surpass such experiments as *Jésus-Christ en Flandre* and *Séraphita*.

One of Wordsworth's noblest sonnets tells us that the world can be too much with a man. Balzac's descendants—Flaubert, Henry James, Proust—affirm the contrary. They proclaim that the world cannot be too much with a novelist; in its concreteness and secular profusion, it is the matrix of his art. By the close of the century, moreover, that rich intimacy with theological values and the vocabulary of religion which informed the minds of such writers as Coleridge and George Eliot had passed from general currency into the preserve of theologians and scholars. In consequence, the treatment of religious themes throughout the major tradition of the European novel tends to be either romantic, as in Anatole France's *Thaïs*, or social and political, as in Zola's *Rome*. *Madame Gervaisais*, by the Goncourts, and Mrs. Humphry Ward's *Robert Elsmere* (which so greatly troubled Mr. Gladstone) are exceptions to the norm. As André Gide said, western fiction is social; it portrays the interrelations of men in society, "but never, nearly never, a man's relations to himself or to God." [3]

The very opposite is true of Tolstoy and Dostoevsky. They were religious artists in the sense of the cathedral-builders or of Michelangelo when he wrought his image of eternity in the Sistine Chapel. They were possessed by the idea of God and travelled their lives like roads to Damascus. The thought of God, the enigma of His being, had seized upon their souls with blinding, constraining force. In their fierce, proud humility, they regarded themselves not as mere inventors of fiction or men of letters, but as seers, prophets, watchmen in the night. "They seek salvation," wrote Berdiaev, "that is the characteristic of Russian creative writers, they seek salvation . . . they suffer for the world." [4]

Their novels are fragments of revelation. They say to us, as Laertes to Hamlet, "Have at you now," and engage our innermost convictions in mortal trial. When we read Tolstoy and Dostoevsky well (to paraphrase

[3] André Gide: *Dostoïevsky* (Paris, 1923).
[4] N. A. Berdiaev: *L'Esprit de Dostoievski* (Paris, 1946).

Richards), questions of belief or disbelief arise incessantly, not through their "fault" or our own, but through their greatness and our humanity.

How, then, should we read them? As we would Aeschylus and Dante rather than, say, Balzac or even Henry James. Commenting on the close of *The Golden Bowl*, which comes so very near to being a religious novel, Fergusson writes: "Maggie does not have a God to refer the Prince to, any more than James did." [5] Such reference to God and His awesome proximity to the life of the soul, are the very centre and foundation of the art of the Russian masters. The cosmology of *Anna Karenina* and *The Brothers Karamazov*, like that portrayed on the antique and medieval stage, is open on either hand to the peril of damnation and the ministry of grace. We cannot say the same of the world of *Eugénie Grandet*, *The Ambassadors*, or *Madame Bovary*. This is a statement not of value but of fact. Tolstoy and Dostoevsky demand from us habits of sensibility and forms of understanding which had, on the whole, lapsed from European literature after the mid-seventeenth century. Dostoevsky poses a further problem; his world view is steeped in the vocabulary and symbolism of a semi-heretical version of Eastern Orthodoxy. Most western readers have little knowledge of his primary material.

A contemporary critic has said that literature and religion, "with their different authorities and different revelations," give us the principal "theoretic forms" and images of our lives.[6] They give to our vision of mortality perhaps its sole enduring focus. On eminent occasions such as the *Oresteia*, the *Divine Comedy*, and the novels of Tolstoy and Dostoevsky, these authorities and revelations are joined in a single harness. Their conjunction—the approach to the logos through the two principal avenues of reason—was celebrated during the early Middle Ages by the inclusion in the Church cal-

[5] Francis Fergusson: "*The Golden Bowl* Revisited" (*The Human Image in Dramatic Literature*, New York, 1957).

[6] R. P. Blackmur: "Between the Numen and the Moha" (*The Lion and the Honeycomb*, New York, 1955).

endar of a St. Virgil-Poet. It is under his patronage that I would proceed.

II

The history of Tolstoy's mind and of the growth of Tolstoyan Christianity has often been misread. Tolstoy's condemnation of literature in the winter of 1879–80 was so emphatic that it suggested a radical dissociation between two eras in his life. Actually, most of the ideas and beliefs expounded by the later Tolstoy appear in his earliest writings and the live substance of his morality was plainly discernible during the years of apprenticeship. As Shestov points out, in his essay on *Tolstoy and Nietzsche*, the remarkable fact is not the seeming contrast between the early and the late Tolstoy, but rather the unity and consequentiality of Tolstoyan thought.

But it would also be erroneous to distinguish three chapters in Tolstoy's life—a period of literary creation circumscribed on either hand by decades of philosophic and religious activity. In Tolstoy we cannot separate the two shaping powers; the moralist and the poet co-exist in anguished and creative proximity. Throughout his career, the religious and the artistic impulse grappled for supremacy. The struggle was particularly acute at the time when Tolstoy was in the midst of writing *Anna Karenina*. At one moment his capacious spirit inclined towards the life of the imagination; in another it yielded to what Ibsen called the "claims of the ideal." One has the impression that Tolstoy found tranquillity and equilibrium only through physical action and in the wild play of physical energy; through exhaustion of body he was able to silence momentarily the debate raging in his mind.

In *The Hedgehog and The Fox*, Isaiah Berlin says of Tolstoy:

His genius lay in the perception of specific properties, the almost inexpressible individual quality in virtue of which the given object is uniquely different from all others. Nevertheless he longed for a universal explanatory principle; that

242

is the perception of resemblances or common origins, or single purpose, or unity in the apparent variety of the mutually exclusive bits and pieces which compose the furniture of the world.

The perception of the specific and integral is the characteristic mark of Tolstoy's artistry, of his unrivalled concreteness. In his novels each piece of the world's furniture is distinctive and stands with individual solidity. But simultaneously Tolstoy was possessed by the hunger for final understanding, for the all-inclusive and justifying disclosure of the ways of God. It was this hunger which impelled him to his polemic and exegetic labours.

In rare moments of sensuous experience or in the recollection of natural delights, Tolstoy harmonized his warring impulses. But in the end the polarity of his genius brought on intolerable strains. He set out, in darkness of reason, to discover the final reconciling vision. Three times, in *Anna Karenina*, railway platforms are the scene of momentous actions. The choice was prophetic, and at Astapovo Tolstoy's life ended in imitation of his art.

This coincidence between imagined and experienced reality symbolizes the cyclical pattern of Tolstoy's evolution, the recurrence of a small number of decisive motifs and emblematic actions. In his *Journées de lecture*, Proust remarked:

In spite of everything, it would seem that Tolstoy repeated himself in his apparently inexhaustible creations; apparently he had at his disposal only a few themes, disguised and renewed, but always identical. . . .

The reason is that the quest for unity, for the revelation of total meaning, underlies Tolstoy's art even where his sensuous perception is most enthralled by the boundless diversity of life.

The principal motifs were apparent from the outset. In January 1847, when he was only nineteen, Tolstoy wrote down rules of behaviour which clearly prefigure the mature precepts of Tolstoyan Christianity.

In the same month he began his diary—that lifelong witness to the dialogue between exacting spirit and rebellious flesh. During that winter also, he attempted to ameliorate the condition of his peasants. In 1849, Tolstoy founded on his estate a school for peasant children and experimented with pedagogic theories similar to those which were to busy his old age. In May 1851, he recorded in his journal that the life of Moscow high society filled him with revulsion; we read that his mind was beset by a "constant inner struggle." In September of the following year, Tolstoy began writing an early version of *The Morning of a Landed Proprietor*; nothing conveys the unity of his endeavours more aptly than the fact that the hero should bear the same name as the hero of *Resurrection*. Prince Nekhlioudov stands at the beginning and at the end of Tolstoy's literary career; at both extremes he is beset by similar religious and moral dilemmas.

In March 1855, Tolstoy explicitly formulated the thought which was to govern him until the hour of his death. He conceived of a "stupendous idea," the foundation of a new religion corresponding to the present state of mankind: the religion of Christ, but purged of dogmas and mysticism, promising not a future bliss but giving bliss on earth." This is the Tolstoyan credo; the works which he wrote and published after 1880 are merely elaborations on it.

Even before he produced his major novels, Tolstoy had considered rejecting *belles lettres* altogether. In November 1865, he expressed profound disgust with "literary life" and the social milieu in which it flourished. In the same month he wrote a letter to Valeria Arsenyeva (to whom he deemed himself engaged); in it we find a rather tragic, but arch-Tolstoyan, commandment: "Don't despair of becoming perfect."

The foundations for his mature program of religious and moral reform were laid in the period from March 1857 to the latter part of 1861. On April 6, 1857 (new style), in Paris, Tolstoy witnessed an execution. He left the city with a sense of outrage; his reverence of life had been cruelly affronted. He drew the consequence that "the ideal is anarchy," and wrote to the Russian critic Botkin:

I have seen many grim and terrible sights in the war, as well as in the Caucasus, but had they hewn a man in pieces before my eyes, the shock would not have been so terrible as was the sight of this ingenious and elegant machine by means of which a young, strong, and healthy man was done to death in an instant. . . . On one point I am resolved: from this day forward not only will I not assist at any such spectacles, but never again under any circumstances will I take service under any form of Government whatsoever.

In October 1859 Tolstoy informed Chicherin, the well-known publicist and reformer, that he was renouncing literature once and for all. The death of his brother, a year later, seemed to confirm his resolution. In 1861, he quarrelled bitterly with Turgeniev, whom he tended to regard as the champion of pure and mundane art, and plunged into a systematic study of education.

In his *Confession*, the novelist tells us that the sight of the guillotine and the death of Nicholas Tolstoy were the two crucial impulses towards his religious awakening. It is interesting to recall that two precisely analogous experiences—public execution and the death of a brother—were instrumental in Dostoevsky's "conversion." The passage in the *Confession* brings to one's mind Prince Muishkin's account of how he saw a criminal being put to death in front of a gaping crowd in Lyons. Tolstoy conveyed his inner crisis through a traditional image, yet one which could reflect his memories of the Caucasus or a reading of Dante: "In my search for answers to life's questions I experienced just what is felt by a man lost in a forest." But instead of entering the Inferno or turning at once to theology, Tolstoy began gathering notes for "a book about the period 1805." It was to become *War and Peace*.

Thus we may say that Tolstoy's novels are raised on a foundation of moral and religious forces at least some of which were hostile to literature. The austerities we associate with the later Tolstoy—the denunciation of *belles lettres,* the conviction that most art lacked moral seriousness, the suspicion of beauty—were characteristic of his outlook long before he composed his main works. In *War and Peace* and *Anna Karenina* an imperfectly liberated imagination surmounted racking doubts concerning the validity of art. As Tolstoy pursued his inquiries into the purpose of human life, into its authentic ends, these doubts gathered force. "The thought which beyond others most often and conspicuously gnaws at him," said Gorky, "is the thought of God." In *Resurrection* that thought burns with intolerable brightness and all but consumes the structure of narrative.

It was Tolstoy's peculiar tragedy that he should have come to regard his poetic genius as corrupt and as an agent of betrayal. By virtue of their comprehensiveness and vitality, *War and Peace* and *Anna Karenina* had splintered yet further an image of reality in which Tolstoy was determined to discover a single meaning and a perfect coherence. They had opposed the disorder of beauty to his desperate search for the philosopher's stone. Gorky saw him as an aged and baffled alchemist:

The old magician stands before me, alien to all, a solitary traveller through all the deserts of thought in search of an all-embracing truth which he has not found. . . .

The crossing of the deserts had clearly begun prior to the two decades in which Tolstoy seemed to live most wholly the life of the imagination. But can we say that *War and Peace* and *Anna Karenina* actually reflect Tolstoy's metaphysical anguish? Are they not typical of the secular point of view dominant in nineteenth-century fiction?

Anyone familiar with Tolstoy's personal life and with the history of his mind will be sensible—perhaps too sensible—to the problematic and doctrinal implications inherent in everything he wrote. Perceived in their total context, the novels and tales play the part of poetic tropes and exploratory myths in an essentially moral and religious dialectic. They are stages of vision in the long pilgrimage. But if we set *Resurrection* to one side, it is clear that religious themes and acts of a religious character occupy a minor place in Tolstoyan fiction. Both *War and Peace* and *Anna Karenina* are images of the empiric world and chronicles of men's temporal works and days.

Even a momentary glance at Dostoevsky provides the contrasting note. In the novels of Dostoevsky, images and situations, the names of the characters and their habits of speech, the general terms of reference, and the qualities of action are prevailingly and dramatically religious. Dostoevsky portrayed men in crises of belief or denial, and often it is through denial that his characters bear witness most forcefully to the incursions of God. "Whoever attempts to deal with the religious element in Dostoevsky's work, soon realizes that he has taken for his subject no less than the totality of the Dostoevskyan world." [7] The same cannot be asserted of Tolstoy. One may read *War and Peace* and *Anna Karenina* as the foremost of historical and social novels with only a vague awareness of their philosophic and religious tenor.

To the majority of critics the pre-eminent aspect of Tolstoy's art has been its sensuous vitality, its vivid, detailed image of military, social, and rural life. Out of the fine-drawn torment of his own infirmity, Proust looked to Tolstoy as to "a serene God." Thomas Mann saw in him, as in Goethe, a favourite of nature, an Olympian graced with inexhaustible health. He invoked "the mighty sensuality of the Tolstoyan epic," its Hellenic joy in the play of light and wind. As we have seen, Russian critics of a religious cast drew a more radical inference: Merezhkovsky declared that Tolstoy had the soul of "a born pagan," and Berdiaev argued that "all his life long Tolstoy sought God as a pagan seeks him."

Must we suppose that the conventional image of Tolstoy is, after all, accurate? Was there a decisive break (possibly in the period from 1874 to 1878) between

[7] Romano Guardini: *Religiöse Gestalten in Dostojewskis Werk* (Munich, 1947).

the "pagan" creator of *War and Peace* and the Christian asectic of *Resurrection* and the later years? I think not. Tolstoy's biography and the record he has left us of his spiritual life bear out the impression of an underlying unity. If we are right in supposing that *War and Peace* and *Anna Karenina* are nearer to Homer than to Flaubert, then the notion of paganism is not unexpected; indeed, it becomes a vital part of the metaphysics to which the analogies between Homer and Tolstoy refer us. There are in Tolstoyan Christianity, and particularly in Tolstoy's image of God, pagan elements; if the *Iliad* and *War and Peace* are comparable on formal grounds (as we have seen them to be), then their governing mythologies are comparable also. By keeping our attention responsive and uncommitted, we shall, I think, come to realize that Tolstoyan paganism and Tolstoyan Christianity were not diametrical opposites, but successive and interrelated acts in the drama of a single intelligence. *War and Peace*, *Anna Karenina*, and the tales of the early and middle years, sensuous, wondrously serene in their effect, were nevertheless forerunners and preparers of Tolstoy's sacrificial theology. They establish the world image which that theology will seek to interpret. Conversely, the doctrines of the later Tolstoy carry to the folly of conclusion premises laid down in the writings of his golden period.

When we consider the modulations from abstract thought to artistic embodiment and from poetic forms to new mythologies, we tend to oversimplify. We see straight lines and direct sequences where there are, in actual fact, arabesques. This is why the testimony of Gorky, himself a creator of forms, is so invaluable. He says of Tolstoy:

no one was more complicated, contradictory, and great in everything—yes, in everything. Great in some curious sense, broad, indefinable by words, there is something in him which made me desire to cry aloud to every one: "Look what a wonderful man is living on the earth!"

Doubtless, a contradictory nature, but also one that was strangely united and had at its centre an ancient dilemma: God is a creator—the poet of the arch-mythology; but a mortal artist is a creator also. What, then, of the relations between them?

III

I do not propose to attempt a systematic outline of Tolstoyan theology. Its teachings are expounded in lapidary tracts. Tolstoy was a polemicist and pamphleteer who believed in the virtues of clarity and repetition. He was a master in the art of presenting complex ideas through simple images and graphic parables, and his primary meanings are rarely obscure. Lenin and Bernard Shaw may have learnt from him some of the arts of vehemence. I will restrict myself to those aspects of Tolstoy's metaphysics which can be most securely related to the poetics of the Tolstoyan novel.

It follows from what has been said earlier that in every mature and completed work of art a totality of vision is implicit. Even a short lyric poem makes defining statements about two spheres of reality—the poem itself and that which lies outside it (in the sense that a vase defines two areas in space). But in the majority of instances we cannot wholly document the continuities between a mythology and its aesthetic embodiment. We conjecture, we read "between the lines" (as if the poem were a screen and not, as it must be, a lens), or we extrapolate from what we know of the writer's biography and of the intellectual climate of his time. Often such divinations fail us altogether. The magnitude of Shakespeare's art, for example, the steadiness and breadth of illumination which he throws upon the principal themes of the human condition, suggest that he had achieved a philosophy of profound authority and articulateness. Of all the "criticisms of life" put forward in literature, that of Shakespeare impresses one as probably the most comprehensive and prophetic. Yet if we attempt to systematize Shakespeare's insights, if we seek to isolate a metaphysical program from the perpetual mobility of the dramatic medium, we come up with a chap-book of famous lines which have little in common except perfection of utterance. Shakespeare's speculative universality led the romantics to identify him with Hamlet. At present, we are inclined to study the Duke in *Measure for Measure* and Prospero in *The Tempest*, supposing that in these characters the poet's personal philosophy has been declared and has been given the structure of a sustained argument. Thus Fergusson imagines that Shakespeare may have assumed the guise of the Duke of Vienna, "lighting his great theme from several sides at once." [8] But how can we say that in *Measure for Measure* Shakespeare is not Angelo as well? Goethe remarked, in a short paper written in the summer of 1813, that "a man naturally pious, such as Shakespeare was, had the liberty to develop his inner being religiously without reference to any specific religion." But this too is conjecture and there are scholars who believe that the key to Shakespeare's interpretation of life, to his "provisional faiths," lies not in catholicity but in hidden Catholicism.

On the other hand, there are writers in whose works the kinship between a specific philosophy and the literary performance is clear and can be demonstrated in the actual texts. Among them one would count Dante, Blake, and Tolstoy. In Tolstoy's letters, drafts, and journals we may follow a line of thought from the glimmerings of awareness to the final edifice of doctrine. Sometimes we may follow it all too clearly through the fabric of the novels. The elements of abstraction have not everywhere been transposed into the key of fiction. In *Resurrection*, and even in *War and Peace*, moral imperatives and fragments of theory stand out like meteoric boulders in the imagined landscape. The tract invades the poem. In *Anna Karenina*, on the contrary, the accord is perfect: the purgatorial unfolding through tragic recognition to ultimate grace is exactly rendered by the movement of the fable.

In the theology of Tolstoy there are four principal

[8] Francis Fergusson: *"Measure for Measure"* (*The Human Image in Dramatic Literature*, New York, 1957).

themes: death, the Kingdom of God, the person of Christ, and the encounter of the novelist himself with God the Father. It is not always possible to determine Tolstoy's final judgment of these matters. His convictions altered in some measure between 1884 and 1889. Moreover, he professed his meanings in various ways appropriate to the intellectual grasp of the particular audience. Hence Berdiaev's feeling that Tolstoyan theology is often simple-minded. But in the essential canon—in *A Confession, The Gospel in Brief, What I Believe, On Life, The Christian Teaching*, and the journals, notably for the period from 1895 to 1899 —a consequent and firmly wrought metaphysics is put forward. There were elements in it that moved Gorky to say of Tolstoy: "Surely, he has some thoughts of which he is afraid."

Like Goya and Rilke, Tolstoy was haunted by the mystery of death. This hauntedness deepened with the years, for in him, as in Yeats, life burnt hotter and more mutinous with old age. Tolstoy's experience of physical and intellectual life was on so heroic a scale that his whole being rebelled against the paradox of mortality. His terrors were not primarily those of the flesh (he had been a soldier and hunter of great audacity); he suffered from a despair of reason at the thought that men's lives were doomed through illness or violence or the ravenings of time to irremediable extinction, to that inch-by-inch disappearance into the "dark sack" which Ivan Ilych records in his last agonized moments.

In diametric opposition to Dostoevsky, who confessed that he would remain with Christ even if "someone had proved that Christ is outside the truth," Tolstoy declared: "I love truth more than anything in the world." His relentless veracity compelled him to recognize that there is no definitive proof for the immortality of the soul or the survival of any form of consciousness whatever. When Anna Karenina dies under the charging wheels, her being passes irretrievably into the hands of darkness. Like Levin—who so often holds up a mirror to the novelist—Tolstoy was harassed to the edge of self-destruction by the apparent absurdity of human existence. In his diary he examined the possibility of suicide:

A few exceptionally strong and consistent people act so. Having understood the stupidity of the joke that has been played on them, and having understood that it is better to be dead than to be alive, and that it is best of all not to exist, they act accordingly and promptly end this stupid joke, since there are means to do so: a rope round one's neck, water, a knife to stick in one's heart. . . .

Out of this desperate meditation grew a consoling myth. Declaring that "God is life," and that "To know God and to live is one and the same thing," Tolstoy came to deny the reality of death. He wrote in his journal for December 1895 that man is "never born and never dies and always is." And even where he was prepared to recognize in death a definable experience, he saw that experience as a consecration of the life-force. Writing to Countess Tolstoy in May 1898, he described a walk through a forest burgeoning with early summer:

And I thought, as I constantly do, about death. And it was so clear to me that on the other side of death it will be as good, though in a different way, and I understood why the Jews represented paradise as a garden.

In the following month, with the glory of the season upon him, and in terms drawn uncharacteristically from the world of the theatre, Tolstoy recorded one of his finest visions:

Death is the crossing-over from one consciousness to another, from one image of the world to another. It is as if you go over from one scene with its scenery to another. . . . At the moment of this crossing-over, there becomes evident, or at least one feels, the most actual reality.

I do not suppose that this belief, with its Oriental and quietistic overtones, altogether removed Tolstoy's anguish. But as metaphysics, the denial of time and of the terrible chasm between the quick and the dead throws sharp light on the mystery of poetic creation.

Tolstoy perceived in the act of fiction an analogue to the labour of the Deity. In the beginning was the word —for both God and the poet. The personages of *War and Peace* and *Anna Karenina* had sprung from Tolstoy's consciousness fully armed with life and bore within themselves seeds of immortality. Anna Karenina dies in the world of the novel; but each time we read the book she attains resurrection; and even after we have finished it she leads yet another life in our remembrance. In each literary figure there is something of the undying Firebird. Through the after- and onward-lives of his characters, Tolstoy's own existence had its beginnings of eternity. If we marvel, therefore, at the vitality of his inventions and at the formal "unendingness" of his novels, we must bear in mind that he was intent on mastering death. Long after he had condemned his literary works, Tolstoy cherished the secret belief that they were a challenge to mortality. He confessed in his journal for October 1909 that he "would like to come back to writing literature," and to the very last jotted down plans for novels, tales, and dramas as if these were talismans of longevity.

Tolstoy's conception of the Kingdom of God arose directly out of his stubborn attempts to entrap the death-drawn soul and to retain it everlastingly within the confines of the tangible world. He emphatically rejected the notion that the Kingdom lay "elsewhere," that we accede to it through a transcendence of life itself. Much of western thought is founded on a Platonic division between the shadow-world of the mortal senses and the "true," unchanging realm of ideas and absolute light. Entrenched in our poetics is the belief that art reveals to us, through allegory and metaphor, the "real" world of which our own is but a corrupt or fragmentary image. Dante's ascent to the rose of light is an imitation—probably the subtlest and most coherent that we possess—of the principal action of the western mind as a whole: the ascent from the transitory to the real through philosophy or science or the sudden illuminations of poetry and grace.

There is in the Tolstoyan novel a "double consciousness," but both terms of the essential metaphors are of this world. Brought into juxtaposition are not our earthly life and some transcendent, more authentic experience after death, but the good and the bad life here, on earth, in the flux of material time. The art of Tolstoy is anti-Platonic; it celebrates the complete "realness" of the world. It tells us, over and again, that the Kingdom of God must be established here and now, on this earth and in this, the only real life that is accorded us. Behind this conviction lay the program of a practical reformer determined to build the new Jerusalem, and the secretive, tormented faith of a man of letters in the reality and permanence of his imaginings. The poet of *War and Peace* and *Anna Karenina* was not prepared to consider these creations as "but a spume that plays/Upon the ghostly paradigm of things."

Unwearyingly, Tolstoy expounded the lesson that there is no evidence for the existence of another world and that the Kingdom of God must be built by mortal hands. He identified the voice of Christ with "the whole rational consciousness of humanity," and reduced the Sermon on the Mount to five elementary rules of conduct:

The fulfilment of Christ's teaching expressed in the five commandments, would establish the Kingdom of God. The Kingdom of God on earth is the peace of all men one with another. . . . The whole of Christ's teaching consists in giving the Kingdom of God, that is peace, to man.

What is the essence of Christ's ministry? He teaches men "not to commit stupidities." All of Tolstoy's brutal empiricism and aristocratic impatience resound in that extraordinary answer. The Dostoevskyan Christ, on the contrary, teaches men to commit the gravest stupidities. What is wisdom in His eyes may be idiocy in the eyes of the world.

Tolstoy would have no truck with the "dead Church" which accepts the crimes, follies, and inhumanities of terrestrial life in the expectation that justice will be meted out hereafter. The theodicy of compensation, the belief that the tortured and the impoverished shall sit on the right of the Father in another kingdom, seemed to him a fraudulent and cruel legend calculated to preserve the existing social order. Justice must be achieved here and now. The Tolstoyan version of the second coming is an earthly millennium in which men will have awoken to the dictates of rational morality. Is it not

Tolstoi's Excommunication
Hinaus mit ihm! Sein Kreuz ist viel zu groß für unsre Kirche!

"Get him out! His cross is much too big for our Church."

written in the Gospel according to John that the work of God "consists in believing in the life He has given you"? With a sombre instinct Tolstoy felt that He would give no other. The one we have must be rendered as sane and perfect as possible.

Tolstoy affirmed that his doctrines were solidly rooted in Scripture. Earlier commentators had simply misread the relevant texts through perversity or dullness of mind. In 1859, Benjamin Jowett had said with regard to exegetic problems that "The universal truth easily breaks through the accidents of time and place." Tolstoy carried this belief to extremes of assurance:

the common explanation of verses 17 and 18 in Matthew v (which had formerly struck me by their obscurity) must be incorrect. And on re-reading those verses . . . I was amazed by the simple and clear meaning in them which suddenly revealed itself to me.

His solutions are unashamedly dogmatic: "The text confirmed my supposition so that no further doubt about it was possible." This impatient disregard of the philological and doctrinal obscurities of Holy Writ was not an accident of temper; it points to Tolstoy's profound kinship with all the radical and iconoclastic movements which assailed the official Church, between the eleventh and the late sixteenth centuries, in the name of millennial justice and the foundation of the City of God on earth. Each of these insurrections, and the Reformation itself, began by proclaiming that the meaning of the Scriptures was plain and accessible to the common mind. The "inner light" does not recognize the enigmas of textual scholarship.

Throughout history, mythologies of justice and of the ideal state have tended towards one of two directions. Either they postulate the inherent fallibility of man, the permanence of a measure of injustice and absurdity in human affairs, the necessary imperfection of all mechanisms of power, and the consequent perils of attempting to establish a mortal utopia. Or they will affirm that man is perfectible, that reason and will can conquer the inequities of the social order, that the *civitas Dei* must be built now and upon earth, and that transcendental justifications of the ways of God to men are cunning myths intended to stifle the revolutionary instincts of the oppressed. Among adherents to the first alternative are those political thinkers and rulers whom we qualify as empiricists or liberals, all who distrust final solutions and who believe that imperfection is inseparable from historical reality; among them we count those who are inclined to believe that any ideal governance imposed upon the many by the passionate intelligence and outraged humanitarianism of the few will degenerate, by some fatal law of entropy, into hideous misrule. Opposed to this attitude of scepticism and resignation are the partisans of *The Republic*, the chiliasts, the visionaries of the Fifth Monarchy, the Comtians—all the enemies of the open and imperfect society. These men are haunted by the stupidities and evils prevalent in human affairs. They are prepared, at the price of apocalyptic warfare and fanatic self-denial, to uproot the old citadels of corruption and to wade, if need be, through "seas of blood" (the constant image of the medieval Taborites) to the new "city of the sun."

The mystery of the Kingdom of God is central to this conflict. If this Kingdom exists beyond mortality, if we believe that there is a redemptive judgment, then we may accept the persistence of evil in this world. Then we may find it bearable that our present lives do not exemplify perfection, total justice, or the triumph of moral values. In this light, evil itself becomes a necessary adjunct of human freedom. But if there is no "other life," if the Kingdom of God is merely a fantasy born of man's suffering, then we must do everything in our power to purge the world of its failings and build Jerusalem of earthly bricks. To accomplish this, we may have to overthrow existing society. Cruelty, intolerance, fanatical rigour become temporary virtues in the service of the revolutionary ideal. History may have to pass through Armageddon or decades of political terror. But in the end the state shall wither away and man shall awake once again in the first garden.

It is an ancient dream. It was dreamt by the medieval apocalyptics, by the Anabaptists, the Adamites, the Ranters, the more extreme of the Puritan theocrats. In modern guise it inspired the disciples of Saint-Simon, the followers of Cabet, and the religious fringe of the anarchist movement. Though chiliasm often declared its adherence to the Gospel and claimed that it was enacting the true message of Christ, the established churches have perceived in it an arch-heresy. For what need shall there be of a consoling and redeeming God if men achieve perfect justice and repose in their mortal lives? Is the very notion of God not fostered by the suffering of the flesh and the agonies of the spirit? In 1525, Thomas Müntzer attempted to rule Mülhausen in the image of the city or Revelation. Luther condemned the experiment with harsh clear-sightedness. He said of Müntzer's articles of constitution:

they aim to make all men equal, to make of the spiritual realm of Christ a kingdom of this earth, an outward kingdom—and this is impossible.[9]

Much of the irreconcilable conflict between Tolstoyan and Dostoevskyan theology, between the hope of *Resurrection* and the tragic prophecy of *The Possessed*, is implicit in this judgment. "To make of the spiritual realm of Christ a kingdom of this earth" was Tolstoy's principal endeavour. In *The Possessed* and *The Brothers Karamazov*, Dostoevsky asserted not only that "this is impossible," but that the attempt would end in political bestiality and in the destruction of the idea of God.

In our own time this conflict has erupted with apocalyptic violence. The "thousand-year" *Reich* of National Socialism and the classless, ultimately disappearing, state of Soviet Communism are eschatological images and new goals in the ancient pursuit of the millennium.[1] The eschatology is secular in that it arises out of a denial of God. But the underlying vision is that of all chiliastic and utopian movements: man must either create the good life here on earth or resign himself to suffering his term in a chaotic, unjust, and frequently incomprehensible journey between two poles of darkness. The Kingdom of God must be realized as the Kingdom of Man. This is the theology of the totalitarian utopias. Whether it will vanquish its imperfect and divided opponents appears to be the inescapable question of our afflicted century. Another way of asking it is to inquire whether Tolstoy or Dostoevsky gave the truer image of human nature and the more prophetic account of history.

[9] Martin Luther: *Ermahnung zum Frieden auf die zwölf Artikel* (1525).
[1] The relations between modern totalitarian philosophies and the chiliastic tradition are set forth in Norman Cohn: *The Pursuit of the Millennium* (London, 1957).

Clearly, Tolstoy envisaged a terrestrial Kingdom of God; his actual conception of this Kingdom is, however, more difficult to determine. The apostolic succession to which he often referred is equivocal:

Moses, Isaiah, Confucius, the early Greeks, Buddha, Socrates, down to Pascal, Spinoza, Fichte, Feuerbach and all those, often unnoticed and unknown, who, taking no teachings on trust, thought and spoke sincerely upon the meaning of life.

During the earlier stages in his philosophic inquiries, Tolstoy certainly believed that his image of the good life was an integral part of his Christian faith. But later on his mind became more secretive and there were moments in which he seems to have been afraid of pursuing his passionate longing for justice and social reform to its final logic. When he came to write that "The desire for universal welfare . . . is that which we call God," Tolstoy had moved considerably closer to Feuerbach than to Pascal. Lenin described Tolstoy as a "mirror of the Russian revolution," and in November 1905 Tolstoy seems to have adopted some of the special theories of Marxism about the coming insurrection and the ultimate "withering away" of the state. But on all these points, his self-lacerating intelligence and lucidity led to contradictions. Even at a time when he was preaching most vehemently on the text of the perfectibility of men and the foundation of the radical utopia, he glimpsed that possibility of disaster which haunted Herzen and Dostoevsky. He noted in his journal for August 1898:

Even if that which Marx predicted should happen, then the only thing that will happen is that despotism will be passed on. Now the capitalists rule, but then the directors of the working people will rule.

On sifting the complex mass of evidence, one receives the impression that Tolstoy, like so many chiliasts and prophets of the impending apocalypse, was clearer on the need for reform and on the ultimate ideals to be achieved than on the method of achievement or the transitory stages of organization. In his moments of most cogent analysis it becomes apparent that "the ideal is anarchy" rather than temporal theocracy. But on the essential point he was unwavering: the covenant of grace and justice must be executed in this world and through the ministry of reason.

I have insisted on these political aspects of Tolstoyan metaphysics because they dramatize the root antagonism between Tolstoy and Dostoevsky. Tolstoy's eschatology, moreover, was directly related to the point of view and techniques of the Tolstoyan novel. He condemned the notion that a work of art is a reflection of transcendent reality. The match must be played out here and now within the confines of rational and historical experience. This held true for both the philosopher and the novelist. The earth is our sole province and, at times, our prison. In his diary for February 1896, Tolstoy devised a terrifying parable:

If you go away from the conditions here, if you kill yourself, then the same thing will be put before you again there. So there is nowhere to go. It would be good to write the history of what a man lives through in this life who committed suicide in a past life; how, coming up before the same requirements which were placed before him in the other life, he comes to the realization that he must fulfil them.

But in his periods of poetic creation, Tolstoy did not wish to leave "conditions here." He rejoiced in the sensible world, in its infinite variety, in the solidity of things. Berdiaev said of Dostoevsky that "nobody was less preoccupied with the empirical world . . . his art is completely immersed in the profound realities of the spiritual universe." [2] The art of Tolstoy, on the contrary, is steeped in the reality of the senses; no imagination was more carnal or more serenely possessed of what D. H. Lawrence called "blood wisdom." Tolstoy wrote fiction as he hunted wolves or hewed birch-wood, with a physicality and grasp of the "thingness" of things

[2] N. A. Berdiaev: op. cit.

which make the inventions of other novelists seem
ghostly.

In the notebooks for *The Possessed*, Dostoevsky set
down, with evident sarcasm, a fragment of dialogue:

> Liputin: We are not far from the kingdom of God.
> *Nechaiev*: Yes, in June.

That month, or the expectation of it, loomed large in
the Tolstoyan year. Through his art and through his
religious mythology, he celebrated the world—its golden
past and its revolutionary becoming. He would not believe that those who dwell in it are merely insubstantial
shadows.

Despite its follies and evils, moreover, it was a world
accessible to reason. In fact, reason was the supreme
arbiter of reality. Tolstoy asked Aylmer Maude: "How
is it . . . that these gentlemen do not understand that
even in the face of death, two and two still make four?"
The "gentlemen" in question were members of the Orthodox hierarchy who were endeavouring to bring the
novelist back into the fold. But the challenge is addressed even more crucially to the metaphysics of the
irrational put forward by Dostoevsky. "What have *I* to
do with the Laws of Nature," demanded the narrator
in the *Letters from the Underworld*, "or with arithme-
tic, when all the time those laws and the formula that
twice two make four do not meet with my acceptance?"
Much is at stake in this contrariety: a theory of knowledge, an interpretation of history, an image of God—
but also a conception of the novel. We cannot separate the one from the others. Therein lies the stature
and dignity of Tolstoyan and Dostoevskyan fiction.

Nowhere are Tolstoy's imaginative genius and his
philosophic speculations more closely interwoven than
in his attitude towards the person of Christ and the
mystery of God. We touch here on the very heart of
his creative life, where the powers of the writer, the convictions of the theologian, and the temper of the
man were indivisible. Christ and God the Father are
immensely present in the background of Russian litera-

ture. From *Dead Souls* to *Resurrection*, the Russian novel tells of a civilization many of whose keenest minds were engaged in an anguished quest for a redeemer and lived in terror of Antichrist. Here again, the Tolstoyan position can be most accurately defined in contrast to that of Dostoevsky.

In what are among his final notes, Dostoevsky observed:

The Saviour did not descend from the cross because he did not wish to convert men through the compulsion of an outward miracle, but through freedom of belief.

In that refusal, in that supreme liberality, Tolstoy saw the origin of the chaos and blindness afflicting the human mind. Christ had infinitely complicated the task of those who would establish His kingdom by placing the enigma of His silence across the straight path of reason. Had Christ shown Himself in messianic splendour, men's beliefs might, in a sense, have been constrained; but they would have been purged of doubt and removed from daemonic temptation. Christ's policy appeared to Tolstoy like that of a monarch who would go about in rags and obscurity, allowing his realm to fall into disorder, so as to sanctify those few among his subjects acute enough to recognize him even in disguise. Gorky tells us:

When he speaks about Christ, it is always peculiarly poor— no enthusiasm, no feeling in his words, and no spark of real fire. I think he regards Christ as simple and deserving of pity; and although at times he admires him, he hardly loves him.

Tolstoy could not have loved a prophet who declared that His kingdom was not of this world. The aristocratic temper of the man, his love of physical energy and heroism, rebelled at Christ's meekness and pathos. Certain art historians point out that in Venetian painting (with the exception of Tintoretto) the figure of Jesus is pallid and unconvincing. They attribute this fact to the exuberant worldliness of Venice, to the refusal of a culture which had turned water into marble to believe that the riches of the earth were mere dross or that slaves should pass before Doges in some other life. Similar refusals were at work in Tolstoy. They impelled him towards thoughts of which he was evidently afraid. He confessed in *What I Believe*:

It is terrible to say, but it sometimes appears to me that if Christ's teaching, with the Church teaching that has grown out of it, had not existed at all, those who now call themselves Christians would have been nearer to the truth of Christ—that is to say, to a reasonable understanding of what is good in life—than they now are.

In plainer language, this means that if Christ had not existed it would have been easier for men to arrive at rational, Tolstoyan principles of conduct and thus to realize God's Kingdom. Through His humble ambiguity and through His unwillingness to reveal Himself in militant glory, Christ had made human affairs infinitely more difficult.

Seven years later, when replying to the edict of excommunication promulgated against him by the Holy Synod, Tolstoy stated his public creed:

I believe that the will of God is most clearly and intelligibly expressed in the teachings of the man Jesus, whom to consider a God and pray to I esteem the greatest blasphemy.

It is doubtful whether he would have conceded even this much in the privacy of his thoughts. Furthermore, what Tolstoy signified by "the teachings of the man Jesus" was an intensely personal and often arbitrary reading of the Gospels.

Of recorded dramas of the soul, that of Tolstoy's relations to God is among the most absorbing and majestic. In contemplating it one is haunted by the notion that the forces engaged on either side were not infinitely disparate in magnitude. This is a notion which a number of great artists bring to mind. I have heard students of music infer a similar confrontation from the late compositions of Beethoven, and there are pieces of statuary by Michelangelo which hint at awesome encounters between God and the more god-like of

His creatures. To have carved the figures in the Medici Chapel, to have imagined Hamlet and Falstaff, to have heard the Missa Solemnis out of deafness is to have said, in some mortal but irreducible manner: "Let there be light." It is to have wrestled with the angel. Something of the artist is consumed or mutilated in the combat. Art itself has its emblem in the image of Jacob limping away from the banks of the Jabbok, blest, wounded, and transformed by his dread match. This, perhaps, is why one fancies that there was in Milton's blindness, in Beethoven's deafness, or in Tolstoy's final, hunted pilgrimage towards death some terrible but appropriate justice. How much mastery over creation can a man achieve and yet remain unscathed? As Rilke proclaimed, in the First Duino Elegy: *"Ein jeder Engel ist schrecklich."*

Tolstoy's dialogue with God, like that of Pascal and Kierkegaard, had all the elements of drama. There were crises and reconciliations, exits and alarums. He wrote in his journal for January 19, 1898:

Help, Father. Come and dwell within me. You already dwell within me. You are already "me." My work is only to recognize Thee. I write this just now and am full of desire. But nevertheless I know who I am.

It is a strange plea. Tolstoy was inclined to believe that self-knowledge led immediately to the recognition of God. An alien glory had invaded him. And yet, there were strains of doubt and rebellion in the half-despairing, half-exultant assertion, "nevertheless I know who I am." Tolstoy could reconcile himself neither to the absence of God nor to His independent reality outside Tolstoy himself. With awed insight, Gorky captured this divided mood:

In his diary which he gave me to read, I was struck by a strange aphorism: "God is my desire."

Then on returning him the book, I asked him what it meant.

"An unfinished thought," he said, glancing at the page and screwing up his eyes. "I must have wanted to say: God is my desire to know him. . . . No, not that. . . ." He began to laugh, and rolling up the book into a tube, he put it into the big pocket of his blouse. With God he has very suspicious relations; they sometimes remind me of the relations of "two bears in one den."

It is through some such rebellious and secret image that Tolstoy himself may have conceived of the relation in his moments of truth. Time and again, as in his diary for May 1896, he referred to "this God who is enclosed in man." The very existence of God appears to have been acceptable to him only in terms of human identity. This idea, compounded of poetic egotism and spiritual *hauteur*—Tolstoy was every inch a king—led him into various paradoxes. Recollecting an experience that took place in the summer of 1896, he wrote:

I felt God clearly for the first time; that He existed and that I existed in Him; that the only thing that existed was I in Him: in Him like a limited thing in an unlimited thing, in Him also like a limited being in which He existed.

It is this kind of passage students of Tolstoy have in mind when they relate his thought to Oriental theosophy and Taoism. But in the main, Tolstoy was obsessed with reason and a desire for clear understanding. The part of Voltaire in him was too prominent to accept for very long shadowy intimations of the divine presence. If God existed, He was "other" than man. The enigma of His realness tormented Tolstoy's proud and searching intellect. "The man Jesus" could, in the wake of Renan and Strauss, be diminished to a human scale. God was a more redoubtable opponent. Hence, perhaps, the Tolstoyan demand that His kingdom be realized on earth. If this could be accomplished, God might be tempted into walking once again in the garden. There Tolstoy would await Him in an ambush of desire. The two bears would be at last in the same den.

But despite the revolutionary stirrings of 1905 and Gandhi's progress in India, which Tolstoy followed with passionate attention, the Kingdom of God was no nearer fulfilment. God Himself seemed to withdraw before Tolstoy's arduous longing. In Tolstoy's final abandonment of home there is both a specific, material protest against the "bad life" and a more secret pilgrimage of the maddened soul in pursuit of an elusive deity. But was Tolstoy the hunter or the hunted? Gorky imagined him as one

of those pilgrims who all their life long, stick in hand, walk the earth, travelling thousands of miles from one monastery to another, from one saint's relic to another, terribly homeless and alien to all men and things. The world is not for them, nor God either. They pray to Him from habit, and in their secret soul they hate Him—why does He drive them over the earth, from one end to the other?

This alternation of love and hatred, of epiphany and scepticism, makes it difficult to define Tolstoyan theology with any rigour. Through its image of the human Christ, through its speculations on God's enclosedness in man, and by virtue of its chiliastic program, it can be related to some of the major heresies of the early and medieval Church. But the real difficulty lies far deeper and it is one which few commentators, have been prepared to examine seriously. In the religion of Tolstoy the principal terms are dangerously fluid: "God is deliberately replaced by 'the Good' and 'the Good' is in turn replaced by brotherly love among men. Actually, such a creed excludes neither complete atheism nor total disbelief." [3] This is undeniably true; the defining conceptions are interchangeable and through a gradual process of equation we arrive at a theology without God. Or, rather, we arrive at an anthropology of mortal greatness in which men have created God in their own image. He is the uttermost projection of their own nature; at times a titular guardian, at other times an enemy full of ancient cunning and sudden vengeance. Such a vision of God and the drama of encounters between God and man which it entails are neither Christian nor atheist. They are pagan.

I do not suppose that this anthropomorphic theology

[3] Léon Shestov: *Tolstoi und Nietzsche* (trans. by N. Strasser, Cologne, 1923).

determined the whole of Tolstoyan metaphysics. Over considerable periods his image of God was doubtless nearer to that of established Christian doctrine. But in Tolstoy's complex and changeable mind there were very strong elements of what Dostoevsky would have called the idea of the "man-God." A similar idea governed the Homeric world. Before the gates of Troy, men and gods meet in equal commerce and well-matched antagonism. The gods are men enlarged in courage or brute force or ruse or desire. Between gods and men we find the gradations of ultra-heroism and semi-divinity. This lack of an essential qualitative difference between human and divine made possible some of the archetypal myths: the descent of the gods upon mortal women, the deification of heroes, Hercules' wrestling match with death, the mutinies of Prometheus and Ajax, the dialogue between music and material chaos in the legend of Orpheus. But, above all, the humanity of the gods signifies that reality—the controlling pivot of man's experience—is immanent in the natural world. The gods inhabit Olympus; but the latter is merely a high mountain subject to the assaults of daemons and giants. The voices of the divine are heard murmuring through earthly trees and terrestrial waters. These are some of the conventions of belief that we invoke when we refer to a pagan cosmology.

Translated into warier, more ambiguous terms, such a cosmology is implicit also in the art of Tolstoy. Where he did not envisage God as a metaphoric equivalent for a social and rational utopia, Tolstoy saw Him, through some covert blasphemy of solitude or love, as a being rather similar to himself. This, I feel, was the central enigma in his philosophy and the thought of which he was most afraid. In a letter to the dramatist and editor A. S. Suvorin, dated December 11, 1891, Chekhov touched with great precision on the pagan quality of Tolstoyan grandeur. "Oh, that Tolstoy, that Tolstoy! He, at the present time, is not a human being, but a superman, a Jupiter." Tolstoy conceived of God and man as comparable artificers or antagonists. Whatever its bearing on the grace of his soul, this pagan and truly Homeric representation was inseparable from his genius as a novelist.

It is on the genius that I have, until now, insisted: on its sensuous range, on its authority and capaciousness, on the fecundity and humaneness of Tolstoy's invention. But if the mythology of an artist is directly instrumental in the virtues and technical accomplishments of his art, it is implicated also in its failures or incompletions. Where we observe a recurrent or characteristic defect, an instability of treatment or inadequacy of realization, we may find a corresponding failure of metaphysics. Thus, contemporary critics have said of the romantic poets that weaknesses in their poetic technique and imprecisions in their use of language point directly to incoherencies in the philosophic equipment of the romantic period.

Confronted with particular narrative themes and specific modes of action, the novels of Tolstoy reveal unmistakable imperfections or losses of power. There are definable areas in which the composition is blurred and the presentation falters. In each instance we shall find that the narrative has engaged values or types of material to which Tolstoyan philosophy was hostile or of which it had taken insufficient account. Significantly, these are areas in which Dostoevsky excels.

IV

I would like to consider three passages from *War and Peace*. The first is the famous portrayal of Prince Andrew in the moment in which he is struck down at Austerlitz:

"What's this? Am I falling? My legs are giving way," thought he, and fell on his back. He opened his eyes, hoping to see how the struggle of the Frenchmen with the gunners ended, and whether the cannon had been captured or saved. But he saw nothing. Above him there was nothing but the sky—the lofty sky, not clear yet immeasurably lofty, with grey clouds gliding slowly across it. "How quiet, peaceful, and solemn, not at all as it was when I ran," thought Prince Andrew—"not as we ran, shouting and fighting, not at all as the gunner and the Frenchman with frightened and angry faces struggled for the mop: how differently do those clouds glide across that lofty infinite sky! How was it that I did not see that lofty sky before? And how happy am I to have found it at last! Yes! All is vanity, all falsehood, except that infinite sky. There is nothing, nothing but that. But even it does not exist, there is nothing but quiet and peace. Thank God! . . ."

The second passage (from the twenty-second chapter of Book VIII) is an account of Pierre's feelings as he drives home in his sledge after assuring Natasha that she is worthy of love and that life lies all before her:

It was clear and frosty. Above the dirty ill-lit streets, above the black roofs, stretched the dark starry sky. Only looking up at the sky did Pierre cease to feel how sordid and humiliating were all mundane things compared to the heights to which his soul had just been raised. At the entrance to the Arbat Square an immense expanse of dark starry sky presented itself to his eyes. Almost in the centre of it, above the Perchistenka Boulevard, surrounded and sprinkled on all sides by stars but distinguished from them all by its nearness to the earth, its white light, and its long uplifted tail, shone the enormous and brilliant comet of the year 1812—the comet which was said to portend all kinds of woes and the end of the world. In Pierre, however, that comet, with its long luminous tail aroused no feeling of fear. On the contrary he gazed joyfully, his eyes moist with tears, at this bright comet which, having travelled in its orbit with inconceivable velocity through immeasurable space, seemed suddenly—like an arrow piercing the earth —to remain fixed in a chosen spot, vigorously holding its tail erect, shining, and displaying its white light amid countless other scintillating stars. It seemed to Pierre that this comet fully responded to what was passing in his own softened and uplifted soul, now blossoming into a new life.

Finally, I want to cite a short passage from the relation of Pierre's captivity in Book XIII:

The huge endless bivouac that had previously resounded with the crackling of camp-fires and the voices of many men had grown quiet, the red camp-fires were growing paler and dying down. High up in the lit sky hung the full moon. Forests and fields beyond the camp, unseen before, were now visible in the distance. And farther still, beyond those forests and fields, the bright, oscillating, limitless distance lured one to itself. Pierre glanced up at the sky and the twinkling stars in its far-away depths. "And this is me, and all that is within me, and it is all I!" thought Pierre. "And they caught all that and put it into a shed boarded up with planks!" He smiled, and went and lay down to sleep beside his companions.

These three passages illustrate how "in the novel, as elsewhere in the literary arts, what is called technical or executive form has as its final purpose to bring into being—to bring into performance, for the writer and for the reader—an instance of the feeling of what life is about." [4] In all three the technical form is a great curve of motion speeding outward from a conscious centre—the eye of the character through which the scene is ostensibly perceived—and returning decisively to earth. This motion is allegorical. It communicates plot-values and visual actualities in its own right; but it is at the same time a stylistic trope, a means of conveying a movement of the soul. Two gestures mirror one another: the upward vision of the eye and the downward gathering of the human consciousness. This duality aims at a conceit which is characteristically Tolstoyan: the three passages draw a closed figure, they return to their point of departure—but that point itself has been immensely widened. The eye has returned inward to find that the vast, exterior spaces have entered into the soul.

All three episodes articulate around a separation between earth and sky. The vastness of the sky extends above the fallen prince; "dark" and "starry," it fills Pierre's eyes as he tilts his head against his fur collar; the full moon hangs in it and draws his glance into far-away depths. The Tolstoyan world is curiously Ptolemaic. Celestial bodies surround the earth and reflect the

⁴ R. P. Blackmur: "The Loose and Baggy Monsters of Henry James" (*The Lion and the Honeycomb*, New York, 1955).

emotions and destinies of men. The image is not unlike that of medieval cosmography, with its stellar portents and symbolic projections. The comet is like an arrow transpiercing the earth, and this image hints at the perennial symbolism of desire. The earth is emphatically at the centre. The moon hangs above it like a lamp and even the distant stars appear to be a reflection of the camp-fires. And central to the earth is man. The entire vision is anthropomorphic. The comet, "vigorously holding its tail erect," suggests a horse in a terrestrial landscape.

The thematic movement, after reaching the "immeasurably lofty" sky, the "immense expanse of the night," or the "oscillating" distances, is brought downward, to earth. It is as if a man had widely cast his net and were drawing it in. The vastness of the sky collapses into Prince Andrew's bruised consciousness, and his physical position is nearly that of burial, of enclosedness in the earth. The same is true of the third example: the "shed boarded up with planks" stands for more than the hut in which Pierre is being held captive—it evokes the image of a coffin. The implication is reinforced by Pierre's gesture: he lies down beside his companions. The effect of contraction in the second passage is richer and more oblique: we pass rapidly from the comet to Pierre's "softened and uplifted soul, now blossoming into a new life." Softened and uplifted like newly turned earth; blossoming like an earth-rooted plant. All the implicit contrasts, between celestial motion and earth-bound growth, between the uncontrollable play of natural phenomena and the ordered, humanized cycles of agriculture, are relevant. In the macrocosm, the tail of the comet is uplifted; in the microcosm, the soul is uplifted. And then, through a crucial transformation of values, we are given to realize that that universe of the soul is the larger.

In each instance, a natural phenomenon moves the observing mind towards some form of insight or revelation. The sky and the grey clouds gliding over Austerlitz tell Prince Andrew that all is vanity; his numbed senses cry out in the voice of Ecclesiastes. The splendour of the night rescues Pierre from the trivialities and malevolence of mundane society. His soul is literally raised to the heights of his belief in Natasha's innocence. There is irony in the motif of the comet. It did portend "all kinds of woes" to Russia. And yet, though Pierre cannot know it, these woes will prove to be his salvation. He has just told Natasha that if they were both free he would offer her his love. When the comet shall have vanished into the depths of the sky and the smoke have settled over Moscow, Pierre is destined to realize his impulse. Thus the comet has the classical ambiguity of oracles and Pierre is both prophetic and mistaken in his interpretation of it. In the final passage the expanding spectacle of forests and fields and shimmering horizons evokes in him a sense of all-inclusiveness. Outward from his captive person radiate concentric circles of awareness. Momentarily, Pierre is hypnotized by the magic of sheer distance—like Keats in the *Ode to a Nightingale*, he feels his soul ebbing away towards dissolution. The net drags the fisherman after it. But then there flashes upon him the insight—"all that is within me," the joyous affirmation that outward reality is born of self-awareness.

This progress through outward motion and the threat of dissolution to solipsism is arch-romantic. Byron scoffed at it in *Don Juan*:

> What a sublime discovery 't was to make the
>   Universe universal egotism,
> That's all ideal—*all ourselves*. . . .

In the art of Tolstoy, however, this "discovery" has social and ethical implications. The calmness of the cloud-blown sky, the cold clarity of the night, the unfolding grandeur of field and forest reveal the sordid irreality of mundane affairs. They show up the cruel stupidity of war and the cruel emptiness of the social conventions which have brought Natasha to grief. With dramatic freshness they proclaim two ancient pieces of morality: that no man can be altogether another man's captive, and that forests shall murmur long after the armies of invading conquerors have gone to dust. The circumstances of weather and physical setting in Tolstoy act both as a reflection of human behaviour and as a commentary upon it—as do those scenes of pastoral repose with which Flemish painters surrounded their depictions of mortal violence or agony.

But in each of these three passages, so illustrative of Tolstoy's genius and of his principal beliefs, we experience a sense of limitation. Lamb wrote a famous gloss on the funeral dirge in Webster's *The White Devil*:

I never saw anything like this Dirge, except the Ditty which reminds Ferdinand of his drowned Father in the Tempest. As that is of water, watery; so this is of the earth, earthy. Both have the intenseness of feeling, which seems to resolve itself into the elements which it contemplates.

War and Peace and *Anna Karenina* are "of the earth, earthy." This is their power and their limitation. Tolstoy's groundedness in material fact, the intransigence of his demand for clear perceptions and empirical assurance, constitute both the strength and the weakness of his mythology and of his aesthetics. In Tolstoyan morality there is something chill and flat; the claims of the ideal are presented with impatient finality. This, perhaps, is why Bernard Shaw took Tolstoy for his prophet. In both men there were a muscular vehemence and a contempt for bewilderment which suggest a defect of charity and of imagination. Orwell remarked on Tolstoy's leaning towards "spiritual bullying."

In the three examples cited, we come to a point at which the tone falters and the narrative loses something of its rhythm and precision. This occurs as we pass from the portrayal of action to the interior monologue. Every time, the monologue itself strikes one as inadequate. It takes on a forensic note, a neutral resonance, as if a second voice were intruding. The stunned uncertainty of Prince Andrew's consciousness, his attempt to rally the sudden *débâcle* of his thoughts, are beautifully rendered. Suddenly the narrative lapses into the abstract pronouncement of a moral and philosophical maxim: "Yes! All is vanity, all falsehood, except that infinite sky. There is nothing, nothing, but that." The change of focus is important: it tells much of Tolstoy's inability to convey genuine disorder, to commit his style to the portrayal of mental chaos. Tolstoy's genius was inexhaustibly literal. In the margin of his copy of *Hamlet*, he placed a question mark after the stage direction "Enter Ghost." His critique of *Lear* and his presentation of Prince Andrew's collapse into unconsciousness are of a piece. When he approached an episode or condition of mind not susceptible to lucid account, he inclined to evasion or abstraction.

The sight of the comet and the immediate impressions arising out of his meeting with Natasha provoke a complex response in Pierre's mentality and in his vision of things. The proposal of love, which he made out of an impulse at once generous and prophetic, is already exerting influence over Pierre's feelings. But little light is thrown on these changes by Tolstoy's flat assertion that the soul of his hero was "now blossoming into a new life." Consider how Dante or Proust would have conveyed the inner drama. Tolstoy was perfectly capable of suggesting mental processes before they reach the simplification of awareness: one need only refer to the famous instance of Anna Karenina's sudden revulsion at the sight of her husband's ears. But in all too many cases he conveyed a psychological truth through a rhetorical, external statement, or by putting in the minds of his characters a train of thought which impresses one as prematurely didactic. The moralizing generality of the image—the soul as a blossoming plant —fails to convey responsibly the delicacy and complication of the underlying action. The technique is impoverished by the thinness of the metaphysics.

Knowing Tolstoy's approach to the theory of knowledge and to the problem of sense perception, we can reconstruct the genesis of Pierre's declaration: "And all that is me, all that is within me, and it is all I!" But in the narrative context (and the latter alone is decisive),

Pierre's assertion has an intrusive finality and a ring of platitude. So great a surge of emotion should, one supposes, culminate in a moment of greater complexity and in language more charged with the individuality of the speaker. This applies to the entire treatment of Pierre's relations with Platon Karataev:

But to Pierre he always remained what he had seemed that first night: an unfathomable, rounded, eternal personification of the spirit of simplicity and truth.

The weak writing here is revelatory. The figure of Platon and his effect on Pierre are motifs of a "Dostoevskyan" character. They lie on the limits of Tolstoy's domain. Hence the series of abstract epithets and the notion of "personification." What is not altogether of this earth, what is to be found on either hand of normality—the subconscious or the mystical—seemed to Tolstoy unreal or subversive. When it forced itself upon his art, he tended to neutralize it through abstraction and generality.

These failings are not solely, or even primarily, matters of inadequate technique. They are consequential on Tolstoyan philosophy. This can be clearly seen when we examine one of the main objections put forward to Tolstoy's conception of the novel. It is often argued that the characters in Tolstoyan fiction are incarnations of their author's own ideas and immediate reflections of his own nature. They are his puppets; he knew and had mastered every inch of their being. Nothing is seen in the novels that is not seen through Tolstoy's eyes. There are novelists who believe that such narrative omnipotence violates cardinal principles of their craft. One would cite Henry James as the foremost example. In the Preface to *The Golden Bowl*, he recorded his predilection

for dealing with my subject-matter, for "seeing my story," through the opportunity and the sensibility of some more or less detached, some not strictly involved, though thoroughly interested and intelligent, witness or reporter, some person who contributes to the case mainly a certain amount of criticism and interpretation of it.

The Jamesian "point of view" implies a particular conception of the novel. In this conception the supreme virtue is dramatization and the author's ability to remain "outside" his work. In contrast, the Tolstoyan narrator is omniscient and tells his story with unconcealed directness. Nor is this an accident of literary history. At the time when *War and Peace* and *Anna Karenina* were being written, the Russian novel had developed a high sophistication of style and had exemplified various modes of indirection. Tolstoy's relation to his characters arose out of his rivalry with God and out of his philosophy of the creative act. Like the Deity, he breathed his own life into the mouths of his personages.

The result is a matchless amplitude of presentation and a directness of tone which recall the archaic liberties of "primitive" art. Percy Lubbock, himself an exponent of Jamesian obliquity, writes:

With less hesitation apparently, than another man might feel in setting the scene of a street or parish, Tolstoy proceeds to make his world. Daylight seems to well out of his page and to surround his characters as fast as he sketches them; the darkness lifts from their lives, their conditions, their outlying affairs, and leaves them under an open sky. In the whole of fiction no scene is so continually washed by the common air, free to us all, as the scene of Tolstoy.[5]

But the cost was considerable, especially in terms of explored depths.

In each of the three passages we have been examining, Tolstoy passes from the exterior to the interior of the particular character; with each inward movement there occurs a loss of intensity and a certain naïveté of realization. There is something disturbing about the effortless manner in which Tolstoy addresses himself to the notion of the soul. He enters too lucidly into the consciousness of his creations and his own voice pierces through their lips. The fairy-tale conceit, "from that day on he was a new man," plays too broad and uncritical a

[5] Percy Lubbock: *The Craft of Fiction* (New York, 1921).

role in Tolstoyan psychology. We are required to grant a good deal regarding the simplicity and openness of mental processes. On the whole, we do grant it because Tolstoy enclosed his characters with such massiveness of circumstance and elaborated their lives for us with such patient warmth that we believe all he says of them.

But there are effects and depths of insight to which these splendidly rounded creations do not lend themselves. Generally, they are effects of drama. The dramatic arises out of the margin of opaqueness between a writer and his personages, out of their potential for the unexpected. In the full dramatic character lurks the unforeseen possibility, the gift for disorder. Tolstoy was omniscient at a price; the ultimate tension of unreason and the spontaneity of chaos eluded his grasp. There is a snatch of dialogue between Pyotr Stepanovich Verkhovensky and Stavrogin in *The Possessed*:

"I am a buffoon, but I don't want you, my better half, to be one! Do you understand me?"

Stavrogin did understand, though perhaps no one else did. Shatov, for instance, was astonished when Stavrogin told him that Pyotr Stepanovich had enthusiasm.

"Go to the devil now, and tomorrow perhaps I may wring something out of myself. Come tomorrow."

"Yes? Yes?"

"How can I tell! . . . Go to hell. Go to hell." And he walked out of the room.

"Perhaps, after all, it may be for the best," Pyotr Stepanovich muttered to himself as he hid the revolver.

The intensities achieved here lie outside Tolstoy's range. The tightness, the high pitch of drama, are brought on by the interplay of ambiguous meanings, of partial ignorance with partial insight. Dostoevsky conveys the impression of being a spectator at his own contrivings; he is baffled and shocked, as we are meant to be, by the unfolding of events. At all times he keeps his distance from "backstage." For Tolstoy this distance did not exist. He viewed his creations as some theologians believe that God views His: with total knowledge and impatient love.

In the moment in which Prince Andrew falls to the ground, Tolstoy enters into him; he is with Pierre in the sleigh and in the encampment. The words spoken by the characters spring only in part from the context of action. And this brings us once again to the main problem in Tolstoyan criticism—what Professor Poggioli has described as the reflection of Molière's moralizing and didactic Alceste in Tolstoy's own nature.

No aspect of Tolstoy's art has been more severely condemned than its didacticism. Whatever he wrote seems to have, in Keats's phrase, a "palpable design" upon us. The act of invention and the impulse towards instruction were inseparable, and the technical forms of the Tolstoyan novel clearly reproduce this duality. When Tolstoy's poetic faculties worked at highest pressure, they brought in their wake the abstract generality or the fragment of theory. His distrust of art came sharply to life where the narrative, through its energy or lyric warmth, threatened to become an end in itself. Hence the sudden breaks of mood, the failures of tone, the downgradings of emotion. Instead of being realized through the aesthetic forms, the metaphysics made their own rhetorical demands on the poem.

This occurs in the instances which we are considering. The downward shift is delicate, and the pressure of Tolstoy's imagination is so constant that we scarcely notice the fracture. But it is there—in Prince Andrew's meditations, in the flat assertion about Pierre's soul, and in Pierre's sudden conversion to a philosophic doctrine which, as we know, represented a specific strain in Tolstoyan metaphysics. In this regard the third passage is the most instructive. The outward movement of vision is arrested and drawn back abruptly to Pierre's consciousness. He exclaims to himself: "And all that is me, all that is within me, and it is all I!" As a piece of epistemology this statement is rather problematic. It expresses one of a number of possible suppositions about the relations between perception and the sensible world. But does it arise out of the imaginative context? I think not, and the proof is that the idea which

278

Pierre expounds runs counter to the general tone of the scene and to its intended lyric effect. This effect is latent in the contrast between the calm eternity of physical nature—the moon in the lofty sky, forests and fields, the bright limitless expanse—and the trivial cruelties of man. But the contrast vanishes if we assume that nature is a mere emanation of individual perception. If "all that" is inside Pierre, if solipsism is the most legitimate interpretation of reality, then the French have succeeded in putting "all" into "a shed boarded up with planks." The explicit philosophic statement runs against the grain of the narrative. Tolstoy has sacrificed to the speculative bent of his mind the logic and particular colouring of the fictional espisode.

I realize that Pierre's language may be read more loosely, that it may be interpreted as a moment of vague pantheism or Rousseauist communion with nature. But the change of pace is unmistakable, and even if we take the end of the passage in the most general sense, the voice would seem to be Tolstoy's rather than Pierre's.

When a mythology is realized in painting or sculpture or choreography, thought is translated from language into the relevant material. The actual medium is radically transformed. But when a mythology is embodied in literary expression, a part of the underlying medium remains constant. Both metaphysics and poetry are incarnate in language. This raises a crucial problem: there are linguistic habits and techniques historically appropriate to the discourse of metaphysics even as there are linguistic habits and techniques more naturally appropriate to the discourse of imagination or fancy. When a poem or a novel is expressive of a specific philosophy, the verbal modes of that philosophy tend to encroach on the purity of the poetic form. Thus we are inclined to say of certain passages in the *Divine Comedy* or *Paradise Lost* that in them the language of technical theology or cosmography overlies the language of poetry and poetic immediacy. It is this kind of interposition which De Quincey had in mind when he distinguished between the "literature of knowledge" and the "literature of power." Such encroachments occur whenever an explicit world view is argued and set forth in a poetic medium—when one agency of language is translated into another. They occur with particular acuity in the case of Tolstoy.

Didacticism and the bias towards hortatory argument appeared in Tolstoyan fiction from the time that he began writing. Little he wrote later on was more of a tract than *The Morning of a Landed Proprietor* or the early story *Lucerne*. It was scarcely conceivable to Tolstoy that a serious man should publish a piece of fiction for no purpose but entertainment or in the service of no cause better than the free play of invention. That his own novels and tales should convey so much to readers who neither know nor care about his philosophy is an ironic wonder. The supreme and notorious instance of a divergence of attitudes between Tolstoy and his public arises over the parts of historiography and philosophic disquisition in *War and Peace*. In a well-known letter to Annenkov, the literary critic and editor of Pushkin, Turgeniev denounced these sections of the novel as "farcical." Flaubert exclaimed: "*Il philosophise*" and suggested that nothing could be more alien to the economy of fiction. And most of Tolstoy's Russian critics, from Botkin to Biryukov, have considered the philosophical chapters in *War and Peace* as an intrusion—valuable or worthless, as the case might be—on the proper fabric of the novel. And yet, as Isaiah Berlin says,

there is surely a paradox here. Tolstoy's interest in history and the problem of historical truth was passionate, almost obsessive, both before and during the writing of *War and Peace*. No one who reads his journals and letters, or indeed *War and Peace* itself, can doubt that the author himself, at any rate, regarded this problem as the heart of the entire matter—the central issue around which the novel is built.

Unquestionably this is so. The ponderous and unadorned statements of a theory of history weary most readers or seem to them extrinsic; to Tolstoy (at least at the time that he was writing *War and Peace*) they were the pivot of the novel. As I have mentioned earlier, moreover, the problem of history is only one of the philosophic questions raised in the work. Of comparable significance are the search for the "good life"—dramatized in the sagas of Pierre and Nicholas Rostov—the gathering of material towards a philosophy of marriage, the program of agrarian reform, and Tolstoy's life-long meditation on the nature of the state.

Why is it, then, that the intrusion of metaphysic practices on literary rhythms and the consequent failures of realization—such as occur in the three passages under discussion—do not constitute a more drastic barrier to the success of the novel as a whole? The answer lies in its dimensions and in the relation of individual parts to the complete structure. *War and Peace* is so spaciously conceived, it generates so strong an impetus and forward motion, that momentary weaknesses are submerged in the general splendour; the reader can skim over ample sections—such as the essays on historiography and tactics—without feeling that he has lost the primary thread. Tolstoy would have regarded such selectivity as an affront to his purpose even more than to his craft. Much of his later rancour towards his own novels, the state of mind which induced him to describe *War and Peace* and *Anna Karenina* as representative instances of "bad art," reflects his recognition that they had been written in one key and were being read in another. They had partly been conceived in a cold agony of doubt and in haunted bewilderment at the stupidity and inhumanity of worldly affairs; but they were being taken as images of a golden past or as affirmations of the fineness of life. In this controversy, Tolstoy may well have been mistaken; he may have been blinder than his critics. As Stephen Crane wrote in February 1896:

Tolstoy's aim is, I suppose—I believe—to make himself good. It is an incomparably quixotic task for any man to undertake. He will not succeed; but he will succeed more than he can ever himself know, and so at his nearest point to success he will be proportionately blind. This is the pay of this kind of greatness.[6]

Much of the perfection of *Anna Karenina* lies in the fact that the poetic form resisted the demands of the didactic purpose; thus there is between them a constant equilibrium and harmonious tension. In the double plot the duality of Tolstoy's intent is both expressed and organized. The Pauline epigraph initiates and colours the story of Anna but does not utterly control it. Anna's tragic fate yields values and enrichments of sensibility that challenge the moral code which Tolstoy generally held and was seeking to dramatize. It is as if two deities had been invoked: an ancient, patriarchal God of vengeance and a God who sets nothing above the tragic candour of a bruised spirit. Or to put it otherwise: Tolstoy grew enamoured of his heroine, and through the liberality of his passion she achieved a rare freedom. Nearly alone among Tolstoyan characters, Anna appears to develop in directions which point away from the novelist's control and prescience. Thomas Mann was right in asserting that the commanding impulse behind *Anna Karenina* is moralistic; Tolstoy framed an indictment against a society which seized for its own upon a vengeance reserved to God. But for once, Tolstoy's own moral position was ambivalent; his condemnation of adultery was rather close to current social judgment. Like the other spectators at the opera —however mundane or acrimonious they may appear— Tolstoy could not help being shocked by Anna's behaviour, by her tentative advances towards a freer code. And in his own perplexity—in the lack of a perfectly lucid case such as is argued in *Resurrection*—lay opportunities for narrative freedom and for the predominance of the poet. In *Anna Karenina* Tolstoy succumbed to his imagination rather than to his reason (always the more dangerous tempter).

But if the parts of the novel immediately concerned

[6] *Stephen Crane's Love Letters to Nellie Crouse* (ed. by H. Cady and L. G. Wells, Syracuse University Press, 1954).

with Anna were freed from the weight of doctrine, it was also because the story of Levin and Kitty acted as a lightning-rod upon which the energies of didacticism were discharged. The balance of the work is, therefore, rigorously dependent on its double plot structure. Without it Tolstoy could not have portrayed Anna with such largesse and with the poetic justice of love. But in many respects *Anna Karenina* marks the end of the period in which the contrary impulses in Tolstoy's genius were maintained in creative equilibrium. As we have seen, Tolstoy experienced difficulty in completing the book; the artist in him, the technician of fiction, was retreating before the pamphleteer.

After *Anna Karenina*, the moralistic and pedagogic strains in Tolstoy's inspiration, with their attendant techniques of rhetoric, became increasingly dominant. Shortly after its completion, Tolstoy set to work on some of his most urgent tracts in *paideia* and religious theory. When he turned again to the art of the novel, his imagination had taken on the dark fervour of his philosophy. Both *The Death of Ivan Ilych* and *The Kreutzer Sonata* are masterpieces, but masterpieces of a singular order. Their terrible intensity arises not out of a prevalence of imaginative vision but out of its narrowing; they possess, like the dwarf-figures in the paintings of Bosch, the violent energies of compression. *The Death of Ivan Ilych* is a counterpart to the *Letters from the Underworld*; instead of descending into the dark places of the soul, it descends, with agonizing leisure and precision, into the dark places of the body. It is a poem—one of the most harrowing ever conceived—of the insurgent flesh, of the manner in which carnality, with its pains and corruptions, penetrates and dissolves the tenuous discipline of reason. *The Kreutzer Sonata* is, technically, less perfect because the elements of articulate morality have become too massive to be entirely absorbed into the narrative structure. The meaning is enforced upon us, with extraordinary eloquence; but it has not been given complete imaginative form.

The artist in Tolstoy continued to be alive very near the surface; a reading of *The Charterhouse of Parma* in April 1887 re-awoke in Tolstoy the desire to write a major novel. In March 1889, he referred specifically to the thought of composing a "vast and free" piece of fiction in the manner of *Anna Karenina*. Instead, he went on to write *The Devil* and *Father Sergius*, two of his most sombre parables against the flesh. It was only in 1895, eighteen years after the completion of *Anna Karenina*, that he returned to the grand form.

It is difficult to think of *Resurrection* as a novel in the ordinary sense. The preliminary sketches for it go back to December 1889; but Tolstoy could not reconcile himself to the idea of fiction, particularly on a large scale. It was only when he saw in the work a chance to convey his religious and social program in an accessible and persuasive form that he could compel himself to the task. Had it not been, finally, for the needs of the Dukhobors (to whom the royalties of *Resurrection* were destined), Tolstoy might never have completed the book. It reflects these changes of mood and a puritanical conception of art. But there are wondrous pages in it, and moments in which Tolstoy gave rein to his unchanging powers. The account of the eastward transportation of the prisoners is handled with a breadth of design and aliveness which transcend any programmatic purpose. When Tolstoy opened his eyes on actual scenes and events, instead of keeping them fixed inward on the workings of his anger, his hand moved with matchless artistry.

This is no accident. In a full-length novel, even the late Tolstoy could allow himself a measure of freedom. Through the repeated exemplifications that a long novel makes possible, abstractions assume a colour of life. Ample flesh surrounds the bones of argument. In a short story, on the contrary, time and space are lacking. The elements of rhetoric cannot be absorbed into the fictional medium. Thus, the didactic motifs, the mythology of conduct in Tolstoy's late stories remain visible and oppressive. Through their sheer length, *War*

and Peace, Anna Karenina, and *Resurrection* enable
Tolstoy to approach that ideal of unity which he pursued with such obstinate passion. In the imaginary landscape of his three principal novels (as Marianne Moore
would say) there was room for both a real hedgehog
and a real fox.

Perhaps we touch here upon a more general law of
literary form—a law of necessary amplitude. Where a
complex philosophy is involved, the poetic structure
through which it is expressed must be of a certain
length. In contrast, Strindberg's late plays suggest that
the drama cannot accord its severely contracted forms
with the systematic exposition, the "arguing out," of a
metaphysical position. On the actual stage—as distinguished from the ideal theatre of the Platonic dialogues
—there is not time or place enough. Only in the long
poem or the long novel can "the element of thought"
be allowed an independent role.

Tolstoy has had one student and successor in whom
the sense of epic form and philosophic concept were as
pronounced and as closely allied as in Tolstoy himself.
Thomas Mann was the more sophisticated metaphysician, the more deliberate user of myths. But in his confident use of history and the massive forms, the example
of Tolstoy was decisive. Both writers were, to use an
ancient and vulnerable distinction, poets of the reason-
ing mind as well as of the sentient heart. In *Doktor
Faustus,* Mann achieved the synthesis of a myth of history, a philosophy of art, and an imagined fable of rare
solemnity. In this book, meditation arises wholly out of
the fictional circumstance. Tolstoy's transitions from
poem to theory were, as we have observed in specific
instances, more laboured and more visible to the reading eye. But Tolstoy and Mann stand together in a
tradition of philosophic art. They have restored to our
awareness an understanding of how the complex structures of metaphysics—the formal mythologies embody-
ing men's beliefs about heaven and earth—are translated into the truths of poetry.

Tolstoy's genius was that of a prophet and religious reformer, but not, as Berdiaev observed, that of a theologian in the traditional or technical sense. He regarded the ceremonial and the liturgical rites of the established churches with contempt; theological disputations, in their formal and historically consecrated mode, impressed him as vain quibbles. In him, as in Rousseau and Nietzsche, the current of iconoclasm ran strong. Hence his abiding concern, both as artist and as religious teacher, with the nature of social behaviour and the establishment of a plain rational code for the affairs of the world. He tended to regard Christianity "neither as a divine revelation nor as a historical phenomenon, but as a teaching which gives us the meaning of life." In the words of a recent critic, Tolstoy produced a Gospel "devoid of irrationality, deprived of metaphysical and mystical vision, despoiled of metaphors and symbols, mutilated of its miracles, and sometimes of its parables as well." [7] Consequently, Tolstoy's handling of religious material was free from the strain of iconography which is so prevalent in Russian thought. He saw in symbolic and anagogical presentations of religious ideas a deliberate obscurantism, an attempt by priests and false teachers to keep from the common people the simple and irrefutable truths of the good life. In *The Christian Teaching*, Tolstoy wrote that love is present in every man "like steam confined in a boiler: the steam expands, drives the pistons and performs the work." It is a curious simile—so pedestrian and literal that it might have come out of a revivalist sermon. One cannot imagine it in the mouth of Dostoevsky.

Dostoevsky's metaphysics and his theology constitute a formidable subject. Even if his novels were of lesser magnitude than they are, we would be reading them still as seminal works in the history of ideas.

[7] R. Poggioli: "A Portrait of Tolstoy as Alceste" (*The Phoenix and the Spider*, Harvard, 1957).

Around Dostoevsky's radical theology, and in commentary or opposition, there has grown up a literature which is complex and brilliant in its own right. It includes the writings of Vasili Rozanov, Leon Shestov, Vladimir Soloviev, Merezhkovsky, Vyacheslav Ivanov, Constantine Leontiev, and Berdiaev. From the point of view of contemporary philosophy, of existentialism in particular, Dostoevsky's works are among the sibylline books. The author of *The Brothers Karamazov* was, as Berdiaev says, "a great thinker and a great visionary as well as a great artist, a dialectician of genius and Russia's greatest metaphysician." The formula is worth noting; it throws into high relief the image of the artist as conceiver and interpreter of myths. Berdiaev goes on: "Dostoevsky cannot be understood—indeed, his books had better be left alone—unless the reader is prepared to be immersed in a vast strange universe of ideas."

I shall touch only on some of its more salient features. In contrast to Tolstoy, the metaphysics of Dostoevsky assumed their mature form within the novels themselves. The expository and polemic writings are of historical interest. But it is in the novels that the Dostoevskyan world view is most coherently and fully set forth. In reading *Crime and Punishment*, *The Idiot*, *The Possessed*, and, above all, *The Brothers Karamazov*, we cannot separate philosophic interpretation from literary response. The theologian and the student of fiction, the critic and the historian of philosophy meet on common ground. To each, Dostoevsky offers a rich domain.

In Chapter III of *The Possessed*, Kirillov says to the narrator:

I know not how it is with the others, and I feel that I cannot do as others. Everybody thinks and then at once thinks of something else. I think all my life of one thing. God has tormented me all my life. . . .

The words are very nearly those used by Dostoevsky about himself. Writing to Maikov in 1870, with reference to the projected *Life of a Great Sinner,* the novelist confessed: "The fundamental idea, which will run through each of the parts, is one that has tormented me, consciously and unconsciously, all my life long: it is the question of the existence of God." This torment was at the heart of Dostoevsky's genius; his secular instincts—the power of the story-teller, the inborn sense of drama, his fascination with politics—were profoundly conditioned by the religious cast of his mind and by the essentially religious quality of his imagination. Of few lives can it be said with more assurance that they were God-haunted or that God's presence invaded their own identity with more tangible force. Around "the question of the existence of God," Dostoevsky's novels elaborate their special vision and their dialectic. They raise it now by affirmation and now by denial. The problem of God was the constant impulse behind Dostoevsky's apocalyptic and ultra-nationalist theories of history; it made moral discriminations of the utmost insight a necessary art; it gave the activities of intellect their pivot and tradition. As Alyosha says to Ivan, in *The Brothers Karamazov*:

Yes, for real Russians the questions of God's existence and of immortality, or, as you say, the same questions turned inside out, come first and foremost, of course. . . .

At times, the novelist went even further. He believed that the human person, as such, derived its only reality from the existence or deprivation of God: "For man exists only if he is an image and reflection of God, he exists only if God exists. Let God be non-existent, let man make of himself a god and no longer a man—his proper image will perish. The only solution to the problem of man lies in Christ." [8]

The Dostoevskyan world has its characteristic architecture: the plane of man's experience runs narrowly between heaven and hell, between Christ and Antichrist. The agents of damnation and of grace assail our spirits, and the assaults of love are the more consuming. In

[8] N. A. Berdiaev: op. cit.

Dostoevskyan terms, the salvation of man depends on his vulnerability, on his exposure to sufferings and crises of conscience which compel him to face unequivocally the dilemma of God. To make them more liable to ambush, the novelist stripped his personages of sheltering impediments. When God's shadow falls across their paths, the dread intensity of the challenge is diminished neither by the routine of social life nor by temporal involvement. Dostoevskyan characters have little else to do but be themselves to the utmost degree. We rarely observe them asleep or at table (when Verkhovensky devours his raw beefsteak, the singularity of the action shocks us as much as the symbolic brutality of his manner). Like the agents of tragic drama, Dostoevsky's *dramatis personae* move in the nakedness of a Last Judgment. Or as Guardini puts it: the Dostoevskyan landscape is everywhere bounded by a narrow rim "on whose other side stands God." [9]

The novels of Dostoevsky mark successive stages of an inquiry into the existence of God. In them is elaborated a profound and radical philosophy of human action. Dostoevsky's heroes are intoxicated with ideas and consumed by the fires of language. This does not mean that they are allegoric types or personifications. No one, with the exception of Shakespeare, has more fully represented the complex energies of life. It means simply that characters such as Raskolnikov, Muishkin, Kirillov, Versilov, and Ivan Karamazov feed on thought as other human beings feed on love or hatred. Where other men burn oxygen, they burn ideas. This is why hallucinations play so large a role in Dostoevsky's narratives: hallucinations are the state in which the rush of thought through the human organism and the dialogues between self and soul are exteriorized.

What were some of the raw materials of ideology and religious doctrine from which Dostoevsky drew his particular vision? In what terms did he put to himself this "question of the existence of God"?

[9] Romano Guardini: op. cit.

In terms rather less eccentric and unique than a western reader might suppose. Much of what has seemed to non-Russians as most personal and autonomous in Dostoevskyan mythology was, in fact, characteristic of the time and place of utterance. The context is thoroughly national, and behind Dostoevsky's great illuminations lies a long tradition of Orthodox and messianic thought a major part of which dates back to the fifteenth century. Too often Dostoevsky has been seen as one of a small group of isolated visionaries such as Blake, Kierkegaard, and Nietzsche. But this is only one perspective. The Dostoevskyan setting is richly historical. Significant elements in his world view derive from St. Isaac the Syrian, whose works lie at Smerdyakov's bedside during the latter's final meeting with Ivan Karamazov. Tiutchev's conception of Christ and of the Christ-bearing mission of the Russian people passed nearly unchanged through the Dostoevskyan crucible. Without Nekrasov's poem *Vlas*, Dostoevsky might not have hit with such fine directness on his image of the "meek ones," the wandering beggars of blighted intelligence and sanctified spirit who whisper God's secrets across the land. Had Bakunin not declared: "God exists —and man is a slave; if man is free—God does not exist," the dialectic of Kirillov in *The Possessed* might well have been less trenchant. Wherever we inquire into the principal themes of Dostoevskyan metaphysics, the variety and explicitness of their origins become manifest; the indictment against God pronounced by Ivan Karamazov deepens and ennobles a page in Belinsky; Danilevsky's *Russia and Europe* inspired the novelist's beliefs in the messianic and theocratic role of the czar and suggested to him the spiritual meaning of the reconquered Byzantium; an essay by Strakhov gave him the terrifying notion that experience may be cyclical and ever-recurrent. This is not to question the originality of Dostoevsky's genius; it is to affirm that some awareness of the Orthodox and national background is indispensable for any serious reading of his novels.

In the Dostoevskyan world, the image of Christ is

the centre of gravity. Whereas Tolstoy cited with approval Coleridge's warning against those who love "Christianity better than truth," Dostoevsky asserted in his own name and through the mouths of his characters that, in the event of contradiction, Christ was infinitely more precious to him than either truth or reason. His imagination dwelt on the figure of the Son of God with such passionate scrutiny that it is possible to read a major portion of Dostoevskyan fiction as a gloss on the New Testament. Dostoevsky's conception of Christ originates in the Augustinian injunction: *"per hominem Christum tendis ad Deum Christum."* But, like most artists, he was by instinct a Nestorian. He inclined to that powerful fifth-century heresy which distinguished the human from the divine Saviour. It was Christ the man whom he sought to envision and glorify. Unlike Tolstoy, Dostoevsky was ardently persuaded of Christ's divinity, but that divinity moved his soul and solicited his intelligence most forcefully through its human aspect.

Here the technical approach of the novelist to the old problem of how goodness may be dramatized and yet shown in its purity coincided with the faith of the believer. Dostoevsky's endeavours to incorporate something of the tone or effulgence of Christ into his portrayals of the human person are of the highest interest: they are exercises in delimitation, instructing us of the fact that the possibilities of art are finite. We are similarly instructed by Dante's blindness at the climax of vision. Dostoevsky's physical imagining of Christ was influenced by Holbein's "Descent from the Cross," which the novelist had seen in Basle and which had profoundly moved him. A reproduction of the painting hangs in Rogojin's house:

I know that the Christian Church laid it down, even in the early ages, that Christ's suffering was not symbolical but actual, and that His body on the Cross was therefore fully and completely subject to the laws of nature. In the picture the face is fearfully crushed by blows, swollen, covered with fearful, swollen and blood-stained bruises, the eyes are open and squinting: the great wide-open whites of the eyes glitter with a sort of deathly, glassy light.

To Dostoevsky this rendition of the Messiah was more than an act of realism. He saw the painting as an icon in the medieval sense of the word, as a "real form" of that which had actually existed. It posed with graphic urgency the problem of whether Christ had, in truth, been the son of God as well as of man and whether there could be any redemption for a world in which a being such as He had been tortured to death. If Dostoevsky answered both questions in the affirmative, it was only after a long evolution of spirit and a lacerating exposure to every species of disbelief. At the very end of his life, we find the novelist conceding that he had come to God through the heart of "the hell-fire of doubt." Dostoevsky made several major studies and sketches for a portrayal of Jesus: Prince Muishkin, Makar Ivanovich in *Raw Youth*, Alyosha Karamazov. The only completed picture is that of the returned Christ in the Legend of the Grand Inquisitor. His beauty and ineffable grace are subtly evoked, but He does not speak. This silence is not, as D. H. Lawrence perversely argued, a sign of acquiescence; it is a parable of the artist's humility and one of the truest insights given us into the necessary defeats of language.

The conception of Christ which is hinted at in the figure of Muishkin is rooted in Russian folk-lore and in the hagiography of the Eastern Church. As Dostoevsky notes in *The Diary of a Writer*:

It is being passed from generation to generation, and it has merged with the heart of the people. Perhaps, Christ is the only love of the Russian people, and they love His image in their own way, to the limit of sufferance.

It is the image of the wandering and persecuted Son of Man whom we may mistake for an idiot, of the hidden prince recognized by the children, the holy beggars, and the epileptics. Dostoevsky caught sight of Him in Siberia, in the house of the dead, and believed, contrary to Roman dogma, that He would end time itself and thus revoke the eternity of damnation. And He would do so not as Christ *Pantokrator*, the all-consuming Lord of Revelation, but with the unquenchable charity of the insulted and the injured.

Prince Muishkin is, as I have said before, a composite figure with borrowings from Cervantes, Pushkin, and Dickens. His meekness, his unworldly wisdom, his immaculateness of heart—all of which are traits of the implicit Christ—are conveyed in the course of action. But there is too little in him of mortal substance. The image we retain from *The Idiot* is pale, with that rather morbid pallour found in depictions of Jesus by painters of the German romantic school. Alyosha Karamazov is a more plausible invention. Dostoevsky observed in the Preface to the novel that Alyosha had confronted him with technical difficulties. Even after completing the book, he was not certain whether he had succeeded in representing the proper alloy of purity and intelligence, of angelic grace and human passion. If Alyosha is taken to be an allegory of Christ, Dostoevsky's doubts were justified. He fulfils the role no less imperfectly than Muishkin, but for the contrary reason. There is too much blood in him, too much Karamazov blood. But he is, nevertheless, a rare and convincing instance of how goodness may be rendered dramatic. Alyosha performs Christ's commandment, "Let the dead bury their dead: but go thou and preach the Kingdom of God." In so doing, he descends deeper and deeper into the condition of humanity, but Dostoevsky persuades us (at least in those fragments of the intended saga which were actually completed) that the enigmatic radiance of grace will continue to surround his person. In him "behaviour might for once, through the moment of a life-time, wholly incarnate its inspiration." [1]

But, for all their fineness of conception, or perhaps because of it, both Prince Muishkin and Alyosha Karamazov embody essentially canonic and traditional

[1] R. P. Blackmur: "Between the Numen and the Moha" (*The Lion and the Honeycomb*, New York, 1955).

representations of Christ. I believe that there were invoked in the creation of Stavrogin revelations of a subtler, more radical, and more harrowing kind. The figure of Stavrogin stands at the heart of darkness of the Dostoevskyan world. But all paths lead to him, for there too the sensibility of the poet and the revolutionary, apocalyptic argument of "Russia's greatest metaphysician" are most closely united. Stavrogin embodies Dostoevsky's ultimate explorations both in the techniques of the novel and in the creation of myth. But before we may approach him a summary view of the surrounding dialectic is essential.

Dostoevskyan theology and Dostoevsky's science of man were founded on the axiom of total freedom. Man is free—wholly and terrifyingly free—to perceive good and evil, to choose between them, and to enact his choice. Three exterior forces—the trinity of Antichrist, which offered itself to Jesus in triple temptation—seek to relieve man of his freedom: miracles, the established churches (Roman Catholicism in particular), and the state. If miracles occurred in any but a psychological, private, and inward sense, if Christ had descended from the cross or if Zossima's body exhaled sweet odours, man's acceptance of God would no longer be free. It would be enforced by mere evidence as the obeisance of slaves is enforced by material power. The churches deprive men of their essential liberty by interposing between God and the agony of the individual soul the assurance of absolution and the mysteries of ritual. The functions of the priest diminish the nobility and solitude of the God-tormented worshipper. Roman Catholicism and the political state, when they act in what Dostoevsky took to be a natural concert, threaten to make human salvation impossible through their promise of an earthly millennium. The program put forward by Shigalov in *The Possessed*— the perfect society run by the lonely few for the material beatitude of the soul-deprived millions—is monstrous not because it destroys legal and civil rights (about which Dostoevsky cared little), but because it transforms men into satisfied brutes. By filling their bellies it suffocates their souls.

With dark insight Dostoevsky perceived that there are affinities between material want and religious faith. Hence his life-long polemic against the "crystal palace" of socialism, against Rousseau, Babeuf, Cabet, Saint-Simon, Fourier, Proudhon, and all the positivists who believe in the reality of secular reform and who preach justice at the expense of love. Hence his hatred of Claude Bernard, whose rational physiology seemed to encroach upon the hiddenness and daemonic autonomy of the spirit. Dostoevsky detested the belief of Tolstoy and of all social radicals that men may be persuaded to love one another through reason and utilitarian enlightenment. The notion seemed to him fraudulent on psychological grounds. He affirmed in the *Diary of a Writer* for December 1876 "that love of mankind is unthinkable, unintelligible and *altogether impossible without the accompanying faith in the immortality of man's soul.* . . . I even assert and venture to say that love of mankind *in general, as an idea,* is one of the most incomprehensible ideas for the human mind." And in a meditation on Christ, written on April 16, 1864, next to the dead body of his first wife, Dostoevsky argued that " 'love everything as thyself' is impossible on earth, because it contradicts the law of the development of personality."

This law is not immutable. There are private apocalypses, moments of illumination in which the human soul is riven and sanctified. In these moments, which may have the tenor and outward symptoms of epilepsy, a criminal such as Raskolnikov is overwhelmed with universal love; mastered by grace, Alyosha is freed from the agony of doubt and falls to the ground in adoration of all men and of all sensible nature. These flashes of revelation are the only authentic miracles. Dostoevsky entitled his narrative of Alyosha's experience "Cana in Galilee"—water is turned into wine or, to paraphrase Platon Karataev's prayer in *War and Peace*, we lie down like a stone and wake like fresh bread. Only if man is free, only if neither exterior wonders nor ecclesiastical dogmas nor the material achievements of the utopian state have shielded him from the assaults of God, can these epiphanies occur. Man's freedom is his vulnerability to God. Anything that robs him of it dooms his soul to the captivity of blindness.

From this dialectic, with its psychological precision and its fierce poetry, arises the Dostoevskyan theory of evil. Without evil there would be no possibility of free choice and none of the torment which impels man towards the recognition of God. Berdiaev, who penetrated Dostoevsky's intentions most acutely on this point, states the essential paradox:

The existence of evil is a proof of the existence of God. If the world consisted wholly and uniquely of goodness and righteousness there would be no need for God, for the world itself would be god. God is, because evil is. And that means that God is because freedom is.

If the freedom to choose God is to have any meaning, the freedom to refuse Him must exist with equal reality. Only through the chance of committing evil and experiencing it can man attain a mature grasp of his own freedom. The supreme liberty of the criminal act throws a violent but true light on the parting of the ways; the one road leads to the resurrection of the soul, the other to moral and spiritual suicide. The pilgrimage towards God can have real significance only so long as men may choose the way of darkness. As Kirillov inexorably demonstrates, those who are possessed by freedom but cannot accept the existence of God are compelled to self-destruction. To them the world is a chaotic absurdity, a cruel farce in which inhumanity wreaks havoc. Only those who can come to terms, in the very marrow of their being, with the paradox of total freedom and the omnipotence of Christ and of God will be able to live with the knowledge of evil. There is something they will fear even beyond torture and the monstrous injustices of human affairs; it is God's indifference, His ultimate withdrawal from a world which the

Shigalovs or the Tolstoys have made materially perfect and in which men look earthward with the eyes of contented brutes.

Like the protagonist of a morality play, Dostoevskyan man is poised between the ministrations of grace and the subversions of evil. Daemonic powers occupy an eminent place in Dostoevskyan cosmology, but it is not entirely clear how he conceived of their nature. As far as can be ascertained, he did not believe in spiritism in the usual sense. Mediums sought to persuade him that voluntary communications with the dead were possible, but he denounced them as charlatans. His image of psychic reality was subtler. Dostoevsky's multiple vision of the soul allowed for the likelihood of occasional fragmentation. In Thomistic terms, "ghosts" could be manifestations of the human spirit when the spirit acts as pure energy, divorcing itself from the coherent government of reason or faith in order to sharpen the dialogue between different facets of consciousness. Whether we refer to the consequent phenomenon as schizophrenic or preternatural is, as yet, a matter of terminology rather than complete knowledge. What counts is the intensity and quality of the experience, the shaping impact of the apparition upon our understanding. Like Henry James in his ghostly tales, Dostoevsky surrounded his personages with a zone of occult energies; forces are attracted towards them and grow luminous in their vicinity, and corresponding energies erupt from within and take palpable form. In such awesome studies of the unnatural as Ivan Karamazov's colloquies with the Devil, we see a perfect coalescence between the techniques of Gothicism and Dostoevsky's myth of the unstable soul.

Correspondingly, he drew no firm barrier between the world of ordinary sense-perception and other, potential worlds. As Merezhkovsky said:

For Tolstoy there exists only the eternal antagonism of life and death; for Dostoïevski only their eternal oneness. The former looks at death from within the house of life with the eyes of this world; the latter, with the eyes of the spirit world, looks on life from a footing which, to those who live, seems death.[2]

To Dostoevsky the plurality of worlds was a manifest truth. Often he saw empirical reality as insubstantial and phantasmic. The great cities are a cunning mirage; the white nights over St. Petersburg are proof of the spectral illumination which plays around material things; what positivists take to be solid fact or laws of nature are merely thin webs of supposition thrown over an abyss of irreality. In this regard, Dostoevsky's cosmology was medieval and Shakespearean. But whereas his successors, such as Kafka, came to see in the witchery and hauntedness of things a symptom of psychological damnation, Dostoevsky himself perceived in the daemonic a mark of man's especial proximity to God.

Despite its carnal husk and its gross immersion in temporal life, man's spirit retains its vulnerability to grace or perdition. The destitute, the infirm, and the epileptic have important advantages: through their material nakedness and in their seizures they suffer totalities of perception which rend apart the obscuring armour of sensuality and normal health. Muishkin and Kirillov are epileptics; their confrontation with the problem of God has a privileged immediacy. But daemonic claims and temptations surround every man. We are all bidden to sup at Cana in Galilee.

Like the epileptic, the criminal and the atheist play a primary role in Dostoevskyan theodicy. They stand at the outermost limits of freedom; their next step must lead either to God or to the pit of hell. They have rejected the trimmer's wage as it was devised by Pascal. Pascal proposed that men should live piously whether or not they believed in God; if God existed, their piety would be eternally rewarded; if not, their lives would nevertheless have been decorous and rational. Dostoevsky's heroes rebel at such equivocation. To them God's existence or non-existence is tantamount to the mean-

[2] D. S. Merezhkovsky: *Tolstoi as Man and Artist, with an Essay on Dostoïevski* (London, 1902).

ing of life. He must be found or it must be shown past doubt that He has withdrawn from creation, leaving human beings, as Versilov suggests in *Raw Youth*, with the dread liberty of the abandoned. The search for God may well lead through the kingdoms of night and abomination. This idea is reflected in the legends and symbolism of the Christian church. Thieves and harlots occupy a consecrated place even in the Latin tradition. In the Orthodox view their place is very near the centre. Slavonic theologians delight in the paradox of Christ's pre-eminent love for those who come to Him from the edge of damnation. To this doctrine Dostoevsky added his personal experience of servitude and redemption. When the elders bow before Stavrogin and Dimitri Karamazov, they pay prophetic homage to the sacredness of evil, to infernal temptations so destructive that in them the power of God's challenge and the infinity of His forgiveness are doubly manifest.

But if man's freedom provides the only access to God, it also provides the conditions of tragedy. The possibility of the false choice, of the denial of God, lies always at hand. A world in which the problem of the existence of God would no longer preoccupy the human soul would, by Dostoevskyan definition, be a world without tragedy. It might be a social utopia achieved through Shigalov's formula of "unlimited despotism." In it the material "good life" might be attained. But in the playhouse of the Grand Inquisitor there could be no tragic drama. "As soon as man has vanquished nature," announced Lunacharsky, the first Soviet commissar of education, "religion becomes superfluous; thereupon the sense of the tragic shall vanish from our lives." Everyone, with the exception of a handful of incurable madmen, would know and rejoice in the certainty that twice two equals four, that Claude Bernard had penetrated to the centre of the vascular system, and that Count Tolstoy was building model schools on his estates. Foremost among the insane would be Dostoevsky and his principal characters. They stand in radical antagonism to worldly utopias, to all paradigms of secular reform which would lull man's soul into a sleep of comfort and material satiety, thus banishing from it the tragic sense of life. In the Comtian phrase, Tolstoy was a "servant of Humanity." Dostoevsky bitterly distrusted the humanitarian creed and preferred to remain with the anguished, infirm, and at times criminally deranged "servants of God." Between these two servitudes great hatreds may prevail.

VI

In the novels of Dostoevsky, religious thought and religious experience are presented in two principal modes, the one being essentially explicit and orthodox, the other covert and heretical. Under the explicit mode I would include the wealth of citations from Scripture, the theological dialectic and terminology, the elements of plot founded on the life of the actual church, the liturgical motifs, and those numberless allusions to Biblical analogues which give the Dostoevskyan scene its specific iconography. The novels literally bristle with religious matter which is often communicated in rather primitive forms. Dostoevsky gave his personages characterizing and allegoric names. Raskolnikov, the "heretic," the one who dwells in schism; Shatov, the "waverer"; Stavrogin, who bears in his name the Greek word for "cross"; Aglaya, the "ardent one." *The Brothers Karamazov* is built around a nomenclative symbolism much of which Dostoevsky derived from the Saints' calendar of the Orthodox Church. Alyosha is both "helper" and "man of God"; Ivan is named after the evangelist of the Fourth Gospel, for he too is intoxicated with the mystery of the Word; in Dimitri we hear the echo of Demeter, the goddess of earth, and this echo refers us back to the Johannine epigraph of the novel—"*nisi granum frumenti cadens in terram mortuum fuerit, ipsum solum manet.*" Fyodor Pavlovich conceals the name signifying "God's gift"; in trying to elucidate this ironic and paradoxical hint we would find ourselves precisely on the border between Dostoevsky's open use of symbolic devices and his more private and unorthodox mythology. In "Karamazov" itself we find the Tatar word for "black."

Comparable allegories are implicit in the names of Dostoevskyan heroines. The notion of *sophia*, of intellection through grace, is a cardinal point in Orthodox theology. Dostoevsky associated the term with the attainment of wisdom through humility and suffering. Hence the Sofya (Sonia) Marmeladova of *Crime and Punishment*, the Sofya Ulitin who travels the land selling the Gospel in *The Possessed*, the Sofia Dolgoruki of *Raw Youth*, and Alyosha's saintly mother, Sofya Karamazov. In the name of Marya Timofeyevna, the Cripple of *The Possessed* and perhaps the purest figure in Dostoevsky's God-haunted creation, there lies an entire Christology. Names bear witness to man's place in the drama of salvation, in what Nemirovich-Danchenko called, with reference to his staging of *The Brothers Karamazov* at the Moscow Art Theatre in 1911, the "spectacle-mystery" of Dostoevskyan fiction.

The spectacle and the mystery (in both the metaphysical and the technical sense) had been first presented to men through Holy Scripture. Thus, Biblical quotations or allusions were to Dostoevsky what the shaping background of myth had been to the Greek dramatists. The holy words, inexhaustibly familiar and, until recent times, encrusted in the very fabric of the western and the Russian mind, give the Dostoevskyan text its particular tonality. A special study could be made of Dostoevskyan citations from the Gospels and Pauline epistles. As Guardini observes, the novelist was at times purposefully inaccurate: there are, for example, deliberate confusions between the designation of abstract evil and the personalized references to Satan in some of the scriptural tags in *The Brothers Karamazov*. But in most instances, Dostoevsky quoted scrupulously and with a high sense of drama. He was not afraid of matching the Biblical passage to his narrative as a master of mosaic might place jewels among his stones. Many examples come to mind; among the finest are the moments of conversion and epiphany in *Crime and Punishment* and *The Possessed*.

Sonia reads the eleventh chapter of St. John to Raskolnikov:

> She was trembling in a real physical fever. . . . She was getting near the story of the greatest miracle and a feeling of immense triumph came over her. Her voice rang out like a bell; triumph and joy gave it power. The lines danced before her eyes, but she knew what she was reading by heart. At the last verse, "Could not this man who opened the eyes of the blind . . ." dropping her voice she passionately reproduced the doubt, the reproach and censure of the blind disbelieving Jews, who in another moment would fall at His feet, as though struck by thunder, sobbing and believing. . . . "And *he—he*, too—is blinded and unbelieving, he, too will hear, he, too will believe, yes, yes! At once, now," was what she was dreaming, and she was quivering with happy anticipation.
>
> "Jesus therefore again groaning in himself cometh to the grave. It was a cave and a stone lay upon it.
>
> Jesus said: Take ye away the stone. Martha, the sister of him that was dead, saith unto him, Lord, by this time he stinketh: for he hath been dead four days."
>
> She laid emphasis on the word *four*.

The Biblical and the narrative representations are in precise accord. The memories and faith solicited by the story of Lazarus announce the raising of Raskolnikov from the grave of the spirit. Sonia herself associates the sceptical blindness of the Jews with that of the hero and in a profoundly moving ambiguity links the image of the dead Lazarus to that of the murdered Lizaveta. Raskolnikov's spiritual resurrection foreshadows the ultimate resurrection of the dead. The parallel vision informs each detail. Sonia's voice rings out like the church bells which annually proclaim the resurrection of Christ. The story of Lazarus, moreover, is cited in proof of Dostoevsky's conception of miracle; without committing himself to its historical truth (which, on the whole, would run counter to his notion of human freedom), Dostoevsky is suggesting that the scriptural account prefigures the authentic and recurrent miracle that comes to pass every time a sinner returns to the life of God.

A similar interweaving of Biblical and fictional motifs is the ordering principle in the final section of *The Possessed*. When Stepan Trofimovich meets the Gospel-woman, he has not read the New Testament for thirty years "and at most had recalled some passages of it, seven years before, when reading Renan's *Vie de Jésus*." But now he is wandering, homeless and ill, and the agents of grace lie in wait for him on the road. First, Sofya Matveyevna reads the Sermon on the Mount. Then, opening the book at random, she begins the famous passage from Revelation: "And unto the angel of the church of the Laodiceans. . . ." It culminates in the words: "and thou knowest not that thou art wretched and miserable, and poor and blind, and naked." "That too . . . and that's in your book too!" exclaims the old liberal. As death draws near, he asks Sofya to read to him the passage "about the pigs." It is the parable from the eighth chapter of Luke. In it the vast energies and thematic range of *The Possessed* are wholly concentrated. It is both epigraph and epilogue. With the clarity of delirium—a signally Dostoevskyan condition—Stepan Trofimovich interprets the words of the evangelist in the light of Russian experience. The devils shall enter into the swine:

"They are we, we and those . . . and Petrusha and *les autres avec lui* . . . and I perhaps at the head of them, and we shall cast ourselves down, possessed and raving, from the rocks into the sea, and we shall all be drowned. . . ."

The political foresight and dramatic propriety are Dostoevsky's but the governing myth, the shaping image, stems from the New Testament.

It might be argued that Dostoevsky infringed "the rules of the game," that he amplified and solemnized the impact of his novels through the use of Biblical citations and analogues. But in fact he heightened the risks of artistic failure. A strong quotation can destroy a weak text; in order to incorporate a scriptural passage and give it pertinence, a narrative design must *per se* be of great firmness and nobility. The quotation brings with it a train of echoes and is overlaid with previous interpretations and usages. These will obscure or corrode the effect which the novelist is aiming at unless this effect is inherently spacious and dynamic. Thus *The Possessed* can sustain the weight of its majestic epigraph, and when the words of Luke are invoked a second time they have acquired a special resonance through their use in the novel.

Dostoevsky did not always quote directly. At times the narrative, through its rhythm and tonality, points towards a Biblical or liturgical resolution as we say that a musical chord points towards the dominant. In his important study of the novelist, A. L. Zander gives a number of examples. The chapter heading "Cana in Galilee" and the terms in which Alyosha's ecstasy is recounted seem to lead to the canonic definition of a miracle. Similarly, Marya Timofeyevna's invocation of the "Mother of God, the damp earth" echoes the first canticle of the rite of preparation for Holy Communion in the Orthodox liturgy so closely that the question arises whether the words of the Cripple are not intended as a paraphrase.

Personages such as Marya, Makar Ivanovich in *Raw Youth*, or Father Zossima (who was himself called Makary in the early drafts of *The Brothers Karamazov*) speak a language saturated with Biblical phrases and allusions. When seeking to understand their meanings, we face a problem comparable to that posed for us by Milton or Bunyan. This fact alone distinguishes Dostoevsky's conception of the novel from that of his European contemporaries. He participated intimately in a live religious tradition and in its habits of thought and rhetoric; he relied on anagogical devices of a kind which had passed out of currency in western literature after the seventeenth century. In so doing he magnified beyond all previous attainments except Melville's the potentialities and resources of the craft of prose fiction.

The art of Dostoevsky possesses in eminent degree what Matthew Arnold called "high seriousness." It touches on areas traditionally reserved to poetry and, in particular, to the poetry of religious emotion. There is nothing in the European novel to surpass it in ferocity of observation or in compassion of treatment. One cannot imagine, with any assurance, how a page in *Madame Bovary* or even in *The Wings of the Dove* would fare when exposed to the consuming light of Biblical speech. In a very real sense, Dostoevsky's quotations define the range of his powers.

This does not mean, however, that his handling of religious themes was autonomous or exclusively Russian in inspiration. Here, as elsewhere, European influences are discernible. The figure of Zossima derives mainly from the actual figure of Tikhon Zadonsky. But it owes a good deal to Prior Leonardus in E. T. A. Hoffmann's *Die Elixiere des Teufels* and to Père Alexis in George Sand's *Spiridion*. The relationship between Zossima and Alyosha is modelled on George Sand's treatment of Alexis and Angel; Ambroise, an ascetic and fanatical monk, is the immediate prototype for Father Ferapont. Sand put forward ideas which were to become of the first importance in *The Brothers Karamazov*: Alexis recognizes in the assertion of human freedom a proof of the existence of God and equates suicide with the surrender of the soul to the void of atheism. At the close he says to Angel, precisely as Zossima will say to Alyosha: "Now receive my farewell, my child, and prepare yourself to quit the monastery and to re-enter into the world." But whereas *Spiridion* remains a curio, a neglected piece of Gothic fantasy, *The Brothers Karamazov* stands among the great poems of belief.

In addition to passages from Scripture and to motifs drawn from ecclesiastical life, the novels of Dostoevsky include excursions of considerable depth and authority into theological and oecumenical speculation. Dostoevsky may have been a less forceful polemicist than Tolstoy, but he was a much finer craftsman of abstraction.

In his reading of Aristotle's *Poetics*, Humphry House glossed "the element of thought" as signifying the "internal deliberative casuistry of the individual." In Dostoevskyan fiction, this casuistry is externalized. We find it in the harrowing disputations on the existence of God in *The Possessed* or in the argument over church and state at the beginning of *The Brothers Karamazov*. But the dialectic is never divorced from the dramatic context: each of the Karamazovs enacts, in the course of events, one of the possible moralities discussed in a generalized manner in Father Zossima's cell.

By adding to the complications of setting, which Balzac had mastered, and to the complications of feeling, which Henry James and Proust were so passionately concerned with, the world of ideas—ideas lived and expounded in their extremity of statement and compulsion—Dostoevsky enlarged the confines of his medium. He made of it a mirror adequate to the entirety of man and to the ideological temper of the age. Perhaps it will be objected that this enlargement had already been accomplished by Stendhal. But although Stendhal did extend the art of the novel to include the full play of argumentative and philosophic intelligence, his rendering of the mind was, compared with Dostoevsky's, diffident and, in the main, restricted to the life of reason.

I have, so far, dealt with the more classical and straightforward expressions of Dostoevsky's religiosity. The material embodied in the narrative (allegoric names, Biblical citations, references to liturgy) is of an explicit and traditional order. The context of fiction can of itself act as a species of commentary and enrichment. By virtue of the dramatic moment a quotation acquires new overtones, and new inferences may crystallize around it. But in the examples I have given, the structure of meaning and historically established connotation is not altered. We may gloss, in an orthodox vein, the image of Christ which shimmers through Prince Muishkin. The material, as Coleridge says with reference to the workings of Fancy, is "ready made from the law of association."

But if we move inward into the world of Dostoevsky we shall come upon a covert, idiosyncratic, and revolutionary mythology with its own habits of speech, its own iconography, and its own re-creation of value and fact. At this centre of vision, historical beliefs and traditional symbols have been fused or wholly transformed into something radical and private. Ivanov describes this change in a concise formula: the art of Dostoevsky leads "from the real to the more real." The techniques of presentation alter correspondingly; in the domain of the "more real" the principal means are paradox, dramatic irony, and a sombre, heretical ambivalence.

The two orders of realization are not at every point distinguishable. Smerdyakov, in *The Brothers Karamazov*, partakes of both. In the outward design he is repeatedly associated with Judas (he receives a symbolically numbered sum of money, hangs himself after his major betrayal, and so on). But as the fourth and "true" son of Karamazov he enacts in the mystery of parricide, in the primary fable, a role which can only be understood by inward reference. The terms of symbolic action, such as his epilepsy, have no equivalence outside Dostoevsky's specific, and in part concealed, mythology. Here, as Coleridge says of the poetic Imagination, all previously extant material is dissolved and recast. In particular instances Dostoevsky's passage "from the real to the more real" is unmistakable; the logic of causation seems temporarily suspended and action yields to the logic of myth. I have in mind the difference between the discussion on church and state in Zossima's cell and the elder's sudden, mysterious homage to Dimitri; between the humble, romantic faith of Sonia in *Crime and Punishment* and the eschatology of pure grace which is manifest in Stavrogin's holy and crippled bride; between Makar Ivanovich's gospel of love and the secret workings of sensuality in Alyosha Karamazov. The image of Christ evoked in *The Idiot* is of "the real"; the Lord of the Second Coming whom we glimpse in the uncertain light of *The Possessed* is of "the more real." When exemplifying this ultimate realism, Dostoevsky proceeds somewhat like Shakespeare in the late plays. He seems in possession of a tragic revelation, and yet, of a revelation that may carry us beyond tragedy; he concentrates his purpose around gestures and symbols drawn from the well-spring of a central mythology; he delights in contradiction and plays with ironic freedom on the plodding conventionality of our ordinary modes of thought.

But in attempting to follow Dostoevsky to the core of meaning we become drastically aware of the insufficiencies of criticism. The very richness of symbolic material offers temptations which one must guard against. In I. A. Richards's phrase, "We need here both a free eye and a light hand." The personage of Marya Timofeyevna poses searching problems in critical tact. They have not always been resolved. Her family name contains an allusion to the theme of the pure white swan prevalent in the folklore of Russian heretical sects. She is a cripple, like Lise in *The Brothers Karamazov*, and feeble-minded in a more extreme measure than Prince Muishkin. Mysteriously, she is at once mother, virgin, and bride. Lebyadkin flogs her with a cossack whip, and yet she is telling the truth when she declares "he's my footman." She has lived in a convent where an old woman "doing penance for prophecy" (Dostoevsky would have us know that there are sins of insight) has confirmed to her that the Mother of God "is the Great Mother—the damp earth." Marya treasures this assurance, and it clothes her in strange majesty. Father Bulgakov may be justified in saying that this association between the Virgin and the *Magna Mater* of the ancient east makes of the Cripple a pre-Christian figure. But Marya also incarnates Dostoevsky's consummate reflections on the New Testament and she appears to foreshadow a post-historical, authentic Catholicism in which the worship of the nurturing earth shall play an essential part. These theological overtones are clearly intended and must be taken into account. But Marya Timofeyevna is, at the same time, totally involved in the specific iconography of *The Possessed*. When interpreted through an external symbolism, she retreats into contradiction and obscurity. Ivanov argues that through the Cripple, Dostoevsky

tried to show how the eternally-feminine principle in the Russian soul has to suffer violence and oppression at the hands of those Daemons who in the people contend against Christ for the mastery of the masculine principle in the people's consciousness. He sought to show how these Daemons, in their attack upon the Russian soul, also wound the Mother of God herself (as shown in the symbolic episode of the desecration of the ikon), although their vilifications cannot reach her invisible depths (compare the symbol of the untouched silver garment of the Virgin Undefiled in the home of the murdered Marya Timofeyevna).

The commentary is ingenious and erudite, but it proceeds from the real to the less real. The "meanings" of Marya Timofeyevna cannot be translated accurately into a previous body of myth or dialectic; they inhere in the self-consistent entirety of the poem. And it is with poetry, in the full sense, that we are confronted.

Let us consider one of the most riddling, yet luminous passages in the novel. It deals with Marya's dreams of motherhood, with her memories of a secret flowering of consciousness, of an "annunciation":

"Sometimes I remember it was a boy, and sometimes it was a girl. And when he was born, I wrapped him up in cambric and lace, and put pink ribbons on him, strewed him with flowers, got him ready, said prayers over him. I took him away unchristened and carried him through the forest, and I was frightened, and what I weep for most is that I had a baby and I never had a husband."

"Perhaps you had one?" Shatov queried cautiously.

"You're absurd, Shatushka, with your reflections. Perhaps I had, but what's the use of my having had one if it is just the same as though I hadn't. There's an easy riddle for you, guess it," she smiled.

"Where did you take your baby?"

"I took it to the pond," she said with a sigh.

Shatov nudged me again: "And what if you never had a baby and all this is only a wild dream?"

"You ask me a hard question, Shatushka," she answered dreamily, without a trace of surprise at such a question. "I can't tell you anything about that. Perhaps I hadn't: I think it's only your curiosity. I shan't leave off crying for him; anyway, I couldn't have dreamt it. . . ." And big tears glittered in her eyes.

This is sheer poetry, not unlike the feverish dream-poetry of Ophelia. What Marya calls "an easy riddle" is, I think, the crux of *The Possessed*. We cannot un-ravel it through a glossary of symbols and equivalences outside the novel. The terms of reference point inward to the ritual actions of Stavrogin and the ambiguity of his marriage to the Cripple. In Marya's reverie there is both the notion of an immaculate conception and the older mythology of earth spirits bedecking the child with flowers and carrying it through the forest in some rite of purgation and sacrifice. But the tears are real, harrowingly real; they lead back from the dream-world into the grievous destinies of the plot.

Marya Timofeyevna's riddle can be apprehended only in terms of the novel itself and of its poetic forms. But which version of *The Possessed* do we regard as authoritative? Shall we include the famous chapter entitled "Stavrogin's Confession"? There are substan-tial grounds for not doing so. The work was issued repeatedly in Dostoevsky's lifetime and under condi-tions in which the original objections of Katkov (who had published the book in serial form) could no longer have prevailed; yet the novelist himself never embodied Chapter IX into the text. Much of Stavrogin's narra-tive, moreover, was transferred into the mouth of Versilov in *Raw Youth*. Would Dostoevsky have ex-pended on a later novel material which he judged in-tegral to *The Possessed*? Finally, as Komarovich has pointed out, the Stavrogin of the "Confession" and the Stavrogin of the novel as we know it are signifi-cantly different. The former is the projected hero of

The Life of a Great Sinner. Traces of that grand design may be found in its two principal fragments, *The Possessed* and *The Brothers Karamazov*. But in the process of composition each of these two novels developed its own dynamics. Through this development, as it can be followed in the drafts and notebooks, the personage of Stavrogin took shape.

Much has been written of him. As I have suggested earlier, he represents a Dostoevskyan variant on the Satanic heroes of Byronism and the Gothic. But he is much more than that. He is the supreme example of how the religious imagination enters into the art of the novel. As so often with Dostoevsky, the character is introduced against a background of drama and in the image of a particular play. Stavrogin is first referred to as "Prince Harry." The princely title is borne by Muishkin and by Alyosha Karamazov (in several preliminary drafts and once in the novel itself). In Dostoevskyan mythology it would seem to have gnostic and messianic connotations. But as is made plain by specific allusion, Dostoevsky is here referring to Shakespeare's Prince Hal. Stavrogin is presented to us in the image of the wild Prince of Wales. Like his Shakespearean prototype, he has been rioting in the underworld of crime and debauchery. Throughout *The Possessed* he will be surrounded by a mock-court of parasites and ruffians. Like Hal, he is an enigma to his intimates and to outside observers. They do not know whether he will

> be more wond'red at
> By breaking through the foul and ugly mists
> Of vapours that did seem to strangle him

or whether he will everlastingly

> permit the base contagious clouds
> To smother up his beauty from the world.

There is beauty in Stavrogin, and a dark royalty. As Irving Howe writes in his essay on Dostoevskyan politics: "Stavrogin is the source of the chaos that streams through the characters; he possesses them but is not himself possessed." [3] Even in his early pranks there is a kind of desperate wisdom, suggesting another Shakespearean prince. A fatuous citizen affirms that he cannot be led by the nose. Stavrogin seizes upon his literal meaning and translates the cliché into a grotesque pantomime. There is something of Hamlet in that, of Hamlet's interest in the nature of language and of his acid wit. The analogy is reinforced by various speculations as to whether or not Stavrogin was in his "right mind" when he performed his bizarre and cruel tricks. He is banished from the town and undertakes a long voyage. His itinerary is significant. He visits Egypt, the traditional place of gnostic mysteries, and Jerusalem, the site of messianic fulfilment. He travels to Iceland, recalling to our minds that there are eschatologies in which hell is imagined not as a world of fire but as an eternity of ice. Like the Prince of Danemark and Faust (a figure with whom Ivanov seeks to identify him), Stavrogin spends some time at a German university. But deep longings and fierce expectations solicit his return.

Suddenly he appears, on that tremendous occasion in Varvara Petrovna's house, and the Cripple, whom Dostoevsky has endowed with the ultimate clarities of unreason, asks: "may I . . . kneel down . . . to you now?" Gently Stavrogin denies her. But there is every implication that the query is a natural one, that there is something in Stavrogin's person to justify submission and the primordial gesture of worship. Shatov, who is also among the authentic carriers of Dostoevsky's vision, confirms Marya's action. He says to Stavrogin: "I've waited too long for you. I've been thinking of you incessantly." He asks: "Shan't I kiss your footprints when you've gone?" The attitudes of the other characters towards "Prince Harry" are similarly excessive. Each has his own image of Stavrogin and seeks to invoke Stavrogin's powers in behalf of some private lust or sacrificial intent. But, like Zeus in the myth of

[3] Irving Howe: "Dostoevsky: The Politics of Salvation" (*Politics and the Novel*, New York, 1957).

Semele, Stavrogin destroys those who draw too near to him in passion or observance. Pyotr Verkhovensky knows this; his cult is wary and treacherous:

"Why do you look at me? I need you, you; without you I am nothing. Without you I am a fly, a bottled idea; Columbus without America."

True, but Columbus was the discoverer, perhaps even the contriver of the new world. Pyotr is puzzled to the last whether it was not he who had "invented" Stavrogin. He says to him: "You are proud and beautiful as a god." But this god is strangely dependent on men's worship even where they kneel to him in corruption or greed. Do Verkhovensky's frantic posturings direct our thoughts to a paradox often put forward by modern existentialism: "It is God who is in need of man" (*Dieu a besoin des hommes*)?

Many aspects of Stavrogin belie the notion of theophany, the idea that he performs, in some tragic and secret manner, the role of God in Dostoevsky's final mythology. He bears the marks of a false Messiah and is shown to us in the guise of Antichrist. When outlining his insane plans for insurrection and the establishment of the millennial kingdom, Verkhovensky observes that there "are Skoptsi here in the neighbourhood." Verkhovensky himself draws a parallel between the orgiastic cult of the Skoptsi and the revelation of Stavrogin as the messianic Czarevich. In a moment of agonized intelligence, Marya Timofeyevna bitterly rejects Stavrogin's claims to authentic royalty. He is not the "Sacred Bridegroom" and "Falcon" of the impending apocalypse, the hieratic redeemer of Byzantine iconography. He is "an owl, an impostor, a shopman." She refers to him as Grishka Otrepyev, the monk who pretended to be Dimitri, the murdered son of Ivan the Terrible. And this identification of Stavrogin with the false Czar—who plays so rich a part in Russian poetry and religious thought—is hinted at throughout *The Possessed*. In a tone of characteristic ambivalence, half in homage and half in derision, Pyotr salutes Stavrogin as Ivan the Czarevich. When Marya Shatov's son is born, she names him Ivan, for he is Stavrogin's child and secret heir to the kingdom. Like Antichrist, moreover, Stavrogin dangerously resembles the true Messiah; in him darkness itself burns with a peculiar radiance. "You're like him, very like, perhaps you're a relation," says the Cripple. It is she alone, with the penetrating gaze of folly, who sees Stavrogin's nakedness; he is wearing a false mask of brightness, he is a bird of night pretending to the soaring majesty of the falcon. In the end Stavrogin hangs himself. Vladimir Soloviev, one of the intimates of Dostoevsky's thought, believed that this final action is conclusive proof of Stavrogin's true nature. He is Judas or Antichrist, and the devils at his command are legion. He embodies Dostoevsky's expectations of a premature and daemonic second coming in which false saviours shall appear from the east to deceive the hearts of men and plunge the world into chaos.

This interpretation is founded on strong evidence both from the novel and from Dostoevsky's philosophic writings. But it leaves too much unexplained. Stavrogin's name has in it not only the Russian word for "horns" but also the word signifying a cross. Would Dostoevsky have pronounced through the mouth of a false Messiah one of the cardinal articles of his personal creed: "rather with Christ than with the truth"? Why is it that Stavrogin, in veiled but unmistakable semblance to the Son of Man and in analogy to the Idiot, should allow himself to be slapped and publicly insulted? We know that Dostoevsky regarded such sufferance as one of the outward marks of sanctity. When we consider Stavrogin's relations to women, dilemmas of central meaning and the need for a comprehensive understanding crowd on us. Referring to the Cripple, he says to Shatov: "She never had a baby and couldn't have had. Marya Timofeyevna is a virgin." Yet he insists that she is his bride, and it is her death which finally pierces his cold and wanton reserve. Between Stavrogin and Marya Timofeyevna prevails the double sacrament of espousal and virginity. "There's an easy riddle for you, guess it," says Marya. Perhaps we have not done so because the solution is somewhat fantastic and blasphemous. The motif of chastity obtrudes again on the encounter between Stavrogin and Liza Nikolaevna. "A complete fiasco," suggests Verkhovensky. "I'll bet anything that you've been sitting side by side in the drawing room all night wasting your precious time discussing something lofty and elevated." How shall we accord this image with that of Antichrist, who is traditionally portrayed as the embodiment of ravenous lust? Unlike Muishkin, Stavrogin is not impotent. But the one instance in the novel in which his involvement is clearly sexual is of a strange and sacred character.

Marya Shatov bears Stavrogin's son, and Shatov receives the infant with ecstatic humility. We are led to believe that what hopes for the future *The Possessed* allows us are founded on this child. But why the name Marya and the mystery of transferred fatherhood? The evidence is too urgent and close-knit to be denied. The birth of Christ is relevant to the birth of Stavrogin's son. And this relevance is not one of parody. Shatov's rapture and the sudden ground-swell of emotion which affects Kirillov are communicated to us as authentic values. If Stavrogin were merely, or predominantly, a false Messiah, all the wonders and stirrings of spirit that attend on this nativity would add up to a sardonic farce.

The antinomies in the role of Stavrogin are baffling. He is a "traitor in the sight of Christ," affirms Ivanov, but "he is also disloyal to Satan." His plane of action would appear to lie, in the most literal sense, outside human morality. In imagining him, Dostoevsky may have succumbed to an ancient and desperate suspicion. If God is the creator of the universe, He is by the same token of entirety the creator of evil. If all grace is encompassed in His being, so is all inhumanity. Stavrogin does not incarnate this sombre mythology at all points in the novel. But his actions and his relevance to the symbolic placing of Marya Timofeyevna and Marya Shatov preclude the notion that he represents a scheme of pure malignity or a straightforward portrayal of the Prince of Darkness. There seem to be moments in the novel in which Stavrogin conveys to us a tragic apprehension of the duality of God. To use the language of the alchemists (with its appropriateness to the logic of myth and of poetry), we may read in the figure of Stavrogin a tetragrammaton, an occult cipher expressing or invoking a revelation of the attributes of God. Dostoevsky's censors and critics were quick to note that his official theodicy—the metaphysics of freedom argued by Alyosha Karamazov—failed to give an adequate answer to Ivan Karamazov's fierce recital of the horrors and evils of the world. I wonder whether Dostoevsky's final answer, the "more real" of his meaning, may not be found in Stavrogin, in the hint that evil and the violation of human values are inseparable from the universality of God.

Few figures in literature draw us closer to the limits of understanding. None persuades us more forcibly that the consoling distinctions between good and evil, between the sacred and the monstrous, are of human contrivance and restricted application. Stavrogin exemplifies Kierkegaard's belief that the categories of morality and of religion may not be identical—that they may, indeed, be bewilderingly different. As one considers Stavrogin, one comes to marvel at Dostoevsky's nerve—taking nerve to signify constancy of vision into an abyss of thought or that faculty which moved Dante to proceed through the flames of hell though, as legend has it, they darkened his skin.

The trials of nerve are recorded in the drafts. "With regard to the Prince," Dostoevsky confided to himself, "all things are in question." He saw from the outset that Stavrogin would bear on the problem of the existence of God "even," as a fragmentary sentence tells us, "to the point of overturning God, of taking His place." What Coleridge said of Shakespeare is true of Dostoevsky: he possessed "that sublime faculty by which a great mind becomes that on which it meditates." The notebooks for the novel bear the mark of this total absorption; in them we may observe Dostoevsky proceeding beyond his original beliefs to new ideas and sudden flashes of perception. The drafts detail for us the essential structure of *The Possessed*, the manner in which Stavrogin is the catalyst of action. He bares the infirmity of Shatov's religious faith and drives Kirillov to the extremity of reason. He calls out the assassin in Fedka and awakens Liza's hysterical sensuality. He is the pivot of Verkhovensky's life, through the entanglement here is so close that we cannot always determine where the principle of motion lies.

In his portrayal of the relations between Stavrogin and the other characters, Dostoevsky reverted to one of his arch-themes: the advent of folly and evil through the aberration of love. Where it is love of God that is being perverted, the folly and the evil are correspondingly greater. On this point Dostoevskyan thought reflects Carl Gustav Carus's *Psyche*. The novelist may have read this rather eccentric but brilliant treatise even prior to his imprisonment in Siberia. In partial anticipation of Freud, Carus argued that there are reciprocities (what we might call "transferences") between immature religiosity and immature sexuality. The eruption of religious feeling or erotic passion in what Carus designated as "the unripe soul" could lead to similar depravities. Out of an excess of desire, ill conceived or imperfectly objectified, the mind may succumb to sudden and irrational hatreds. The character and performance of Verkhovensky dramatize this state of malevolent infatuation. But nearly all the personages revolving around Stavrogin are comparably infected. Much of the evil that darkens *The Possessed* arises from a desecration or perversion of love. Men and women surrender themselves to "Prince Harry," but he neither honours nor reciprocates their offering. In turn, this failure of requital, which is rooted in his essential inhumanity, breeds disorder and hatred.

The way in which Stavrogin drains men's souls so

that the devils can enter into them is shown, with extraordinary force and dramatic poise, in the episode of the meeting at Virginsky's house. The scene is a Last Supper, and the mode of treatment lies midway between the ironic and the elegiac. Pyotr Verkhovensky has hinted that someone will betray the conspiracy, that there is a Judas among the disciples. Amid the chorus of denial and protestation, Stavrogin—the Czarevich himself—remains silent. The conspirators turn to him, seeking reassurance, demanding to know the extent of his own commitment:

"I see no necessity to answer the question which interests you," muttered Stavrogin.
"But we've compromised ourselves and you won't," shouted several voices.
"What business is it of mine if you have compromised yourselves?" laughed Stavrogin, but his eyes flashed.
"What business? What business?" voices exclaimed.
Many people got up from their chairs.

The Prince departs, followed by his false prophet, abandoning the apostles to a pathetic and sinister emptiness of spirit. In Verkhovensky's subsequent desire to precipitate events we may discern a heretical supposition nearly as old as Christianity itself: that Judas betrayed Christ in order to bring on the hour of revelation.

Whatever one may say of Stavrogin and of the mythology of *The Possessed* is bound to be incomplete by that great margin which separates the critical from the poetic. We can no more exhaust the significations of Stavrogin than we can those of Hamlet or King Lear. In matters of poetry and of myth there are no solutions, merely attempts to make our responses more adequate and of a more precise modesty. Dostoevsky talks out "queer and clear," says Empson. Often the clarity lies in the strangeness. Not all critics are prepared to concede as much. The enigma of the central character and the formal complications of *The Possessed* have been interpreted as failures of technique: "Dostoevsky has in this work dropped anchor in such depths that he cannot completely raise it again. To clear his vessel, he had to cut more than one cable. Only in part could he give artistic form to what he had beheld. . . ." [4] This point of view is developed in Jacques Rivière's essay on "Dostoevsky and the Unfathomable." At the heart of every Dostoevskyan figure, claims Rivière, there is "an x," an irreducible unknown: "Nothing will persuade me that, given sufficient intuition, one may not endow a character with both profundity and logical coherence." "True depth," he concludes, "is explored depth."[5] Contracted to an aphorism, and set in the period prior to *Finnegans Wake*, this is the ablest defence of the European against the Russian novel.

But it is a defence founded on retrenchment. In the great atlas of the experienced or dreamt-of world there are chasms of which we can take no soundings and altitudes beyond direct ascent. To use once again the instance of the *Paradiso*: at the limits of vision we find light in blindness, not in further exploration. But the *Divine Comedy* and the literature on which Rivière founded his principles of logic reflect different conceptions. The distinction lies in the inclusion or absence of the religious element—taking "religious" in its most spacious connotations. In the absence of it, certain reaches of poetic achievement would appear to be unattainable. We define these reaches by virtue of Greek and Elizabethan tragedy, of the lineage of the serious epic, and, I submit, in reference to the novels of Tolstoy and Dostoevsky. Where European fiction falls short of the notion of supremacy which we associate with *War and Peace*, *Anna Karenina*, *The Idiot*, *The Possessed*, and *The Brothers Karamazov*, it does so in the range and inclusiveness of its mythologies.

The craft of the novel, as practised by Balzac, Stendhal, Flaubert, and James, bears on the middle part of

[4] V. Ivanov: *Freedom and the Tragic Life: A Study in Dostoevsky* (New York, 1957).

[5] Jacques Rivière: *"De Dostoïewski et de l'insondable"* (*Nouvelles Etudes*, Paris, 1922).

the spectrum of reality. Beyond it, on either hand, lie great depths and elevations. That this middle domain, primarily the social order of things, can, through force of scrutiny, comprise rich and mature portrayals of life is shown in the case of Proust. *A la recherche du temps perdu* bears witness to the longest recorded flight of the secular imagination. A temporal world view could yield no more complex or inclusive imitation of life. Substantiality of technique nearly makes up for thinness of metaphysics. But in the final analysis, the work sets its own limits within a narrower scope than either Tolstoy or Dostoevsky. The betraying instance is the sullied and reduced manner in which Proust dismisses from the scene his noblest figure, Robert de Saint-Loup (his military cross is found lying on the floor of a *maison de passe*). In their tragic hours Proust's characters, like Emma Bovary before them, stoop a little as if the ceilings were too low. Even in dirty socks—a particularly harsh symbol of abasement—Dimitri Karamazov stands before us with contrasting grandeur; even then he directs our imaginings to the thought that God may, after all, have created man in His own image.

Three of the foremost novelists of the "post-Russian" era, D. H. Lawrence, Thomas Mann, and James Joyce, have enlarged the inheritance of fiction. It was precisely towards a religious or transcendent mythology that they moved. That Lawrence's endeavours concluded in the ferocities of a new witchcraft and that neither Mann nor Joyce arrived at the wholeness of revelation attained by Dostoevsky is immaterial. The significant fact lies in the nature of their experiments. *Ulysses*, in particular, is the firmest bid for an ordered view of the world that any European poet has made since Milton; as in Milton, moreover, the terms of governance are those of religious myth. Blackmur writes in *Anni Mirabiles*:

Stephen is the image of Lucifer, an outcast by his own will, and intransigent to the last bite on the nail. Bloom is Christ (or, as the book says, "another"), is an alien by definition, and is supremely transigent in response to every twist of experience.

Both are, of course, many other things as well, but that these categories should pertain at all points to a marked expansion in the range of the prose novel.

Joyce's stubborn pilgrimage, his attempt to build an *ecclesia* for civilization, ended, so far as we may judge, in partial frustration. European and, for that matter, American masters of the twentieth century have been able to draw neither on the authoritative and encompassing creed in which Dostoevsky struck roots nor on Tolstoy's solitary, self-intoxicated, and yet rational paganism. The contemporaneity of religious fervour and poetic imagination in nineteenth-century Russia, the dialectical relationship between prayer and poetry, was a specific historical circumstance. It was no less rooted in a moment of time than was that coalescence of occasion and genius which made possible Greek tragedy and Elizabethan drama.

VII

The works of Tolstoy and Dostoevsky are cardinal examples of the problem of belief in literature. They exercise upon our minds pressures and compulsions of such obvious force, they engage values so obviously germane to the major politics of our time, that we cannot, even if we should wish to do so, respond on purely literary grounds. They solicit from their readers fierce and often mutually exclusive adherences. Tolstoy and Dostoevsky are not only read, they are believed in. Men and women from all over the world undertook pilgrimages to Yasnaya Polyana in quest of illumination, in the hope of receiving some message of oracular redemption. Most of the visitors, Rilke being a notable exception, sought out the religious reformer and prophet rather than the novelist whom Tolstoy himself had seemingly repudiated. But the two were, in fact, inseparable. The expounder of the new Gospel and the teacher of Gandhi was by virtue of essential unity—or, if we prefer, by definition of his own genius—the author of *War and Peace* and of *Anna Karenina*. In contrast to those who proclaim themselves "Tolstoyans," yet also in analogy, there are the disciples of Dostoevsky, the believers in the Dostoevskyan vision of life. Joseph Goebbels wrote a curious but not ungifted novel, *Michael*. In it we find a Russian student saying: "We believe in Dostoevsky as our fathers believed in Christ." [6] His statement is borne out by what Berdiaev, Gide, and Camus have recorded of the role of Dostoevsky in their own lives and *prises de conscience*. Gorky said that the simple fact of Tolstoy's existence made it possible for other men to be writers; existentialist metaphysicians and some of the poets who survived the death camps have testified that the image of Dostoevsky and their remembrance of his works made it possible for them to think intelligibly and endure. Because it is the crowning action of the soul, belief demands a commensurate object. Could one say that one "believes in Flaubert"?

Merezhkovsky was probably the first to consider Tolstoy and Dostoevsky in contrast to each other. The antinomies in their respective world views seemed to him a saddening commentary on the divided state of the Russian conscience. He hoped that there would come a time when Tolstoyans and Dostoevskyans would join forces:

There is a handful of Russians—certainly no more—hungering and thirsting after the fulfilment of their new religious Idea: who believe that in a *fusion* between the thought of Tolstoy and that of Dostoïevski will be found the Symbol—the union—to lead and revive.[7]

It appears unlikely that either novelist would have condoned this expectation. The only common ground between them was a wary and at times suppressed recognition of each other's genius. The tenor of their respective greatness and its forms of being set them irremediably at odds.

Tolstoy and Dostoevsky never met or, more pre-

[6] Joseph Goebbels: *Michael* (Munich, 1929). I am indebted to Professor Sidney Ratner of Rutgers University for drawing my attention to this work.

[7] D. S. Merezhkovsky: op. cit.

cisely and significantly, they were convinced that they had never met although they realized that they had, at one period, frequented the same literary circle. Indeed, their outward biographies and the histories of their religious opinions came very near to touching at various times and occasions. Both were in contact with the Petrashevsky group, Dostoevsky in 1849, Tolstoy in 1851; capital punishment, the death of a brother, and the impression made upon them by the spectacle of urban life in western Europe played comparable parts in the shaping of their beliefs; both men were passionate gamblers; both paid repeated visits to the renowned monastery at Optin; both were fascinated by the populist movement in the 1870's and wrote for Mikhailovsky's journal; they had mutual friends intent on bringing about a meeting between them. As far as is known, no such encounter took place. Perhaps the two masters feared that it would end in a drastic clash of tempers or, more grievously, in total failure of communication (such as marred the one brief meeting between Joyce and Proust).

Shortly after receiving news of Dostoevsky's death, Tolstoy wrote to Strakhov:

I never saw the man, had no sort of direct relations with him; but when he died, I suddenly realized that he had been to me the most precious, the dearest, and the most necessary of beings. It never even entered my head to compare myself with him. Everything that he wrote (I mean only the good, the true things) was such that the more he did like that, the more I rejoiced. Artistic accomplishment and intellect can arouse my envy; but a work from the heart—only joy. I always regarded him as my friend, and reckoned most confidently on seeing him at some time. And suddenly I read that he is dead. At first I was utterly confounded, and when later I realized how I had valued him, I began to weep—I am weeping even now. Only a few days before his death, I had read with emotion and delight his *Injury and Insult*.

Writing under the shock of the event, Tolstoy was doubtless being sincere. But in claiming that he had confidently reckoned on seeing Dostoevsky "at some time," he was either deceiving himself or yielding to a sense of the occasion. One is reminded of a similar failure of encounter in the lives of Verdi and Wagner. Legend has it that Verdi reached Wagner's palazzo in Venice, for what was to have been their first meeting, in the moment of Wagner's death—the moral being that neither as man nor as musician could he have reached it before.

Even in its grief, the letter betrays Tolstoy's real feelings. What did he regard as "the good, the true things" in Dostoevskyan fiction? Like Turgeniev, he tended to rank *The House of the Dead* above all other of Dostoevsky's writings. He thought it a "fine, edifying book"; no doubt it is, but it represents Dostoevsky neither in his mature vein nor, primarily, as a novelist. It is the most Tolstoyan of Dostoevsky's works. What delighted Tolstoy in *The Insulted and the Injured* was the element of Christian pathos, the quality of Dickensian sentiment. The major Dostoevsky repelled him. Gorky noted that he spoke of him "reluctantly, constrainedly, evading or repressing something," Sometimes the essential antagonism broke out in flashes of injustice:

He was suspicious without reason, ambitious, heavy and unfortunate. It is curious that he is so much read. I can't understand why. It is all painful and useless, because all those Idiots, Adolescents, Raskolnikovs, and the rest of them, they are not real; it is all much simpler, more understandable. It's a pity people don't read Leskov, he's a real writer. . . .[8]

To Gorky, Tolstoy made the bizarre comment that "there was something Jewish" in Dostoevsky's blood. To invoke one of the images of a divided world proposed by St. Jerome, it was as if Athens (the city of reason, of scepticism, and of pleasure in the free play

[8] Tolstoy to Gorky, in Gorky: *Reminiscences of Tolstoy, Chekhov and Andreev* (trans. by Katherine Mansfield, S. S. Koteliansky, and Leonard Woolf, London, 1934).

of secular energies) had confronted the transcendent eschatology of Jerusalem.

Dostoevsky's attitudes towards Tolstoy were equivocal and exceedingly complex. He acknowledged in *The Diary of a Writer* that "Count Leo Tolstoy, unquestionably, is the most beloved writer among the Russian public of all shades." He assured his readers that *Anna Karenina*, of whose politics he bitterly disapproved, was a masterpiece beyond the reach of western European literature. But he suffered constant irritation at the thought of the privileged circumstances in which Tolstoy worked. Even at the outset of his career, at the time of his return from Semipalatinsk, Dostoevsky felt that the rate of pay Tolstoy commanded in literary periodicals was excessive. Writing to his niece in August 1870, he exclaimed:

Do you know that I am absolutely *aware* that if I could have spent two or three years at that book—as Turgeniev, Goncharov, and Tolstoy can—I could have produced a work of which men would still be talking in a hundred years from now!

The leisure and wealth which seemed to Dostoevsky to make Tolstoy's work possible seemed to him responsible also for its particular tone and character. He referred to Tolstoy's novels as "Landed-proprietor's Literature" and declared in a letter to Strakhov in May 1871:

that kind of literature has said all it has to say (particularly well in the case of Leo Tolstoy). It has spoken its last word, and is exempt from further duty.

In the *Diary of a Writer* for July–August 1877, Dostoevsky described much of Tolstoy's work as "nothing more than historical pictures of times long past." He asserted repeatedly that Tolstoy's achievements fell short of Pushkin's, who had both initiated and perfected the historical genre. In Dostoevskyan aesthetics this comparison implicates a whole range of values and ideals. Pushkin was the national poet and prophet, the very incarnation of Russia's destiny; in contrast, both Turgeniev and Tolstoy appeared to Dostoevsky (as he remarked in a note for *The Life of a Great Sinner*) as somehow alien.

Tolstoy and Tolstoyan thought are referred to at several points in Dostoevsky's fiction and polemical writings. During the Balkan war, his Pan-Slavism and messianic expectations assumed hysterical tones. He wrote in *The Diary*: "God bless the Russian volunteers with success!—It is rumoured that Russian officers by the dozens are again being killed in battle. You, dear ones!" Tolstoy's condemnation of the war in the last Book of *Anna Karenina* seemed to Dostoevsky proof of "apostasy" and of cynical alienation from "the all-Russian great cause." In the personage of Levin he recognized Tolstoy's authentic spokesman and he perceived in Levin a love of the "holy earth" comparable to his own. What shocked Dostoevsky was the fact that such love could be divorced from nationalism. Yasnaya Polyana had been made into a closed world; through the image of Levin's estate, Tolstoy was exalting private over public life. To Dostoevsky, with his vision of the reconquered Constantinople, such a cultivation of one's own garden was a form of treason. His critique of *Anna Karenina* in *The Diary* ends on a note of accusing rhetoric: "Men, such as the author of *Anna Karenina*, are teachers of society, our teachers, while we are merely their pupils. What then, do they teach us?"

But the quarrel ran deeper than politics. With his uncanny insight into the anatomy of the intellect, Dostoevsky had recognized in Tolstoy a disciple of Rousseau. Beyond Tolstoy's professions of love for mankind, Dostoevsky prophetically discerned the alliance between a doctrine of social perfectibility, a theology built on reason or the primacy of individual feeling, and a desire to eliminate from men's lives the sense of paradox and tragedy. Long before Tolstoy's other contemporaries, perhaps before Tolstoy himself, Dostoevsky obscurely made out where Tolstoyan thought would lead—to a Christianity without Christ. In Tolstoyan humanitarianism he devined a central, Rousseauist egotism: " 'Love for humanity,' " he observed in A *Raw Youth*, "is to be understood as love for that humanity which you have yourself created in the soul." Persuaded of the Orthodox creed and enthralled by the mysteries and tragedies of faith, Dostoevsky sensed in Tolstoy an arch-opponent.

But Dostoevsky was too great a novelist, too passionate an inquirer into men, not to be drawn to Tolstoy's genius. Only in terms of some such divided impulse may we account for the oddest allusion to Tolstoy in all of Dostoevskyan fiction. Critics have long pointed out that the name of the "idiot," Prince Lyov Nikolaevich Muishkin, echoes that of Count Lyov Nikolaevich Tolstoy. Both Muishkin and Tolstoy, moreover, refer their names to an ancient lineage. The resemblance may indicate a shadowy and perhaps unconscious process of dialectic in Dostoevsky's mind. Was he saying that the Tolstoyan conception of Christ (what could he have known of it at the time *The Idiot* was being written?), like Muishkin himself, was doomed to impotence through some radical defect of insight or excess of humanity? Or was Dostoevsky pointing to the notion that individual sainthood without the sustaining structure of a church is a form of self-indulgence destined to end in catastrophe? We cannot tell, but this kind of echo is rarely an accident; beneath it lie the hidden candours of the imagination.

A less mysterious and finely ironic allusion to Tolstoy occurs in the dialogue between Ivan Karamazov and the Devil. That "gentleman" is attempting to persuade Ivan that he is real:

"Listen, in dreams and especially in nightmares, from indigestion or anything, a man sees sometimes such artistic visions, such complex and real actuality, such events, even a whole world of events, woven into such a plot, with such unexpected details from the most exalted matters to the last button on a cuff, as I swear Leo Tolstoy has never invented. . . . The subject is a complete enigma. A statesman confessed to me, indeed, that all his best ideas came to him when he was asleep. Well, that's how it is now, though I am your hallucination, yet just as in a nightmare, I say original things which had not entered your head before."

The Devil quotes not only Scripture but also Tolstoy. And Dostoevsky implies, doubtless with tongue in cheek, that the massive and detailed realism of Tolstoyan fiction is as prone to hallucination as the spectral world of *The Brothers Karamazov*.

R. Fülöp-Miller has said that Dostoevsky was projecting an "anti-Tolstoy novel." If so, no trace of it remains. Nor has any Walter Savage Landor written an imaginary conversation between the two novelists. Yet I wonder whether we do not possess what might, in fact, be regarded as a fragment of this imaginary dialogue. In the architecture of Dostoevskyan art and mythology the Legend of the Grand Inquisitor occupies something of the place which *King Lear* and *The Tempest* occupy in the world of Shakespeare. In poetry and intent the Legend is of such manifold complexity that we may, with profit, approach it from many points of view and recognize in it many planes of meaning. Through it Dostoevsky gave the final measure of his thought, and significant elements of its form and metaphysics may have arisen out of some polemic meditation on Tolstoy. In proposing to read the Legend of the Grand Inquisitor as an allegory of the confrontation between Dostoevsky and Tolstoy, I am suggesting a design which is meant to be neither dogmatic nor of persistent gravity. I am putting forward a myth of criticism, a fancy through which to re-direct our imaginings to one of the most famous yet enigmatic of literary works.

The Legend is the culminating stage, the episode of ultimate crisis and resolution, in the disputation between Ivan and Alyosha Karamazov. Immediately before recounting what he designedly calls his "poem," Ivan has professed his rebellion against God. He cannot accept the knowledge of the bestialities inflicted upon innocent children. If God exists while allowing children to be killed and maimed in purposeless inhumanity, He must be either malevolent or powerless. The notion of a final theodicy, of redemptive justice, is not worth "the tears of that one tortured child who beat itself on the breast with its little fist and prayed in its stinking outhouse, with its unexpiated tears to 'dear, kind God.'" And then Ivan tenders his abdication:

"too high a price is asked for harmony; it's beyond our means to pay so much to enter on it. And so I hasten to give back my entrance ticket, and if I am an honest man I am bound to give it back as soon as possible. And that I am doing. It's not God that I don't accept, Alyosha, only I most respectfully return Him the ticket."

Ivan's argument is closely modelled on Belinsky's attack against the Hegelians in a well-known letter to Botkin:

with all the respect due to your philosophic philistinism, I have the honour of making it clear to you that if ever I happen to attain the highest rung on the ladder of evolution, I would there demand that account be rendered to me for all human beings whom circumstances and history have made into martyrs, for all the victims of hazard, of superstition, of the Inquisition, of Philip II. . . . If they are not accounted for, I shall hurl myself from my eminence head first. I do not wish the happiness which is dispensed to me if I am not, beforehand, reassured about each of my brothers. . . . It is said that dissonance is the condition of harmony; that may be delightful and profitable from the point of view of the music lover, but surely it is much less so for whomever is destined to play the role of dissonance.

In this passage lies the germ of the Legend: the association between a general critique of theodicy and the specific theme of the Inquisition.

But the net of memory had been cast in many directions. The motif of the returned "ticket of admission" points to one of Schiller's most profound allegories, *Resignation*. In this poem the speaker relates how he traded youth and love from the vain promise of harmony and understanding in the life to come. Now he charges Eternity with deceit. No man has ever returned from death with proof that there is in another world a just compensation for the torments and inequities of man's condition. An omniscient voice answers his indictment. Human beings are accorded either hope or bliss (*Genuss*). They cannot have both. He that chooses to hope for some revelation of transcendent justice will have been compensated in the act of hoping. No further reward should be asked for. I cite only those stanzas which bear directly on the Dostoevskyan text:

> *Da steh ich schon auf deiner finstern Brücke,*
> > *Furchtbare Ewigkeit.*
> *Empfange meinen Vollmachtbrief zum Glücke!*
> *Ich bring ihn unerbrochen dir zurücke,*
> > *Ich weiss nichts von Glückseligkeit.*
>
> *Vor deinem Thron erheb ich meine Klage,*
> > *Verhüllte Richterin.*
> *Auf jenem Stern ging eine frohe Sage,*
> *Du thronest hier mit des Gerichtes Waage*
> > *Und nennest dich Vergelterin.*
>
> *Hier, spricht man, warten Schrecken auf den Bösen*
> > *Und Freuden auf den Redlichen.*
> *Des Herzens Krümmen werdest du entblössen,*
> *Der Vorsicht Rätsel werdest du mir lösen*
> > *Und Rechnung halten mit den Leidenden.*

> Upon thy bridge the shadows round me press,
> > O dread Eternity!
> And I have known no moment that can bless;—
> Take back this letter meant for Happiness—
> > The seal's unbroken—see!
> Before thee, Judge, whose eyes the dark-spun veil
> > Conceals, my murmurs came;
> On this our orb a glad belief prevails,
> That, thine the earthly sceptre and the scales,
> > Requiter is thy name.
> Terrors, they say, thou dost for Vice prepare,
> > And joys the good shall know;
> Thou canst the crooked heart unmask and bare;
> Thou canst the riddle of our fate declare,
> > And keep account with Woe.
>
> (in the version of Lord Lytton)

Both Ivan Karamazov and the speaker of the poem have been given a "ticket of admission," a *Vollmachtbrief zum Glücke,* but neither is prepared to pay the price. The darkness of the world is beyond their acquiescence.

Two elements had now been brought into contact by what Livingston Lowes would have called "the hooked atoms" of Dostoevsky's memory: the poem by Schiller and the theme of Philip II as he was referred to by Belinsky. The next step was nearly inevitable: Schiller's *Don Carlos* moved centrally into the imaginative process. It is in *Don Carlos* that Ivan Karamazov's Grand Inquisitor first appears. The stage direction and the account of him in the Legend are almost identical:

The Cardinal Grand Inquisitor, an old man aged ninety and blind, leaning on a staff and led by two Dominicans. As he proceeds through their ranks, the grandees all cast themselves down before him. . . . He accords them his blessing.

. . . .

He is an old man, almost ninety. . . . The crowd instantly bows down to the earth like one man, before the old Inquisitor. He blesses the people in silence and passes on.

But Schiller's drama gave Dostoevsky more than the physical image of the Inquisitor. Like the Legend, *Don Carlos* turns on the dialectic of freedom and solitary power; it exposes the murderous integrity of the few—the lonely tyrants whom Shigalov portrays in *The Possessed*—to the temptations of mercy and liberality. The possibility of human freedom and of the spontaneous play of human affection momentarily subverts Philip II; it induces in his sombre and self-denying autocracy an instant of vertigo. The Dostoevskyan text looks back to this trial and to the two contrasting dialogues between the King and the Marquis of Posa, and between the King and the Inquisitor. Some of Schiller's motifs are translated nearly unchanged into Ivan's poem. When justifying his momentary spell of humaneness, Philip says of the Marquis: "I looked into his eyes." The same recognition passes between the Grand Inquisitor and

Christ; after gazing into His eyes, the priest lets Christ depart in peace.

But although the Legend is indebted to Belinsky, to Schiller, and, as we shall have occasion to note, to Pushkin, its special force and tonal quality derive from the immediate fictional context. This fact is sometimes overlooked both because Ivan's narration is couched in a heightened and somewhat archaic style—as if to set it apart from the surrounding prose—and because it is so well known in its own right. But the poem is an integral part of the dialogue between the two Karamazovs and much of its meaning is inseparable from its dramatic purpose. Ivan inquires of Alyosha whether there is anyone in the world empowered to forgive those who torture helpless children. Alyosha replies:

"there is a Being and He can forgive everything, all and for all, because He gave His innocent blood for all and everything. You have forgotten Him, and on Him is built the edifice, and it is to Him they cry aloud, 'Thou art just, O Lord, for Thy ways are revealed!' "

But Ivan has not forgotten Him and proceeds to tell his fable of Christ's visit to Seville. After hearing the monologue of the Grand Inquisitor, Alyosha says: "Your poem is in praise of Jesus, not in blame of Him—as you meant it to be." But he mistakes Ivan's tragic conception. The Legend was never imagined as an attack on Christ. It is the crowning symbol and primary conveyor of Ivan's indictment of God. A few moments later, Alyosha realizes this: " 'You don't believe in God,' he added, speaking this time very sorrowfully." That is the heart of the matter. Ivan believes in Christ with a fierce, covert passion. He cannot commit his lucid soul to a belief in God. It would be difficult to conceive of a subtler or more agonizing heresy.

But what I propose is a narrower reading, leaving unconsidered the relations between the Legend and the structure of *The Brothers Karamazov* as a whole. Through an artifice of criticism, I shall regard Ivan's fable as an imaginary encounter between Tolstoy and

Dostoevsky, as a clash between two world views which were expressed, with genius and a high sense of rhetoric, in crucial aspects of Tolstoyan and Dostoevskyan thought. The poem of the Grand Inquisitor concentrates and radicalizes an enmity of beliefs that is elsewhere muted through dispersal or the cautions of debate. It is here that what Berdiaev called the "insoluble controversy" between the two novelists, the antagonism between "fundamental conceptions of existence," can be followed with utmost clarity. In the drafts Dostoevsky enunciated, through rigorous self-examination, the ideas and challenges which are central to his mythology. Few chapters in fiction were more elaborately "thought out." The fascination of the process lies in the detail.

Let us consider first one of the earliest preliminary entries in the notebooks:

cut off all their heads
The inquisitor: what need have we of "over there"? We are more human than you. We love the earth—Schiller sings to joy, John Damascene. What price joy? With what torrents of blood, of torture, of degradation and of unbearable ferocity [is it purchased?]. No one talks of that. Oh the crucifixion is a dread argument.
The inquisitor: *god like a merchant*. I love humanity better than you.

Here, truly, is the workshop of the mind, with the sudden leaps and gaps of reason and the secret languages of intuition. Only a part of the design can be reconstructed. The broken sentence at the start points back to a preceding train of thought on tyranny, on Shigalov's despotic utopia. Does it refer to Caligula's famous wish that all his subjects should have but one neck so that they might all be exterminated with a single blow of the axe? Or should we see in it an allusion to an earlier fragment in which Dostoevsky simply wrote down and underlined the name of Louis XVII, the lost Dauphin? The next sentence is easier to make out and its significance is clear. The Grand Inquisitor states his case in terms which may reasonably be characterized as

Tolstoyan. His metaphysic has no need of a transcendent reality—of "over there." It acts within the material and secular world. He is "more human" than Christ in the sense both of imperfection and humaneness. He is more genuinely animated than was Christ by a desire for reason and order and social tranquillity. Hence the Tolstoyan affirmation "we love the earth." On it must be established, through asceticism or violence if need be, the true kingdom.

In the next few lines Dostoevsky plunged into a tangle of private associations and fragmented references. First we are directed to Schiller's ode, *An die Freude*. Going back to the poem, we note a number of passages that bear on Ivan's philosophy. The quatrain of the sixth stanza is particularly relevant:

> *Duldet mutig, Millionen!*
> *Duldet für die bessre Welt!*
> *Droben überm Sternenzelt*
> *Wird ein grosser Gott belohnen.*

> (Suffer bravely, oh ye millions!
> Suffer for the better life!
> For beyond the stars' pavilions
> God shall compensate your grief.)

In essence, this is the theodicy of Idealism. Let us suffer to achieve a better world. Even if we fail, God shall reward the endeavour. In a manner which we cannot elucidate, the ode to joy led Dostoevsky to John Damascene, whose *De fide orthodoxa* played an important role in the doctrinal history of the eastern churches. Dostoevsky probably knew the work. But it appears more plausible that Schiller's ode suggested to the novelist one of John Damascene's famous hymns. In the hymn *In Dominicam Pascha*, the Church Father celebrated the joyous paradox of the Passion, the benefit which came to all men through the cruel death of the Lord:

> *Resurrectionis dies: splendescamus, populi;*
> *Pascha Domini, Pascha.*

E morte enim ad vitam, et ex terra ad coelum,
Christus nos traduxit, victoriam canentes.

(Day of resurrection: let us rejoice, ye people;
Lamb of God, Lamb.
From death even unto life, from earth to heaven,
Christ has led us, singing alleluia.) [9]

Thus two memory clusters were, if we may put it in so gross an image, at neighbouring points in Dostoevsky's mind: Schiller's joy in human progress and final harmony and John Damascene's celebration of Christ's redemptive sacrifice. In the following, apparently unfinished sentence, Dostoevsky reflects on both ideas. Must millions suffer (*dulden*) for the sake of some unknown and perhaps illusory compensation? That is the crux of Ivan Karamazov's challenge. "Oh the crucifixion is a dread argument." But against whom? At this stage in the drafts Dostoevsky may not have known. It could be an argument for those who doubt Christ's immortality or God's willingness to forgive a world in which His only begotten Son was tormented to death. But the crucifixion is also Alyosha's principal evidence that through self-sacrifice Christ had made all compassions possible. The end of the note is cryptic. One fails to construe what the italicized phrase, "*god like a merchant*," signifies or refers to. But the force and direction of the Inquisitor's claim that he loves humanity better than Christ does is obvious. This claim will be amplified in the definitive text; the Inquisitor is a defender of mankind against the violence and paradox of grace, a justifier of the ways of man to a remote or incomprehensible Deity. In obscuring brevity, and with the indirections of a mind turned towards its own secret workings, this entry in the notebooks prefigures the major design of the Legend.

It is followed by a series of jottings—fragments of sentences, snatches of dialogue, citations. In them we

[9] In these remarks on Dostoevsky's allusion to John Damascene, I am indebted to the guidance of Professor John J. O'Meara of University College, Dublin.

may perceive Dostoevsky becoming more familiar with his material and imposing upon his theme mastery of treatment. At times he leapt too far and arrived at finalities that were then discarded from the actual novel. In the drafts Ivan states categorically that he is on the Grand Inquisitor's side, "for he is the better lover of humanity." In *The Brothers Karamazov* there is an ironic equivocation:

"Why it's all nonsense, Alyosha. It's only a senseless poem of a senseless student, who could never write two lines of verse. Why do you take it so seriously?"

In its early contours the dialectic of the Grand Inquisitor is exceedingly close to that of Shigalov and of the egalitarian socialism satirized in *The Possessed*. "We shall have to wait a long time yet until we organize the Kingdom," confides the nameless voice in the notebooks:

A swarm of locust will rise from the earth crying that we are enslavers, that we corrupt virgins—but the wretched creatures shall submit. In the end they will submit and the greatest among them will join with us and understand that we take on suffering for the sake of power.—
But these damned ones do not really know what burden we are assuming—we are taking knowledge—and suffering.

Nowhere was Dostoevsky a truer prophet than in these drafts, in this long discourse between his hesitant imagination and the darting certitudes of his intelligence. The Inquisitor grows to all his sombre majesty out of Shigalov's vision of the lonely oligarch, out of the personage of the priest in *Don Carlos*, and out of Belinsky's portrayal of Marat as a "lover of humanity." As he becomes himself, we observe in him attitudes of mind and forms of sensibility which are markedly Tolstoyan: an encompassing and autocratic love of humanity, that arrogance of reason when it believes itself to be in possession of assured knowledge, the strain of asceticism, and the prevailing loneliness. Ivan's portrait of "that accursed old man who loves mankind so obstinately" is strangely prophetic. Dostoevsky was dead long before Tolstoy reached the age of the Grand Inquisitor; but the premonitions of the Legend were in great measure fulfilled. Tolstoy aged into a fierce solitude of spirit.

After these prefatory notes in which the mind had, as it were, sharpened its pen, Dostoevsky advanced into the massive sweep of his argument. Here again the drafts are illuminating. In them the Inquisitor puts his case more openly than in the novel and we can follow in detail those articulations of thought which were subsequently masked by the lyricism of the poem. The Inquisitor accuses Christ of having abandoned men not only to freedom but also to doubt:

For in beginning to live, men seek tranquillity above all else. . . . You, on the contrary, have proclaimed that life is rebellion and have abolished tranquillity for ever. Instead of giving solid, plain and clear principles you have taken everything away.
And the second thesis, the second secret of human nature was founded on the necessity of establishing a common understanding of good and evil for all men. He who shall teach, he who will guide, is a true prophet.

In *The Brothers Karamazov* the same charge is made more poetically:

And behold, instead of giving a firm foundation for setting the conscience of man at rest for ever, Thou didst choose all that is exceptional, vague and enigmatic. . . .

As we have seen, this is Tolstoy's essential indictment of the New Testament and, in a different range of judgment, it is his principal critique of the Dostoevskyan novel. Gorky shrewdly remarked that Tolstoy arranged his own version of the Gospels "in order that we might forget the contradictions in Christ." He sought to replace the "exceptional, vague and enigmatic" by thorough, unhesitating common sense. Like the Inquisitor, he could not accept the paradoxes and riddling obscurities in Christ's teaching. Both Tolstoy and the Dostoevskyan priest were fanatic believers in the powers of the mind, in the capacity of reason to throw a plain and steady light on that which Christ had left in the penumbra of allegory. "The most important thing lies in thoughts," wrote Tolstoy in his journal for June 1899: "Thoughts are the beginning of everything. And thoughts can be directed. And therefore the principal task of perfection is—to work on thoughts." Dostoevsky held precisely the contrary view. He defined nihilism as "servility of thought. A nihilist is a lackey of thought." As Gide said: in the psychology of Dostoevsky "that which is opposed to love is not primarily hatred but the rumination of the brain." [1]

In the drafts the Inquisitor gives a terrifying account of what happens to the human soul when it is delivered into the hands of doubt:

For the secret of man's being is not only to live . . . but to live for something definite. Without a firm notion of what it is that he is living for, man will not accept life and will rather destroy himself than remain on earth. . . .

This is exactly the condition to which Tolstoy bore witness in his *Confession*: "I could not live, and, fearing death, had to employ cunning with myself to avoid taking my own life."

Men are racked by doubt and metaphysical anguish because Christ has allowed them the freedom to choose between good and evil, because the tree of knowledge has once again been left dangerously unguarded. This is the central theme of the Legend. The Inquisitor accuses Christ of having tragically overestimated the stature of man or his ability to bear the agonies of free will. Men prefer the brute calm of servitude. Much of Ivan Karamazov's dialectic is anticipated in Pushkin's "Parable of that Moderate Democrat Jesus Christ" (1823):

> With freedom's seed the desert sowing,
> I walked before the morning star;
> From pure and guiltless fingers throwing—
> Where slavish plows had left a scar—
> The fecund seed, the procreator;
> Oh, vain and sad disseminator,

[1] André Gide: op. cit.

338

I learned then what lost labors are . . .
Graze if you will, you peaceful nations,
Who never rouse at honor's horn!
Should flocks heed freedom's invocations?
Their part is to be slain or shorn,
Their dower the yoke their sires have worn
Through snug and sheeplike generations.[2]

The Grand Inquisitor draws the consequence: men shall know happiness only when a perfectly regulated kingdom shall have been established on earth under the governance of miracles, authority, and bread. The ideas thrust forward by Shigalov in *The Possessed*, the mythology of the total state, are expounded and detailed in the ardent prophecy of the old priest:

Then we shall give them the quiet humble happiness of weak creatures such as they are by nature. . . . We shall show them that they are weak, that they are only pitiful children, but that childlike happiness is the sweetest of all. . . . They will marvel at us and will be awe-stricken before us, and will be proud of our being so powerful and clever, that we have been able to subdue such a turbulent flock of thousands of millions. . . . Yes, we shall set them to work, but in their leisure hours we shall make their life like a child's game, with children's song and innocent dance. . . . And they will have no secrets from us. We shall allow or forbid them to live with their wives and mistresses, to have or not to have children—according to whether they have been obedient or disobedient—and they will submit to us gladly and cheerfully. The most painful secrets of their conscience, all, all they will bring to us, and we shall have an answer for all. And they will be glad to believe our answer, for it will save them from the great anxiety and terrible agony they endure at present in making a free decision for themselves. And all will be happy, all the millions of creatures except the hundred thousand who rule over them.

Recent history has made it difficult to read this passage from *The Brothers Karamazov* with detachment. It testifies to a gift of foresight bordering on the dae-

[2] The translation is by Babette Deutsch.

339

monic. It lays before us, in precise detail, a summation of the disasters peculiar to our times. Even as earlier generations opened the Bible or Virgil or Shakespeare to find epigraphs for experience, so ours may read from Dostoevsky the lesson for the day. But let us not mistake the meaning of this "senseless poem of a senseless student." It does foreshadow, with uncanny prescience, the totalitarian regimes of the twentieth century—thought control, the annihilating and redemptive powers of the élite, the brutish delight of the masses in the musical and dancelike rituals of Nuremberg and the Moscow Sports Palace, the instrument of confession, and the total subordination of private to public life. But like 1984, which may be understood as an epilogue to it, the vision of the Grand Inquisitor points also to those refusals of freedom which are concealed beneath the language and outward forms of industrial democracies. It points to the tawdry cheapness of mass culture, to the pre-eminence of quackery and slogans over the rigours of genuine thought, to the hunger of men—a hunger no less flagrant in the west than in the east—after leaders and magicians to draw their minds out of the wilderness of freedom. "The most painful secrets of their conscience, all, all they will bring to us"—"us" being either the secret police or the psychiatrists. Dostoevsky would have discerned in both comparable attainders to the dignity of man.

But may we legitimately extend to this text our allegory of an encounter between Dostoevsky and Tolstoy? Not altogether. A Tolstoyan would point out that the master's utopian hopes were founded on nonviolence, on the maintenance of perfect concord within the ideal republic. This is true, but it does not necessarily contrast with the expectations of the Inquisitor. It is of the essence of his prophecy that men will yield voluntarily to their guardians, that the kingdom of reason will also be the kingdom of peace. Tolstoyans might urge that we can find nowhere in their canon any pronouncement to suggest the division of humanity into rulers and ruled. Narrowly considered, they would be right. But we misread Tolstoy's genius and the cast of his mind if we underrate its inherent aristocracy. Tolstoy loved men from above. He spoke of their equality before God and of the generality of common sense. But he conceived of himself as a teacher, as someone subject to the privileges and obligations of eminence. No less than the Inquisitor he saw in paternalism an ideal mode of relationship. There was nothing in him of that nearly untranslatable Dostoevskyan concept of "humility." In his shrewd empiricism, Tolstoy must have known that the pure and rational ethics which he expounded would be freely accepted only by a handful of chosen and kindred spirits.

Much turns on our understanding of the Tolstoyan Christ. A Christ the "whole" of whose teaching consisted in "giving the Kingdom of God, that is peace, to man," and who enjoined human beings "not to commit stupidities," would in no manner have been intolerable to the Grand Inquisitor. The Dostoevskyan Christ, whom the aged priest first threatens to burn and then banishes for ever, was precisely that enigmatic, paradoxical, and transcendent personage whom Tolstoy sought to remove from the new Christianity.

Finally, there is the problem of God as it arises in Ivan Karamazov's poem and in Tolstoyan metaphysics. It is generally assumed that the Inquisitor is an atheist. But the evidence is ambiguous. There is a gnomic passage in the drafts:

Euclid's geometry. That is why I shall accept God, all the more as it is the everlasting old God and one cannot resolve Him [or make Him out]. Let Him be the good Lord. It is more shameful that way.

This appears to signify that the speaker—Ivan or the Inquisitor—is prepared to accept the existence of some kind of ineffectual and incomprehensible deity, if only because this existence would make the state of the world yet more bewildering and outrageous. Or it may refer back to the riddle of Stavrogin, to the grim suspicion that "the everlasting old God" is a God of evil.

This possibility is borne out by the statement of the Inquisitor, in the novel itself, that he believes in "the wise spirit, the dread spirit of death and destruction." Hence the irony of the phrase: "Let Him be the good Lord." Neither of these attitudes is, to be sure, analogous to Tolstoyan theology. But one can say this: both the Grand Inquisitor and the later Tolstoy stood in mysterious rivalry to their images of God. Both were intent upon establishing utopian kingdoms in which God would be a rare or unwelcome guest. In their different ways, they exemplified one of Dostoevsky's essential theses: that humanitarian socialism is, fatally, a prelude to atheism.

I repeat that this reading of the Legend is a critical fancy, an attempt to use criticism metaphorically. It cannot be enforced on the whole text. Those aspects of Tolstoyan thought which may most justly be compared with the theories of the Grand Inquisitor were expressed in writings and private speculations of which Dostoevsky could have had no knowledge. In great measure they belong to the late and more obscure strains in Tolstoy's metaphysics. In this imaginary dialogue, moreover, we are given only one side of the argument. The Dostoevskyan position is gathered into the silence of Christ; it is realized not in language, but in a single gesture—the kiss which Christ bestows on the Inquisitor. Christ's refusal to engage in the duel yields a dramatic motif of great majesty and tact. But from the philosophic point of view, it has about it something of evasion. Dostoevsky's patrons in the Orthodox hierarchy and in court circles were disturbed by the one-sidedness of the poem. The fact that the Inquisitor had not been answered seemed to give his argument an unanswerable force. Dostoevsky promised that Alyosha or Father Zossima would, in subsequent episodes of the novel, clearly refute Ivan's heretical mythology. Whether they actually succeed in doing so is a moot point.

But once we allow for these facts, this interpretation of the Legend as an allegory of an encounter between

Tolstoy and Dostoevsky does retain a certain pertinence. Sir Geoffrey Keynes has drawn attention to a strikingly similar dialogue at cross-purposes between Blake and Francis Bacon. In the margin of Bacon's essay "Of Truth," Blake wrote—as Dostoevsky might have done—"Rational Truth is not the Truth of Christ, but of Pilate." The essay concludes on the theme of Ivan Karamazov's fable: "it being foretold that when Christ cometh, he shall not find faith upon the earth." Blake interjected: "Bacon put an End to Faith." [3] Such exchanges across time or in the divided mind produce moments of summation and special clarity. They point, through stress of contrast and antagonism, to the recurrent contradictions in our philosophic and religious heritage.

By virtue of divination or hazard, the close of the Legend of the Grand Inquisitor is strangely prophetic of the history of Tolstoy's life. Ivan depicts the Inquisitor as an old man "who has wasted his whole life in the desert yet could not shake off his incurable love of humanity." Gorky may have had this image in mind when he spoke of Tolstoy as "a man seeking God, not for himself, but for men, so that God may leave him, the man, alone in the peace of the desert chosen by him." And what has more bearing on the late Tolstoy than Ivan Karamazov's account of one "who had himself eaten roots in the desert and made frenzied efforts to subdue his flesh to make himself free and perfect"?

VIII

The contrarieties between Tolstoy and Dostoevsky did not cease with their deaths. Indeed, they were sharpened and dramatized by subsequent events. They had written their works in one of those periods of history which seem particularly favourable to the creation of great art—a period in which a civilization or traditional

[3] See the signed article by Sir Geoffrey Keynes in *The Times Literary Supplement* for March 8, 1957.

culture is on the verge of decline. "Then the vital force of this civilization meets with historical conditions which cease being appropriate to it, but it is still intact, for one moment, in the sphere of spiritual creativity, and it gives its last fruit there, while the freedom of poetry avails itself of the decay of social disciplines and ethos." [4] Less than forty years after the Grand Inquisitor had prophesied to Christ that the kingdom of man was at hand, some of Tolstoy's hopes and most of Dostoevsky's fears were realized. An eschatological despotism, the lonely, visionary rule foretold by Shigalov in *The Possessed*, was imposed upon Russia.

Dostoevsky and his writings were honoured during the brief dawn of power newly attained and energies newly liberated. Lenin thought *The Possessed* "repulsive but great," and Lunacharsky described Dostoevsky as "the most enthralling" of all Russian novelists. The centenary of his birth was marked during 1920–1 by official and critical tributes.[5] But with the triumph of Shigalovism in its radical forms, Dostoevsky came to be recognized as a dangerous foe, as an engenderer of subversion and heresy. The new inquisitors accused him of being a mystic, a reactionary, a sick mind endowed with rare gifts of imagination but crucially devoid of historical insight. They were prepared to tolerate *The House of the Dead* for its portrayal of czarist oppression and *Crime and Punishment* for its account of how a revolutionary intellectual may be destroyed by the "internal contradictions" of a pre-Marxist society. But to Dostoevsky's major works, to *The Idiot*, *The Possessed*, and *The Brothers Karamazov*, the men of the Stalinist era said, as the Inquisitor to Christ: "Go, and come no more . . . come not at all, never, never!" In July 1918, Lenin had decreed that statues should be erected of both Tolstoy and Dostoevsky. By 1932 the hero of Ilya Ehrenburg's *Out of Chaos* had to admit that only Dostoevsky had told the full truth about the people.

[4] Jacques Maritain: *Creative Intuition in Art and Poetry* (New York, 1953).
[5] See Irving Howe: op. cit.

But it is a truth with which one cannot live. "It can be given to the dying as formerly they gave last rites. If one is to sit down at a table and eat, one must forget about it. If one is to raise a child, one must first of all remove it from the house. . . . If one is to build a state one must forbid even the mention of that name."

Tolstoy, on the contrary, was securely enshrined in the revolutionary pantheon, rather as Rousseau had been sanctified in Robespierre's Temple of Reason. Lenin considered him to be the greatest of all writers of fiction. In the hands of Marxist criticism the difficult aristocrat, the *barin* of whose arrogance Gorky had written with affectionate awe, became the champion of proletarian nationalism. In him the Russian revolution had, according to Lenin, found its true mirror. Dostoevsky, the injured and humbled artisan of letters, the condemned radical and survivor of Siberia, the man who had been familiar with every species of economic and social degradation, was posthumously exiled from the "homeland of the proletariat." Tolstoy, the patrician chronicler of high society and rural wealth, the advocate of pre-industrial paternalism, was accorded the freedom of the new millennial city. It is an instructive paradox, suggesting that our interpretation of Ivan Karamazov's poem, however incomplete and metaphoric, is of historical relevance. What the Marxists have discerned in Tolstoy is many of the elements which Dostoevsky imagined in the Inquisitor: a radical belief in human progress through material means, a belief in pragmatic reason, a rejection of mystical experience, and a total absorption in the problems of this world to the near-exclusion of God. They have understood Dostoevsky, on the other hand, very much as the Inquisitor understands Christ, seeing in him the eternal "disturber," the disseminator of freedom and tragedy, the man to whom the resurrection of an individual soul was more important than the material progress of an entire society.

Marxist literary criticism has dealt richly, though in a selective manner, with the genius of Tolstoy. It has either condemned or ignored the bulk of Dostoevsky. George Lukács is a case in point. He has written extensively about Tolstoy; in treating of *War and Peace* and *Anna Karenina* his critical powers are vigorously at ease. But throughout his voluminous pronouncements, Dostoevsky makes only infrequent appearances. Lukács's early book *Die Theorie des Romans* refers to him in its final paragraph; we are told in a burst of obscure rhetoric that the Dostoevskyan novel falls outside the complex of nineteenth-century problems with which Lukács has been dealing. In 1943 he at last wrote an essay on the author of *The Brothers Karamazov*. Significantly, Lukács chose for his motto Browning's verse: "I go to prove my soul!" But little came of the venture. The piece is indecisive and superficial.

It could scarcely be otherwise. Dostoevsky's works embody a total denial of the world view held by a Marxist revolutionary. Moreover, they contain a prophecy which a Marxist must reject if he is to believe in the ultimate triumph of dialectical materialism. The Shigalovs and the Grand Inquisitors may, according to Dostoevsky, achieve temporary dominion over the kingdoms of the earth. But their rule is destined, through its own fatally determined inhumanity, to end in chaos and self-slaughter. To a perceptive and believing Marxist, *The Possessed* must read like a horoscope of disaster.

During the Stalinist period, Soviet censorship acted on this insight. The spell of anti-Stalinism has brought with it a revaluation of Dostoevsky and a resumption of Dostoevskyan studies. But it is evident that even a liberalized version of a proletarian and secular dictatorship cannot allow too many of its subjects to read and ponder the adventures of Prince Muishkin, the parable of Shigalov and Verkhovensky, or the "Pro and Contra" chapters in *The Brothers Karamazov*. Once again, Dostoevsky's may become the voice from the underground.

Outside Russia the reverse has, on the whole, been true. Dostoevsky has penetrated more deeply than Tolstoy into the fabric of contemporary thought. He is one of the principal masters of modern sensibility. The Dostoevskyan strain is pervasive in the psychology of modern fiction, in the metaphysics of absurdity and tragic freedom which emerged from the Second World War, and in speculative theology. The wheel has come full circle. The "Scythian" whom Vogüé introduced to European readers as a remote barbarian has become the prophet and historian of our own lives. Perhaps this is because barbarism has drawn so much nearer.

Thus, even beyond their deaths, the two novelists stand in contrariety. Tolstoy, the foremost heir to the traditions of the epic; Dostoevsky, one of the major dramatic tempers after Shakespeare; Tolstoy, the mind intoxicated with reason and fact; Dostoevsky, the contemner of rationalism, the great lover of paradox; Tolstoy, the poet of the land, of the rural setting and the pastoral mood; Dostoevsky, the arch-citizen, the master-builder of the modern metropolis in the province of language; Tolstoy, thirsting for the truth, destroying himself and those about him in excessive pursuit of it; Dostoevsky, rather against the truth than against Christ, suspicious of total understanding and on the side of mystery; Tolstoy, "keeping at all times," in Coleridge's phrase, "in the high road of life"; Dostoevsky, advancing into the labyrinth of the unnatural, into the cellarage and morass of the soul; Tolstoy, like a colossus bestriding the palpable earth, evoking the realness, the tangibility, the sensible entirety of concrete experience; Dostoevsky, always on the edge of the hallucinatory, of the spectral, always vulnerable to daemonic intrusions into what might prove, in the end, to have been merely a tissue of dreams; Tolstoy, the embodiment of health and Olympian vitality; Dostoevsky, the sum of energies charged with illness and possession; Tolstoy, who saw the destinies of men historically and in the stream of time; Dostoevsky, who saw them contemporaneously and in the vibrant stasis of the dramatic moment; Tolstoy, borne to his grave in the first civil burial ever held in Russia; Dostoevsky, laid to rest in the cemetery of the Alexander Nevsky monastery in St. Petersburg amid the solemn rites of the Orthodox Church; Dostoevsky, pre-eminently the man of God; Tolstoy, one of His secret challengers.

In the stationmaster's house at Astapovo, Tolstoy reportedly had two books by his bedside: *The Brothers Karamazov* and the *Essais* of Montaigne. It would appear that he had chosen to die in the presence of his great antagonist and of a kindred spirit. In the latter instance he chose aptly, Montaigne being a poet of life and of the wholeness of it rather in the sense in which Tolstoy himself had understood that mystery. Had he turned to the celebrated twelfth chapter of Book II of the *Essais* while composing his fierce genius to tranquillity, Tolstoy would have found a judgment equally appropriate to himself and to Dostoevsky:

C'est un grand ouvrier de miracles que l'esprit humain. . . .

Bibliography

QUOTATIONS from the novels, tales, dramas, and essays of TOLSTOY are taken from the translations by Louise and Aylmer Maude in the Centenary Edition (1928–39). There are two exceptions to this: in the case of *Anna Karenina*, I have used the translation by Constance Garnett, and in that of *The Christian Teaching*, I have quoted from the translation by Vladimir Chertkov (New York, 1898).

Quotations from Tolstoy's letters, journals, and unfinished writings are taken from the following:

P. I. Biryukov: *Leo Tolstoy: his life and work* (London, 1906); *The Journals of Leo Tolstoi, 1895–1899* (trans. by R. Strunsky, New York, 1917); *Tolstoi's Love Letters* (trans. by S. S. Koteliansky and Virginia Woolf, London, 1923); *Lettres inédites de L. Tolstoy à Botkine* (trans. by J. W. Bienstock in vol. 66 of *Les œuvres libres*, Paris, 1926); *The Private Diary of Leo Tolstoy 1853–1857* (trans. by Louise and Aylmer Maude, London, 1927); *The Letters of Tolstoy and his Cousin Countess Alexandra Tolstoy* (trans. by L. Islavin, London, 1929); *New Light on Tolstoy, Literary Fragments, Letters and Reminiscences Not Previously Published* (ed. by R. Fülöp-Miller, London, 1931); *Léon Tolstoï et Sophie Tolstoï. Journaux intimes, 1910* (trans. by J. Chuzeville, Paris, 1940).

Quotations from the notebooks and drafts for *Anna Karenina* and *Resurrection* are taken from the translations into French by Henri Mongault, S. Luneau, and E. Beaux published in

the Bibliothèque de la Pléiade (Paris, 1951). I have also con-
sulted Henri Mongault's translation of *War and Peace* published, together with a preface by Pierre Pascal, in the same
collection (Paris, 1944).

QUOTATIONS from the novels and tales of DOSTOEVSKY
are taken from the translations by Constance Garnett (Lon-
don, 1912–20) except in the following cases: I have used
C. J. Hogarth's translations of *Poor Folk*, *The Gambler*,
Letters from the Underworld, *The Gentle Maiden*, and *The
Landlady*, as they have appeared in Everyman's Library.
Quotations from *The Diary of a Writer* are taken from the
translation by Boris Brasol (London, 1949).

Quotations from Dostoevsky's letters, reminiscences, and
literary fragments are taken from the following:

Letters of Fyodor Michailovitch Dostoevsky (trans. by E. C.
Mayne, London, 1914); *Letters and Reminiscences* (trans.
by S. S. Koteliansky and J. Middleton Murry, London, 1923);
Dostoevsky: Les Inédits (trans. by J. W. Bienstock, Paris,
1923); *Der unbekannte Dostojewski* (ed. by R. Fülöp-Miller
and F. Eckstein, Munich, 1926); *Dostoevsky: Lettres à sa
femme* (trans. by J. W. Bienstock, Paris, 1927); *New Dostoevsky Letters* (trans. by S. S. Koteliansky, London, 1929);
The Letters of Dostoyevsky to His Wife (trans. by E. Hill
and D. Mudie, London, 1930).

Quotations from the notebooks and drafts for Dostoevsky's
novels are taken from W. Komarovitch: *Die Urgestalt der
Brüder Karamasoff. Dostojewskis Quellen, Entwürfe und
Fragmente* (Munich, 1928), and from the translations into
French as they have appeared in the Bibliothèque de la
Pléiade:

Les Frères Karamazov, *Les Carnets des Frères Karamazov*,
Niétotchka Niezvanov (trans. by H. Mongault, L. Désor-
monts, B. de Schloezer, and S. Luneau, Paris, 1952); *L'Idiot*,
Les Carnets de L'Idiot, *Humiliés et offensés* (trans. by A.
Mousset, B. de Schloezer, and S. Luneau, Paris, 1953);
Crime et châtiment, *Journal de Raskolnikov*, *Les Carnets
de Crime et châtiment*, *Souvenirs de la maison des morts*
(trans. by D. Ergaz, V. Pozner, B. de Schloezer, H. Mon-
gault, and L. Désormonts, Paris, 1954); *Les Démons*, *Les
Carnets des Démons*, *Les Pauvres Gens* (trans. by B. de
Schloezer and S. Luneau, Paris, 1955); *L'Adolescent*, *Les
Nuits blanches*, *Le Joueur*, *Le Sous-sol*, *L'Éternel Mari*
(trans. by Pierre Pascal, B. de Schloezer, and S. Luneau,
Paris, 1956).

(THE following list includes only works cited or used as direct sources. It does not include specific editions of classical or standard texts such as, for instance, the poems of Schiller or Matthew Arnold's *Essays in Criticism*.)

Charles Andler: *"Nietzsche et Dostoïevsky"* (in *Mélanges Baldensperger*, Paris, 1930).

Vladimir Astrov: "Dostoievsky on Edgar Allan Poe" (*American Literature*, XIV, 1942).

N. A. Berdiaev: *Les Sources et le sens du communisme russe* (trans. by A. Nerville, Paris, 1951).

——: *L'Esprit de Dostoievski* (trans. by A. Nerville, Paris, 1946).

Isaiah Berlin: *The Hedgehog and the Fox* (London, 1953).

——: *Historical Inevitability* (Oxford, 1954).

Rachel Bespaloff: *De Iliade* (New York, 1943).

Marius Bewley: *The Complex Fate* (London, 1952).

R. P. Blackmur: *The Double Agent* (New York, 1935).

——: *Language as Gesture* (London, 1954).

——: *The Lion and the Honeycomb* (London, 1956).

——: *Anni Mirabiles, 1921–1925* (Library of Congress, Washington, 1956).

N. von Bubnoff, ed.: *Russische Religionsphilosophen: Dokumente* (Heidelberg, 1956).

Jakob Burckhardt: *Weltgeschichtliche Betrachtungen* (*Gesammelte Werke*, IV, Basel, 1956).

Kenneth Burke: *The Philosophy of Literary Form* (New York, 1957).

E. H. Carr: *Dostoevsky (1821–1881)* (London, 1931).

C. G. Carus: *Psyche* (Jena, 1926).

J.-M. Chassaignon: *Cataractes de l'imagination* (Paris, 1799).

V. Chertkov: *The Last Days of Tolstoy* (trans. by N. A. Duddington, London, 1922).

N. Cohn: *The Pursuit of the Millennium* (London, 1957).

Stephen Crane's Love Letters to Nellie Crouse (ed. by H. Cady and L. G. Wells, Syracuse University Press, 1954).

R. Curle: *Characters of Dostoevsky* (London, 1950).

D. Čyževśkyj: *"Schiller und 'Die Brüder Karamazov'"* (*Zeitschrift für Slavische Philologie*, VI, 1929).

Ilya Ehrenburg: *Out of Chaos* (trans. by A. Bakshy, New York, 1934).

T. S. Eliot: *Selected Essays, 1917–1932* (London, 1932).

——: *Notes towards the Definition of Culture* (London, 1948).

Francis Fergusson: *The Idea of a Theater* (Princeton University Press, 1949).

——: *The Human Image in Dramatic Literature* (New York, 1957).

Gustave Flaubert: *Correspondance de* (Paris, 1926–33).

E. M. Forster: *Aspects of the Novel* (London, 1927).

Sigmund Freud: "Dostoevsky and Parricide" (in preface to the translation of *Stavrogin's Confession* by Virginia Woolf and S. S. Koteliansky, New York, 1947).

D. Gerhardt: *Gogol' und Dostojecskij in ihrem künstlerischen Verhältnis* (Leipzig, 1941).

Gabriel Germain: *Genèse de l'Odyssée* (Paris, 1954).

André Gide: *Dostoïevsky* (Paris, 1923).

Michael Ginsburg: "Koni and His Contemporaries" (*Indiana Slavic Studies*, I, 1956).

Joseph Goebbels: *Michael* (Munich, 1929).

Lucien Goldmann: *Le Dieu caché* (Paris, 1955).

Maxim Gorky: *Reminiscences of Tolstoy, Chekhov and Andreev* (trans. by Katherine Mansfield, S. S. Koteliansky, and Leonard Woolf, London, 1934).

Romano Guardini: *Religiöse Gestalten in Dostojewskis Werk* (Munich, 1947).

J. E. Harrison: *Ancient Art and Ritual* (London, 1914).

F. W. J. Hemmings: *The Russian Novel in France, 1884–1914* (Oxford, 1950).

Alexander Herzen: *From the Other Shore* and *The Russian People and Socialism* (trans. by R. Wollheim, with an introduction by Isaiah Berlin, London, 1956).

Humphry House: *Aristotle's Poetics* (London, 1956).

Irving Howe: *Politics and the Novel* (New York, 1957).

V. Ivanov: *Freedom and the Tragic Life. A Study in Dostoevsky* (trans. by N. Cameron, London, 1952).

Henry James: *Hawthorne* (London, 1879).

——: *Notes on Novelists, with Some Other Notes* (London, 1914).

——: *The Letters of Henry James* (ed. by P. Lubbock, London, 1920).

——: *The Art of the Novel* (ed. by R. P. Blackmur, London, 1935).

——: *The Notebooks of Henry James* (ed. by F. O. Matthiessen and K. B. Murdock, Oxford University Press, New York, 1947).

——: *The Art of Fiction and Other Essays* (ed. by M. Roberts, Oxford University Press, New York, 1948).

Georges Jarbinet: *Les Mystères de Paris d'Eugène Sue* (Paris, 1932).

John Keats: *The Letters of* (ed. by M. B. Forman, Oxford, 1947).

H. D. F. Kitto: *Form and Meaning in Drama* (London, 1956).

G. Wilson Knight: *Shakespeare and Tolstoy* (Oxford, 1934).

Hans Kohn: *Pan-Slavism: Its History and Ideology* (University of Notre Dame Press, 1953).

Reinhard Lauth: *Die Philosophie Dostojewskis* (Munich, 1950).

D. H. Lawrence: *Studies in Classic American Literature* (London, 1924).

——: Introduction to F. M. Dostoevsky: *The Grand Inquisitor* (trans. by S. S. Koteliansky, London, 1930).

——: *The Letters of D. H. Lawrence* (ed. with an introduction by Aldous Huxley, London, 1932).

T. E. Lawrence: *The Letters of* (ed. by David Garnett, London, 1938).

F. R. Leavis: *The Great Tradition* (London, 1948).

——: *D. H. Lawrence, Novelist* (London, 1955).

T. S. Lindstrom: *Tolstoï en France (1886–1910)* (Paris, 1952).

H. de Lubac: *Le Drame de l'humanisme athée* (Paris, 1954).

Percy Lubbock: *The Craft of Fiction* (London, 1921).

George Lukács: *Die Theorie des Romans* (Berlin, 1920).

——: *Balzac und der französische Realismus* (Berlin, 1952).

——: *Deutsche Realisten des 19. Jahrhunderts* (Berlin, 1952).

——: *Der russische Realismus in der Weltliteratur* (Berlin, 1952).

——: *Der historische Roman* (Berlin, 1955).

——: *Probleme des Realismus* (Berlin, 1955).

——: *Goethe und seine Zeit* (Berlin, 1955).

J. Madaule: *Le Christianisme de Dostoïevski* (Paris, 1939).

Thomas Mann: *Adel des Geistes* (Stockholm, 1945).

——: *Neue Studien* (Stockholm, 1948).

——: *Nachlese* (Stockholm, 1956).

Jacques Maritain: *Creative Intuition in Art and Poetry* (London, 1954).

R. E. Matlaw: "Recurrent Images in Dostoevskij" (*Harvard Slavic Studies*, III, 1957).

Aylmer Maude: *The Life of Tolstoy* (Oxford, 1930).

D. S. Merezhkovsky: *Tolstoi as Man and Artist, with an Essay on Dostoïevsky* (London, 1902).

H. Muchnic: *Dostoevsky's English Reputation (1881–1936)* (Northampton, Mass., 1939).

J. Middleton Murry: *Dostoevsky: a Critical Study* (London, 1916).

George Orwell: "Lear, Tolstoy, and the Fool" (*Polemic*, VII, London, 1947).

Denys Page: *The Homeric Odyssey* (Oxford, 1955).

C. E. Passage: *Dostoevski the Adapter: A Study in Dostoevski's Use of the Tales of Hoffman* (University of North Carolina Press, 1954).

Gilbert Phelps: *The Russian Novel in English Fiction* (London, 1956).

R. Poggioli: "Kafka and Dostoyevsky" (*The Kafka Problem*, New York, 1946).

——: *The Phoenix and the Spider* (Harvard, 1957).

Tikhon Polner: *Tolstoy and his Wife* (trans. by N. Wreden, London, 1946).

John Cowper Powys: *Dostoievsky* (London, 1946).

Mario Praz: *The Romantic Agony* (Oxford, 1951).

Marcel Proust: *Contre Sainte-Beuve* and *Journées de Lecture* (Paris, 1954).

I. A. Richards: *Practical Criticism* (London, 1929).

——: *Coleridge on Imagination* (London, 1934).

Jacques Rivière: *Nouvelles Etudes* (Paris, 1922).

Romain Rolland: *Vie de Tolstoï* (Paris, 1921).

——: *Mémoires et fragments du journal* (Paris, 1956).

Boris Sapir: *Dostojewsky und Tolstoi über Probleme des Rechts* (Tübingen, 1932).

Jean-Paul Sartre: "A Propos Le bruit et la fureur, *La temporalité chez Faulkner*" (*Situations*, I, Paris, 1947).

——: "*Qu'est-ce que la littérature?*" (*Situations*, II, Paris, 1948).

George Bernard Shaw: *The Works of* (London, 1930–8).

Léon Shestov: *All Things Are Possible* (trans. by S. S. Koteliansky, London, 1920).

——: *Tolstoi und Nietzsche* (trans. by N. Strasser, Cologne, 1923).

——: *Les Révélations de la mort, Dostoievsky–Tolstoy* (trans. by Boris de Schloezer, Paris, 1923).

——: *Dostojewski und Nietzsche* (trans. by R. von Walter, Cologne, 1924).

——: *Athènes et Jerusalem* (Paris, 1938).

E. J. Simmons: *Dostoevski: The Making of a Novelist* (Oxford University Press, New York, 1940).

——: *Leo Tolstoy* (London, 1949).

E. A. Soloviev: *Dostoievsky: His Life and Literary Activity* (trans. by C. J. Hogarth, London, 1916).

André Suarès: *Tolstoï* (Paris, 1899).

Allen Tate: "The Hovering Fly" (*The Man of Letters in the Modern World*, London, 1955).

The Tolstoy Home, Diaries of Tatiana Sukhotin-Tolstoy (trans. by A. Brown, Columbia University Press, 1951).

Alexandra Tolstoy: *Tolstoy: A Life of My Father* (trans. by E. R. Hapgood, New York, 1953).

Ilya Tolstoy: *Reminiscences of Tolstoy* (trans. by G. Calderon, London, 1914).

Leon L. Tolstoy: *The Truth about My Father* (London, 1924).

Lionel Trilling: *The Liberal Imagination* (London, 1951).

——: *The Opposing Self* (London, 1955).

Henri Troyat: *Dostoïevski: l'homme et son œuvre* (Paris, 1940).

L. B. Turkevich: *Cervantes in Russia* (Princeton University Press, 1950).

J. Van Der Eng: *Dostoevskij romancier* (Gravenhage, 1957).

E. M. M. de Vogüé: *Le Roman russe* (Paris, 1886).

Simone Weil: "*L'Iliade ou le Poème de la force*" (under the pseudonym of Emile Novin, *Cahiers du sud*, Marseilles, 1940).

Edmund Wilson: "Dickens: The Two Scrooges" (*Eight Essays*, New York, 1954).

Virginia Woolf: "Modern Fiction" (*The Common Reader*, London, 1925).

A Yarmolinsky: *Dostoevsky. A Life* (New York, 1934).

L. A. Zander: *Dostoevsky* (trans. by N. Duddington, London, 1948).

Emile Zola: *Les Romanciers naturalistes* (*Œuvres complètes*, XV, Paris, 1927–9).

——: *Le Roman expérimental* (*Œuvres complètes*, XLVI, Paris, 1927–9).

Index

Because this book is not biographical in nature, and because including every reference to Tolstoy or Dostoevsky would have made the index unwieldy, the references under their names have been confined to their writings.

v

vi

xiii